"This is a fine collection of essays in honor of the redoubtable theologian, Elizabeth Johnson, with social attention paid to Johnson's lifelong, major contributions to the central issues of God, humankind, and cosmos. A fitting and welcome tribute to a splendid theologian."

—David Tracy
The University of Chicago

"Far more than a *festschrift*, this volume in honor of feminist and ecological theologian Elizabeth Johnson attests to the multi-modal, multi-generational impacts that radiate from the theological work and mentorship of this esteemed scholar. With essays ranging from cosmos to earthly embodiment, from bonobos to the Anthropocene, and from Christology to ethics, *Turning to the Heavens and the Earth* is a delightful testimony to frontiers in theological thinking that have been charted by Elizabeth Johnson. Essays in the book brim with insights, and the volume as a whole coheres beautifully."

—Christiana Z. Peppard
Fordham University

"Younger theologians might call Elizabeth Johnson a 'rock star.' Although that is not a theological category, I think the celestial metaphor is fitting for the stellar scholarship she has generated over the decades and that, in turn, has attracted a constellation of colleagues, peers, students, and others to do theology that simultaneously orbits the tradition while boldly exploring new space(s) for understanding the One in whom we 'live and move and have our being' (Acts 17:28). Humans, nonhuman animals, and indeed all of creation are encompassed in this 'we' as reflected in the light that these essays emit as a tribute to Johnson's gravitas. Now as we face urgent environmental issues and as we extend our human footprint further into our solar system's small corner of the galaxy, the theological work offered in this collection is indeed most welcome."

—Tobias Winright
Saint Louis University

Turning to the Heavens and the Earth

Theological Reflections on a Cosmological Conversion

Essays in Honor of Elizabeth A. Johnson

Edited by
Julia Brumbaugh
and Natalia Imperatori-Lee

Foreword by
Mary Catherine Hilkert, OP

A Michael Glazier Book

LITURGICAL PRESS
Collegeville, Minnesota

www.litpress.org

A Michael Glazier Book published by Liturgical Press

Cover design by Jodi Hendrickson.

1   2   3   4   5   6   7   8   9

Library of Congress Cataloging-in-Publication Data

Names: Johnson, Elizabeth A., 1941– honouree. | Brumbaugh, Julia, editor.
Title: Turning to the Heavens and the Earth : theological reflections on a
  cosmological conversion : essays in honor of Elizabeth A. Johnson / edited
  by Julia Brumbaugh and Natalia Imperatori-Lee ; foreword by Mary Catherine
  Hilkert, OP.
Description: Collegeville, Minnesota : Liturgical Press, 2016. | "A Michael
  Glazier book." | Includes bibliographical references and index.
Identifiers: LCCN 2015048768 (print) | LCCN 2016003108 (ebook) | ISBN
  9780814687727 (pbk.) | ISBN 9780814687604
Subjects: LCSH: Nature—Religious aspects—Christianity. | Human
  ecology—Religious aspects—Christianity. | Cosmology.
Classification: LCC BT695.5 .T87 2016 (print) | LCC BT695.5 (ebook) | DDC
  261.8/8—dc23
LC record available at http://lccn.loc.gov/2015048768

For Elizabeth Johnson
Beloved teacher, mentor, seeker, and sister
Treasure-hunter and whip-cracker,
Friend of God and of the Earth.
Prophet.

Onward!

Contents

Acknowledgments

The work of a *festschrift* is perhaps distinctive in the clarity with which it shows how dependent all our scholarly work is on the thought, support, and labor of many. In this collection honoring Elizabeth A. Johnson, we acknowledge first her inspiration, guidance, and mentoring, which for these editors have been a stable force in our lives for at least twenty years. We have also to acknowledge with gratitude Kathryn Lilla Cox, Erin Lothes Biviano, Gloria Schaab, SSJ, Diane Tomkinson, OFM, and Suzanne Franke, CSJ, all part of a cohort of doctoral students at Fordham in the late 1990s, whose concern that Beth be honored with a *festschrift* got this project started. We thank also Hans Christoffersen, academic publisher at Liturgical Press, whose early enthusiasm gave us courage and enduring support gave us strength. Lauren L. Murphy, managing editor at Liturgical Press, has with humor, precision, intelligence, and care shepherded this book from fragmented essays to a coherent, thoughtful work of theology. Colleen Stiller, production manager at Liturgical Press, has with similar grace and care honed the text into its present format.

We extend heartfelt gratitude to the authors of this collection: Kevin Glauber Ahern, Lisa Sowle Cahill, Collen Mary Carpenter, David Cloutier, Kathy Coffey, Carol Dempsey, OP, Denis Edwards, William French, Ivone Gebara, John Haught, Cathy Hilkert, OP, Erin Lothes Biviano, Sallie McFague, Eric Daryl Meyer, Richard W. Miller, Jürgen Moltmann, Jeanette Rodriguez, and Michele Saracino.

We thank Penguin Press for permission to use Mary Oliver's "Poem of the One World" in Lisa Cahill's essay, and to the Catholic Theological Society of America for the permission to reprint Elizabeth Johnson's

1996 presidential address "Turning to the Heavens and the Earth." We also thank Beth herself for helping us compile a selected bibliography of her extensive published work, which appears at the end of this text.

There is also a parade of generous, compassionate, and witty friends, who have accompanied us, watched our kids, answered our questions, cheered us on, filled our wine glasses, and given us hope. In no particular order: Linda Land-Closson, Grant Gallicho, Jim Keane, Mike and Mary McManus, Rori and Debbie Knudtson, Russ Arnold, Brenna Moore, Maureen O'Connell, Christine Firer Hinze and Brad Hinze.

Julia Brumbaugh acknowledges Regis University, particularly the religious studies department and its chair, Kari Kloos, as well as the dean of Regis College, Thomas Bowie, for support, both personal and professional, and particularly for the gift of a sabbatical. Natalia Imperatori-Lee thanks Manhattan College for the sabbatical grant, as well as the year-round support of her department, chaired by Michele Saracino, that afforded her the time and resources to bring this project to completion.

It goes without saying, though it is not repeated enough, that we both thank our families. Their patience with our partial attention and deadline stress has been extensive, and their support of this project and all our endeavors has been unambiguously enthusiastic. For that, and much else, we are so grateful.

Foreword

Mary Catherine Hilkert, OP

Elizabeth Johnson once remarked that "the gift of a new question may be the best possible present of all."[1] This volume offers ample testimony to the fact that she has been gifting the church, the academy, her students, and a wider reading public with new questions—and creative responses—for over three decades. Rich and diverse as her theological insights have been, her writing always returns to the heart of the matter—the question of God. A true friend of God and a prophet, this disciple of Wisdom has prepared theological feasts and nourished women and men hungry for meaning and hope in a secular, suffering, and violent world since the early 1980s.

The first line of Beth's dissertation set the stage for her theological pilgrimage in the decades to follow: "A crucial, if not the most basic question of all theology is the question of the right way to speak of God."[2] The mystery of God and God's love for all of her beloved creatures—including the Earth and the entire cosmos—has been at the heart of Beth's own lifelong quest for the Living God. The diverse questions that she has engaged along the way also reflect her perceptive attention to the concerns of her many readers who join her in that search, even if they do not always share her faith convictions.

---

[1] Elizabeth A. Johnson, "Pneumatology and Beyond: 'Whatever,'" in *The Theology of Cardinal Walter Kasper: Speaking Truth in Love*, ed. Kristin M. Colberg and Robert A. Krieg (Collegeville, MN: Liturgical Press, 2014), 98–109, at 105.

[2] Wolfhart Pannenberg, "Analogy and Doxology," *Basic Questions in Theology*, vol. 1 (Philadelphia: Fortress Press, 1970), 211, cited in Elizabeth A. Johnson, *Analogy and Doxology and Their Connection with Christology in the Thought of Wolfhart Pannenberg* (PhD diss., The Catholic University of America, 1981), 1.

To borrow a refrain from the litany of thanksgiving at Passover in which the Jewish faith community remembers and celebrates God's many blessings, *it would have been enough* if this gifted theologian had focused her life's work on the key insight that theological speech always falls short of expressing the unfathomable mystery of God.

Likewise, *it would have been enough* had Elizabeth Johnson explored the question at the heart of Christian faith: What does it mean to believe that the God of Love has become one with humankind and the cosmos in the Word become flesh—Jesus, the incarnate Wisdom of God—and to follow in faithful discipleship? When invited by the South African Bishops' Conference to engage those questions with clergy and religious educators in South Africa during the apartheid era, she drew on her many years of studying and teaching Christology in a series of lectures later published in the widely used text, *Consider Jesus* (see Heb 3:1).

In her next step on the quest to find a more inclusive way to "speak rightly of God," Beth forged a new pathway as she set out "to braid a footbridge between the ledges of classical and feminist Christian wisdom" in her groundbreaking volume *She Who Is: The Mystery of God in Feminist Theological Discourse.* The expressed aim of that now-classic work, which received the 1992 Louisville Grawemeyer Award in Religion, describes her broader theological project as well: "My aim in what follows is to speak a good word about the mystery of God recognizable within the contours of Christian faith that will serve the emancipatory praxis of women and men, to the benefit of all creation, both human beings and the earth."[3] *It would have been enough.*

When she was asked to deliver the Madeleva Lecture in Spirituality at St. Mary's College a year later, Beth focused the lens of her theological imagination more explicitly on the connection between pneumatology, feminist theology, and ecological theology in *Women, Earth, and Creator Spirit.* This time her angle of vision highlighted the interconnectedness of the Creator God's love of and concern for plants, animals, the ocean, the blue planet Earth, and all things living with her ongoing concern for the well-being and flourishing of women and girls around the globe who live in systems that fail to recognize their full dignity and the wisdom emerging from their diverse experiences.

---

[3] Elizabeth A. Johnson, *She Who Is: The Mystery of God in Feminist Theological Discourse* (New York: Crossroad, 1992), 8.

Reminding her readers that "we are as large as our loves," she called for a deeper share in the Creator Spirit's compassionate desire for "a flourishing humanity on a thriving earth."

It would have been enough. But Beth's religious sensibilities—at once clearly feminist and deeply Catholic—as well as the questions of her students and wide readership led to her next project: the development of a contemporary theology of Mary of Nazareth within the broader communion of saints, research that resulted in two more award-winning volumes: *Friends of God and Prophets: A Feminist Theological Reading of the Communion of Saints* (winner of the American Academy of Religion's Excellence in the Study of Religion Award in 1999) and *Truly Our Sister: A Theology of Mary in the Communion of Saints* (College Theology Society Book of the Year Award, 2004).

Since the readership of that two-volume exploration of Mary and the broader communion of saints might have been limited primarily to scholars and students, Johnson published the final section of *Truly Our Sister*, a mosaic of feminist biblical insights on Miriam of Nazareth (both her own and those of colleagues whose work she gratefully acknowledged), as a pastoral resource titled *Dangerous Memories: A Mosaic of Mary in Scripture* the following year.

It would have been enough. But Johnson's next sabbatical afforded her the time to return to her abiding theological and pastoral concern in *Quest for the Living God: Mapping Frontiers in the Theology of God* (2007). That volume, which she described fondly as her "little God book," was not intended as an original constructive work. Rather, her expressed purpose was to explore the diverse responses of the broader theological community to the questions of what Christians mean when they profess, "We believe in one God," and what that proclamation demands of Christians situated in a world of religious pluralism as well as atheism and faced with global threats to God's beloved children and endangered creation. When that volume received unexpected criticism and its contents were misrepresented in a public document issued by a committee of US bishops several years later and a media frenzy followed, Elizabeth Johnson did what she has always done best: she wrote a measured, but clear, statement of what it means to be a Catholic theologian charged with the responsibility of speaking of God in the contemporary world. She welcomed criticism of her scholarship, both ecclesial and academic, but also stood her ground, stating, "I am not responsible for what I have not written and do not think."

In the shadow of that controversy and with her many other responsibilities, it would have been understandable if Elizabeth Johnson had chosen to turn her next research leave into a well-deserved personal sabbatical. Instead, she turned her attention to the work that she had been urging her theological colleagues to embrace since the time of her presidential address to the Catholic Theological Society of America in 1996: the pressing theological and ecological need for theologians to "turn to the heavens and the earth." After engaging in a year-long study of Charles Darwin's *Origin of the Species* with an interdisciplinary group of colleagues at Fordham University, Beth crafted her own theological contribution to that dialogue—*Ask the Beasts: Darwin and the God of Love*. In the year before Pope Francis penned his prophetic encyclical *Laudato Sì*, Johnson published her own summons for Christians, other religious believers, and the broader human community to recognize our kinship with all creatures and embrace our shared ecological vocation to care for the living world and all its creatures with special concern for the most vulnerable. Returning to her abiding concern for the living God, now with a more explicit focus on God's own love of the Earth, Beth reminded her readers that the call to ecological conversion is an urgent call "to love in tune with God's abundant love so that all may have life."[4]

In over three decades of creative scholarship Elizabeth Johnson repeatedly has broken new ground, tilled the soil, and planted seeds for future harvesting of the abundant wisdom of the Christian tradition as a source of life and hope for all of creation. *It would have been enough.* Yet Johnson is no ivory-tower academic. Much as she treasures her study, she is equally if not more at home in the classroom and the numerous academic, pastoral, and public settings where she has been invited to "share the fruits of her contemplation with others" (in the language of Thomas Aquinas's Dominican tradition). For that reason it is fitting that this volume of essays in her honor includes not only the voices of colleagues with whom Beth has shared theological conversations over many years but also the insights of newer scholars whom she has mentored and inspired to speak in their own voices of the Living God and of all that God loves, "to practical critical effect."

---

[4] Elizabeth A. Johnson, *Ask the Beasts: Darwin and the God of Love* (London: Bloomsbury, 2014), 285.

Thank you, Beth, and thanks to your colleagues and students, for your questions—and for calling all of us to praise, to lament, and to act on behalf of all of God's beloved creation.

Prologue

A Time for Every Purpose

Kathy Coffey

Elizabeth Johnson writes and speaks about what matters most: the nature of God, the relationships of men and women, the peril to the earth. In her recent writings about the earth, she captures the excitement of the human adventure on this planet. You could get up in the morning—practically whistling—for the sake of such a bold, intriguing vision. Or you could hum "To Everything There Is a Season," with its chorus of "turn, turn, turn." Johnson has initiated or been part of the most important theological turnings in our era.

A pioneer in environmental theology, as in many other fields, Johnson develops the framework and builds the intellectual scaffolding for the hard and genuine work ahead. Her labor to root the current ecological crisis in the long tradition of Catholic theology demonstrates that saving our habitat isn't just sentimental "love the butterflies" drek. Rather, it is a compelling call to honor the Creator of this beautiful, threatened home. Like other prophets before her, she may not be popular. But she's courageous. And she's right.

Furthermore, she anticipated Pope Francis's environmental encyclical *Laudato Sì* by twenty years. She underscores similar themes: the elegance of a complex system; the danger of concentrated greenhouse gases; the risk to the poor; the destruction of biological diversity; the contamination of water, air, and earth; and the condemnation of ruthless exploitation. Most importantly, both prophetic voices see the world not as a problem to be solved but as "a joyful mystery to be contemplated with gladness and praise."

Johnson's current focus stands in a continuum with her previous work. People who'd never read *She Who Is* were nonetheless empowered by her message of women's full personhood and flourishing. I'd present her creative ideas in writing or in talks to diverse audiences: parish groups, diocesan conventions and retreatants, who'd sit up and take notice, even to the work "in translation" from the original, more academic form. So too her bold stand on the environment compels us to popularize it for those who will make a difference: energetic youth, earth care committees, ordinary pew people who wield enormous collective power to turn down the thermostat, walk or cycle—not drive—recycle, boycott, vote, and use alternative energy sources.

One thing that makes Johnson's work so exciting is its emphasis on action: *She Who Is* gave us a dynamic sense of the Spirit's activity through verbs like vivify, sustain, renew, liberate, knit together, heal, ignite, purify, strengthen, cleanse, restore, play music, quicken, warm, bless, and awaken hope. Now Johnson draws our attention to a world exploding with daily discoveries, an "open-ended adventure" full of mystery and enchantment. Nature bears the divine promise, reveals the creator, and is filled with surprise. Creation is a "book" about God or a pathway leading to God; therefore its ruin is a matter for grave concern. Damage to the planet also damages the people, especially the most vulnerable; she underscores the connection between social injustice and ecological destruction, drawing us to a radically improved order.

What we may once have conceived as static hierarchy, she invites us to revision as "a circle of the community of life." So too we may have once thought God was the male atop the patriarchal ladder. She deftly changes our calcified attitudes through uplifting participation in a great adventure, never by coercing. Her style avoids heavy-handed preachiness, or telling us unconvincingly, "eat it; it's good for you" as a glob of slimy, overcooked spinach slides onto the plate. She invites us to become the "cantors of the universe," in Abraham Heschel's phrase, who not only praise its magnificence but do all we can to preserve it. How could we refuse such a charming, invigorating invitation?

As a writer, I appreciate her accessible style and graphic metaphors. Like Teresa of Avila and Therese of Lisieux, she prefers concreteness to abstractions: the Spirit like water in three forms, or the root, shoot, and fruit of a tree. She poses the risk to the planet in stark terms that aren't overly nuanced: wonder or waste. And every now and then she throws in a phrase like "the whole shebang" or "unholy litany" to wake up those accustomed to dozing through theological discourses.

Johnson empowers by reminding that our healthy, thoughtful changes participate in God's lively and gracious being. God's bounty overflows into humans and quickens our life; we are God's partners in helping creation heal and thrive. Just as she softens and adds humor to her CTSA address by including Ellery, the goldfish Annie Dillard bought for twenty-five cents, so I'll end with a personal example. My three-year-old grandson Sawyer and I are big fans of the classes for toddlers offered on San Francisco Bay. We've learned about sharks, snowy egrets, salty pickleweed, sandpipers, and tides.

Having little background in science, I'm just as enthralled as he when a naturalist teaches us to distinguish the male from the female crab. (The former has a triangle on its belly; the latter, a half-circle.) Equipped with nets, the children in the class turn over rocks to find a plethora of life forms beneath. With shouts of glee, they capture snails and crabs, placing them in a large, water-filled pan for closer observation. Then, they carefully return the stones to their original places, and gingerly restore the creatures to their habitat.

That last word wasn't even part of my vocabulary until recently; the toddlers use it with ease and seem to understand it. Predictions of global warming mean the shore and marshlands where we study now will be gone when Sawyer is thirty-three. But part of me greets the predictions with a slight degree of skepticism. The threat, without a doubt, is real. But there is also room for hope. With Elizabeth Johnson, Pope Francis, and the toddler brigade working on the problem, maybe another magnificent turn will occur. By bringing the weight of theologians to bear on this pressing issue, and shifting the axis toward the cosmological agenda, Johnson has moved world attention from a narrow, subjective focus toward a vast and crucial arena. By voicing and orchestrating this graceful turn, she has set us on course toward reverence for the natural world, a hierarchy redesigned as a circle, sustainability, diminished greed, a new flourishing for both humans and the natural order. We, in turn, owe Dr. Johnson our deepest appreciation.

Introduction

Julia Brumbaugh and Natalia Imperatori-Lee

Classical definitions of theology tell us that theology is speech about God and faith seeking understanding. And yet perhaps the most powerful insight Elizabeth Johnson's work argues for is that theology matters for living. Theology is that discipline of intellectual, moral, and spiritual integrity that reflects on Christian belief in the context of the life of the church, the people of God, in the light of the world as it is. Theology develops in the context of that life of faith and in dialogue with it, but it also challenges, cajoles, invites, and inspires believers to live Christian life more fully. Theologians assume that how we talk about God, Christ, the world, and each other matters. Or, as Elizabeth Johnson would put it, "the symbol of God functions."[1] The idea of God and all the ideas that intersect with God—which is everything—matter. Ideas matter, questions matter, science matters, experience matters. Women's experience matters. They matter because the symbols function—they do work. This past month, from where we are writing in the United States in the fall of 2015, this became abundantly clear as Pope Francis's words evoked so powerfully the symbols of our shared life in ways that often jarred or surprised us. "Every life is sacred."[2] "It must be said that a true 'right of the environment' does

---

[1] Elizabeth Johnson, *She Who Is: The Mystery of God in Feminist Theological Discourse* (New York: Crossroad, 1992), 4.

[2] Pope Francis, Visit to the Joint Session of the United States Congress, Address of the Holy Father, United States Capitol, Washington, DC, Thursday, 24 September 2015, http://w2.vatican.va/content/francesco/en/speeches/2015/september /documents/papa-francesco_20150924_usa-us-congress.html.

exist."[3] "Gratitude and appreciation [for the family] should prevail over concerns and complaints."[4] This land, to which we belong, is the whole continent—Alaska to the Atacama Desert.[5] Even when the words are all words we know from our traditions the meaning is changed—expanded in the context of the life of the church, which has no political boundaries. How different is it to think that Americans are the citizens of this continent, not just the citizens of the United States? And, what might happen if we allow this idea to sink deep into our imaginations so that it informs how we see ourselves and our neighbors?

Elizabeth Johnson's theology—her power to reveal (to us) how our symbols function to shape us—is likewise an effort that turns the tradition a few degrees on its own axis to reveal meaning, hope, and promise that had been shadowed or veiled. She *turns* St. Irenaeus of Lyons's phrase *Gloria Dei vivens homo* to *Gloria Dei est vivens mulier*, which jars us into realizing that women—especially poor women and women of color—are not valued in our world. Women's lives—*full* lives—are not celebrated and lifted up as loved by God and as revealing of God as consistently or as exuberantly as they should.[6] Johnson's theology develops not as a rejection of the tradition but as a turning and a lifting, a dance with the tradition that raises questions and proposes ways forward in the confidence that the Living One whom Jesus called *Abba* really desires life for all, but also in the sure knowledge that we as a people have failed women. And, in so doing, Johnson has launched us (though not singlehandedly) into a deep, public, critical, and loving conversation that connects how we think about women to how we think about the Triune God of Christian faith and the life to which Christians are called. Over the last several decades, she has similarly

---

[3] Pope Francis, Meeting with the Members of the General Assembly of the United Nations Organization, Address of the Holy Father, United Nations Headquarters, New York, Friday, 25 September 2015, http://w2.vatican.va/content /francesco/en/speeches/2015/september/documents/papa-francesco_20150925 _onu-visita.html.

[4] Pope Francis, Meeting with Bishops Taking Part in the World Meeting of Families, Address of the Holy Father, St. Charles Borromeo Seminary, Chapel of Saint Martin, Philadelphia, Sunday, 27 September 2015, http://w2.vatican.va/content /francesco/en/speeches/2015/september/documents/papa-francesco_20150927 _usa-vescovi-festa-famiglie.html.

[5] Pope Francis, Visit to the Joint Session of the United States Congress.

[6] Johnson, *She Who Is*, 14–15.

lifted up the tradition around the person of Jesus, the person of Mary his mother, the communion of saints, all creation and its unimaginably ancient story of life, in dialogue with the world as known and the faith Christians believe. Over all of this hovers the mystery of God Who Is! The living one, who is ultimately beyond all names, in and by whose Spirit we live and are transformed.

Most recently, Elizabeth Johnson has turned to the Earth with her book *Ask the Beasts: Darwin and the God of Love*.[7] To some, it may seem that this turn to the Earth, to the cosmos, is a recent addition, an add-on to her more central and urgent work as a feminist theologian, lifting up the experiences of women in light of the central doctrines of Christianity. But the truth is that Johnson has been turning to the cosmos, to the Earth and its creatures, all along. In fact, turning toward women and turning toward the Earth, listening to women and listening to the Earth, valuing women and valuing the Earth are intrinsically related. Speaking in 1993, she said: "I am persuaded of the truth of ecofeminism's insight that analysis of the ecological crisis does not get to the heart of the matter until it sees the connection between the exploitation of the earth and the sexist definition and treatment of women."[8] Even earlier, in her paradigmatic work *She Who Is: The Mystery of God in Feminist Theological Discourse*, she tied the goal of feminist religious discourse to the flourishing of women of color in violent situations and the well-being of the Earth. "For me," she wrote in 1992, "the goal of feminist religious discourse pivots in its fullness around the flourishing of poor women of color in violent situations. Not incidentally, securing the well-being of these socially least of women would entail a new configuration of theory and praxis and the genuine transformation of all societies, including the churches, to open up more humane ways of living for all people, *with each other and the earth*."[9] This turning to women *and* turning to the Earth in their needs is precisely the form the Gospel takes in this world today.

The theological work required for such a tremendous task takes place not in a vacuum but in a web of relationships and communities

---

[7] Elizabeth Johnson, *Ask the Beasts: Darwin and the God of Love* (New York: Bloomsbury, 2014).

[8] Elizabeth Johnson, *Women, Earth, and Creator Spirit*, 1993 Madeleva Lecture (Mahwah, NY: Paulist Press, 1993), 10.

[9] Johnson, *She Who Is*, 11. Emphasis added.

that includes bishops, scholars, and social movements. Her work was preceded and influenced by ecclesiastical treatises at the episcopal level dealing with environmental degradation and stewardship: from the Appalachian bishops' This Land Is Home to Me and At Home in the Web of Life, to similar work by episcopal conferences in Australia, Malaysia, and Latin America. Work by scholars such as Sallie McFague and Jürgen Moltmann (both contributors here), as well as Catherine Keller and other paradigmatic examples—among them Jame Schaefer, Rita Nakashima Brock, Rosemary Radford Ruether, and many others—laid the groundwork for, inspired growth of, and expressed creatively theological responses to the emerging ecological crisis. Broad social movements, the products of a growing consciousness about the contours of our perilous ecological situation, represent a third strand of this web. Initiatives like the Catholic Climate Covenant evidence the cross-pollination of spiritual and ecological concerns and questions into avenues for activism and social change. This is the context out of which Johnson's ecological work emerges and to which it continues to contribute.

Even as we recognize the varied and intertwining contexts that brought Johnson (and us) to this point, this text represents an attempt to move the conversation forward toward a contemplative ecology, allowing for a retrieval of sacramentality and paving the way for creative encounter: with nonhuman animals, with alternative ethical frameworks, with new theological categories. The essays in this text endeavor to exemplify the ways in which turning to the fate of women engenders deeper conversions in the field of ecological global consciousness, and why that consciousness must inform Catholicism.

In 1996, Elizabeth Johnson was the outgoing president of the Catholic Theological Society of America, which was meeting in San Diego, California, on the theme Toward a Spirited Theology: The Holy Spirit's Challenge to the Theological Disciplines. In her address to the members, she enjoined them to *turn to the heavens and the Earth* and in doing so to reimagine, rediscover, and renew the church's understanding of and relationship to the cosmos, and to do so urgently in the context of growing clarity about how human abuse of the world has created a perilous situation for all the inhabitants of our beautiful blue planet.

It is now nearly twenty years later, and the ecological situation is even more urgent. In this collection of essays, written in honor of Johnson's tireless and inspiring theologizing, an array of Johnson's former students, friends, colleagues, and collaborators were challenged to ply the trade of theology in service of urgent and necessary turning to the cosmos in theology. What has resulted from that invitation is a collection about conversion that reflects the web of relationality that characterizes all good scholarship. In the end, conversion is a kind of turning—turning toward nonhuman animals, toward the forests, toward the inspired experience of environmental activists, toward the cosmos as a whole. These are turnings that force us to interrogate our theological institutions, our practice of virtue, our experience of vulnerability, our intellectual frameworks, our understanding of suffering and evil, and our categories of inclusion. Many of the chapters echo a central theme of Johnson's work: the centrality of material reality and embodiment that is a focus of ecotheology is a natural extension of faith seeking understanding. Johnson's own turn to ecotheological concerns, as we've noted, is embedded in its own three-part web of relationality and its own patterns of turning.

The book is divided into three sections, each depicting an invitation to "turn." The first group invites readers to turn to the wild(erness), with essays on the ways in which attention to nonhuman animals and reverence for the forest and wilderness more generally usher us toward new frameworks for anthropological and theological conversation. Denis Edwards and Eric Meyer both lift up nonhuman animals, specifically primates, as important sources for ecological-anthropological reflection. Edwards invites nonhuman animals into his recalibration of the *imago Dei*, while for Meyer, nonhuman animals call humanity to an apophatic moment. Colleen Carpenter's and Carol Dempsey's essays both invite the reader to the wilderness. Carpenter elaborates a forest spirituality, in dialogue with great artists who love the forest like Wendell Berry and the Canadian artist Emily Carr. Dempsey opens up ancient Hebrew texts to recall the wilderness as a place of divine (and human) encounter and challenge.

The second section invites a turn to new, more urgent forms of ethical action in order to respond appropriately to the planetary emergency we now face. Michele Saracino suggests embracing genuine vulnerability, while Kevin Ahern proposes a reinterpretation of magnanimity. David Cloutier develops a cosmological paradigm that will enable moral action commensurate with the moral dilemmas of the present. Finally, William French provides two concrete moral frameworks for the ecological task ahead.

The third and final group of essays invites us to turn to something radically new and includes four proposals for reimagining central theological categories. Erin Lothes Biviano reimagines pneumatology, inspired by the creedal affirmation of the Holy Spirit as Giver of life and drawing on the experiences of religious environmental activists, to reframe a pneumatological trinitarian theology. Lisa Sowle Cahill raises penetrating questions about theodicy and the suffering of the world's creatures in light of evolution and in the context of Johnson's and others' recent work. Jeanette Rodriguez draws together Latina feminist action for justice and ecological concerns in an effort to reimagine a future for the marginalized of the Earth. And Richard W. Miller ponders the theologian's task of thinking the unthinkable as a proper response to planetary emergency.

This collection has two kinds of essays arising out of the fact that Johnson's work reaches across generations, building on earlier work and inviting new work. One group of essays is shorter, more reflective pieces by senior colleagues who have grown to embody the role of elders in our theological community and our world. Sallie McFague, John Haught, Jürgen Moltmann, and Ivone Gebara are all theologians well known for their long and sustained concern that contemporary Christian theology be accountable to the more-than-human world. Kathy Coffey, whose name might be less well known in the academy, is an acclaimed writer and speaker whose work witnesses to the reach of Johnson's thought beyond the academy to people in the pews and in the highways and byways of ordinary Christianity. These elders wrote pieces from the wisdom of their experiences and hope nurtured in their own long labors to turn to the Earth. These elder essays bookend and are woven through the collection.

As a theologian whose work has often been subject to scrutiny, Johnson's tireless response has long been to just keep working. As she has put it so often, you just have to keep doing theology! Her attitude reminds us of that of Peter when Jesus asks him if he wanted to follow another: to whom would we go? This is the answer of a person with a vocation, a person who has been called by name and who knows, through joy and struggle, to what and to whom she is responsible. Beth Johnson is a theologian. This book seeks to honor her theological vocation and the fruit it has borne by bearing witness to the web of relationships of people and thought that Beth's work has challenged, supported, and inspired. In honor of her commitment to advancing theological thought, this work also seeks to extend the field of theology by turning, in a dozen different movements, toward a newly cosmological theology that might help us to restore, transform, reimagine, and otherwise live in new, sustainable relationship within and with the world. We hope you join the dance!

A Word about This Collection's Collaborators

While Johnson may be most known for her scholarship in the forms of writing and public speaking, her legacy cannot be recounted adequately without deep respect for her work as a teacher and her solidarity in friendship. The contributors to this volume reflect but a dim light on the range of relationships that have both nourished Johnson's work and been nourished by her work. Natalia Imperatori-Lee and Kevin Ahern were her students as undergraduates at Fordham University in the Bronx, while Julia Brumbaugh, Erin Lothes Biviano, and Eric Daryl Meyer were her students in the doctoral program there. Catherine Hilkert, OP, Denis Edwards, and Elizabeth Johnson were graduate students together at Catholic University of America; our publisher, Hans Christoffersen, was her graduate student at CUA when Johnson was on the faculty there; and her friendship with Carol Dempsey, OP, also goes back to those days. Relationships with Jürgen Moltmann, Sallie McFague, John Haught, Lisa Sowle Cahill, and Jeanette Rodriguez all go back decades, with lives and work linked though travel, conferences, theological collaboration, critique, and support rooted in mutual regard and a shared love of theology, the church, and the Holy Mystery hovering over all. Younger scholars who were not "officially" her students bear witness to how Johnson's work mentored—through inspiration, challenge, invitation, and vision—a generation of rising scholars, some of whose work is included here: Colleen Mary Carpenter, David Cloutier, Richard W. Miller, and Michele Saracino. Kathy Coffey, whose essay serves as prologue, is not an academic theologian but a writer. Her essay testifies to the reach of Johnson's theologizing to those Johnson most hoped to reach: the people of God.

Without question, the easiest part of bringing this volume to publication was the willingness with which our contributors agreed to a project that would honor Beth. Even those without direct professor-student or colleague ties to her spoke effusively of her profound influence on their work and development. It is our hope that these essays return, even in some small measure, the generosity Beth has shown to generations of scholars.

ONWARD!!!

Turn to the Heavens and the Earth

Retrieval of the Cosmos in Theology[1]

Elizabeth A. Johnson

Prefatory Note. Giving a presidential address is an awesome task, starting with the choice of topic. In the current ecclesial climate I was tempted to focus on the situation of theology or the role of the theologian, both under duress. However, the words of David Power, this year's John Courtney Murray award winner, came to mind. To a faculty demoralized by the unjust removal of one of our colleagues, he, as chair of [the] department, never ceased repeating, "The best offense is to keep on theologizing." Subvert repression by moving ahead. This is not to say that taking a stand on internal matters is not occasionally necessary. It is. But while theologians have life and breath we must keep on pressing forward, practicing our craft, seeking understanding of the faith for the sake of our own and coming generations. Guided by that wisdom, I have chosen to address the Catholic Theological Society of America on a theological issue that quite literally is coming to be a matter of life or death, namely, the natural world.

Introduction

As the twenty-first century rapidly approaches, there is a vital theme largely absent from the thinking of most North American theologians, namely, the whole world as God's good creation. There are a few notable exceptions among our members, but surveying our work as a whole

---

[1] Presidential Address, *CTSA Proceedings* 51 (1996): 1–14. Reprinted with permission.

would quickly make this absence clear. This neglect of "the cosmos" by recent decades of mainstream Catholic theology has two deleterious results. It enfeebles theology in its basic task of interpreting the whole of reality in the light of faith, thereby compromising the intellectual integrity of theology. And it blocks what should be theology's powerful contribution to the religious praxis of justice and mercy for the threatened earth, so necessary at this moment of our planet's unprecedented ecological crisis, thereby endangering the moral integrity of theology. In this address I am going to try to persuade you of the following thesis: as theologians of the twenty-first century, we need to complete our recent anthropological turns by turning to the entire interconnected community of life and the network of life-systems in which the human race is embedded, all of which has its own intrinsic value before God. In a word, we need to convert our intelligence to the heavens and the earth.

Remembering and Forgetting the Cosmos

It is instructive to remember the long-standing Catholic heritage that held high the importance of the cosmos in theology, and to examine how and why it got lost.

Theology is potentially the most comprehensive of fields. If there is only one God, and if this God is the Creator of all that exists, then everything is encompassed in the scope of theology's interest. Traditionally this is expressed in the idea that theology deals with three major areas: God, humanity, and world, a metaphysical trinity, so to speak. Nor can these elements be separated, for, as the history of theology makes evident, every understanding of God corresponds to a particular understanding of the natural world and the human.

Early Christian and medieval theologians took this view of things for granted, interpreting the natural world as God's good creation, a revealing pathway to the knowledge of God, and a partner in salvation. It was common for them to say that God has put two books at our disposal, the book of Sacred Scripture and the book of nature; if we learn how to read the book of nature aright, we will hear God's word and be led to knowledge about God's wisdom, power, and love.[2]

---

[2] For this and what follows, see the study by Max Wilder, *The Theologian and His Universe: Theology and Cosmology from the Middle Ages to the Present*, trans. Paul Dunphy (New York: Seabury, 1982).

The conscious endeavor to integrate the cosmos into theology reached its zenith in the twelfth and thirteenth centuries. Inspired by the translation of ancient Greek scientific works along with works by Jewish and Muslim scholars, medieval theologians applied themselves to constructing an all-embracing Christian view of the world, writing innumerable treatises on the universe, on the world, on the picture of the world, on the philosophy of the world, on the nature of things. Their endeavor to interpret the whole world in the light of Christian faith gave vitality to their work and inspired impressive systems in which cosmology, anthropology, and theology of God formed a harmonious unity. Some examples:

- In her summa of Christian doctrine (*Scivias*) Hildegard of Bingen sees the whole universe imbued with the love of Christ, the sun of justice, who shines with "the brilliance of burning charity of such great glory that every creature is illumined by the brightness of this light."[3] In the midst of this marvelous vision stand human beings, "made in a wondrous way with great glory from the dust of the earth, and so intertwined with the strengths of the rest of creation that we can never be separated from them."[4]

- Bonaventure instructs the soul journeying toward God to see the universe as a wonderful work of art in which one recognizes traces of its Maker:

  > Whoever is not enlightened by the splendor of created things is blind; whoever is not aroused by the sound of their voice is deaf; whoever does not praise God for all these creatures is mute; whoever after so much evidence does not recognize the First Principle is a fool [*stultus est* = an idiot].[5]

---

[3] Hildegard of Bingen, *Scivias*, trans. Mother Columba Hart and Jane Bishop (New York: Paulist, 1980), 94.

[4] Ibid., 98; adapted for inclusivity.

[5] "Qui igitur tantis rerum creatarum splendoribus non illustratur caecus est; qui tantis clamoribus non evigilat surdus est; qui ex omnibus his effectibus Deum non laudat mutus est; qui ex tantis indiciis primum principium non advertit stultus est." *Itinerarium mentis in Deum*, c. 1, no. 15; adapted from *The Mind's Journey to God*, trans. Lawrence Cunningham (Chicago: Franciscan Herald Press, 1979).

- Aquinas believes that theologians ought quite consciously to study nature and include a consideration of nature in their work. His own writing is pervaded with a cosmic sense as well as instructive analogies from the natural world, from fire to urine. Indeed, the whole cosmos itself is an astonishing image of God:

> God brought things into being in order that the divine goodness might be communicated to creatures and be represented by them. And because the divine goodness could not be adequately represented by one creature alone, God produced many and diverse creatures, that what was wanting in one in the representation of divine goodness might be supplied by another. For goodness, which in God is simple and uniform, in creatures is manifold and divided. Thus the whole universe together participates in divine goodness more perfectly, and represents it better, than any single creature whatever.[6]

Medieval theology brought God, humanity, and the world into an ordered harmony. The resulting synthesis not only shaped art, architecture, liturgy, and poetry, it also remained for centuries a guiding influence in Catholic theology even when its underlying world picture was discredited by scientific advance. And scientific advance there was, as the names of Copernicus, Galileo, Newton, and later Darwin, Einstein, Heisenberg, and many others imply. Strange as it may seem in the light of a fifteen-hundred-year-old heritage, after the Reformation neither Catholic nor Protestant theology kept pace with new scientific worldviews. Instead, they focused on God and the self, leaving the world to the side. Why this should have been the case has not been sufficiently studied. One factor frequently cited is the seventeenth-century ecclesiastical censure of Galileo, whose investigations challenged the medieval picture of the universe as geocentric, static, and perfectly ordered. According to John Paul II, speaking on the occasion of Galileo's rehabilitation, at the heart of the conflict was the fact that to church leaders "geocentrism seemed

---

[6] *Summa theologiae* I, q. 47, a. 1. The first chapters of the *Summa contra gentiles* 2 are even entitled this way: "That the consideration of creatures is useful for instruction of faith" (ch. 2); "That knowledge of the nature of creatures serves to destroy errors concerning God" (ch. 3), wherein it is written that "errors about creatures sometimes lead one astray from the truth of faith" (3.1).

to be part of scriptural teaching itself."[7] Wedded as they were to a literal interpretation of Scripture, they thought that since the Bible assumes the centrality of the earth, this was a doctrine of the faith. To have avoided the conflict "it would have been necessary all at once to overcome habits of thought, and to devise a way of teaching capable of enlightening the people of God." But most of them did not know how to do so.

Under pressure of ecclesiastical censure, Catholic theologians largely ignored the questions arising from a heliocentric and evolutionary world. Theology became estranged from ongoing thought about the universe. Even so, even as the medieval world picture disintegrated and was no longer available as a cosmological framework for Christian doctrine, the spirit of that great synthesis lingered like a ghost in the neoscholastic manuals. Those of us in the Catholic Theological Society of America of a certain age, who first studied theology before the Second Vatican Council, imbibed a sense of the cosmos with our first lessons. The implicit world picture may have been untenable, but at least there was a natural world there worthy of some consideration before God.

Vatican II marked a turning point in the saga of Catholic theology, directing thought with new openness toward dialogue with the modern world and with ecumenical and interreligious partners. Far from putting Catholic thought in touch with Christian theology that had kept pace with scientific advance, however, our first contacts with Protestantism heightened our own absorption with anthropology. For under pressure of the Reformation's great *solas*—Christ alone, faith alone, grace alone, Scripture alone—Protestant thought had taken an intensely anthropocentric turn. Revelation discloses a gracious God bent over our sinfulness and justifying us in Christ: theology's vision stays focused on humanity. Furthermore, the Protestant thought we met was grappling with the modern discovery of history. History, interpreted through the lens of the Bible as linear time, was the locus of God's mighty acts. By contrast, nature was the realm of cyclic time where pagan deities were invoked. Nature thus came to be treated as simply a stage on which salvation history was played out. With the outstanding exception of American process thought, cosmology, for all practical purposes, had disappeared as a partner and subject of theology.

[7] Quotations from John Paul II: "Lessons of the Galileo Case," *Origins* 22, no. 22 (12 November 1992): 369–73. For what follows, see also Cardinal Paul Poupard, "Galileo: Report on Papal Commission Findings," ibid., 374–75.

In the decades since the council, Catholic theology has moved rapidly away from neoscholasticism, going through a series of turns: the turn to the subject in transcendental theology; the turn to the subject under threat or defeated, in political theology; the linguistic turn, reintegrating the subject to community; the turn to the nonperson through the praxis of justice in liberation theologies as well as in feminist, womanist, *mujerista*, and Third World women's theologies. In this richness of theology's flourishing, however, it seems to me that something has been lost, namely, even that ghost of outdated cosmology that used to hover in our vision. Today one could go through a whole course of study in college, seminary, or university and never encounter the subject. And yet nature is one of the three main pillars of theology, along with God and humanity. What is needed now, I am convinced, is yet one more turn, a fully inclusive turn to the heavens and the earth, a return to cosmology, in order to restore fullness of vision and get theology back on the track from which it fell off a few hundred years ago. At least two reasons persuade us to make this turn: the intellectual integrity and the moral integrity of theology, one not strictly separable from the other.

Cosmology and the Intellectual Integrity of Theology

Since theology is the study of God and all things in the light of God, shrinking attention to humanity apart from the rest of creation simply does not do justice to theology's intrinsic mission. Even more, ignoring the cosmos has a deleterious effect insofar as it paves the way for theology to retreat to otherworldliness, disparage matter, body, and the earth, and offer interpretations of reality far removed from the way things actually work. We must engage the world. When theology today opens its door to the natural world, it is met with a wondrous array of insights. Medieval cosmology, which saw the world as geocentric, static, and unchanging, hierarchically ordered and centered on humanity, is gone. But gone too is the Enlightenment prejudice that held a mechanistic and deterministic view of nature inimicable in many ways to religious values. Instead, contemporary science is discovering a natural world that is surprisingly dynamic, organic, self-organizing, indeterminate, chancy, boundless, and open to the mystery of reality. There are still many gaps and uncertainties, but enormous discoveries are being made in our day.[8]

---

[8] Several key works that deal directly with scientific concepts are Ian Barbour, *Religion in an Age of Science*, 2 vols. (San Francisco: Harper & Row, 1990–1991);

- The world is almost unimaginably *old*: about fifteen billion years ago a single numinous speck exploded in an outpouring of matter and energy, shaping a universe that is still expanding. Five billion years ago an aging, first-generation star exploded, spewing out elements that coalesced to form our sun and its planets, including Earth. (The human race is only recently arrived.)

- The world is almost incomprehensibly *large*: more than 100 billion galaxies, each comprised of 100 billion stars, and no one knows how many moons and planets, all of this visible and audible matter being only a fraction of the matter in the universe. (We humans inhabit a small planet orbiting a medium-sized star toward the edge of one spiral galaxy.)

- The world is almost mind-numbingly *dynamic*: out of the Big Bang, the stars; out of the stardust, the earth; out of the earth, single-celled living creatures; out of the evolutionary life and death of these creatures, human beings with a consciousness and freedom that concentrates the self-transcendence of matter itself. (Human beings are the universe become conscious of itself. We are the cantors of the universe.)

- The world is almost unfathomably *organic*: everything is connected with everything else; nothing conceivable is isolated. In the words of scientist and theologian Arthur Peacocke, "Every atom of iron in our blood would not have been there had it not been produced in some galactic explosion billions of years ago and eventually condensed to form the iron in the crust of the earth from which we have emerged."[9] (We are made of stardust.) We are also biologically interconnected: human genetic structure closely parallels the DNA

Arthur Peacocke, *Theology for a Scientific Age: Being and Becoming—Natural, Divine, and Human* (Minneapolis: Fortress Press, 1993); Ted Peters, ed., *Cosmos as Creation: Theology and Science in Consonance* (Nashville: Abingdon, 1989); John Polkinghorne, *One World: The Interaction of Science and Theology* (Princeton, NJ: Princeton University Press, 1986); and the series edited by Robert Russell et al. and published by the Vatican Observatory (Vatican City) and the Center for Theology and the Natural Sciences (Berkeley): *Physics, Philosophy, and Theology: A Common Quest for Understanding* (1988), *Quantum Cosmology and the Laws of Nature: Scientific Perspectives on Divine Action* (1993), and *Chaos and Complexity: Scientific Perspectives on Divine Action* (1995).

[9] Arthur Peacocke, "Theology and Science Today," in Peters, *Cosmos as Creation*, 32.

of other creatures—bacteria, grasses, bluebirds, horses, the great gray whales. We have all evolved from common ancestors and are kin in the shared history of life.

These and other discoveries of contemporary science coalesce into a picture of the world calling for new interpretations, especially as classical dualisms can no longer be maintained. What, for example, is the proper relationship of spirit and matter if they are in effect the inside and outside of the same phenomena?[10] And—a burning question—what is humanity's place in the great scheme of things? The ancient concept of the hierarchy of being ranks things according to their participation in spirit, from nonorganic to grades of organic life, all under the sway of the Source of Being (from the pebble to the peach to the poodle to the person to the powers and principalities). In this hierarchy, human beings with their rational souls are superior to the natural world, a ranking that easily gives rise to arrogance, one root of the present ecological crisis. Consider for a moment, however, green plants. Predating the human race by millennia, green plants take in carbon dioxide and give off oxygen. Through this process of photosynthesis they create the atmosphere that makes the life of land animals possible. Human beings could not exist without these plants that neither think nor move. They, on the other hand, get along fine without us. Wherein, then, lies superiority?[11] In an interdependent system, no part is intrinsically higher or lower. Yes, more complex life represents critical evolutionary breakthrough, but not such as to remove humanity from essential dependence on previously evolved creatures. The challenge is to redesign the hierarchy of being into a circle of the community of life. With a kind of species humility,

---

[10] See the insightful essay of Karl Rahner, "The Unity of Spirit and Matter in the Christian Understanding of Faith," *Theological Investigations*, vol. 6, trans. Karl and Boniface Kruger (New York: Crossroad, 1982), 153–77. The works of Teilhard de Chardin are prophetic in this respect: cf. *The Divine Milieu* (New York: Harper & Row, 1960) and *Hymn of the Universe* (New York: Harper & Row, 1965).

[11] This example is taken from Rosemary Radford Ruether, *To Change the World: Christology and Cultural Criticism* (New York: Crossroad, 1981), 67. This scholar has contributed early, insightfully, and voluminously to ecological theology: see her *New Woman, New Earth* (San Francisco: Harper & Row, 1975), chap. 8; *Sexism and God-Talk: Toward a Feminist Theology* (Boston: Beacon, 1983), chaps. 3, 9, 10, and postscript; and *Gaia and God: An Ecofeminist Theology of Earth Healing* (San Francisco: HarperCollins, 1992).

we need to reimagine systematically the uniqueness of being human in the context of our profound kinship with the rest of nature.

In addition to prodding us to rethink basic categories, the new cosmology also offers a new framework within which to consider typical theological questions.[12] Each of our subspecialties is profoundly affected. In such an old, vast, dynamic, and organic world, how and for what reasons does one come to belief in God (foundational theology or apologetics)? What wisdom about the world can be found in biblical and historical authors and the writings of the world's other religious traditions? What does the book of nature in our day teach us about the mystery of God, the Creator of this magnificence, who continues to work creatively within its open and unpredictable systems? How to interpret the irreversible entrance of God into precisely this world through the incarnation of divine Wisdom and the transformation of this flesh in the resurrection of Jesus Christ? How to understand that the love revealed in Jesus' healings and feeding and poured out on the cross is the very same "Love that moves the sun and the other stars,"[13] so that Dante's vision is no pious lyricism but a theological truth? How to interpret the Spirit of the baptismal font as none other than the very Giver of Life to all the creatures of the rain forest (another undeveloped aspect of pneumatology to which this convention's theme has been drawing our attention)? Whence evil in such a self-organizing universe, and how does sin gain a foothold? Why suffering? How to preach salvation as healing and rescue for the whole world rather than an a-cosmic relation to God? How to let go of contempt for matter, the

---

[12] It is good to report that the work has already begun. See, e.g., university symposiums: David Burrell, ed., *God and Creation: An Ecumenical Symposium* (Notre Dame, IN: University of Notre Dame Press, 1990); and Kevin Irwin, ed., *Preserving the Creation: Environmental Theology and Ethics* (Washington, DC: Georgetown University Press, 1994); pivotal essays: David Tracy, "Cosmology and Christian Hope," in his *On Naming the Present* (Maryknoll, NY: Orbis, 1994), 73–81, and Michael Himes and Kenneth Himes, "Creation and an Environmental Ethic," in their *Fullness of Faith* (New York: Paulist, 1993), 104–24; and book-length treatments: John Haught, *The Promise of Nature: Ecology and Cosmic Purpose* (New York: Paulist, 1993); Tony Kelly, *An Expanding Theology: Faith in a World of Connections* (Newtown, Australia: E. J. Dwyer, 1993)—a little summa; and Denis Edwards, *Jesus the Wisdom of God: An Ecological Theology* (Maryknoll, NY: Orbis, 1995).

[13] Dante, *The Divine Comedy*, trans. Dorothy Sayers and Barbara Reynolds (Harmondsworth, England: Penguin, 1962), canto 33, line 145.

body and its sexuality, and revalue them as good and blessed? How to interpret human beings as primarily "earthlings" rather than tourists or aliens whose true home is elsewhere?[14] How to conceive of the church, its mission and structures, in an evolving universe? How to recognize the sacraments as symbols of divine graciousness in a universe which is itself a sacrament? How to hope for the eschatological redemption of the whole material universe, even now groaning? What paths of spirituality does the new cosmology suggest? Not least, how is moral decision making affected? In the classic synthesis, there is a natural order in the world established by God and knowable by the human mind. To act morally or "in accord with natural law" is to transpose the order in the cosmos into human conduct, doing or avoiding acts according to their coherence with that order. How is this pattern of thought affected by the realization that the laws of nature are themselves not eternal principles but only approximations read off from regularities, and that their working is shot through with chance and indeterminacy? Bringing cosmology into view, I am suggesting, shifts the axis of all theological questions, setting an agenda for years to come. Notice that one does not have to deal with the cosmos directly; rather, it provides both framework and substantive insights useful for *fides quaerens intellectum*. The intellectual integrity of theology, as public discourse of a North American community responsible to articulate faith in a global society, requires vigorous response to this intellectual challenge.

Cosmology and the Moral Integrity of Theology

Besides an intellectual reason for theology's turn to the heavens and the earth, there is a compelling moral reason as well. In our day the human race is inflicting devastation on the life-systems and other living species of our home planet, havoc that has reached crisis proportions and even in some places ecological collapse. Due to the unceasing demands of consumerist economies on the one hand and burgeoning population on the other, we are exploiting earth's resources without regard for long-term sustainability.

---

[14] This is the expression of Sallie McFague, "An Earthly Theological Agenda," in *Ecofeminism and the Sacred*, ed. Carol Adams (New York: Continuum, 1993), 84–98.

This assault on the earth results now in damage to the systems that sustain life: holes in the ozone layer; clear-cut forests; drained wetlands; denuded grasslands and soils; polluted air, rivers, and coastal waters; poisoned oceans; disrupted habitats; and hovering over all the threat of nuclear conflagration and the reality of nuclear waste. The wide-scale destruction of ecosystems has as its flip side the extinction of species with a consequent loss of earth's biodiversity. By a conservative estimate, in the last quarter of the twentieth century (1975–2000), 20 percent of all living species will have become extinct. We are living in a time of a great dying off. Life forms that have taken millions of years to evolve, magnificent animals and intricate plants, are disappearing forever, due to human actions. Their perishing sends an early warning signal of the death of the planet itself as a dwelling place for life. In the blunt language of the World Council of Churches Canberra assembly, "The stark sign of our times is a planet in peril at our hands."[15]

This ongoing destruction of God's good earth, when perceived through the lens of theology, bears the mark of deep sinfulness.[16] Through greed, self-interest, and injustice, human beings are violently bringing disfigurement and death to this living, evolving planet which ultimately comes from the creative hands of God who looks upon it as "very good" (Gen 1:31). Ecocide, biocide, geocide—these new terms attempt to name the killing of ecosystems and species that are meant to reflect the glory of God but instead end up broken or extinct. One of the "books" that teaches about God is being ruined, and this is a matter for theological concern, having even the character of a moral imperative.

In light of the devastation, the turn to the heavens and the earth bears the marks of genuine conversion of mind and heart, with repentance for the lack of love and the violence visited on the living planet. As we turn, we will be looking for thought patterns that will transform our species-centeredness and enable us to grant not just instrumental

---

[15] "Giver of Life—Sustain Your Creation," in *Signs of the Spirit*, official report of the WCC's seventh assembly in Canberra, ed. Michael Kinnamon (Geneva: WCC, 1991), 55.

[16] See Sallie McFague's shrewd analysis of ecological sin in her *The Body of God: An Ecological Theology* (Minneapolis: Augsburg/Fortress Press, 1993), 112–29; her earlier work, *Models of God: Theology for an Ecological, Nuclear Age* (Philadelphia: Fortress Press, 1987), is filled with data about the ecological crisis and offers a rethinking of God in its light.

worth but intrinsic value to the natural world. This is a condition for the possibility of extending vigorous moral consideration to the whole earth, now under threat.[17] If nature with its own inherent value before God be the new poor, then our compassion is called into play. Solidarity with victims, option for the poor, and action on behalf of justice widen out from human beings to embrace life-systems and other species to ensure vibrant communion in life for all.

Moral reflection about the natural world under threat becomes more complex when we take into consideration the organic links that exist between exploitation of the earth and injustice among human beings themselves. The voices of the poor and of women bring to light the fact that structures of social domination are chief among the ways that abuse of the earth is accomplished. Attending to these voices prevents retrieval of the cosmos from being tagged as the interest of only a First World, male, academic elite.

The Poor

Economic poverty coincides with ecological poverty, for the poor suffer disproportionately from environmental destruction.[18] In so-called Third World countries, the onset of development through capitalism

---

[17] This intrinsic value is well attested in biblical theologies. God covenants with the earth as well as with humans; prophets invoke judgment over all that destroys life; Wisdom's playful delight in the natural world is not dependent on human participation. As oppressed people cry out to God, so too the earth can groan, lament, and shout out; conversely, rejoicing clothes the hills, the desert blossoms, the meadows and valleys sing with gladness. See Richard Clifford, "The Bible and the Environment," in Irwin, *Preserving the Creation*, 1–26.

[18] See David Hallman, ed., *Ecotheology: Voices from South and North* (Geneva: WCC; Maryknoll, NY: Orbis, 1994); Leonardo Boff and Virgilio Elizondo, eds., *Ecology and Poverty*, Concilium 5 (Maryknoll, NY: Orbis, 1995), esp. Eduardo Gudynas, "Ecology from the Viewpoint of the Poor," 106–14; Leonardo Boff, *Ecology and Liberation: A New Paradigm* (Maryknoll, NY: Orbis, 1995); Mary Heather MacKinnon and Moni McIntyre, eds., *Readings in Ecology and Feminist Theology* (Kansas City, MO: Sheed and Ward, 1995), esp. H. Paul Santmire, "Ecology, Justice, and Theology: Beyond the Preliminary Skirmishes," 56–62, and Vandana Shiva, "Development, Ecology, and Women," 161–71; and Vitor Westhelle, "Creation Motifs in the Search for a Vital Space: A Latin American Perspective," in *Lift Every Voice: Constructing Christian Theologies from the Underside*, ed. Susan Thistlethwaite and Mary Potter Engel (San Francisco: Harper & Row, 1990), 128–40.

brings deforestation, soil erosion, and polluted waters, which in turn lead to the disruption of local cycles of nature and the sustenance economies on which most poor people depend. Sheer human misery results. Again, plantation farming of commodity crops for export not only destroys biodiversity but also creates wealth for a few from the backbreaking labor of a class of poor people. Correlatively, lack of land reform pushes dispossessed rural peoples to the edges of cultivated land where, in order to stay alive, they practice slash-and-burn agriculture, in the process destroying pristine habitat, killing rare animals, and displacing indigenous peoples. To give a North American example, US companies export work to factories across the Mexican border (*maquiladores*) that cheaply employ thousands of young, rural women to make high-quality consumer goods for export while they live in unhealthy squalor in an environment spoiled by toxic waste.

In a global perspective, these conditions result from an economic system driven by profit whose inner logic makes it prey without ceasing on nature's resources and seek cheap labor to turn those resources into consumer products. The beneficiaries are the wealthy classes and nations, including ourselves, who consume without ceasing a disproportionate amount of the earth's resources not out of need to stay alive but out of need to be pleasured and entertained. Even in these wealthy countries, ecological injustice runs through the social fabric. The economically well-off, for example, can choose to live amid acres of green, while poor people are housed near factories, refineries, or waste processing plants that heavily pollute the environment; birth defects, general ill health, and disease result. The bitterness of this experience is exacerbated by racial prejudice as environmental racism pressures people of color to dwell in these neighborhoods. In sum, social injustice has an ecological face: ravaging of people and of the land go hand in hand. To be truly effective, therefore, the turn to the cosmos in theology needs to include commitment to a more just social order within the wider struggle for life as a whole, for healthy ecosystems where all living creatures can flourish.

Women

Exploitation of the earth also coincides with the subordination of women within the system of patriarchy. Female symbolism for nature generally pervades human thought, arising from the fact that women are the lifegivers to every human child as the earth itself, Mother Earth, brings forth fruits. Feminist scholarship today points out how classical Christian theology has consistently used this symbolic affinity to interpret both women and the natural world in terms of hierarchical dualism, separating them from and subordinating them to the men they bring forth and sustain. While granted their own goodness before God, both women and nature are identified with matter, potency, and body more than with spirit, act, and mind. They are assigned mainly instrumental value in this world and excluded from direct contact with the sphere of the sacred, which is construed in analogy with transcendent male consciousness beyond the realm of coming to be and passing away. Women whose bodies mediate physical existence to humanity thus become the oldest symbol of the connection between social domination and the domination of nature.[19]

While the construals of Greek philosophy that undergird traditional subordinationist theologies may be superseded by other philosophies, the mentality that sees nature as something to be dominated continues to draw on the imagery and attitudes of men's domination of women. We speak of "the rape of the earth," revealing the extent to which exploitation of nature is identified with violent sexual conquest of women, and of "virgin forest," as yet untouched by man but awaiting his exploration and conquest. These and other linguistic metaphors point to the reality that ruling man's hierarchy over women extends also to nature, who is meant for his service while he, in his nobility, has a duty to control and a right to use her.

The contribution of women from cultural positions other than white feminists is instructive here. For example, womanist theologian Delores Williams makes a telling connection between the violation of nature and the practice of breeding black women under slavery, both defilements leading to exhaustion of the body and depletion of the spirit created by God.[20] Describing the Chipko Movement to protect local trees in

---

[19] "In addition to the writings of Ruether and McFague, see Anne Primavesi, *From Apocalypse to Genesis: Ecology, Feminism, and Christianity* (Minneapolis: Augsburg/ Fortress Press, 1991); Elizabeth Johnson, *Women, Earth, and Creator Spirit* (New York: Paulist, 1993); Adams, *Ecofeminism and the Sacred*; and MacKinnon and McIntyre, *Readings in Ecology and Feminist Theology*.

[20] Delores Williams, "Sin, Nature, and Black Women's Bodies," in Adams, *Ecofeminism and the Sacred*, 24–29; see also Shamara Shantu Riley, "Ecology Is a

India and the Green Belt Movement for reforestation in Kenya, both led largely by women, Asian theologian Aruna Gnanadason analyzes how the women are affirming the life of their own bodies in the process.[21] Indeed, in our day, women's bodily self-confidence, women's psychological and spiritual self-confidence, flows against the tide of ecological collapse but meets mighty opposition in the process.

In sum, sexism too has an ecological face, and the devastating consequences of patriarchal dualism cannot be fully addressed until the system is faced as a whole. To be truly effective, therefore, the turn to the cosmos in theology needs to cut through the knot of misogynist prejudice in our systematic concepts, shifting from dualistic, hierarchical, and atomistic categories to holistic, communal, and relational ones.

The argument of this section has been that the moral integrity of theology demands that it extend its concern to embrace the great family of earth as a supreme value, now under threat. The vision motivating such theology is that of a flourishing humanity on a thriving earth, both together a sacrament of the glory of God.

Ellery and Participation

Having scanned the history of the cosmological theme in theology and having argued for its retrieval on the grounds of theology's intellectual and moral integrity, I would like to engage you in a simple thought experiment, one that may whet your appetite for the work that lies ahead. Let us juxtapose a goldfish with Aquinas's notion of participation and ask what might result if theology interpreted the former in the light of the latter.

We begin with nature writer Annie Dillard's description of her goldfish Ellery:

> This Ellery cost me twenty-five cents. He is a deep red-orange, darker than most goldfish. He steers short distances mainly with his slender red lateral fins; they seem to provide impetus for going

---

Sistah's Issue Too," in MacKinnon and McIntyre, *Readings in Ecology and Feminist Theology*, 214–29.

[21] Aruna Gnanadason, "Towards a Feminist Eco-Theology for India," in *A Reader in Feminist Theology*, ed. Prasanna Kumari (Madras, India: Gurukul Lutheran Theological College, 1993), 95–105.

backward, up, or down. . . . He can extend his mouth, so it looks like a length of pipe; he can shift the angle of his eyes in his head [to] look before and behind himself, instead of simply out to his side. His belly, what there is of it, is white . . . and a patch of this white extends up his sides . . . as though all his [upper] brightness were sunburn.

For this creature, as I said, I paid twenty-five cents. I had never bought an animal before. It was very simple; I went to a store in Roanoke called "Wet Pets"; I handed the man a quarter, and he handed me a knotted plastic bag bouncing with water in which a green plant floated and the goldfish swam. This fish, two bits' worth, has a coiled gut, a spine radiating fine bones, and a brain. Just before I sprinkle his food flakes into his bowl, I rap three times on the bowl's edge; now he is conditioned, and swims to the surface when I rap. And, he has a heart.[22]

As Sallie McFague comments, "the juxtaposition in this passage of twenty-five cents with the elaborateness, cleverness, and sheer glory of this tiny bit of matter named Ellery is frankly unnerving. For the intricacy of this little creature calls forth wonder, and suddenly we see that it is priceless."[23] What would be an appropriate theological interpretation of Ellery? I suggest that Aquinas's notion of participation is a resource with great and largely untapped potential to help answer that question.

According to Aquinas, all creatures exist by participation in divine being.[24] This is an awesome concept, suggesting an intrinsic, ongoing relationship with the very wellspring of being, with the sheer livingness of the living God who in overflowing graciousness quickens all things. Exemplifying the catholic imagination at work, Aquinas works with a fine analogy to explain this.[25] God's presence among creatures awakens them to life the way fire ignites what it brushes against. We know that fire is present wherever something catches on fire. Just so, everything that exists does so by participation in the fire of divine being. Everything

---

[22] Annie Dillard, *Pilgrim at Tinker Creek: A Mystical Excursion into the Natural World* (New York: Harper & Row, 1974), 124.

[23] McFague, *The Body of God*, 210. I am indebted to this author for her discovery and use of this passage.

[24] For what follows, see Aquinas, *Summa theologiae* I, questions 4 (a. 3), 8, 13, 15 (a. 2), 18, 44, 45 (a. 7), and 104; and *Summa contra gentiles* 3, chs. 17-21, 65-70.

[25] *ST* I, q. 8, a. 1, 2, 3; and *SCG* 3.66, par. 7.

that acts is energized by participation in divine act. Everything that brings something else into being does so by sharing in divine creative power. Every act of resistance to the history of radical suffering is fueled by the inexhaustible source of new being. Conversely, thanks to the relation of participation, we can affirm of God in a surpassing and originating sense all the vitality, radical energy, spontaneity, and charm encountered in the world. In turn, we can see that creatures themselves in some way resemble God.

Does Ellery exist by participation in divine being? Is this glorious little fish in some way an image of God? Is he a word in the book of nature that reveals knowledge of God? Is God intimately present to this goldfish preserving him in existence at every moment? Does he have his own intrinsic value which we are called upon to respect? If so—and I hope you are answering "Yes" to these questions—then we can ill afford to neglect him. Including Ellery, and by extension the whole universe, in theological reflection is of critical importance.

Conclusion

This address has been seeking to persuade you that theology needs to complete the many recent worthy turns to the subject with a turn to the heavens and the earth. Whatever our subdisciplines, we need to develop theology with a tangible and comprehensive ecological dimension. I am not suggesting that we just think through a new theology of creation, but that cosmology be a framework within which all theological topics be rethought and a substantive partner in theological interpretation. There is hard work ahead. We need to appreciate all over again that the whole universe is a sacrament, vivified by the presence of the Creator Spirit. We need to realize that its destruction is tantamount to a sacrilege. And we need to fathom that human beings are part of the mystery and magnificence of this universe, not lords of the manor but partners with God in helping creation to grow and prosper.

Recovering the cosmocentric power of the fuller Christian tradition puts us in line with our ancient and medieval forebears and fosters the intellectual and moral integrity of theology. Not doing so would be to make our theologizing increasingly irrelevant. It would also be to fail in responsibility to our profession, to the Church, and to generations yet unborn, human and nonhuman species alike. Doing so sets theology off on a great intellectual adventure, one where both wisdom and prophecy will intertwine on the way to a new theological synthesis and praxis. This, friends and colleagues, is a monumental challenge as the Catholic Theological Society of America begins its second half-century of Catholic talk.[26]

---

[26] See Peter Steinfels, "Fifty Years of Catholic Talk," *New York Times* (20 June 1995), A12, on the fiftieth-anniversary convention.

Part 1

Turning

To the Wild(erness)

Chapter 1

Turn to the Earth

Some Reflections on Elizabeth Johnson's Contributions

Sallie McFague

Elizabeth Johnson and I, as they say, "go back a long way." I have admired her work for many years and cherished her friendship just as much. She is, I believe, one of the most important theological voices of our generation, and I am honored to write a few words about her distinctive contributions. There are many, but I will focus on just one, which is epitomized in our mutual love for a little goldfish named Ellery and its implications for a theological response to global climate change. In Beth's presidential address in 1996 for the Catholic Theological Society of America, titled "Turn to the Heavens and the Earth: Retrieval of the Cosmos in Theology," she called on all theologians not merely to "think through a new theology of creation" but to reframe all theological topics from a cosmological perspective. She notes how demanding this task will be, for "we need to appreciate all over again that the whole universe is a sacrament, vivified by the presence of the Creator Spirit." What a challenge! And, believe it or not, she insists that we include Ellery the goldfish. In fact, Ellery becomes the main example of Aquinas's notion that all creatures exist through their participation in the divine being. What an awesome assignment for

3

a little goldfish that Annie Dillard has told us cost "twenty-five cents" in a store called Wet Pets in Roanoke, Virginia. As Dillard writes, "This fish, two bits' worth, has a coiled gut, a spine radiating fine bones, and a brain. Just before I sprinkle his food flakes into his bowl, I rap three times on the bowl's edge; now he is conditioned, and swims to the surface when I rap. And, he has a heart."[1]

Beth and I both see Ellery as an example of Aquinas's notion of participation in God. Ellery stands for what is true of every creature, no matter how humble—"its ongoing relationship with the very well-spring of being, with the sheer livingness of the living God who in overflowing graciousness quickens all things." If we can see Ellery as "within" God, then we will also see other events as within God, as Beth tells us: "every act of resistance to the history of radical suffering" as well as "all the vitality, radical energy, spontaneity, and charm encountered in the world." In other words, does this include such events as climate change and financial inequality? Does the suffering as well as the insight and energy needed to tackle such matters also participate somehow in God? I think Beth is telling us that it does.

From the microscopic to the macroscopic, *everything* participates, both in its joys and sufferings, *within* God. By using Ellery the goldfish as the example of the most important direction for theology in the twenty-first century, Beth is telling us that one thing needful is for us *to wake up*. She is telling us to see the whole world "within God's hands," every scrap of it. At the heart of this call to theologians is *a new way to see the world*. We are called to wake up to both the glory and the horror of life on planet Earth, the glory of the intricacy, beauty, and cleverness of Ellery *and* the horror of the brief lives of suffering that most creatures undergo. Beth is calling us to *wake up and stay aware* that we live daily and in all ways and at all levels in a world that is awesome and wonderful beyond expression and *also* a world that is more gruesome, selfish, depressing, and mean-spirited beyond what we can endure. But all of this world, the cosmos with its joys and sufferings, is "within God's hands," participating in the divine being both to gain insight and energy for its beauty, life, and love *and* to endure its most despicable human atrocities.

[1] Annie Dillard, *Pilgrim at Tinker Creek: A Mystical Excursion into the Natural World* (New York: Harper and Row, 1974), 124.

As we step further into the twenty-first century, a time notable so far for challenging us with fearful climate change and gross financial inequality, we realize that in order to bear both its beauty and its terrors, we will need this new way of seeing, the *wide awake aware gaze* that encourages us to see each and every creature and event as participating in God. Everything lives within God, not in a general or generic way, but in its own most particular and distinctive manner and ways. Ellery, as Dillard tells us, is not any old goldfish but a *particular* one with unique features: "He is a deep red-orange, darker than most goldfish. He steers short distances mainly with his slender red lateral fins; they seem to provide impetus for going backward, up, or down. . . . He can extend his mouth, so it looks like a length of pipe; he can shift the angle of his eyes in his head [to] look before and behind himself, instead of simply out to his side. His belly, what there is of it, is white . . . and a patch of white extends up his sides . . . as though all his [upper] brightness were sunburn."[2] As we read this seemingly endless passage describing in detail the peculiarities of this particular goldfish, we may wonder, "Do we really need to know *so much* about one measly goldfish?" Apparently, we do, since Aquinas's understanding of participation is not some general mushy stew but the acknowledgment and appreciation for each and every particular creature, object, and event in the cosmos. So, glory to God for difference, diversity, and peculiarity! Apparently, we are to wake up to and love marvelous, messy planet Earth in all the glorious detail of its most humble members.

So, what an assignment Beth has given the upcoming generation of theologians! We do not know what this new century will bring us. Many of us fear the worst. The Anthropocene Era, the human era, is characterized by the end of human innocence and ignorance: *we know that we know.* We know who we are in the scheme of things (as Beth's book on evolution illustrates), and we know that we are responsible for the planetary mess at both ecological and financial levels. We may not want to wake up and stay aware, but it is our fate as well as the most important challenge facing us. Beth reminds that "every creature and *event*" participates in God; hence, we know that we must also include such "events" as climate change and financial inequality. It is not that God causes such events, but if Ellery is within God then so are these

[2] Ibid.

results of our actions. As we tackle the most difficult challenges that human beings have ever faced, we need to recall that "Retrieval of the Cosmos" for theology includes *everything*, even such monstrous, enigmatic, complex, and daunting events. We do not face these events alone—hallelujah!

Chapter 2

Humans, Chimps, and Bonobos
Toward an Inclusive View of the Human as Bearing the Image of God

Denis Edwards

For Elizabeth Johnson, faithful explorer into the mystery of God and the community of creation

In her recent theological anthropology, Celia Deane-Drummond seeks to go beyond the idea of the divine image as associated with unique characteristics of the human, such as reason or freedom. Focus on the uniqueness of such characteristics has often involved marking a sharp separation of humans from other animals, and in some cases of men from women, which can then provide an excuse for oppressive behavior. She explores, instead, what she calls a liminal theology that celebrates what links humans together with other animals in evolutionary and ecological relationships.

Deane-Drummond seeks to show "that we have become ourselves and importantly become ourselves in evolutionary terms through navigating boundary relationships with each other, in both a temporal and a spatial sense, including relationships with other species."[1] These

---

[1] Celia Deane-Drummond, *The Wisdom of the Liminal: Evolution and Other Animals in Human Becoming* (Grand Rapids, MI: Eerdmans, 2014), 4.

boundaries do not have hard edges, she says, but are somewhat "fuzzy."[2] They can show up as distinctive marks of the human, but only through communal relationships with others, including other animals. She sees humans as becoming more distinctively and properly themselves, and taking their proper God-given role in the divine theo-drama, through encounters with other species.

It is my hope to contribute to this discussion by focusing particularly on our evolutionary relationship with our nearest living relatives, the great apes, and bringing this relationship into dialogue with the early Christian tradition of humans as made in the image of God. Perhaps it is significant to note that the Judaeo-Christian tradition arose, and particularly in Europe continued to develop, with little or no awareness of other primates. When a chimpanzee and an orangutan were first put on display at the London Zoo in 1835, people were shocked and offended at their likeness to humanity, and Queen Victoria judged the apes to be "painfully and disagreeably human."[3]

I will begin by engaging with two scientists, Frans de Waal and Michael Tomasello. Both have contributed to the recent body of work on the evolution of cooperation, and both explore the connections between humans and other apes, particularly chimpanzees and bonobos. Their science is work in progress and controversial, and I will not be able to track all the biological discussion of their work. But I will point to some real differences between them. I have chosen them not only because they are influential figures in the field but also because they stand in opposing places in some of the controversies.

The aim here is to bring some of their key scientific insights into dialogue with the theological tradition, in the quest to further the theological understanding of the human in relation to other creatures. In particular, I will explore a view of the human as bearing the divine image in a way that is not only distinctive but also inclusive of other animals, rather than exclusive of them. In developing this position, I will take up theological concepts from the Greek patristic tradition, particularly from Athanasius.

---

[2] Ibid.

[3] Frans de Waal, *The Bonobo and the Atheist: In Search of Humanism among the Primates* (New York: Norton, 2013), 101. Charles Darwin saw and felt a connection where the queen felt a threat (p. 107).

Frans de Waal

Frans de Waal is the C. H. Chandler Professor of Primate Behavior at Emory University and the director of the Living Links Center at the Yerkes Primate Center. In his early work, of the mid-1970s, he discovered and explored reconciliation among primates and pioneered the study of conflict-resolution in animals.[4] Chimpanzees make up after a fight by kissing and embracing. High status male chimps can be seen to come between disputing parties to put an end to a confrontation and to the looming violence. Female chimps drag males together to make up after a fight and remove weapons from their hands. Although de Waal is well aware of how aggressive and violent chimps can be to each other, and to humans, he also sees them as engaging in self-control to avoid confrontation and in peacemaking after conflict occurs. He points to the work of Christophe Boesch, who documents ten instances of wild male chimps that have been observed to adopt juveniles who have lost their mothers.[5] De Waal opposes, then, the unrelieved bleak picture of nature "red in tooth and claw," as well as the behaviorist theory of B. F. Skinner, and contemporary ideas of genetic determinism.

In his more recent work, he has been exploring what he sees as the basis of human morality in the lives of primates. He fully accepts that humans possess a unique ability to cooperate across large, highly organized populations, and they have a complex and well-developed morality. Nevertheless, based on intensive observation of chimpanzees and bonobos, he argues that these other species can also be highly cooperative and that they possess an emotional capacity for empathy.[6] He proposes that this capacity for empathy, and the resulting cooperation, shared by various mammal species, is the evolutionary foundation for human morality.[7]

---

[4] Frans de Waal, *Peacemaking among Primates* (Cambridge, MA: Harvard University Press, 1989).

[5] De Waal, *The Bonobo and the Atheist*, 46.

[6] See Frans de Waal, *Our Inner Ape: A Leading Primatologist Explains Why We Are Who We Are* (New York: Riverhead, 2005); *The Age of Empathy: Nature's Lessons for a Kinder Society* (New York: Harmony Books, 2009); Frans B. M. de Waal and Malini Suchak, "Prosocial Primates: Selfish and Unselfish Motivations," *Philosophical Transactions of the Royal Society B* 365, no. 1553 (September 12, 2010): 2711–22.

[7] De Waal, *The Bonobo and the Atheist*.

As an example of such empathy, de Waal describes his observation of an elderly female chimpanzee, Peony, who sometimes has trouble walking and climbing because of arthritis. This makes it difficult for her to get up into the climbing frame where other chimps are gathered for a grooming session. When she is struggling to get up to the frame, a younger, unrelated, female moves behind her, and puts both hands on her behind to push her up so that Peony can join the rest. Another example is that when Peony is thirsty and has a long way to walk for water, younger females run ahead to the water source, take up water in their mouths and come to spit it out into Peony's mouth.[8]

De Waal describes an experiment between Peony and an unrelated chimp, Rita, which, he claims, first demonstrated that chimpanzees care about each other's welfare.[9] A bucket was filled with green and red tokens. Peony was asked to pick one at a time and hand it to those conducting the experiment. Each time she did this she was rewarded with food. If she chose a green token, Rita was also rewarded, but if she chose a red one, Rita missed out. Peony began to select more green tokens. She made more prosocial choices than choices for herself alone. This was repeated with other pairs of chimps. Sometimes the partner would try to influence the choice by aggressive and intimidating behavior or by begging. This proved to be counterproductive, resulting in fewer prosocial choices, as if the one choosing the tokens were punishing the bad behavior of the partner. Fear was ruled out as an explanation for prosocial choices, because the highest-ranking chimps, with least to fear, proved to be the most generous. It seems that chimpanzees are capable of prosocial choices based on a feeling for the other.

According to de Waal, recent studies of cooperation among primates have led researchers to three important conclusions: (1) Cooperation does not require family ties; unrelated chimpanzees and bonobos travel together, hunt together, share food, and groom one another. (2) Cooperation is often based on mutuality and reciprocity; chimps will share food with another who had earlier groomed them. (3) Cooperation can be motivated by empathy; primates identify with others in distress, arousing emotions that can lead to helping action. De Waal sees empathy as a characteristic of all mammals from rodents to elephants. He

---

[8] Ibid., 4–5.
[9] Ibid., 120–21.

suggests that it may have evolved from the maternal care demanded of mammals. Mothers need to respond to the signals of hunger or distress of their young. This sensitivity, along with the neural and hormonal processes that enable it, was then transferred to other relationships, enabling empathy, bonding, and cooperation in the wider group.[10]

Rejecting old models of animals as stimulus-response machines, or as instinct driven, de Waal insists that the animals he studies operate from emotions. He sees no sharp dividing line between human and animal emotions. While our brains are three times larger than those of chimpanzees, they have the same structure and the same parts. A special kind of neuron, known as a spindle cell, thought to be involved in self-awareness, empathy, and self-control, is found not only in humans but also in the brains of other animals, including apes.[11] Scientists from Parma in Italy have explored mirror neurons, which connect humans as well as other animals at a bodily level, as when one's yawn or hand movement causes the same reaction in another. It seems empathy is a bodily characteristic of humans and other mammals. Emotions can be channelled from one mammal to another in a kind of bodily contagion. Put a needle in a woman's arm and the pain center in her husband's brain lights up.

As a further example of this kind of bodily channelling of emotion, de Waal describes an observation of the birth of a chimpanzee. May, the delivering mother, stands half upright, with her open hand cupped between her legs ready to catch the baby. Others stand gathered quietly by. An older female, Atlanta, standing next to May, adopts the same position, as if she too were expecting the baby. When May's baby emerges, one chimpanzee screams, others embrace. Atlanta grooms the new mother almost continuously for the next week.[12]

De Waal suggests that it is helpful to think of three levels of empathy in mammals. At the core is what he describes as emotional contagion, the capacity to match another's emotional state. At a second level is the capacity to feel concern for others. This is expressed among chimpanzees and bonobos when consolation is offered to an ape in distress,

---

[10] Frans de Waal, "One for All: Our Ability to Cooperate in Large Societies Has Deep Evolutionary Roots in the Animal Kingdom," *Scientific American* 311, no. 3 (September 2014): 54–55.

[11] De Waal, *The Bonobo and the Atheist*, 80.

[12] Ibid., 139.

by hugging, grooming, or carefully inspecting an injury. The third level, according to de Waal, found in species such as dolphins, elephants, and apes, is the capacity to take the perspective of another and offer targeted help to them.

He describes a test carried out at the Primate Research Institute of Kyoto University. Shina Yamamoto gives a chimpanzee a choice between two ways to obtain orange juice. The chimp can use a rake to bring it closer or suck it up through a straw. But the chimp has no tools, while a nearby chimp in a separate area has a whole range of tools. This second chimpanzee takes one look at the first one's problem and immediately hands over precisely the right tool. However, if the second chimp is unable to see the first, he simple picks tools at random. De Waal concludes that this experiment indicates not only that chimpanzees readily assist one another but also that they take the specific needs of the other into account. While he acknowledges that we still know little about the capacities of apes, he insists that "they are not nearly as selfish as has been assumed."[13]

De Waal sees human cooperation as grounded in the mutualistic cooperation that is shared by other species. He sees both humans and other animals as highly sensitive to the fair divisions of food and other valued goods. He recognizes that humans are the only species to cooperate widely with outsiders. This out-group cooperation, he suggests, can be seen as extension of the in-group cooperation of our evolutionary past. What is truly unique to humans, he proposes, is the highly organized and large-scale nature of their cooperation. Humans also enforce cooperation by punishing freeloaders and advancing the good reputation of cooperators.[14] What sets human morality apart, according to de Waal, is the development of a logically coherent and universal system of moral standards. Because this is lacking in chimps, he is not inclined to call a chimpanzee a "moral being."[15]

While de Waal advocates a tolerant stance toward religion, he attempts to develop a bottom-up view of human morality that does not depend on religious faith. His argument is that morality, in fact, predates religion: "The moral law is not imposed from above or derived from

---

[13] Ibid., 147.
[14] De Waal, "One for All," 55.
[15] De Waal, *The Bonobo and the Atheist*, 17.

well-reasoned principles; rather, it arises from ingrained values that have been there since the beginning of time."[16]

As a theologian I am far from convinced that we can do without God, and without a theology of grace and sin. In an earlier work, I have discussed the extremely dangerous other side to our inherited tendency to cooperate with insiders, namely, our tendency to make outsiders into scapegoats and enemies and so to do violence to them.[17] I see this tendency as profoundly connected to traditional Christian understandings of original sin and grace. Nevertheless, if de Waal is broadly right in the scientific insights he advances, I can see every reason to embrace the idea that human compassion for others unites us in an evolutionary relationship with the cooperation and empathy found among chimpanzees and bonobos, and more broadly in mammals and other animals. Here, too, grace can be understood to build on nature.

Michael Tomasello

Michael Tomasello is the codirector of the Max Planck Institute for Evolutionary Anthropology in Leipzig, Germany. He and his colleagues have been engaged in carefully designed comparative experiments with great apes and with very young children. His experiments are particularly concerned with the evolutionary origins of human cooperation.

He sees humans as the paradigmatically cultural species. He points to two clearly observable characteristics of human culture. The first is its cumulative nature, so that an invention is quickly taken up by others and improved on in ever new ways. Tomasello calls this the "ratchet" effect: humans inherit cultural artifacts and practices that accumulate modifications, which then ratchet up in complexity over time. The second observable characteristic is the creation of social institutions, behavioral practices guided by mutually agreed upon rules, which confer rights and responsibilities and are supported by sanctions. The result is a diverse range of culturally defined entities, including husbands and wives, systems of exchange, money, chiefs, and presidents. According to Tomasello, no other species has been observed to possess anything

---

[16] Ibid., 228.

[17] Denis Edwards, *Partaking of God: Trinity, Evolution and Ecology* (Collegeville, MN: Liturgical Press, 2014), 130–46.

like the cultural ratchet effect or the social institutions found among humans.[18]

Underlying these characteristics is what Tomasello sees as a species-unique level of cooperation. Because of cultural niche construction, and gene-culture coevolution, humans possess highly developed motivations and skills for cooperation with one another. Borrowing a term from the philosophy of action, Tomasello calls the psychological processes involved in the human level of cooperation "shared intentionality."[19] This phrase indicates a capacity to create joint attention and joint commitment with others in cooperative endeavours.

The shared intentionality thesis is central to Tomasello's recent book, which sets out to answer the question: what makes human thinking unique? He begins from two sets of empirical discoveries of recent decades. The first concerns the nonhuman great apes: There is new evidence for the sophisticated nature of their cognitive abilities, which makes it clear that they think in human-like ways and can understand causal and intentional connections in their physical and social worlds. This suggests that important aspects of human thinking derive from the same problem-solving abilities that are possessed by great apes. The second concerns very young children who do not yet partake fully of the language and the culture that surrounds them: they are found to operate with some cognitive processes that are not evident in great apes, in the way they engage cooperatively with others in joint attention and in cooperative communication. They possess a joint intentionality.

Based on these and other empirical findings concerning apes and young children, Tomasello sets out to offer a natural history of human knowledge, an evolutionary account of its emergence. His shared intentionality hypothesis structures this account. He describes three components of thinking: cognitive representation, inference, and self-monitoring. The shared intentionality thesis proposes that all three components were transformed at least twice in human evolution, as humans were forced to find new ways to cooperate. I will trace, briefly, Tomasello's account of the evolutionary movement from individual intentionality to joint intentionality and from joint intentionality to collective intentionality.

---

[18] Michael Tomasello, with Carol Dweck, Joan Silk, Brian Skyrms, and Elizabeth Spelke, *Why We Cooperate* (Cambridge, MA: Boston Review, 2009), xii.
[19] Ibid., xiii.

Like de Waal, Tomasello insists that great apes are far from being the stimulus-response machines they were thought to be by many theorists. They not only operate in an intentional way, but also understand others as intentional agents.[20] They operate with abstract cognitive representations, to which they assimilate particular experiences. They make causal, intentional, and productive inferences from these cognitive representations and can imagine non-actual situations. And they self-monitor their behavioral decision-making process. This implies a kind of "executive" oversight of their own decision making. Great apes operate in a flexible, intelligent, and self-regulating way.[21]

Tomasello assumes that this kind of consciousness existed in the common ancestors of humans and apes, who lived about six million years ago. He puts forward the hypothesis that not only these common ancestors but also the hominin species of the next four million years, such as the various species of australopithecines, possessed this kind of intelligence, which he names individual intentionality. He calls this intentionality individual because he sees it as intelligence that has evolved mainly in competitive situations within social groups. Although Tomasello acknowledges that great apes cooperate in various ways—in traveling together, foraging in small groups, forming alliances, and in defense against outsiders and predators—he sees them as generally highly competitive rather than cooperative in many facets of life, including eating, mating, and dominance.

He acknowledges that there is the appearance of a level of cooperation in the way that some bands of chimpanzees hunt for monkeys. But while other researchers like de Waal and Christophe Boesch (colleague of Tomasello from the Max Planck Institute) interpret this activity as an example of chimpanzees possessing a joint goal and coordinated roles, Tomasello interprets the hunt differently.[22] He thinks that each chimp is attempting to capture the monkey for its own benefit, even as it takes into account the behavior and perhaps the intentions of others. In his view, even in the hunt, chimps operate from an "I" intentionality rather than from the "We" of joint intentionality.

[20] Michael Tomasello, *A Natural History of Human Thinking* (Cambridge, MA: Harvard University Press, 2014), 20.

[21] Ibid., 30.

[22] Christophe Boesch, "Joint Cooperative Hunting among Wild Chimpanzees: Taking Natural Observations Seriously," *Behavioral and Brain Sciences* 28 (2005): 692–93. See Tomasello, *A Natural History*, 35.

By contrast he finds strong empirical evidence that very young children operate from a "We" intentionality. Infants from fourteen to eighteen months will engage in a joint activity with an adult, such as working together to obtain a toy by each operating one side of an apparatus. He notes that should an adult stop cooperating without explanation, the children regularly attempt to reengage the adult. By the time they are three, children show ongoing commitment to joint activities in the face of distractions. When one child is rewarded halfway through an experiment, the lucky child delays the consumption or her rewards until the partner receive hers. No such findings are observed in similar experiments with chimpanzees.[23]

Tomasello relates these experiments with children to evolutionary history, to the emergence of a new cognitive model, which he calls joint intentionality. In Tomasello's account, the move beyond individual intentionality begins when a change in ecology leads to new forms of collaboration. He speculates that it may have begun in an initial, preparatory way soon after the emergence of the species *Homo* around two million years ago. This coincided with an expansion of terrestrial monkeys, like baboons, who may have out-competed hominins for fruits and forced them into a new foraging niche, perhaps into scavenging meat. This may have culminated about four hundred thousand years ago with *Homo heidelbergensis*.[24] Current evidence suggests that this was the first hominin to engage in a systematic way in collaborative hunting of large game. Thus began a lifestyle in which early humans were interdependent with others in foraging for food and where there was social selection, where individuals began to evaluate others as collaborative partners. This created selection pressure for the skills and motivations associated with joint intentionality.

The capacity to help one another systematically requires new forms of communication, beginning, Tomasello argues, with informative gestures and iconic gestures—such as warning of a snake with a slithering hand movement. Cooperation in joint intentionality requires new forms of symbolic thinking. Intellectual representation is transformed, since participants must now come to represent each other's perspective on the situation they face. Inference is transformed: it becomes socially

---

[23] Tomasello, *A Natural History*, 38–43.
[24] Ibid., 48.

recursive, as individuals make inferences about their partner's intentions in relation to their own intentional states. Self-monitoring is transformed as individuals come to imagine the perspective of their partner as well as monitoring their own. This kind of "I" and "You" perception involves, simultaneously, jointness and individuality. It is these two characteristics together that define Tomasello's notion of joint intentionality. He sees this kind of joint intentionality as the necessary intermediate step toward the collective intentionality of modern humans.[25]

Collective intentionality, Tomasello argues, appeared when human populations began growing in size and competing with one another. Group life as a whole became one collaborative activity, creating a permanent shared world, a culture, based on collectively known cultural conventions, norms, and institutions. Tomasello acknowledges that many species, from whales to capuchin monkeys, and above all the great apes, engage in forms of social learning and possess a form of culture. But human culture is based on a far more developed group way of knowing and acting.

Individuals can now reason from the transpersonal, "objective," or "agent-neutral" point of view of the group. It is in this context that cooperative communication begins to operate not only through gesture and pantomime but also in language. Modern humans participate in collective intentionality not just with other individuals but with the whole social group. This leads to cognitive representation that is conventional and objective, to processes of inference that are reasoned and aimed at truth, to self-monitoring in which individuals adjust their thinking in relation to that of the group.[26]

Tomasello thinks that the step toward collective intentionality probably evolved in a population of modern humans in Africa before they migrated to other parts of the world after one hundred thousand years ago.[27] As they settled in new local ecological niches, on top of their species-wide cognitive capacity of individual, joint, and collective intentionality, they began to develop culturally specific cognitive and linguistic skills, which in a ratchet effect built on one another in cumulative cultural evolution.

Tomasello believes that in the case of human children, ontogeny follows phylogeny: at about their first birthday they cooperate with others

[25] Ibid., 78.
[26] Ibid., 141.
[27] Ibid.

in joint intentionality, and about their third they engage in collective intentionality. But these skills emerge only in constant interaction with the social environment. Thus, for Tomasello, the skills of shared intentionality are neither simply innate nor simply learned. They spring from biological adaptations but require, for their flourishing, growing up in a preexisting cultural collective with its conventions, norms, institutions, and language.[28]

Toward an Inclusive Theology of the Divine Image in Creatures

There are some obvious differences between the positions of de Waal and Tomasello. De Waal emphasizes what is common to humans and other apes, while Tomasello focuses more sharply on what is distinctive to humans. De Waal is clearly convinced that chimpanzees and bonobos are less selfish and more cooperative than Tomasello's experiments indicate. Tomasello sees de Waal and Christophe Boesch as, at times, "anthropomorphizing apes."[29] He has challenged experimental results of de Waal and Sarah Brosnan that claim to show that capuchin monkeys possess a "sense of fairness."[30]

My theological focus is not on these differences but on the broader picture that emerges from their work: that human beings can be understood only in terms of evolutionary primate history; that the evolution of large-scale cooperation is fundamental to the emergence of modern humans; that humans have profound similarities to chimpanzees and bonobos but also have distinct human qualities; that human qualities, including emotions like empathy, the capacity for moral decision making, large-scale cooperation, intelligence, culture, and language are all related to qualities found in chimps and other apes; that these human qualities can be seen as based on evolutionary adaptations from our common inheritance but also as requiring a rich social and cultural environment for their development and flourishing.

---

[28] Ibid., 146–47.

[29] Garry Stix, "The 'It' Factor," *Scientific American* 311, no. 3 (September 2014): 63.

[30] See, for example, Juliane Brauer, Josef Call, and Michael Tomasello, "Are Apes Really Inequity Averse?," *Proceedings of the Royal Society B* 273, no. 1605 (2006): 3123–28.

How might all of this be brought into dialogue with the theological tradition and its understanding of the human being as made in the image of God? This tradition has often understood the image of God in terms of qualities that seem to separate humans from other animals, as located, for example, in human reason, human freedom, or the human soul. More recently the International Theological Commission has seen the image of God in humans as woven from two major strands, communion and stewardship: first, humans are "persons oriented towards communion" with the triune God and with one another;[31] second, human beings occupy the unique place of "sharing in the divine governance of visible creation."[32]

This document of the International Theological Commission contains many rich insights, and in my judgment its vision of humans as persons oriented toward communion is deeply meaningful. The document has important things to say about evolution and also about human responsibility toward other creatures. But when talking about human stewardship of other creatures, it insists on kingly language that I think needs questioning, above all, in the context of the ecological crisis of the twenty-first century. It speaks of humans as participating in God's "governance" and "lordship" over the universe, of human "rule" and "sovereignty" over other creatures, and of humans as "the summit" of visible creation.[33] Importantly, the document qualifies its kingly language by pointing out that the kingship of Jesus is one of service and of the cross.

In my view the biblical concept of the human person made in the image of God needs to be understood in a broader biblical context in which human beings are called to cosmic humility before God and the wonders of God's creation, and in which human beings are called to praise God with other creatures as part of the one community of creation.[34] In the light of the insights of scientists like de Waal and Tomasello, and their findings about what is common to humans and

---

[31] International Theological Commission, *Communion and Stewardship: Human Persons Created in the Image of God*, par. 25.

[32] Ibid., par. 57.

[33] Ibid., pars. 57–58.

[34] On this, see Richard Bauckham, *Bible and Ecology: Rediscovering the Community of Creation* (London: Darton, Longman & Todd, 2010). This theme is developed by Elizabeth Johnson in her *Ask the Beasts: Darwin and the God of Love* (London: Bloomsbury, 2014), and also in my *Partaking of God*.

other members of the great ape family, as well as about what is distinctive to humans, I think we need a more inclusive concept of the image of God.

Are there resources in the Christian tradition that can help theologians today affirm that humans are made in the image of God, in a distinctive way, not as over against other creatures, but precisely in our evolutionary interrelationship and ongoing relations with them? Can these resources help us to affirm that other creatures, such as bonobos, also in their own distinctive way, bear the image of God? And can resources from the tradition help us see that part of what is distinctive about the way humans bear the image is that they are persons called to communion, not only with one another and the triune God, but also with the community of life on Earth and the wider universe?

I find some such resources in Athanasius. The concept of the image of God is central to Athanasius's theological anthropology as it was for his predecessor Irenaeus, although Athanasius does not follow Irenaeus's distinction between image and likeness. Athanasius reserves the word "image" to the eternal Word. Christ, for him, is the Image, the Wisdom, the Radiance, the Word, and the Son of the Father. Humanity, then, is "in the image" of the Image. Athanasius situates humanity in the midst of God's creation, all of which is completely dependent on the creative Word for its existence. Within this wider creation he has a strong view of humanity's uniqueness. In his *On the Incarnation* he writes:

> Because he does not begrudge the gift of existence, he made all things from nothing through his proper Word, our Lord Jesus Christ. And among these creatures, of all creatures he was especially merciful towards the human race. Seeing that by the logic of its own generation it would be unable to remain forever, he granted it a further gift, not simply creating humanity like all irrational animals on the earth, but making them in his own image and granting them also a share in the power of his proper Word, so that having as it were, shadows of the Word and being made rational, they might be able to remain in blessedness and live the true life in paradise, which is really that of the saints.[35]

---

[35] Athanasius, *On the Incarnation* 3, in *Contre Gentes and de Incarnatione*, ed. and trans. Robert W. Thomson, Oxford Early Christian Texts (Oxford: Oxford University Press, 1971), 138–40.

Held in being, like all other creatures, by the Word of God, humans are granted a "further gift," a special grace. This special grace is specified as making them in the image of the Word. This grace enables humans to participate in the Logos as creatures of reason (*logikos*) and thus to "actively and intentionally" participate in the Word and to rejoice in this participation.[36] Through this grace human beings were meant from the beginning to share eternally in the divine communion. The concept of the human made in the image of God is always, for Athanasius, a relational concept, concerned with the uniquely human way of participating in this communion.

Athanasius has a highly developed concept of humans as made in a distinctive way according to the true Image, who is the Word and Wisdom of the Father. He sees humans, at their creation, as given the grace of participating in the Image and, in knowing the Image, also knowing the Father. But humans chose to reject God, forfeited the grace of eternal life, and damaged their relationship to the Image. Out of the abundance of divine generosity, the Image of the Father becomes flesh to seek out the lost, to bring forgiveness of sins, to abolish the debt to death, and to repair and wonderfully renew the image of God in human beings.

Such an exalted view of the human as bearing the divine image might lead one to suspect that Athanasius's view of being in the image would be an exclusive one. But in fact, in his *Orations Against the Arians*,[37] he defends the concept of other creatures as bearing the imprint of the divine Image. The context is his long treatment of Proverbs 8:22, where Wisdom is found to say: "The Lord created me as a beginning of his ways for his works." This was the foundational text for anti-Nicene theology in the fourth century, constantly used as a biblical warrant for claiming that Wisdom had a beginning and is created. Any defense of Nicaea had to deal with this text. Athanasius responds to this challenge by attempting to show that the overall pattern of scriptural language identifies the Wisdom/Word as uncreated and truly divine. With regard to Proverbs 8:22, he argues that it refers not to the divine identity of

---

[36] Khaled Anatolios, *Athanasius*, The Early Church Fathers Series (London: Routledge, 2004), 42.

[37] My quotations from *Orations Against the Arians* are from the translation by Khaled Anatolios, *Athanasius*, 110–75.

Wisdom but to the economy of the incarnation, where Wisdom is made flesh in the created humanity of Jesus.

In this context, he speaks of the created imprint and image of uncreated divine Wisdom in all creatures. As divine Wisdom is the Creator of all things, the whole creation reflects uncreated Wisdom. It is precisely the presence of Wisdom, and the imprint of this divine Wisdom, that enables creatures to exist and to flourish: "But in order that creatures may not only be but also thrive in well-being, it pleased God to have his own Wisdom condescend to creatures. Therefore he placed in each and every creature and in the totality of creation a certain imprint [*typon*] and reflection of the Image of Wisdom, so that the things that come into being may prove to be works that are wise and worthy of God."[38]

All the creatures we see around us bear the imprint and reflection of the Image of Wisdom. In human beings, Athanasius goes on to say, this imprint of Wisdom is manifest in our human wisdom: "The wisdom that comes into being within us is an image of his Wisdom."[39] Because we have this gift of wisdom, Athanasius says, we possess the God-given capacity to recognize the image of Wisdom in other creatures: "Thus did the imprint of Wisdom come to be in created things, so that the world, as I have said, may come to know its Creator and Word, and through him, the Father."[40]

So Athanasius's interpretation of "the Lord created me" in Proverbs 8:1 is that it is said not of Wisdom, who is Creator, "but on account of his image that it is in created works."[41] He notes too that in Sirach Wisdom is said to be "poured forth" upon on all God's works (Sir 1:9). Again, he interprets this as pointing to the fact that "his image and his imprint is created in the works, although he himself is not one of the things created."[42] It is not eternal Wisdom, but Wisdom's created image that is poured out in all creatures. It is through this created wisdom that "the heavens declare the glory of God, and the stars proclaim the work of his hands" (Ps 19:2).

Athanasius then offers an image. The son of a king builds a city to fulfill his father's wishes. He inscribes his name on each of the works of

---

[38] *Arians* 2.78.
[39] Ibid.
[40] Ibid.
[41] Ibid.
[42] Ibid.

the building project, so that each stone may be secured and preserved. And because of the inscription of his name each inhabitant will be able to remember both him and his Father. For Athanasius, then, animals and plants, mountains and rivers are made according to the image of Wisdom, and they all bear Wisdom's imprint: "For while Wisdom herself is Creator and Maker, her imprint is created in the works and is made according to the image of the Image."[43]

Athanasius says that the perception of the imprint and image of Wisdom in creatures is "the beginning" and "paradigm," or symbol, of the knowledge of God. When one begins by embarking on this primary path of creation and is guided by Wisdom, and "then ascends by intelligence and understanding and perceives in creation the Creator Wisdom," such a one "will perceive in her also her Father, as the Lord himself has said, 'The one who has seen me has seen the Father'" (John 14:9).

Athanasius notes, however, with Paul, that in spite of the imprint of the Wisdom of God being evident in creatures, humans have failed to recognize God's attributes in creatures and have instead made them into false gods (Rom 1:19-25). Nevertheless, God does not abandon what God has created. Out of the abundance of divine generosity, God sends divine Wisdom, through whom all things are created, to be made flesh:

> For God willed to make himself known no longer as in previous times through the image and shadow of wisdom, which is in creatures, but has made the true Wisdom herself take flesh and become a mortal human being and endure the death of the cross, so that henceforth all those who put their faith in him may be saved. But it is the same Wisdom of God, who previously manifested herself, and her Father through herself, by means of her image in creatures—and thus is said to be "created"—but which later on, being Word, became flesh (John 1:14) as John said.[44]

Thus in Athanasius we find a theology that sees the eternal Wisdom/Word of God, and this Wisdom/Word made flesh as the one true Image of the Father. He has a profound theology of human beings as distinctively created according to the Image, as having damaged their relationship to the Image, and as through the incarnation of the divine

---

[43] Ibid., 2.80.
[44] Ibid., 2.81.

Image, being repaired and renewed in their being according to the Image. But this is not an exclusive view of humans as bearing the divine image. He sees other creatures, through God's creative act, as participating in divine Wisdom, and as created icons of the eternal Image of God. He sees human beings as called to recognize the imprint of Wisdom in the creatures around them and thus be led to a knowledge of Wisdom, and through Wisdom to her Father.

Conclusion

This dialogue between contemporary science and early theology's insights into the image of God suggests a more inclusive way of thinking about human beings as made according to the Image of God. It might be summarized in four statements:

1. Humans are made by God according to the Image only in and through their evolutionary relationships with other creatures such as chimpanzees and bonobos. The process of becoming human, and thus being made according to the Image, is to be understood not as something separating humans from other creatures but as occurring only in relationship with them.

2. Chimps and bonobos too can be said to be made according to the Image of God, in their own distinctive ways. They too, along with other creatures, are created icons of God in our world. With human beings they form part of the community of life on Earth, a community in which all creatures are united in a communion of praise of their Creator.

3. Essential to what is distinctive about the way that humans bear the image of God, the International Theological Commission has affirmed, is their communion with one another and with the triune God. The proposal made here is that this communion is to be seen as embracing not only other humans and the triune God of life but also bonobos and chimpanzees, and the whole community of life on Earth.

4. The concept of stewardship, discussed by the International Theological Commission, can then be understood within such a wider idea of the community of creation (Pss 148; 104), as responsible care for each species, and for the well-being of each living creature.

To be humanly according to the Image is to be committed to the well-being of the community of creatures of Earth, all of which are created icons of the living God. Such an inclusive view suggests an expansion of our love to embrace all our neighbours. As Elizabeth Johnson writes at the end of her *Ask the Beasts*: "Inspired by the Spirit who pervades and sustains the community of creation, the human imagination grows to encompass 'the other' and the human heart widens to love the neighbors who are uniquely themselves, not humans."[45] Such an inclusive view does not diminish the human but brings out what is distinctive to humans in bearing the divine image, as it allows other creatures to take their specific and distinctive identities as icons of holy Wisdom.

[45] Johnson, *Ask the Beasts*, 284.

Chapter 3

They Fell Silent
When We Stopped Listening
Apophatic Theology and "Asking the Beasts"[1]

Eric Daryl Meyer

Introduction

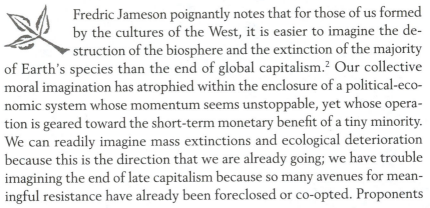 Fredric Jameson poignantly notes that for those of us formed by the cultures of the West, it is easier to imagine the destruction of the biosphere and the extinction of the majority of Earth's species than the end of global capitalism.[2] Our collective moral imagination has atrophied within the enclosure of a political-economic system whose momentum seems unstoppable, yet whose operation is geared toward the short-term monetary benefit of a tiny minority. We can readily imagine mass extinctions and ecological deterioration because this is the direction that we are already going; we have trouble imagining the end of late capitalism because so many avenues for meaningful resistance have already been foreclosed or co-opted. Proponents

[1] This title paraphrases Laurel Kearns, "Foreword," in *Divinanimality: Animal Theory, Creaturely Theology*, ed. Stephen Moore (New York: Fordham University Press, 2014), xii.

[2] Fredric Jameson, *The Seeds of Time* (New York: Routledge, 1994), xii.

of even the grittiest realism still negotiate daily complicity with the economic empires that pollute, despoil, and colonize the resilience of the land and its creatures. To use a threatened metaphor, this is a stream against which it is exceedingly difficult to swim. Going with the flow, though, charts a course toward "manmade omnicide."[3]

The urgency of this framing perhaps balances the eccentricity of my constructive proposal below. This essay highlights Elizabeth Johnson's theological work as a passage toward terrain in which our collective moral imagination might outgrow the constraints of its current formation. Specifically, it explores the apophatic impulse in Johnson's work as an avenue toward new forms of shared creaturely life through extended encounters with nonhuman animals. In other words, I chart a course from Johnson's adaptation of apophatic theology toward attitudes and practices that would enable us to "ask the beasts" themselves (Job 12:7-9). Such asking, it turns out, will require more listening than we humans have yet had patience for. My wager here is that cultivating passionate communicative curiosity toward our nonhuman neighbors would transform human relations to the biosphere generally, insofar as nonhuman animals often function as representatives and condensations of the natural world.

The essay's itinerary runs as follows: First, I offer a brief exposition of the apophatic impulse in Elizabeth Johnson's theological work. Second, I take a more focused look at the way that this apophatic impulse is at work in *Ask the Beasts: Darwin and the God of Love*, particularly in relation to what "the beasts" are thought to be saying and who is authorized to speak for them. Third, I take a constructive turn, setting a creaturely apophaticism in conversation with the science of ethology to seek after forms of theological knowledge that transgress species boundaries. Learning how to name God from our nonhuman neighbors would necessarily expand our moral imagination, enabling us to see modes of exchange that do not presume endless exploitation.

---

[3] Catherine Keller, *Apocalypse Now and Then: A Feminist Guide to the End of the World* (Minneapolis: Fortress Press, 1996), 148.

Elizabeth Johnson's Apophatic Impulse: Fidelity to Mystery[4]

Apophaticism is a methodologically sophisticated approach to the unavoidable but impossible questions that drive the discipline of theology. Wendy Farley rightly notes that "awareness of the inadequacy of language exposes every attempt to draw the divine into the structure of thought as a failure."[5] Theologians are those fortunate few who find great value in failing endlessly and publicly. In its ancient roots, apophatic theology emerges from practices of mystical contemplation seeking communion with God beyond the interference of language, concepts, and images. As a theological *discourse*, however, apophaticism demands an intensified attention to language's limits and slippage. Apophatic theology, then, is not an escape from discourse into pure knowledge but a disciplined, self-reflexive awareness of language's inadequacies and structural contradictions.

Elizabeth Johnson's writing evinces a strong apophatic impulse.[6] Drawing on Thomas Aquinas, she enumerates three principles for speaking about God: (1) God is a mystery beyond all imagination, beyond every "grasp" of thought or language; (2) therefore, no description or name for God can be taken literally; (3) the inadequacy of language and thought necessitates a proliferation of images for God.[7] Human beings can name and describe God only through faltering metaphors that liken God to familiar aspects of created life (including highly abstract realities like being or time). Even the christological mediation of the *communicatio idomatum*—which warrants claims that creation bears the weight of God's self-revelation (*finitum capax infiniti*)—does not collapse the

---

[4] The phrase "fidelity to mystery" comes from Wendy Farley, "And What Is a Merciful Heart? Apophatic Theology and Christian Ethics," *Theology Today* 67, no. 4 (2011): 415.

[5] Ibid., 409.

[6] For example, Elizabeth Johnson, *Consider Jesus: Waves of Renewal in Christology* (New York: Crossroad, 1990), 27, 46–47; idem, *She Who Is: The Mystery of God in Feminist Theological Discourse* (New York: Crossroad, 1992), 79–103, 108, 117–20, 273; idem, *Truly Our Sister: A Theology of Mary in the Communion of Saints* (New York: Continuum, 2003), 89–91; idem, "Does God Play Dice? Divine Providence and Chance," *Theological Studies* 57, no. 1 (1996): 17.

[7] Elizabeth Johnson, "Female Symbols for God: The Apophatic Tradition and Social Justice," *International Journal of Orthodox Theology* 1, no. 2 (2010): 43–44; see also *She Who Is*, 7–9.

infinite difference between God and creation. Every carefully crafted description of God communicates genuine knowledge about the divine, yet every description of God simultaneously requires erasure insofar as it misleads hearers into accepting a false equivalence, some presumptive point (however minute) at which language stitches God into creation.[8] Apophatic theology, then, proceeds by multiplying names for God (*via affirmativa*) while also subjecting all names for God to negation (*via negativa*), in recognition that God escapes and exceeds every cognitive or linguistic grasp (*via eminentiae*). Johnson's three principles invert this pattern, but the difference is minimal insofar as, forward or backward, the apophatic method is a cyclic discipline requiring endless repetition.

Johnson's theological work is so compelling because she employs apophasis in a new way. Guided by her watchword, "The symbol of God functions," Johnson places calcified language under apophatic negation in order to call attention to the ways in which habituated patterns of speech about God cement power differentials into a supposedly natural order.[9] Apophasis becomes a tool working toward the transformative justice of the Realm of God. A strong apophatic critique cultivates socio-political change where overused names for God harden into conduits that validate hierarchy (as in Mary Daly's words, "If God is male then the male is God").[10] Using feminine pronouns for God or insisting that God is black shifts the socio-political function of theological discourse precisely by exposing the sexism and racism latent in the theological common sense that finds such speech jarring.[11] Apophasis—an impulse rooted deeply within the Christian tradition—serves as a countervailing force that resists the tradition's tendency to maintain naturalized political hierarchies.

Who Answers for the Beasts?

In *Ask the Beasts*, Johnson's apophatic impulse breaks open stale images of divine transcendence—the God who is untouchably separate

---

[8] Farley, "Merciful Heart," 412.

[9] Johnson, *She Who Is*, 38; "Female Symbols," 41.

[10] Mary Daly, *The Church and the Second Sex* (New York: Harper and Row, 1979), 38; see Johnson, *She Who Is*, 17–18, 33–34, 273; *Truly Our Sister*, 40–43, 68–70, 88–92; "Female Symbols," 41.

[11] See James Cone, *A Black Theology of Liberation* (New York: J. B. Lippincott, 1970), 120–21.

from creation—in order to find the Spirit pulling creation forward from within, fomenting the chance variations shaped into new species by creation's regularity. She recovers symbols for God adequate to the Spirit's work in the cosmic processes which have multiplied creaturely diversity and creaturely beauty.[12] Working from Scripture and tradition, she unfolds images of God as wind, as water, as fire, as a bird, and (philosophically) as the source of all participatory existence. These images transpose Darwin's curious wonder at the natural world into a theological key, perceiving a "profoundly religious" impulse in his attention to creatures while respectfully recognizing that Darwin himself did not understand the "grandeur in this view of life" from within a religious frame.[13] Simultaneously, Johnson works to *unsay* the image of God as an imperturbable grey-haired man, the eternal advocate for stability and keeping everything in its place. The apophatic maneuvers of *Ask the Beasts* establish common ground between Darwin's testimony regarding the complex entanglement of evolving species and the testimony of Job's beasts, for whom "the hand of the Lord has done this. In God's hand is the life of every creature (Job 12:9)."[14]

Johnson's apophaticism allows her to move past the prevalent cultural assumption of an interminable conflict between science and theology toward dialogue and practical cooperation.[15] Darwin's discoveries and the scientific discoveries of those in his wake become an unintentional witness to the work of the "God of love"—and conversely, theology becomes concerned with patient observation of (and care for) fellow creatures. Johnson calls Christians to see as Darwin saw and, in such curious attention, to encounter God in new images and with new names. The apophatic turn toward evolutionary transformation, then, also effects an ecological transformation of theology itself, providing the basis for a pragmatic solidarity with those scientists who are concerned with conservation, restoration, and rehabilitation. Here too, Johnson's apophatic impulse expands fidelity to divine mystery, while simultaneously seeking after a much-needed cosmic justice.

---

[12] Elizabeth Johnson, *Ask the Beasts: Darwin and the God of Love* (New York: Bloomsbury, 2014), 134–52.

[13] Johnson, *Ask the Beasts*, 41; Charles Darwin, *The Origin of Species* (New York: P. F. Collier and Son, 1909), 528–29.

[14] Johnson, *Ask the Beasts*, 179.

[15] Ibid., 12.

Following the scriptural suggestion from Job that lends *Ask the Beasts* its title, Johnson repeatedly gives voice to the animals in her text: "The hand of the Lord has done this." "We are created." "We are finite and will end." The book concludes with the beasts asking "no less" of us than an effective response to ecological degradation in creative fidelity to God's Spirit.[16] In turning toward the constructive work below, I want to note two aspects of Johnson's beastly inquiry. First, as with Job's own injunction, the book's question and answer takes place with animals *en masse*. If panthers and pika have diverse or divergent responses, those perspectival differences regarding "what the Lord has done" disappear within a summing up of the beastly collective. Second, setting theology in conversation with Darwin's evolutionary biology entails that the primary spokesperson for the beasts—Darwin himself—is a creature with questionable beastly credentials. That is not to question Darwin's place in kingdom *Animalia* but to note that the scriptural injunction to "ask the beasts" would seem to push the seeker beyond the boundaries of the human community. In Darwin's wake, fields of scientific inquiry—ethology, for one—have developed that allow for greater attention to the communication of the beasts themselves. A theological dialogue with ethology could enable a more literal (perhaps perversely literal) approach to the task of asking the beasts, each according to their kind. The purpose of raising these points is not to suggest that *Ask the Beasts* should have been a different book so much as to gratefully acknowledge Johnson's path-breaking work toward further apophatic engagement with the life sciences.

Johnson allows Darwin to take the podium as spokesperson for the beasts, partly on the rationale that his inquiry (and human inquiry more generally) has produced the scientific tradition with the most advanced understanding of our shared creaturely origins.[17] The preface to *Ask the Beasts* begins with Holmes Rolston's assertion that the development of human consciousness is a "third Big Bang." Just as space-time-matter qualitatively differs from the hyper-dense formation that produced our universe, and just as living creatures qualitatively differ from the organized collections of matter that preceded them, Rolston claims that human consciousness differs qualitatively from the consciousness

---

[16] Ibid., 155, 214–15, 219, 286.
[17] Ibid., 241.

of all other animals.[18] Though Rolston's scheme provides license for a strong human exceptionalism, Johnson's text sits uneasily with such a position. On one hand, Johnson acknowledges that recent scientific work has made clear that the difference between human beings and other creatures is "less absolute" than previously thought.[19] Likewise, human consciousness remains the product of a common evolutionary history as (in Karl Rahner's terms) the highest expression of matter's tendency toward self-transcendence under the guidance of the Spirit.[20] On the other hand, *Ask the Beasts* holds shades of exceptionalism in the claim that human self-reflection and symbolic expression entail that the human is not "simply one more sibling" in the family of living creatures.[21] Such a claim qualifies the kinship metaphor from Johnson's earlier book, *Women, Earth, and Creator Spirit*, in which Johnson argues that human intelligence and human freedom do not "break the kinship" of human beings with other creatures.[22]

At issue here is how to understand Johnson's designation of humanity as a "singularity."[23] Do human beings differ from other creatures in a manner analogous to the ways that other species differ from one another, so that *every* species is a singularity? Or, are human beings categorically different from all other living creatures, such that "animal" is a coherent category that can be opposed to "human." The overwhelming majority of the Christian theological tradition has subscribed to the latter position, while the force of Johnson's text certainly pushes toward the former. Rooted in apophatic sensibilities, the remainder of this essay looks for theological insight where categorical human exceptionalism is abandoned altogether.

[18] Ibid., xiii; Holmes Rolston III, *Three Big Bangs* (New York: Columbia University Press, 2010), xi.

[19] Johnson, *Ask the Beasts*, 240–41.

[20] Ibid., 175–77, 237; *Women, Earth, and Creator Spirit* (New York: Paulist Press, 1993), 38; see also "Does God Play Dice?," 6–7, 13.

[21] Johnson, *Ask the Beasts*, 240–41.

[22] Johnson, *Women, Earth, and Creator Spirit*, 37; for other metaphors expressing humanity's inseparability from the natural world, see *Ask the Beasts*, 195–96, 240–41.

[23] Johnson, *Ask the Beasts*, 237, 240.

They Fell Silent When We Stopped Listening

Apophatic theology has excelled at marking the limits of discursive thought in any approach to God. In its long history, however, apophaticism has generally been guided by some version of the great chain of being, recognizing discourse's limits only in considering realities that are "above" human existence. If we can shake the great chain of being loose for a moment, however, we recognize other frontiers that persistently repel the intrusion of thought and language. Catherine Keller has recently argued that apophaticism provides an alternate approach to our knowledge of fellow creatures. "The ancient *via negativa* now offers its mystical unsaying, which is a nonknowing *of God*, to the uncertainty that infects our knowing of anything that is *not* God."[24] Turning apophaticism toward "lower" creaturely relations cultivates respectful awareness regarding just how little we know about the pluriform and variegated lives of Earth's many animals.

Do we need justification for transforming apophaticism from a mystical strategy for knowing God to a relational strategy for interacting with others? One approach particularly amenable to Johnson's work could combine a Thomistic account of creaturely participation with Gregory of Nyssa's insight that creaturely being participates not only in God's virtue but also in God's incomprehensibility.[25] Just as theological apophaticism does not deny the knowledge of God altogether but shapes a strategic fidelity to God's mystery as it exceeds every discursive approach, so also creaturely apophaticism is an unknowing meant to expand the terrain in which mutual knowledge dwells.[26]

A few starting points: Within their social networks (which, in many cases bridge multiple species) animals communicate regularly and effectively. It remains controversial to refer to these longstanding, culturally inflected, socially transmitted patterns of communication as *languages*, but the connection is both justifiable and illuminating.[27] Of course,

---

[24] Catherine Keller, *Cloud of the Impossible: Negative Theology and Planetary Entanglement* (New York: Columbia University Press, 2014), 5; see also Farley, "Merciful Heart," 407, 417.

[25] Johnson, "Does God Play Dice?," 12; Gregory of Nyssa, *De hominis opificio* 11.3.

[26] Keller, *Cloud of the Impossible*, 23.

[27] Gregory Bateson, "A Theory of Play and Fantasy," in *Steps to An Ecology of Mind* (Chicago: University of Chicago Press, 1972), 323, 327; Cary Wolfe, *Animal Rites: American Culture, the Discourse of Species, and Posthumanist Theory*

these patterns of communication do not have the same complexity, structure, or function within the social networks that employ them. The wiggle-dance of a bee follows a different logic, has a different range of communicative possibility, and serves a different purpose from the trunk-to-mouth greeting of an elephant. Accordingly, no creaturely language can be translated into another without loss or remainder—a difficulty that explicitly includes expressing any animal communication within the logic, structure, purpose, and emotional range of human language. I begin from the supposition, then, that human communication does not categorically differ from all other creaturely communication any more or less than dolphin communication does but represents a highly specialized and intricate form.[28] Human languages are highly variable sets of audible, written, and/or corporeal practices constrained by particular social-cultural contexts that (falteringly) communicate meaning inflected by a wide range of actual or assumed postures, gesticulations, phonic/tonic variations, and interpersonal histories. On such a definition, patterns of nonhuman animal communication are analogous.

Following this understanding of language, an apophatic approach to "asking the beasts" begins with two convictions: First, we human beings are largely ignorant of vast tracts of animal interiority, worlds (or experiences of the world) that find some form of expression through animal communication. Second, access to any one of these worlds requires immense patience, careful study, a highly refined creative empathy,

---

(Chicago: University of Chicago Press, 2003), 79, 86–87; Brian Massumi, *What Animals Teach Us about Politics* (Durham, NC: Duke University Press, 2014), 8–13; Mary Midgley, *Beast and Man: The Roots of Human Nature* (New York : Routledge, 1995), 243–46; Jacques Derrida, "'Eating Well' or the Calculation of the Subject," in *Points . . . Interviews 1974–1994*, ed. Werner Hamacher and David Wellbery, trans. Peter Connor and Avital Ronell (Stanford: Stanford University Press, 1995), 284–85; idem, *The Animal That Therefore I Am*, ed. Marie Louise Mallet, trans. David Wills (New York: Fordham University Press, 2008), 48, 122–24, 127–29, 133–35; Cynthia Willett, *Interspecies Ethics* (New York: Columbia University Press, 2014), 42–43; see also Ursula K. LeGuin, "Author of the Acacia Seeds," in *Compass Rose* (New York: Harper, 2005), 3–14.

[28] Louise Westling, *The Logos of the Living World: Merleau-Ponty, Animals, and Language* (New York: Fordham University Press, 2013), 113; Wolfe, *Animal Rites*, 86–87; Massumi, *What Animals Teach Us*, 8; cf. Alasdair MacIntyre, *Dependent Rational Animals: Why Human Beings Need the Virtues* (Chicago: Open Court, 1999), 30.

and something akin to social generosity on the part of fellow creatures. Even so, such access will be partial, obscure, and immensely prone to misunderstanding.

The first conviction acknowledges animal interiority—what Jakob von Euxküll called *Umwelt*. Nonhuman animals have rich conscious experiences of the world(s) that they inhabit corresponding to their own drives, physiology, sociality, and interests. Again, extending interiority and mindfulness beyond the human species does not posit consciousness as a homogenous quality that creatures participate in to varying degrees (slugs hardly at all, chimpanzees quite a lot). *Pace* Heidegger, every perceptive creature is *Weltbildend* (world-building) because "the world" is not a single, objective experience to which creatures have varying amounts of access but a reflection of the structured, contextual interests of each species. Likewise, every conscious creature is *Weltarm*—poor in the "worlds" of other species.[29] For example, decades of study convinced Joyce Poole that elephants have rich emotional lives that partially overlap with the emotions familiar to us, but they are also filled with emotions that we humans cannot experience, since our social formation and interests differ drastically.[30] A good acknowledgment with which to begin a creaturely apophaticism would be that we humans are poor in elephant-world (among so many others).

The second conviction recognizes that because of our intractable differences, the minds of nonhuman creatures will necessarily remain partially opaque to us. We may devote our attention to the details of interactive behavior and hone our capacity for empathy, but the differences in our drives, senses, and socialization will necessarily always set an abyss between us and fellow creatures, which description and understanding can never fully cross. As Anthony Paul Smith perceptively argues, nature is always perverse with respect to human thought; no

[29] Derrida argues for this nonstandard reading of Heidegger in *The Beast and the Sovereign II*, trans. Geoffrey Bennington (Chicago: University of Chicago Press, 2011), 197–98; see also Tim Ingold, "Hunting and Gathering as Ways of Perceiving the Environment," in *Animals and the Human Imagination: A Companion to Animal Studies*, ed. Aaron Gross and Anne Vallely (New York: Columbia University Press, 2012), 46.

[30] Marc Bekoff, *The Emotional Lives of Animals: A Leading Scientist Explores Animal Joy, Sorrow, and Empathy—and Why They Matter* (Novato, CA: New World Library, 2007), 6.

campaign of thought can escape nature in order to grasp it in determinate form.[31]

The confidence, unflagging across millennia, that human intelligence really is the high-water mark for cognitive capacity on Earth has been asserted more often than tested when it comes to nonhuman communication. Are human beings intelligent enough to learn—even rudimentarily—the languages of chimpanzees, corvids, cetaceans, or prairie dogs? We have tested a long entourage of creatures for the capacity to learn human language but hardly allowed the obverse question to gain traction on our imagination. We have presumed to be teachers without challenging our minds as students, only occasionally acknowledging the bias inherent in using ourselves as the measure of intelligence.[32] Since many animals communicate regularly, we must acknowledge that they have something to say—even when it is not *to us*. Even so, our barely conscious habits of projection, interruption, and interpretation functionally deny language to animals by another route. We too often assume that we already know what an animal *would be saying*, and we speak it for them, foreclosing their expression by containing it within a familiar language that already reflects human interests and concerns.[33] Apophasis negates the projections that rush to extend human thought and language beyond their limits, an unsaying that knows there is more to be said than we yet perceive. As such, disciplined apophasis remains particularly appropriate for any effort to ask the beasts.

Stephen Clark offers a reminder that many of our religious practices are meant to shut up our "relentless ego," our "self-critical monologue," our rationalizations, and our linguistic fixations. In this light, irony pervades the Christian theological tradition's insistence that human language and human consciousness are a privileged conduit for relation with God, a conduit that remains closed to other creatures.[34] Perhaps our prejudices regarding human exceptionalism have obscured many of the more significant differences among creatures, and as Clark suggests,

---

[31] Anthony Paul Smith, *A Non-Philosophical Theory of Nature: Ecologies of Thought* (New York: Palgrave MacMillan, 2013), 13–15.

[32] Willett, *Interspecies Ethics*, 46; Midgley, *Beast and Man*, 207–13.

[33] Derrida, *Animal*, 18, 48.

[34] Stephen Clark, "Ask Now the Beasts and They Shall Teach Thee," in *Animals as Religious Subjects: Transdisciplinary Perspectives*, ed. Celia Deane-Drummond, Rebecca Artinian-Kaiser, and David Clough (New York: Bloomsbury, 2013), 28, 31.

perhaps one difference is that many animals are *more* religious than we humans are—or, to eschew linear comparison, *differently* religious.[35]

The worlds of many nonhuman creatures may not include a God or gods. Those that do may not associate divinity with transcendence, norms, origins, and ends. Yet, there may be as many names for God as there are animal languages. We cannot know without asking. Learning about such names would require something like a quotidian spiritual ethology. I will sketch the possibilities for such inquiry by turning to ethologist Marc Bekoff, philosopher Val Plumwood, and stories of feral children.

Through his work on canids (i.e., wolves, coyotes, foxes, dogs), Marc Bekoff has earned recognition as a leading figure in ethology, a field that includes well-known scientists such as Konrad Lorenz, Niko Tinbergen, Jane Goodall, Dian Fossey, and Frans de Waal. Ethology is the study of animal behavior patterns within their own social-ecological context, with attention to adaptive-evolutionary function. Building on his scientific work, Bekoff makes philosophical arguments repudiating the idea that morality and emotion belong to human life alone. Bekoff has discerned norms that govern fairness, empathy, cooperation, and generosity along with manifestations of richly textured emotional experiences particular to the social formations and interests of each species. The wholesale denial of morality and emotion to nonhuman species is, in Bekoff's words, "bad biology."[36] Bekoff is careful not to claim that the emotions and morality of caribou or coyotes map seamlessly onto human morality and emotions—or even that they occupy the same spectrum. Rather, he argues for a species-relative view of morality because the social structures of different species (and occasionally interspecies communities) reward and censure behaviors according to a variety of norms and through a variety of mechanisms.[37] Bekoff's work reveals

---

[35] Ibid., 17–18.

[36] Bekoff, *Emotional Lives*, xviii, 15, 162–63; Marc Bekoff and Jessica Pierce, *Wild Justice: The Moral Lives of Animals* (Chicago: University of Chicago Press, 2009), 7–16.

[37] Bekoff, *Wild Justice*, xi–xiii, 31, 56. Celia Deane-Drummond similarly argues for a species relative notion of morality from a theological perspective in "Are Animals Moral? Taking Soundings Through Vice, Virtue, Conscience, and *Imago Dei*," in *Creaturely Theology: On God, Humans, and Other Animals*, ed. Celia Deane-Drummond and David Clough (London: SCM Press, 2009), 204–9.

how much we have to learn about the interiority and sociality of fellow creatures and begins to demonstrate how we might go about learning it.

Val Plumwood encourages us to attend to our "familiars." Familiars include companion animals, but especially the individual creatures that we encounter (and who encounter us) on a daily basis, be it while walking through a park, on a subway platform, or across campus.[38] We have the chance with our familiars to listen, observe, and develop an empathetic curiosity about the worlds they inhabit. Doing so, Plumwood argues, requires abandoning the homogenous Cartesian conception of mind, which functions according to an on/off binary incapable of recognizing structural difference: Are you a thinking thing or a not-thinking thing?[39] Conceiving creaturely mindfulness as pluriform—not subject to measurement upon a single (human) scale—inculcates curiosity about these "other nations" living according to their own moral, emotional, linguistic, social, and mental attunements.[40] It would also place human beings in relationships where we have as much to learn from fellow creatures as we have to teach.[41] Our narrowest definitions of rationality are too cramped to take in the longstanding ecological intelligence of so many of our creaturely neighbors. Further, it is the "rational decisions" of *homo economicus* that drive ecocidal human behavior, legally binding corporate boards (for one example) to prioritize shareholder profit over workers' well-being, the survival of threatened species, and long-term ecological resilience.[42] An everyday spiritual ethology would place

---

Lisa Sideris offers prudent caution regarding the sorts of moral connections I am working with in *Environmental Ethics, Ecological Theology, and Natural Selection* (New York: Columbia University Press, 2003), 169.

[38] Kate Rigby, "Animal Calls," in Moore, *Divinanimality*, 119; Val Plumwood, *Environmental Culture: The Ecological Crisis of Reason* (New York: Routledge, 2002), 165.

[39] Val Plumwood, *Feminism and the Mastery of Nature* (New York: Routledge, 1993), 122–23. Jean Christophe Bailly's focus on animal "pensivity" does much the same work, *The Animal Side*, trans. Catherine Porter (New York: Fordham University Press, 2011), 15.

[40] Plumwood, *Feminism*, 137–38; Ingold, "Hunting and Gathering," 32.

[41] Plumwood, *Environmental Culture*, 176–79.

[42] Plumwood, *Feminism*, 133; *Environmental Culture*, 14. See also David Loy, "The Religion of the Market," in *Visions of a New Earth: Religious Perspectives on Population, Consumption, and Ecology*, ed. Harold Coward and Daniel Maguire (Albany: State University of New York Press, 2000), 15–28.

human beings in *social* and *political* relationships with fellow creatures where we currently see (at best!) managerial responsibility or (more often) colonial control and exploitation.[43]

Another entryway into a quotidian spiritual ethology might be found in the documented stories of feral children—human children living with bears, leopards, wolves, monkeys, gazelles, and even birds. These stories limn the possibilities for communicative encounters with nonhuman animals and perhaps indicate a trajectory of escape from exploitative human relations with fellow creatures.[44] For these exceedingly rare children, human kinship with nonhuman creatures is not simply a metaphor for deep ecological interdependence but a life-sustaining material and social bond. What might these kinship relationships teach us about what it might mean to "ask the beasts"?

Most stories of feral children are framed in tragedy.[45] Whatever cruel events bring human children to their animal kin, as H. Peter Steeves notes, when children are discovered living with animals, the animals who cared for the human children are often killed. Violence also pervades attempts to socialize and civilize the children according to human norms. One boy, discovered living with gazelles, was subjected to surgery cutting the tendons in his legs after his caretakers/captors found his persistent leaping and bounding unnerving.[46] In another case, Amala and Kamala, siblings eighteen months and eight years old, were discovered living with wolves in India; "rescued" by a minister, Reverend Singh; and taken to an orphanage where Amala died within a year.[47] This tragic plot line

[43] Keller, *Apocalypse Now*, 175.

[44] See Johnson, *Women, Earth, and Creator Spirit*, 29–34, for a development of kinship metaphors for ecotheology.

[45] For accounts of feral children, see Douglas Keith Candland, *Feral Children and Clever Animals: Reflections on Human Nature* (New York: Oxford University Press, 1993).

[46] H. Peter Steeves, *The Things Themselves: Phenomenology and the Return to the Everyday* (Albany: State University of New York Press, 2006), 19.

[47] Because the account of Amala and Kamala comes primarily from a diary kept by Reverend Singh (later published in collaboration with an American academic R. M. Zinng), there have been suspicions that the story was fabricated. Other people did, however, provide accounts of visiting the orphanage and meeting Kamala, including a local bishop. Though other stories could serve in its place, I use their story here (without making claims on its veracity) because it is relatively famous and well documented. See Candland, *Feral Children*, 54–55, 375 n. 40.

repeats itself in stories of feral children because their familiar human corporeal form is perceived as a promise that is betrayed by nonhuman movement and socialization. Feral children, by their very existence, pull back the curtain on the operative normativity of "humanity" as a cultural production.[48]

The unnecessary cruelty and tragedy of their stories aside, these children demonstrate that in the absence of "proper" human socialization, humans are plastic enough to be socialized as gazelles, as wolves, as bears. Even after years of reeducation, Kamala was still, in many senses, a wolf: "She learned few words, raced around on all fours, preferred the company of dogs to humans, and frightened the other orphans by prowling at night, sniffing and growling near their beds in the moonlight."[49] When her young sister died, she mourned by remaining in one corner of the orphanage, "moving only to smell all of the places that Amala had frequented."[50] Kamala's world took shape according to a wolfish use of the senses. She did not simply *act* like a wolf, she perceived the world as a wolf; she inhabited a wolf's world.[51] Through wolf-approximations and wolf-adaptations in their human bodies, Amala and Kamala communicated well enough to become kin with wolves. As far as one can tell, these children saw their real kin as wolves and their real sense of themselves was that of a wolf—their animal formation was no veneer.[52] What can be said theologically about Amala, Kamala, and their wolf-kin?

Even in outline, the feral children's stories can teach us quite a lot. On the one hand, it seems, human beings *are* intelligent enough to learn languages in use among fellow creatures. On the other hand, what is required for such communication is considerably more immersive than developing a lexicon or a science-fiction translation device. One must become wolf to learn to communicate with wolves, and this becoming is a (re)construction of the world as much as it is a (re)construction of the

---

[48] Giorgio Agamben, *The Open: Man and Animal*, trans. Kevin Attell (Stanford, CA: Stanford University Press, 2004), 15–16, 21; Kelly Oliver, *Animal Lessons: How They Teach Us to Be Human* (New York: Columbia University Press, 2009), 20–21; Judith Butler, *Frames of War: When Is Life Grievable?* (New York: Verso, 2010), 76–77, 94–95.

[49] Candland, *Feral Children*, 59–62; Steeves, *Things Themselves*, 19.

[50] Candland, *Feral Children*, 66.

[51] Ibid., 27.

[52] Steeves, *Things Themselves*, 33; see also Oliver, *Animal Pedagogy*, 226–27.

self. Beckoff, Plumwood, and feral children help us to see a transformation that Aldo Leopold described as the difference between "man [*sic*] the conqueror" and "man the biotic citizen."[53] Leopold likely conceived the "social approbation and social approval" that govern his famous land ethic as functions of *human* society but, as Cynthia Willett argues (and feral children demonstrate), there is no reason why humans could not expand our socio-moral sensitivity beyond our species boundary.[54] To become sensitive to our socio-political-ecological interdependence on our creaturely neighbors, we would need, as Jane Bennett puts it, to "devise new procedures, technologies, and regimes of perception that enable us to consult nonhumans more closely, or to listen and respond more carefully to their outbreaks, objections, testimonies, and propositions."[55] Apophatic theology, with its attention to the limits of human thought and language and its exploration of alternate modes of knowing, can undoubtedly offer some of the "procedures, technologies, and regimes of perception" that would be necessary to learn to listen differently. Hard as it may be for our untrained noses to follow, the promise of apophatic theology in relation to other creatures tracks along the scent of this pathway. To ask the beasts is to give up on the notion of an easy translation, a simple extraction of wolf-knowledge that can be theologically thematized. Yet, it is arbitrary to insist that *only* the structure of human consciousness, perception, intelligence, and emotion allow for experience of God as creator. In Scripture, Job calls our bluff: "Ask the beasts and they will tell you, the hand of the Lord has done this." We have yet to learn to frame the question.

Conclusion

Apophatic theology multiplies descriptions for God, trusting that each name communicates something truthful, while simultaneously placing every name under negation because creaturely thought and language (in all its forms) remains inadequate to the task. If the chimpanzees' famous waterfall dance orients them in wonder and reverence—by

[53] Aldo Leopold, *A Sand County Almanac: And Sketches Here and There* (New York: Oxford University Press, 1949), 204, 223.

[54] Ibid., 224–25; Willet, *Interspecies Ethics*, 6, 132–33.

[55] Jane Bennett, *Vibrant Matter: A Political Ecology of Things* (Durham, NC: Duke University Press, 2010), 108.

no means a settled question—then apophatic theology offers no reason to discount the accuracy and perspicacity of such a symbolic experience simply because its experiential subject is a chimpanzee.[56] Whatever chimpanzee experience of God might be (and we would have to ask to know), it is surely structured differently from the wide range of human religious experiences. Traditionally, that structural difference has been a reason to dismiss animal experience as theologically irrelevant; it could also, however, represent an enticement. What could we learn from such an experience of God? And here, we circle back toward Johnson's theological project: Expositing Scripture and tradition in connection with the widest range of creaturely experience would surely raise up forgotten symbols for God, and new ones too—symbols that function differently within their eco-socio-political context, opening a more expansive vision of justice and creaturely flourishing. I will conclude with theological rationale—both warrants and potential results—for a creaturely apophasis laboring to ask the beasts.

We can begin by returning to the book of Job. Job's text gives the final dramatic speech to God, who answers Job's lamenting inquisitions by pushing Job back toward his fellow creatures—Leviathan, lions, mountain goats, and all the rest. The significance of this divine speech has been variously understood by its many interpreters, but its content is surely an elaborate repetition of Job's words from chapter 12. God does not presume to speak for the creatures but calls Job to attend to the creaturely experience of all his nonhuman neighbors, effectively saying, "ask the beasts and they will tell you, the hand of the Lord has done this."[57] Practicing his own apophasis, Job realizes that he has been speaking too much and places his words under erasure to listen more carefully (Job 42:1-6). Catherine Keller is surely correct that Genesis's notion of human dominion stands in stark tension with Job's humbler positioning of humanity among God's creatures.[58] Moreover, Christian theology has surely taken guidance from Genesis's arrangement rather

---

[56] Jane Goodall, "Primate Spirituality," in *The Encyclopedia of Religion and Nature*, ed. Bron Taylor (New York: Thoemmes Continuum, 2005), 1303–6; Willett, *Interspecies Ethics*, 100–107; Donovan Schaefer, *Religious Affects: Animality, Evolution, and Power* (Durham, NC: Duke University Press, 2015).

[57] Johnson, *Ask the Beasts*, 271.

[58] Catherine Keller, *Face of the Deep: A Theology of Becoming* (New York: Routledge, 2003), 136–40.

than Job's. Given the deleterious ecological effects of even our most benevolent stewardship, it is high time for a corrective emphasis on Job's creaturely entanglement. Animal apophaticism could provide an introduction to long-overdue apprenticeships in creaturehood, an escape hatch from the constrained rationality of capitalism toward cultural/political transformations that reconfigure human goods and goals into resonance with the resilient thriving of fellow creatures.[59]

Second, Christian theology ought to note that the New Testament's loftiest christological statements—John's prologue and the first chapter of Colossians, for example—connect Jesus' life, death, and resurrection with the entire cosmos. Stephen Moore notes that the Christology in Revelation—arguably the New Testament's strongest links between Jesus and divinity—reaches its highest pitch precisely where it is an *animal* Christology.[60] Jesus is worshiped as a lamb by a host of other strange creatures (Rev 4–5). It required real work, then, for the Christian theological tradition to constrict its purview to human concerns alone while also reading the New Testament. Johnson proposes an emphasis on "deep resurrection" to match recent interest in "deep incarnation," a notion that takes stock of the cosmic implications of God's life in flesh. Creaturely apophaticism represents one concrete way to examine "the risen Christ's affiliation [with] the whole natural world."[61] The Spirit draws creatures into the life of the resurrection wherever she blows and the whole creation groans with the Spirit (Rom 8). What might we learn by attending to these groans with an empathetic, rather than a managerial, ear?

Third, the eccentricity of a creaturely apophaticism pairs well with the eccentricities of Christian hagiography. In over a millennium of hagiographic tradition, the ability to communicate with wild animals has signified sanctity and spiritual clarity. The examples are plentiful: lions help Anthony to bury the body of Paul in the Egyptian desert, a stag preaches to Eustathios/Eustace, birds and wolves attend to the words of Francis of Assisi, and a bear brings honey to Seraphim of Sarov. It is true that the communication largely takes place in human languages and that

---

[59] Cf. Catherine Keller, *From a Broken Web: Separation, Sexism, and Self* (Boston: Beacon Press, 1986), 203.

[60] Stephen Moore, "Ecotherology," in Moore, *Divinanimality*, 209.

[61] Johnson, *Ask the Beasts*, 208–9.

hagiography is dubious (at best) as a record of historical events, but these stories testify to a longstanding theological conviction largely abandoned in the present: that individual animals bear a substantial connection to God internal to the structure of their own perception, intellection, and experience. In hagiography, cross-species communication functions to forge bonds of cooperation, but contemporary theological discourse has lost the capacity for such imaginative possibilities. Nevertheless, asking the beasts through a quotidian spiritual ethology would hardly be novel within the Christian tradition.

Fourth, a creaturely apophaticism represents the first step of an ecotheology that addresses the pitfalls of mainstream environmentalism. In practice, environmentalism tends to enshrine the same managerial approach to the natural world (albeit in a chastened and respectful mode) that produced the ecological overreach it redresses. That is to say, the operative notion of human identity and agency within mainstream environmentalism still celebrates the hallmarks of enlightenment humanism. Very little in our social formation allows us to think of our relationships to fellow creatures as constitutive of our personalities, our subjectivity, and our agency. In part, it is this ecologically detached self-concept that constrains our collective moral imagination to responding to ecological degradation through conscientious consumerism, wildlife preserves, and superficial changes to economic policy.[62] An apophatic reconception of human agency and human entanglement with fellow creatures offers a significant alternative and a rich starting point for ecotheology.[63]

Indebted to Elizabeth Johnson's model of putting apophasis to work in service of those whose experience and speech have been invalidated, I have sketched a creaturely apophasis adequate to the vocation of asking the beasts. The first step toward such a vocation is to cultivate passionate curiosity about the many minds and tongues shaped differently from our own, yet no less enmeshed in God's creation. What shape those minds and tongues (or tails, postures, colors, and scents) give to the knowledge of God is a question that has almost never been asked.

Ask the beasts? Admittedly, we still lack the words.

---

[62] These changes are commendable, to be sure, but woefully incommensurate to the scale of anthropogenic ecological degradation.

[63] Bennett, *Vibrant Matter*, 110–11; Peter Scott, *A Political Theology of Nature* (Cambridge: Cambridge University Press, 2003), 13, 242.

Chapter 4

The Woods Are Lovely, Dark, and Deep

Cultivating a Forest Spirituality in a Clearcut World

Colleen Mary Carpenter

Writer and naturalist Janisse Ray grew up in south Georgia, surrounded by "mobile homes, junked cars, pine plantations, clearcuts, and fields"—in other words, she grew up "among the lost forests," the devastated remains of the great longleaf pine forests that once blanketed the region.[1] The ugliness of her home led her to conclude that "God doesn't like a clearcut," and she warns of retribution: "If you clear a forest, you'd better pray continuously. . . . [W]hen a forest is falling it's easy for God to determine who to spank. Quid pro quo."[2] Her warning is at least slightly tongue-in-cheek; she does not believe that loggers run any more risk than the rest of humanity when it comes to suffering the consequences of our destruction of the world around us—but she certainly does believe that there are consequences to clearcuts. And all around the world, we are not

[1] Janisse Ray, *Ecology of a Cracker Childhood* (Minneapolis: Milkweed Editions, 1999), 3.
[2] Ibid., 123–24.

only clearcutting forests but also burning them down; we are pumping huge amounts of carbon into our atmosphere; we are filling the oceans with plastic trash and emptying them of fish; and we are causing the extinction of 150 to 200 species of plant, insect, bird, and mammal life every twenty-four hours,[3] a rate that means we are in the midst of what biologists are calling the world's sixth great extinction, the most devastating loss of life and diversity on Earth since dinosaurs became extinct 65 million years ago.[4]

While the scope of the devastation wrought by human beings has become only widely understood and accepted in the last few years, Elizabeth Johnson has been sounding the alarm for decades, describing in her 1993 Madeleva Lecture the "ecocide" that we were committing against the planet and its life.[5] More than twenty years later, human actions continue to lay waste to the world around us, and Johnson's words ring ever more terrifyingly true: "Our blue planet as a habitat for life stands in jeopardy due to atmospheric damage, deforestation, pollution of the seas, disruption of ecosystems, destruction of habitat, extinction of species, loss of biodiversity, overpopulation, resource exhaustion, and nuclear proliferation."[6] We are turning our lovely blue planet into a wasteland—a desert.

And confronting the desert we are creating is a frightening task: a desert, after all, is hostile, barren, and dangerous. With stark emptiness of the desert threatening to overwhelm the Earth as we have known it, what might it mean for Christian spirituality to "turn to the heavens and the earth" today? One option would be a turn to the apocalyptic: the world is spinning rapidly toward a horrifying end, and whatever spirituality we embrace must confront (and perhaps even find a way to embrace) the death and destruction we are bringing on ourselves. Despite the prevalence of apocalyptic rhetoric in many of today's environmental discussions, however, this is not the only choice available

[3] John Vidal, "Protect Nature for World Economic Security, Warns UN Biodiversity Chief," *The Guardian* (16 August 2010).

[4] Gerardo Ceballos, Paul R. Ehrlich, et al. "Accelerated Modern Human-Induced Species Losses: Entering the Sixth Mass Extinction," *Science Advances* 1:e1400253 (19 Jun 2015).

[5] Elizabeth A. Johnson, "The Crisis: Ecocide," in *Women, Earth, Creator Spirit* (New York: Paulist Press, 1993), 5–9.

[6] Ibid., 7–8.

to us. Instead of leaping forward to a focus on the terrors the future might hold, we could choose to focus on what we need to do here and now in order to shape a completely different future. This is Johnson's path; this is what she means by turning to the heavens and the earth:

> In light of the devastation, the turn to the heavens and the earth bears the marks of genuine conversion of mind and heart, with repentance for the lack of love and the violence visited on the living planet. As we turn, we will be looking for thought patterns that will transform our species-centeredness and enable us to grant not just instrumental worth but intrinsic value to the natural world. This is a condition for the possibility of extending vigorous moral consideration to the whole earth, now under threat. . . . Solidarity with victims, option for the poor, and action on behalf of justice widen out from human beings to embrace life-systems and other species to ensure vibrant communion in life for all.[7]

With the earth under threat, then, we are called not to despair but to conversion. The spirituality that shapes our lives must widen our vision and broaden our actions so that "vibrant communion in life for all" applies not simply to all human beings but to all creatures and indeed to all "life-systems." Our spirituality must engage the nonhuman world in a way that helps us make the shift from seeing ourselves as the crown of creation, separate from and better than everything else, to understanding ourselves as one part of the greater community of life. Indeed, Johnson speaks not just of community but of kinship—and not just kinship with our nearest relatives, the great apes, nor even with mammals, nor animals in general. Instead, in speaking of kinship, the example Johnson reaches for is the human kinship to trees:

> Take, for example, trees. Their process of photosynthesis creates oxygen, the most essential, life-sustaining element in the air we breathe. Without trees there would be no animal or human life on this earth; we would all be asphyxiated. Now, biologically speaking trees do not need human stewardship. Without human beings they existed very well for millennia. Human beings, however, positively need trees in order to breathe. Who, then, needs whom more? By

---

[7] Elizabeth A. Johnson, "Turn to the Heavens and the Earth: Retrieval of the Cosmos in Theology," *CTSA Proceedings* 51 (1996), 9–10.

what standard do human beings say that they are more important than trees? At this point in evolutionary history we form one mutually interdependent community of life. We are all kin.[8]

Yes, we are all kin; there is but one community of life. But why choose trees to illustrate this point? It seems an odd choice for a theologian to make, especially because the Christian relationship with trees and forests is conflicted at best: certainly trees have been beloved of the occasional saint, but more often, "dualistic strands of Western Christian thought have helped sustain the image of the tree as threatening and idolatrous."[9] Even decorating trees at Christmas is a tradition only a few hundred years old, while cutting down sacred groves in an effort to spread the faith is a Christian action at least a thousand years older. On the other hand, it is also true that in recent years scientists who study trees have begun writing not just about the biological connections between human beings and trees but about the symbolic and religious connections as well.[10] For example, canopy biologist Nalini Nadkarni, who has studied forest canopies and the complex ecosystems they create for over three decades, argues that human beings have "a clear affinity" for trees and that "although we are not of the same family, trees and humans are in a sense married into each other's families, with all the challenges, responsibilities, and benefits that come from being so linked."[11]

For Nadkarni, this link is both a physical, ecological connection and a spiritual one. She uses the image of marriage to point us not just toward family but also toward the spiritual, even the sacramental. The suggestion that we might have a sacramental connection to trees might seem surprising, perhaps even bizarre, but the idea that trees and forests can reveal the presence of God to us in a particular way is worth investigating, especially in the context of our increasingly deforested

[8] Johnson, *Women, Earth, Creator Spirit*, 31.

[9] Belden C. Lane, *Ravished by Beauty: The Surprising Legacy of Reformed Spirituality* (New York: Oxford University Press, 2011), 125.

[10] Some of these include biologists Nalini Nadkarni, Joan Maloof, Jeff Gillman, Bruce Macdonald, Jane Goodall, and Wangari Maathai (who was a professor of veterinary anatomy before founding the Green Belt Movement), and mathematician Karen French.

[11] Nalini M. Nadkarni, *Between Earth and Sky: Our Intimate Connections to Trees* (Berkeley: University of California Press, 2008), 11.

world. Certain contexts and images, after all, capture the imagination and shape the spirituality of any given age. In the third century, for example, the excesses of Rome led some Christians to flee into the desert and seek God in the naked simplicity of that landscape. Desert spirituality has a long and rich history and an honored place in Christian tradition—and yet we no longer live in a time when embracing the idea of the desert seems wise. We live in an age of deforestation and desertification: the desert is no longer a refuge but a threat. Our context has changed; the symbol of the desert functions differently today than it did then.[12] In the end, I believe that both Nadkarni and Johnson—and many others, including biologists/environmental activists Jane Goodall and Wangari Maathai; artists Emily Carr and Stephanie Hunder; farmers Gene Logsdon and Wendell Berry; and poets Mary Oliver and Louise Glück—have made the decision to highlight the human relationship to trees not simply out of individual quirkiness but as a manifestation of the spiritual longings peculiar to our environmentally disastrous context and ecocidal age. The signs of our times call for us to cultivate *a forest spirituality*, a spirituality that recognizes and celebrates our kinship with trees—and with all of God's creation.

Spirituality and Landscape

The easiest way to grasp the link between spirituality and landscape is to return to the idea of the desert and look at how that landscape came to be the basis for a particular kind of Christian spirituality. Deserts live in our imaginations as "forbidding wasteland[s]—sun-seared and

---

[12] According to Whitney Bauman, Richard R. Bohannon, and Kevin J. O'Brien, one of the central tasks in religion and ecology today is to ask how "religious symbols change and evolve in an era of environmental degradation" (Bauman, Bohannon, and O'Brien, eds., *Grounding Religion: A Field Guide to the Study of Religion and Ecology* [New York: Routledge, 2011], 19). Relying on Clifford Geertz's classic understanding of religion as a system of symbols passed down through the generations, Bauman et al. argue that while religions tend to display "impressive periods of consistency as a tradition endures," they also go through "great periods of schism and change" during which the meaning of traditional symbols shift in order to meet the challenges of a new age (18). We are in the midst of such a time of great change, and since the changes we face are ecological (and so are explicitly linked to landscape, and especially to *changing* landscapes), the symbols and meanings we associate with given landscapes are likely to be among those most affected by our changing times.

wind-scoured, waterless and endless, empty of shelter and, except for venomous creatures lurking under the rocks, largely devoid of life."[13] That description is, of course, an exaggeration; its author goes on to point out that while folklore speaks of the desert in such frightening terms, portraying deserts as "utterly hostile" landscapes, in reality human beings have long since learned "how to surmount most of the perils and discomforts of desert existence."[14] Still, survival in a desert is no small thing. The word "desert" itself comes from *desertum*, Latin for "abandoned place," reminding us that the desert is not just a place where human beings find it difficult to live but often a place where human beings have tried and failed to live.[15]

And yet the desert, traditionally, is one of the landscapes most favored in Christian spirituality. A place where God's wild freedom and the human being's smallness and vulnerability are on obvious display, the desert is one of the fierce landscapes in which an encounter with God seems not just possible but likely. Surely Christianity's Jewish roots play a part in this: the desert has long been the site of encounter between God and God's people. The story of the Exodus, of the forty years wandering the desert, and of the giving of the covenant at Mount Sinai all play a role in shaping the desert in the Christian imagination—as does, of course, the story of Jesus being driven out into the desert by the Spirit and fasting there for forty days. To these treasured stories and memories, Christians add the experiences of those who came to be known as the Desert Fathers and Mothers: Antony of Egypt, Abba Poemen, Abba Moses the Black, Amma Syncletia of Alexandria, and many others. These third- and fourth-century hermits and teachers developed an apophatic spirituality, profoundly rooted in the silence and emptiness of their surroundings, that seemed to be "drawn from the desert itself."[16] The Desert Fathers and Mothers emphasized both that "God is a desert whose fullness of glory is hidden from human sight" and that "the self is a desert that must be stripped and made empty before God can be found at its center."[17] This

---

[13] A. Starker Leopold, *The Desert* (Alexandria, VA: Time-Life Books, 1962), 9.

[14] Ibid.

[15] Richard Heinberg, *The End of Growth: Adapting to Our New Economic Reality* (Gabriola Island, Canada: New Society Publishers, 2011), 304.

[16] Belden C. Lane, *The Solace of Fierce Landscapes: Exploring Desert and Mountain Spiritualities* (New York: Oxford University Press, 1998), 11.

[17] Ibid.

understanding of the relationship between God, the self, and the desert proved extraordinarily significant for Christian spirituality—and yet is not unique to Christianity. Indeed, the power of the desert is such that some have argued that "the desert *qua* desert is inevitably a breeding ground for spirituality. . . . Prolonged desert experience irrevocably inclines the soul to questions of faith."[18]

Yet that is too simple; there is in the end no automatic connection between God and the desert. Spirituality scholar Belden Lane argues that this sort of "simplistic geographical determinism . . . makes everything too easy. I do not have to assume the discipline or embrace the *habitus* [of desert contemplatives] if merely 'going' to high desert country irresistibly draws me to an uncomplicated wholeness."[19] It is not just landscape but particular choices about how to engage that landscape that shape one's life and thus one's spirituality. Landscape does indeed "exert an important, sometimes commanding influence upon us,"[20] but it is the landscape *as constructed and interpreted by the human imagination* that ultimately determines how that landscape is understood as a spiritually rich or spiritually dangerous place.

As an example of the interaction between landscape and human imagination and interpretation, theologian David Perrin gives the example of the different reactions of a person living in a desert and another person living on a forested mountain when asked to speak to the idea of Jesus as the "water of life."[21] Because water is both scarce and much needed in the desert, the idea of "water of life" has a much different resonance for a desert-dweller than it does for someone who regularly interacts with rain, snow, and mountain streams. The person who lives on the mountain might focus on the beauty of the rain or the power of water rushing down the mountain; the one who makes a home in the desert is more likely to focus on the absolute and inescapable necessity of water for survival. Thus the idea of water "may evoke different images and feelings, as well as engage different life experiences" for the two people, even as they share the affirmation that "Jesus is the water of life."[22]

[18] Ibid., 14.
[19] Ibid., 15.
[20] Ibid., 16.
[21] David B. Perrin, *Studying Christian Spirituality* (New York: Routledge, 2007), 60.
[22] Ibid.

It is obvious, of course, that those who find challenge, comfort, or profound connection with the Holy through desert spirituality certainly never wished to see the entire world become a desert. Yet if we decide—given our particular context in the world of the twenty-first century—that the desert has less to teach us today than the forest, we still run into the fact that Christianity has an affinity with deserts that it has never had with forests. Forests are too often and too easily associated with the sacred groves of pagans, and chopping down trees is deeply associated with the spread of Christianity. In the sixth century, St. Benedict reputedly cut down a sacred grove in order to build his monastery at Monte Cassino.[23] In the eighth century, St. Boniface famously chopped down a great oak tree and built a chapel from its wood; legend claims that when the German pagans who had revered the oak as sacred saw that he was not struck down by the gods, they converted to Christianity.[24] Such stories are not limited to ancient times: St. Bernard Mizeki cut down trees in a sacred grove in Zimbabwe in 1896.[25]

It would seem, perhaps, that forests are not fertile ground for the Christian imagination, and that it would be unlikely that a "forest spirituality" could be a real possibility. Such a reading of the supposed Christian "hostility" to forests is, however, unwarranted. As Belden Lane points out, "For every story about saints who cut down trees in an act of anti-pagan triumphalism, there are two stories of saints living in hollow oaks, singing the holy office along with their arboreal friends."[26] Christian spirituality can and should investigate the ways that a forest might affect our experience of God and the world. What was it that drew Saints Gerlach, Bavo, and Vulmar to life in hollow oaks, and St. Gudula to pray with poplar trees?[27] More important, what can their experiences offer us today?

---

[23] Nicole A. Roskos, "Felling Sacred Groves: Appropriation of a Christian Tradition for Antienvironmentalism," in *Ecospirit: Religions and Philosophies for the Earth*, ed. Lauren Kearns and Catherine Keller (New York: Fordham University Press, 2007), 485.

[24] Alban Butler, *Lives of the Saints*, quoted in ibid., 483.

[25] Ibid., 485.

[26] Lane, *Ravished by Beauty*, 125.

[27] Ibid., 125, 132.

Elements of a Forest Spirituality

The spare, silent, empty landscape of the desert gave rise to a spirituality that emphasized simplicity, silence, and the soul's nakedness before God. A forested landscape, however, is utterly different from that of the desert. The forest is lush and full of life—even a great variety of life—where the desert is empty; the forest echoes with birdsong and the chattering of squirrels where the desert is silent; and the forest is marked by shade and shadows where the desert is illuminated by a relentless sun. Surely, then, the spirituality that arises from the forest must be different from that of the desert—and yet not so different as to be unrecognizable, for today's human being is not so different from the human being of the fourth century, and the God each seeks is the same.

Farmer, poet, and cultural critic Wendell Berry describes himself as a "forest Christian," a term that is unfamiliar enough that he has been asked repeatedly to explain himself. What in the world is a *forest* Christian? At times his answer is brief and somewhat evasive: "I've called myself a 'forest Christian' because on Sunday mornings when the weather is favorable, my vocation (as it seems to me) has led me to the woods."[28] This might seem to indicate that a forest Christian is nothing but another version of the rather tiresome "spiritual but not religious" person who finds God in the sunset (and the forest), but Berry cannot be dismissed so easily. While it is true that he quite often spends Sundays in the woods—his many Sabbath poems, after all, were written during Sunday walks through the fields and forests of his Kentucky farm—it is also true that Berry takes the demands of the Gospel quite seriously and indeed writes devastatingly of the failures of much of modern Christianity to even pretend to do the same:

> Despite its protests to the contrary, modern Christianity has become willy-nilly the religion of the state and the economic status quo. Because it has been so exclusively dedicated to incanting anemic souls into Heaven, it has been made the tool of much earthly villainy. It has, for the most part, stood silently by while a predatory economy has ravaged the world, destroyed its natural beauty and health, divided and plundered its human communities and households. It

---

[28] From an interview with Gracy Olmstead, "Wendell Berry, Burkean," *The American Conservative* (February 17, 2015), http://www.theamericanconservative.com/articles/wendell-berry-burkean/.

has flown the flag and chanted the slogans of empire. . . . In its
de facto alliance with Caesar, Christianity connives directly in the
murder of Creation.[29]

And yet Berry has no intention of abandoning Christianity as a lost
cause; rather, he seeks to wake up his fellow Christians to the ways in
which modern life betrays the Gospel and to call us to something better.
Berry believes that our central mistake lies in our relationship to the
land, and to the rest of creation. Without a proper understanding of the
human place in the greater scheme of things, we will never understand
our relationship to each other, or to God:

> Until we understand what the land is, we are at odds with every-
> thing we touch. And to come to that understanding it is necessary,
> even now, to leave the regions of our conquest—the cleared fields,
> the towns and cities, the highways—and re-enter the woods. For
> only there can a man encounter the silence and the darkness of his
> own absence. . . . His life will grow out of the ground like the
> other lives of the place, and take its place among them. . . . He
> must reenter the silence and the darkness, and be born again.[30]

Human beings must be born again into Creation; we can no longer
see it as a place we are to conquer and dominate, but one in which we
are connected to and related to everything else. Berry believes that
we must come to understand Creation in a new way—or rather, in a
very old, absolutely traditional way that traces back to Augustine and
Aquinas but is sadly foreign to many Christians today. Creation, Berry
argues, "is not in any sense independent of the Creator, the result of
a primal creative act long over and done with, but is the continuous,
constant participation of all creatures in the being of God."[31] And it is

---

[29] Wendell Berry, "Christianity and the Survival of Creation," in *The Art of the
Commonplace: The Agrarian Essays of Wendell Berry*, ed. Norman Wirzba (Washington, DC: Counterpoint Press, 2002), 319.

[30] Wendell Berry, "A Native Hill," in *The Art of the Commonplace*, 27.

[31] Berry, "Christianity and the Survival of Creation," 308. On continuous creation, see Augustine, *The Literal Meaning of Genesis*, chapter 12, paragraph 22:
"For the power and might of the Creator, who rules and embraces all, makes every
creature abide; and if this power ever ceased to govern creatures, their essences
would pass away and all nature would perish. . . . The universe will pass away in
the twinkling of an eye if God withdraws his ruling hand." On participation, see

this participation that is central to his understanding of what it means to be a forest Christian:

> I used the phrase "forest Christian" to suggest what has been, for me, a necessary shift in perspective on the New Testament: from that of the church to that of the whole Creation. I don't want to sound too positive or knowing about this, because I hope to understand the problem better than I do, but I feel more and more strongly that when St. Paul said that "we are members of one another," he was using a far more inclusive "we" than Christian institutions have generally thought. For me, this is the meaning of ecology. Whether we know it or not, whether we want to be or not, we are members of one another: humans (ourselves and our enemies), earthworms, whales, snakes, squirrels, trees, topsoil, flowers, weeds, germs, hills, rivers, swifts, and stones—all of "us."[32]

As "members of one another," Berry reminds us, we are joined to one another and to God: "we and all other creatures live by a sanctity that is inexpressibly intimate, for to every creature, the gift of life is a portion of the breath and spirit of God."[33] In other words, we and all other creatures are, in Johnson's terms, kin—and that kinship is grounded in our mutual sharing of the spirit of God. Further, Berry extends the notion of "creature" beyond where we might expect: the community of God's creatures is not limited to animals or even beings (such as plants) that are alive. Rather, the community of God's creatures "could not be exclusive but would include all the local neighborhood of creatures—from the rocks, the water, and the air to the microorganisms in the soil to the plants and animals to the humans."[34]

Like Berry, Canadian artist Emily Carr (1871–1945) grounds her spirituality—her understanding of the complex relationships between

---

Johnson's discussion of Aquinas and participation in divine being in "Turn to the Heavens and the Earth." She argues, "According to Aquinas, all creatures exist by participation in divine being. This is an awesome concept, suggesting an intrinsic, ongoing relationship with the very wellspring of being, with the sheer livingness of the living God who in overflowing graciousness quickens all things" (14).

[32] Wendell Berry, in "The Art of Living Right: An Interview with Wendell Berry," by Gregory McNamee and James R. Hepworth, in *Conversations with Wendell Berry*, ed. Morris Allen Grubbs (Jackson: University Press of Mississippi, 2007), 23.

[33] Berry, "Christianity and the Survival of Creation," 308.

[34] Olmstead, "Wendell Berry, Burkean."

God, the world, and herself—in the forest. A native of Victoria, British Columbia, Carr is best known for her stunning modernist paintings of the coastal British Columbian rainforest.[35] In her posthumously published journal, *Hundreds and Thousands*, Carr gives voice to the spiritual vision underlying both her painting and her passion for the forest. God and the forest tangle and merge for Carr, and she speaks passionately of her desire to paint in such a way that the picture "speaks one grand inaudible word—God. The movement and direction of lines and planes shall express some attribute of God—power, peace, strength, serenity, joy."[36] Those attributes are best seen in "the glory of the woods," she says. "See God in every particle of them expressing glory and strength and power, tenderness and protection. . . . See God in it all, enter into the life of the trees."[37]

And yet the great forests of western Canada are inhospitable to human life and flatly dangerous to the unwary or unprepared. Why, then, did Carr insist that "the woods are God's tabernacle. We can see him there . . . [The woods are] the place where He seems nearest"?[38] What was it about the tangled, dark, dangerous forest that spoke to her of the divine? Beauty. "The trees are so inexplicably beautiful!"[39] she exclaims. She also saw in them a life and vitality that she immediately associated with God. "What is beauty?" she asks, and immediately replies to her own question: "God. What is that vital thing, in ugly as well as lovely things and places, the thing that takes us out of ourselves, that draws and attracts us, the unnameable thing claiming kinship with us?—God."[40]

Yes, kinship: like Johnson and Berry, Carr recognizes her kinship with the things around her, "ugly as well as lovely things," and knows that such kinship is grounded in God. She also knows that it is often difficult for us to recognize that kinship, especially perhaps because it

---

[35] For a more detailed analysis of Carr's work and its theological implications, see my "'Surely the Woods are God's Tabernacle': Considering Emily Carr's Ecospirituality Today," in *Spirit and Nature: The Study of Christian Spirituality in a Time of Ecological Urgency*, ed. Timothy Hessel-Robinson and Ray Maria McNamara (Eugene, OR: Wipf and Stock, 2011), 237–54.

[36] Emily Carr, *Hundreds and Thousands* (Vancouver: Douglas and MacIntyre, 2006; originally published by Clarke, Irwin and Co., 1966), 101.

[37] Ibid., 56.

[38] Ibid., 275.

[39] Ibid., 205.

[40] Ibid., 59.

would require recognizing that human beings are not always superior to other beings. "I've been thinking about [trees], how in a way they are better than we humans," she muses. "They are more obedient to God and recognize him clearer. They go straight ahead doing what God tells them; they never pause or question; they grow, always moving in growth, always unfolding, never in a hurry, never behind, doing things in their season."[41]

Carr and Berry are both Christians, albeit unusual ones. Tree canopy biologist Nalini Nadkarni does not identify as Christian,[42] but she does recognize that the forests she studies and the trees she loves are more than material objects with strictly physical relationships to human beings. With the aid of a 2001 Guggenheim Fellowship, Nadkarni studied "how people of different faiths understand trees and forests—as expressed in their holy texts, their religious practices, and the architecture of their places of worship" and then used that information to speak about trees and spirituality, often during worship, to a variety of religious congregations and organizations.[43] "The spiritual teachings of trees are universal,"[44] she argues, and while in many ways that statement sells short both the complexities of the major religions of the world and the great variety of ways that trees interact with human beings, it is also true that she identifies several aspects of a spirituality of trees and forests that do in fact resonate with the particular spiritual yearnings of our time.

First, Nadkarni points out that—just like humans—trees breathe. That is, they respire: they take in oxygen and release carbon dioxide.[45] This fact surprises many people, who know that trees do exactly the opposite: they *take in* carbon dioxide, and *produce* the oxygen we breathe. Human breathing, in this common understanding, is not the same as but complementary to tree breathing: we take in the oxygen that the trees release, and trees take in the carbon dioxide we breathe out. In fact,

---

[41] Ibid., 205–6.

[42] Her father was Hindu; her mother is Jewish; she attended a Unitarian Sunday school; she is married to a Presbyterian and attends Quaker meetings while doing fieldwork in Costa Rica (Nadkarni, *Between Earth and Sky*, 216).

[43] "The congregations I addressed ranged from fundamentalist to progressive and included Episcopalians, Baptists, Unitarian Universalists, Zen Buddhists, Reform Jews, Conservative Jews, Roman Catholics, Methodists, and secular interfaith organizations" (ibid., 217).

[44] Ibid., 242.

[45] Ibid., 22.

however, trees breathe (respire) in the same way that human beings do—oxygen in, and carbon dioxide out—and they do it day and night, continuously. The difference is that during the day, when the sun is shining, trees also engage in photosynthesis, the process by which they produce energy for themselves. Photosynthesis uses carbon dioxide and releases oxygen—and indeed, releases far more oxygen than the tree takes in through respiration.[46] Thus the common understanding is true, but limited—and Nadkarni wants us to pay attention to the full complexity of the breathing relationship between human beings and trees. Nadkarni reminds us that "the word *spirit* derives from the Latin word *spirare*, to breathe," and that when we recognize "a mindful focus on the breath [as] an important spiritual practice," we are in fact connecting ourselves both physically and spiritually to trees.

Next, Nadkarni goes on to discuss the idea that, because their roots are below ground, much of what a tree *is* is hidden.[47] Most people know, of course, that the root systems of trees are vast, usually extending far beyond the diameter of the crown of the tree.[48] The roots are necessary, yet in many ways they are unknown to us. So too do spiritual seekers discover that much about their own selves and interior lives is unknown: spirituality requires self-reflection, and the gradual growth in knowledge of aspects of the self that one has never closely examined or perhaps has even deliberately avoided confronting. Nadkarni points out that tree roots can thus "symbolize that which we keep hidden from ourselves and others: our troubles, our failings, our addictions, our ill health, and our fears. We know that revealing these hidden roots . . . is the first step toward finding the strength to overcome them."[49]

Finally, Nadkarni turns to the idea of connection. Here too she begins with tree roots. Until recently, even scientists did not know much about how roots functioned. "Roots and their associated animals and fungi are the most poorly understood portion of forests," Nadkarni points out, but just as the study of tree canopies (her specialty) has advanced

---

[46] Ibid., 237.

[47] Ibid., 30.

[48] "Typically, the root system of a tree extends outward . . . two to four times the diameter of the average tree's crown." J. M. Sillick and W. R. Jacobi, "Healthy Roots and Healthy Trees," *Fact Sheet* 2.926: Gardening Series: Diseases (Colorado State University Extension, July 1997; revised December 2013).

[49] Nadkarni, *Between Earth and Sky*, 30.

dramatically in recent years, so too has the study of roots. One of the more fascinating discoveries is that "the roots of many tree species can graft to roots of neighboring trees, allowing for the exchange of nutrients and water."[50] This can be problematic, in that it can facilitate the spread of disease,[51] but it can also be a source of strength and resilience: "Researchers have documented that in the tropical lowland forests of the Caribbean, grafted trees grow taller and sustain far less hurricane damage than do nongrafted individuals."[52] Thus trees teach us of the risks and rewards of connection, of sharing, of community.

Trees and the Communion of Saints

Beyond the spiritual resonances of forests for our time, it is also true that for many people, trees are not just "things," even living things, but friends. Jane Goodall, whose work with chimpanzees not only transformed our understanding of chimps but also challenged key ideas about human uniqueness,[53] traces her love of trees back to her earliest childhood. She describes the birch, ash, and chestnut trees surrounding her home in great and loving detail, but her favorite was a beech tree—named, of course, "Beech."

> I spent hours up that tree, perched in my special place. . . . I talked to Beech, telling him my secrets. I often placed my hands or my cheek against the slightly rough texture of his bark. And how I loved the sound of his leaves in summertime: the gentle whispering as the breeze played with them; the joyous, abandoned dancing and rustling as the breeze quickened; and the wild tossing and swishing sounds, for which I have no words, when the wind was strong and the branches swayed. And I was part of it all.[54]

---

[50] Ibid., 29.

[51] Root grafting was one reason that Dutch elm disease spread so quickly (ibid.).

[52] Ibid., 30.

[53] Commenting on Goodall's discovery that chimps made and used tools, anthropologist Louis Leakey famously said, "We must now redefine man, redefine tool, or accept chimpanzees as human!" Quoted in Jane Goodall, *Reason for Hope: A Spiritual Journey* (New York: Warner Books, 1999), 67.

[54] Jane Goodall, with Gail Hudson, *Seeds of Hope: Wisdom and Wonder from the World of Plants* (New York: Grand Central Publishing, 2014), 39.

She was "part of it all," part of the life of the tree and the dance of the wind. She knew Beech as friend, as kin, as one who was inextricably connected to her own life. Goodall is, of course, not the only one to develop an emotional attachment, or even a relationship, with a tree. It seems, actually, to be a rather common experience. Theologian Belden Lane speaks with surprise of the number of his students who tell stories about their relationship with a particular tree, and notes that these stories often "relate to a process of grieving and consoling at some period of crisis in their lives."[55] Lane himself claims relationship with the hundred-year-old cottonwood near his home, a tree he knows as "Grandfather" and describes as one of his spiritual teachers.[56]

Because of his relationship with Grandfather, and his understanding that such a relationship is both spiritually rich and not particularly unusual, Lane goes on to suggest that we should think of trees as part of the communion of saints.[57] While this might seem a rather dramatic leap to make, it is instead a straightforward outgrowth of the experience of the deep relationships that exist between humans and trees. "We must recognize trees as sharing an intimate, even sacramental relation with us in the Body of Christ," Lane argues, adding this plea: "Open the kingdom for a cottonwood tree. Let the green creation sing at the banquet. Love alone demands it. . . . The measure of the authenticity of the communion of Christ is the measurelessness of its power to include. For Christians, loving the natural world isn't any longer a matter of choice. It's required by the community in which they live."[58]

Lane's passionate plea for the inclusion of trees in the communion of saints was made in 2011. Unsurprisingly, given her understanding of the kinship between trees and people, Elizabeth Johnson had made this suggestion over a decade previously. In her 1998 book on the communion of saints, *Friends of God and Prophets*, she points out that "the communion of holy people is intrinsically connected to the community of holy creation, and they stand or fall together."[59] The trees, like the

---

[55] Lane, *Ravished by Beauty*, 129.

[56] Ibid., 124.

[57] Ibid., 130–33.

[58] Ibid., 132, 133.

[59] Elizabeth A. Johnson, *Friends of God and Prophets: A Feminist Theological Reading of the Communion of Saints* (New York: Continuum, 1998), 240.

rest of creation, are our kin and share with us in the community of the holy. As Johnson points out:

> The natural world does not just form a context for the communion of saints but is itself included in the community. Recall that a fascinating ambiguity in the original Latin term *communio sanctorum* supports this understanding, *sanctorum* referring to holy persons (the *sancti*) and also to holy things (the *sancta*). The latter idea, especially in view of the importance of Eucharistic communion, played an important role in shaping the original meaning of this doctrine and its medieval interpretation. The *communion sanctorum* signifies a "communion in the holy": holy people and holy things in interrelationship. Thus from within the symbol itself a way opens to include all beings, sacred bread and wine, certainly, but also the primordial sacrament, the sacred earth itself. The communion of saints has an ecological, cosmic dimension.[60]

To turn to the heavens and the earth, then, we must recognize the inclusion of "the sacred earth itself" and all its creatures in the communion of saints. A forest spirituality teaches us that inclusion through its emphasis on kinship, on connectedness, on the fact that we are members of one another. Those who embrace a forest spirituality will come to know, deeply, that we cannot continue to clearcut the world around us; such destruction would be seen as desecration. Forest Christians, in company with all of the holy people of God and all of God's creation, will understand themselves as part of a "dynamic, sacred community of the most amazing richness and complexity."[61] We will come to see that the woods are indeed lovely, dark, and deep—and we have promises to keep, to one another and to the community of creation of which we are a part. We also have miles to go before we sleep—on a journey of conversion, healing, and hope.[62] Elizabeth Johnson has opened the way before us: let us heed her voice, and enter joyfully into the forest.

---

[60] Ibid., 241.

[61] Ibid., 243.

[62] Robert Frost's beloved poem, "Stopping by Woods on a Snowy Evening," concludes with the following verse: "The woods are lovely, dark, and deep, / But I have promises to keep, / And miles to go before I sleep, / And miles to go before I sleep." Edward Connery Lathem, ed., *The Poetry of Robert Frost: The Collected Poems, Complete and Unabridged* (New York: Henry Holt, 1969), 224.

Chapter 5

The Wilderness

Sacred Space, Endangered Homeland, Hope for Our Planet

Carol J. Dempsey, OP

Introduction

In the 1996 presidential address titled "Turn to the Heavens and the Earth: Retrieval of the Cosmos in Theology," which Distinguished Professor Elizabeth A. Johnson delivered to the Catholic Theological Society of America, Johnson made this point: "As the twenty-first century rapidly approaches, there is a vital theme largely absent from the thinking of most North American theologians, namely, the whole world as God's good creation."[1] Now, twenty years later and well into the twenty-first century, many theologians from around the globe are recognizing the whole world as God's good creation.[2] Johnson herself has published an extraordinary volume titled *Ask*

---

[1] Elizabeth Johnson's Presidential Address was later published under the same title in the *CTSA Proceedings* 51 (1996): 1–14. The quote cited here comes from p. 1 of the published document.

[2] See, e.g., Celia Deane-Drummond and David Clough, eds., *Creaturely Theology: On God, Humans and Other Animals* (London: SCM Press, 2009); John F. Haught, *Is Nature Enough? Meaning and Truth in the Age of Science* (Cambridge:

the Beasts: Darwin and the God of Love that gives voice to a marvelous theology of divine love for all creation.[3]

Most recently some theologians have begun to comment extensively on the plight of planet Earth and the suffering of all of Earth's communities of life, especially those nonhuman communities who, like human women and children, are the most vulnerable among us and who, like the poor, are being forced to migrate and endure the ravages and ramifications of the most perilous planetary crisis today: global climate change.[4] Scientists speak of the web of life of which all that is created is a part; many theologians and biblical scholars have come to appreciate science's contributions and have shifted from an anthropocentric to a cosmological view of the world. A cosmological view recognizes the intrinsic goodness and value of all life, is cognizant that all aspects of creation—including the universe—function interdependently, and celebrates creation as not only the starting point for revelation but also the primary locus and dwelling place of the Sacred.[5] Creation makes

---

Cambridge University Press, 2006); Carol J. Dempsey and Mary Margaret Pazdan, eds., *Earth, Wind, and Fire: Biblical and Theological Perspectives on Creation* (Collegeville, MN: Liturgical Press, 2004); Edward Foley, ed., *The Wisdom of Creation* (Collegeville, MN: Liturgical Press, 2004); Denis Edwards, ed., *Earth Revealing—Earth Healing: Ecology and Christian Theology* (Collegeville, MN: Liturgical Press, 2001); Carol J. Dempsey and Russell A. Butkus, eds., *All Creation Is Groaning: An Interdisciplinary Vision for Life in a Sacred Universe* (Collegeville, MN: Liturgical Press, 1999); among others. Two other significant collections of works that deal with Earth as the interrelated community of God and creatures include Norman Habel's Earth Bible Project and Earth Bible Commentaries.

[3] See Elizabeth A. Johnson, *Ask the Beasts: Darwin and the God of Love* (New York: Bloomsbury, 2014).

[4] See the work of Richard W. Miller, ed., *God, Creation, and Climate Change: A Catholic Response to the Environmental Crisis* (Maryknoll, NY: Orbis Books, 2010); Sallie McFague, *A New Climate for Theology: God, the World, and Global Warming* (Minneapolis: Fortress Press, 2008), among others.

[5] For a full discussion on creation as a circle of a community of life, see the works of Carol J. Dempsey, "Creation, Evolution, Revelation, and Redemption: Connections and Intersections," in Dempsey and Pazdan, *Earth, Wind, and Fire*, 1–23, and "Creation, Revelation, and Redemption: Recovering the Biblical Tradition as a Conversation Partner to Ecology," in Foley, *The Wisdom of Creation*, 53–64. Dempsey's reading of Genesis 1–2 is a cosmological one that takes a synchronic view of the text rather than a diachronic view that posits two versions (the Yahwist [J] and the Priestly [P]) of the creation story.

known who God is, and thus, creation is both sacrament and sacramental. As Johnson states so eloquently, "The Giver of life creates what is physical—stars, planets, soil, water, air, plants, animals, ecological communities—and moves in these every bit as vigorously as in souls, minds, ideas. Earth is a physical place of extravagant dynamism that bodies forth the gracious presence of God. In its own way it is a sacrament and a revelation."[6] Johnson's thought resounds in the thought of Pope Francis, who states: "The entire material universe speaks of God's love, [God's] boundless affection for us all. Soil, water, mountains: everything is, as it were, a caress of God."[7] Additionally, Pope Francis notes: "The bishops of Brazil have pointed out that nature as a whole not only manifests God but is also a locus of [God's] presence. The Spirit of life dwells in every living creature and calls us to enter into relationship with [God]. Discovering this presence leads us to cultivate the 'ecological virtues.'"[8]

As sacrament and sacramental, creation is mysterious, wondrous, beautiful, diverse, creative, and forever evolving. It is a community of life important and endangered enough for Pope Francis to compose an encyclical letter titled *Laudato Sì.*[9] This encyclical addresses the care that needs to be given to our common home. Central to the encyclical is the topic of climate change and its adverse effects on life's countless species.

In celebration of Elizabeth A. Johnson's work and achievements of a lifetime done by a woman theologian so deeply and passionately committed to God and Earth as God's sacred dwelling place, I am proud and privileged to offer this essay as a gift in unison with Beth's voice and efforts with the hope that Beth's prophetic views will become a lived reality for us all. Written from a biblical perspective with an eye toward contemporary realities, this essay focuses on the theme of "wilderness," a part of God's beloved creation. Given the limited space provided for this essay, biblical passages for discussion are highly selective and taken from the Old Testament, which features the wilderness as a place of

---

[6] See Johnson, *Ask the Beasts*, 150.

[7] Pope Francis, *Laudato Sì; An Encyclical Letter of the Holy Father on Care for Our Common Home*, http://w2.vatican.va/content/francesco/en/encyclicals/documents/papa-francesco_20150524_enciclica-laudato-si.html.

[8] Ibid., par. 88.

[9] Ibid., par. 84.

encounter with the Divine, a place where faith is challenged and matures, and a place of refuge that has a significant role in God's vision for the redemption and restoration of ancient Israel.

After grounding the wilderness in the biblical tradition, the essay next looks at how the wilderness as sacred space becomes a source of inspiration for the great naturalist John Muir, who realized and recognized God's immortal Spirit in all things (Wis 11:26), just as many of the ancient biblical people did when they were composing their texts.[10] Finally, the essay looks at the reality of the wilderness today that is being devastated and destroyed by climate change and inordinate human activity. The devastation and destruction of the wilderness has a strong ripple effect: because the wilderness suffers, many species of life who make their home in the wilderness are also being made to suffer with some even being forced into extinction. Ironically, if preserved, the wilderness can assist in reversing the effects of climate change.

The Semantic Range and Significance of the Term "Wilderness" in the Bible

In the Bible and biblical tradition, the term "wilderness" is not clearly defined. In Hebrew, the sematic range for "wilderness" is extensive. Biblical terms include *'arabah, shammah, shemamah, siyyah, haraboth*, and *yeshimen.* The most frequently used word for "wilderness" is *midbar*, which also means "desert." This term *midbar*, however, is not to be understood in the classical sense of desert that implies dry, arid land. While *midbar* does refer to this type of land, it is better known as grazing land, which is found mostly in the foothills of southern Palestine. This area was not used for agriculture; its primary function was for animal grazing. Of note, the prophet Joel refers to the "pastures of the wilderness" (Joel 1:19, 20; 2:22).[11]

Because *midbar* has been understood as both "desert" and "wilderness," the term more generally refers to the sparsely populated open spaces that lie adjacent to more populated areas. The *midbar* not only represents pastureland but also the devastation of war. For example, in

---

[10] All biblical citations are taken from the New Revised Standard Version of the Bible.

[11] Other places in the Hebrew Bible where *midbar* is used in the sense of pasture include Gen 36:24b; 1 Sam 17:28; and 2 Chr 26:10a.

the book of Joel, the prophet speaks of the "day of the Lord," a time of great destruction from warfare when the land, once like the Garden of Eden, becomes a desolate wilderness (Joel 2:3).[12] Thus, *midbar* has a variety of connotations.

Scholars tend to see *midbar* in a variety of ways that range from vast regions to spaces that are limited. Using Exodus 16:10 as a reference, Shemaryahu Talmon suggests that *midbar* is the sparsely populated open spaces near both temporary and permanent settlements. In other words, *midbar* could be an extension of a settlement but not necessarily an integral part of it. Talmon also notes that from time to time *midbar* could refer to the desert or wilderness country.[13]

Peter Addinall points out that when *midbar* is used in the sense of a true desert or wilderness, most often the term refers to a specific place.[14] Robert Funk argues further that *midbar* insofar as it is localized in Palestine, almost always pertains to all or part of the lower half of the Rift Valley, which would be the whole of South Judah east of the central ridge from Jericho along the shores of the Dead Sea to the Gulf of Aqaba.[15] Interestingly, Ulrich Mauser views the *midbar*, the "wilderness-place," as interrelated to the "mountain(s)" because both places are areas of retreat and revelation. They are so closely linked that "the barren mountain regions and the wilderness can become identical."[16] Robert Cohn takes Mauser's point a step further and notes that Mount Sinai/Horeb, which is situated in the wilderness, is the most important sacred space in the entire Pentateuch.[17] Mauser goes on to link the wil-

---

[12] See also Jer 22:6b-7, where the once fertile and inhabited land is destined to become a "desert" and an "uninhabited city."

[13] For further study, see S. Talmon, "The 'Desert Motif' in the Bible and in Qumran Literature," in *Biblical Motifs: Origins and Transformations*, ed. A. Altmann, Philip W. Lown Institute of Advanced Judaic Studies, Brandeis University Studies and Texts 3 (Cambridge, MA: Harvard University Press, 1966), 31–63; see also Talmon, "*Midbar*," in *Theologisches Wörterbuch zum Alten Testament* 4 (Stuttgart: W. Kohlhammer), 660–95.

[14] See Peter Addinall, "The Wilderness in Pedersen's Israel," *Journal for the Study of the Old Testament* 20 (1981): 76–78.

[15] Robert Funk, "The Wilderness," *Journal of Biblical Literature* 78 (September 1959): 209.

[16] Ulrich Mauser, *Christ in the Wilderness*, Studies in Biblical Theology 39 (London: SCM, 1963), 110.

[17] Robert L. Cohen, *The Shape of Sacred Space* (Chico, CA: Scholars Press, 1981).

derness, the mountain, and the sea, stating that these three elements "cannot be isolated one from another."[18] Oftentimes biblical characters in both the Old and New Testaments spend time on the mountains, in the wilderness.

In the New Testament, the Greek word *eremos* (or *eremia*) is often translated not only as "wilderness" but also as "desert" or "place of isolation." In most instances, the New Testament *eremos* refers specifically to the Wilderness of Sinai or the Wilderness of Judea. Unlike the Old Testament, New Testament references to the "wilderness" are few.

Wilderness, then, is not a psychological or social experience; rather, wilderness from the biblical perspective is a locale, a place where the encounter with the Divine—that Sacred Presence that is the ground of all being—occurs. The wilderness is part of the created world, and as part of creation, the wilderness is the locus of divine revelation. The wilderness, then, is sacramental.

Wilderness as a Place of Encounter with the Divine

Within the Bible, and specifically within the Old Testament, the wilderness becomes a place of encounter with the Divine, and as Carol Ochs points out, the wilderness/desert experience "provides the single most informative experience in the creation of the Jewish people."[19] Furthermore, Mauser sees the wilderness as "the womb of a fundamental datum of the religion of the Old Testament without which its development would be unintelligible."[20] Robert Barry Leal in his study on the wilderness in the Bible notes that "All the basic revelations of God's nature and God's will occur in the wilderness: the revelation of the name of God; the establishment of the covenant with Israel; the theophany on Sinai; and the communications of the Ten Commandments. Israel's very belief in its election as a chosen people is grounded in the wilderness experience of its forebears."[21] Thus, Israel's God dares

[18] Mauser, *Christ in the Wilderness*, 141.

[19] Carol Ochs, "The Desert, Biblical Spirituality, and Creation," *Sewanee Theological Review* 36 (1993): 493.

[20] Mauser, *Christ in the Wilderness*, 29.

[21] Robert Barry Leal, *Wilderness in the Bible: Toward a Theology of Wilderness*, Studies in Biblical Literature 3, ed. Hemchand Gossai (New York: Peter Lang, 2004), 52.

to be self-revealing, which often comes as a surprise to those who are the recipients of such a wonderful and often life-changing experience. Several biblical stories showcase the wilderness as a place of encounter with the Divine, one of which is the story of Hagar in Genesis 16 and 21.

A. Hagar (Gen 16 and 21)

In Genesis 16:1-16 Hagar, the maidservant of Sarah and the concubine of Abraham, suffers the disdain of her mistress because she, Hagar, is able to conceive and Sarah (Sarai) is not. Verses 1-6 set the stage for Hagar's encounter with the Divine. Sarah, unable to become pregnant, beseeches her husband Abraham to have relations with Hagar, her maidservant. Abraham complies with Sarah's wishes, Hagar becomes pregnant, and instead of having compassion on Sarah's unfortunate circumstances, Hagar looks with contempt on her mistress (vv. 1-4). This gesture incites anger in Sarah, causing her to deal harshly with Hagar, which results in Hagar running away into the wilderness (vv. 5-6).

In the wilderness, Hagar is found by the angel of the Lord, who gives her a series of commands (vv. 7-11) and a description of her son yet to be born (v. 12). There, in the wilderness, Hagar names the Lord who speaks to her, "You are Elroi," and she is stunned that she has seen God and remains alive (v. 13). Hagar proceeds to name the spring of water where she has had a divine encounter *Beer-lahairoi*. Hagar's encounter with the Divine and subsequent events reassure her that indeed the God of Israel whom she names is with her plight even though she is told to return to her mistress who treated her harshly and upon whom she had had contempt.

Hagar's story continues in Genesis 21:8-21. Here Hagar suffers more abuse by her mistress Sarah. By this time, Sarah has given birth to Isaac and, not wanting him to be associated with Hagar's son Ishmael, Sarah demands that Abraham banish the maidservant and her son (vv. 8-11). Abraham, distraught by such a demand, abides by Sarah's wishes (vv. 11-14): "So Abraham rose early in the morning, and took bread and a skin of water, and gave it to Hagar, putting it on her shoulder, along with the child, and sent her away. And she departed, and wandered about in the wilderness of Beer-sheba" (v. 14). In the wilderness of Beersheba, Hagar cries out to God, pleading with God not to let her look upon the death of the child who is about to die of thirst because the water in the skin she was carrying had been used up completely (vv. 15-16). And God hears and responds to Ishmael's voice and Hagar's pleas. God meets Hagar and Ishmael in the wilderness and provides the water that Ishmael needs to survive (vv. 17-19). The story concludes on a poignant note: "God was with the boy, and he grew up; he lived in the wilderness, and became an expert with the bow. He lived in the wilderness of Paran; and his mother got a wife for him from the land of Egypt" (v. 20). Israel's God whose largeness of heart responds to the plight of an Egyptian woman and her young son is the God who dwells in the midst of the human condition and remains present even in the wilderness which, through divine grace, becomes a place not of peril but of safe haven for the nurturing and maturation of human life (v. 20).

B. Moses (Exod 3 and 19)

Hagar is not the only person to encounter the Divine in the wilderness. Moses receives his life-changing call and divine commission there. Exodus 3 opens with Moses keeping the flock of his father-in-law, Jethro. He leads the flock beyond the wilderness to Horeb,[22] the mountain of God. Horeb is located in the wilderness. At that mountain, Moses encounters God. During that encounter Moses is called by name (v. 4) and God reveals God's identity to Moses: "I am the God of your father, the God of Abraham, the God of Isaac, and the God of Jacob" (v. 6a). God then commissions Moses to set the Israelites free from Egyptian captivity (vv. 7-12). In response to Moses' seeming bewilderment and reluctance, God reveals further God's sacred identity to Moses: "I AM WHO I AM" (v. 14). Moses then receives a series of divine promises (vv. 15-22) and, eventually, Moses embarks on his divinely ordained task and leads the Israelites out of Egypt (Exod 4:1–15:20). In the wilderness, on the mountain of Horeb, Moses encounters his God, who changes his life and the lives of the Israelites, as well as their history, forever.

Under the leadership of Moses and Aaron, the Israelites journey through the wilderness en route to Canaan, the Promised Land. The Exodus story states that:

[22] Horeb and Sinai are interchangeable names for the mountain of God and appear as such in the biblical text on account of different authors. In this article Horeb and Sinai appear interchangeably depending on how the references appear in both the Hebrew and English biblical texts.

> On the third new moon after the Israelites had gone out of the land of Egypt, on that very day, they came into the wilderness of Sinai. They had journeyed from Rephidim, entered the wilderness of Sinai, and camped in the wilderness; Israel camped there in front of the mountain. Then Moses went up to God; the LORD called to him from the mountain, saying, "Thus you shall say to the house of Jacob, and tell the Israelites: You have seen what I did to the Egyptians, and how I bore you on eagles' wings and brought you to myself. Now therefore, if you obey my voice and keep my covenant, you shall be my treasured possession out of all the peoples. Indeed, the whole earth is mine, but you shall be for me a priestly kingdom and a holy nation. These are the words that you shall speak to the Israelites. (Exod 19:1-6)

In the wilderness, Moses once again encounters the Divine. At Mount Sinai, Moses is given a sacred word to speak to the Israelites. In the wilderness, at Mount Sinai, God reveals God's intention, which is to establish a relationship with the Israelites. At Mount Sinai, in the wilderness, God reveals Israel's divine identity. A people are then consecrated to their God (vv. 19-25), and Moses soon after receives the Law that solidifies Israel's and God's covenantal relationship (Exod 20:1–31:18). In the wilderness, God speaks to Moses "face to face as one speaks to a friend" (Exod 33:11a). The wilderness is the place where one encounters the Divine.

C. *Elijah (1 Kgs 19:11-18)*

Another biblical character who, like Moses, encounters the Divine on Mount Horeb is Elijah. Commanded by God to go and stand on the mountain, Elijah does so and has a series of dramatic experiences: a great wind that splits the mountains and breaks the rocks into pieces, an earthquake, a fire, and then the sound of sheer silence (1 Kgs 19:11-12). Suddenly in the midst of the silence, in the place of the wilderness, Elijah meets his God, who enters into dialogue with him and gives him various instructions, one of which is to return on his way to the wilderness of Damascus (1 Kgs 19:13b-18). In the silence of the wilderness, God and humankind meet.

The Wilderness as a Place of Challenge (Exod 16)

Besides being a place for the encounter with the Divine, the wilderness is also a place of challenge where faith can mature and develop.

Ochs, in reflecting on the desert and its traditions, states that "the desert is teaching that to be human is to be vulnerable."[23] Leal adds further that "in the wilds of Sinai the Israelites do in fact soon acquire a consciousness of their vulnerability. How to react to this is the first challenge that they face. Confronted by obvious physical privation, they have a stark choice. On the one hand is the temptation of lapsing back into nostalgia for the well-fed certainties of bondage in Egypt where vulnerability was not normally an issue. On the other hand, they can endure with dogged faith the difficulties of the wilderness, moving forward in faith and trusting in [God] to provide."[24]

Two stories where the wilderness becomes a challenge that leads to faith development and maturation are found in Exodus 16:1-36 and Exodus 17:1-7. In Exodus 16:1-36, the Israelite community, on their sojourn from Egypt, comes into the wilderness of Sin (v. 1). There the whole congregation complains against Moses and Aaron. The people express their ill-desire to have stayed in Egypt—in oppression—because at least there they were being fed. Now, in the wilderness, on their journey to freedom—to the Promised Land—they are hungry and fear starvation (vv. 2-3). In response to their situation, God instructs Moses that manna and quail will be divinely provided for the people, but they are to gather as much as each person needs without leaving any leftovers for morning (vv. 9-19). Fearing they would have no food in the morning and lacking trust in both Moses and their God, the Israelites do not follow Moses' instructions. They leave some of the food for the morning only to discover that it is full of worms and has become foul (vv. 20-21). Their lack of trust continued, and yet, despite their fear and refusal to follow Moses' and God's instructions, God continued to feed the Israelites in the wilderness (vv. 22-36).

After experiencing hunger and God's grace, the Israelites then experience thirst in the wilderness (Exod 17:1-7), and now they quarrel with Moses: "'Give us water to drink.' Moses said to them, 'Why do you quarrel with me? Why do you test the LORD?' But the people thirsted there for water; and the people complained against Moses and said, 'Why did you bring us out of Egypt, to kill us and our children and livestock with thirst?'" (vv. 2-3). God responds to Moses in the wilderness, in the

---

[23] Ochs, "The Presence in the Desert," *Cross Currents* 43 (Fall 1993): 302.
[24] Leal, *Wilderness in the Bible*, 111.

midst of the people's thirst even though they complain against Moses and challenge the care and beneficence of their God. Moses, under God's command, strikes a rock and water flows out of it to quench the people's thirst (vv. 4-7). For the Israelites, the wilderness offers challenges to their faith, a faith that God nurtures with steadfast love, one that Israel time and again needs to be reminded of generation to generation. Thus, Leal observes that "[the wilderness] emerges as a privileged place from which the Israelites are called to make critical judgments about the past and to determine the way of the future. Entry into the wilderness gives the Israelites the opportunity to hold a mirror up to themselves and to decide whether to transform the image that they see. From this perspective the wilderness sojourn becomes a period of challenge and intense testing as they are called upon to decide what really counts in their lives."[25] Finally, Walter Brueggemann notes that "all the faith questions are put to Israel in the wilderness."[26] Thus, the wilderness is a place that challenges faith and calls it into the possibility of deeper maturation.

The Wilderness as a Place of Refuge (1 Sam 23:15-29)

In addition to the wilderness being a place of encounter and challenge, the wilderness is also a place of refuge, as in the case of 1 Samuel 23:15-29, where David eludes Saul in the wilderness. The story opens with David in the wilderness of Ziph at Horesh. Here he learns that Saul is seeking his life (v. 15). Jonathan, Saul's son and David's friend, warns David about his father Saul's motives (vv. 16-18). Some of the Ziphites disclose David's hiding place to Saul, who in turn commands the Ziphites to find David's exact location (vv. 19-24a). Meanwhile, David moves on to the wilderness of Maon in the Arabah to the south of Jeshimon, where he takes refuge against Saul and those with him who were pursuing David (v. 24b). Saul goes to one side of the mountain, and David goes to the other side of the mountain. Here the mountain in the wilderness helps to protect David (vv. 25-26). The pursuit of David comes to an abrupt halt when a messenger tells Saul about the Philistines' raid on the land, which forces Saul to redirect his efforts

---

[25] Ibid., 111–12.

[26] Walter Brueggemann, *The Land: Place as Gift, Promise, and Challenge in Biblical Faith*, 2nd ed., Overtures to Biblical Theology (Minneapolis: Fortress Press, 2002), 35.

toward the Philistines and away from David (v. 27). The story closes with David escaping danger and the place in the wilderness where David took refuge being named the "Rock of Escape" (v. 28).

The Wilderness as Part of the Divine Vision of Redemption and Restoration of Israel

Within the Old Testament canon and particularly in the Prophets, the suffering of the land comes to the fore. The interrelatedness of social sin and the suffering of the natural world is especially apparent in the prophetic books of Isaiah, Hosea, Amos, Jeremiah, Joel, and Zephaniah.[27] It was thought that God struck the land with blight, mildew, pestilence, and drought to chastise wayward Israel and thus destroy the people's food source. What becomes clear in the writings of the Prophets is that as the people are redeemed from their transgressions so the land is restored. Included in this land restoration is the wilderness. When good governance is established in the land, when a king reigns in righteousness and princes rule with justice (Isa 32:1),

> Then justice will dwell in the wilderness,
>   and righteousness abide in the fruitful field.
> The effect of righteousness will be peace,
>   and the result of righteousness, quietness and trust forever.
> My people will abide in a peaceful habitation,
>   in secure dwellings, and in quiet resting places. (Isa 32:16-18)

With envisioned battles waged and won, and the exile over, the poet proclaims a new vision in Isaiah 35:1-2:

> The wilderness and the dry land shall be glad,
>   the desert shall rejoice and blossom;
> like the crocus it shall blossom abundantly,
>   and rejoice with joy and singing.
> The glory of Lebanon shall be given to it,
>   the majesty of Carmel and Sharon.
> They shall see the glory of the LORD,
>   the majesty of our God.

---

[27] For further discussion on the suffering of the land, see Carol J. Dempsey, "The Prophetic Voice: Exposing the Obvious and Unmasking the Implied," in *Hope Amid the Ruins: The Ethics of Israel's Prophets* (St. Louis, MO: Chalice Press, 2000), esp. 74–88.

The coming of the reign of God in glory and majesty will cause the land to celebrate, symbolized by its fertility and lush growth. The execution of God's justice—the removal of all enemies from the land (see also Isa 33:1-16; 34:1-17)—will allow the land to renew itself, making the wilderness glad and the desert rejoice and blossom. In this renewed wilderness, waters will break forth and streams will gush in the desert (Isa 35:6b; cf. Isa 41:18). The cedar, acadia, myrtle, and olive will be placed in the wilderness, and the cypress, plane, and pine will be set in the desert (Isa 41:19). Israel's God will do something new:

> I am about to do a new thing;
>   now it springs forth, do you not perceive it?
> I will make a way in the wilderness
>   and rivers in the desert.
> The wild animals will honor me,
>   the jackals and the ostriches;
> for I give water in the wilderness,
>   rivers in the desert,
> to give drink to my chosen people,
>   the people whom I formed for myself
>   so that they might declare my praise. (Isa 43:19-21)

The wilderness—the desert—once desolate and uninhabitable has become a source of new life for a people redeemed and restored to their God through God's saving grace. As the people are redeemed from their transgressions, so the land is redeemed from its pain and suffering. As the people are restored to their God, so the land is restored to the people and the people to the land (cf. Amos 8:11-15). The wilderness, a place now healed, has the potential to become a place of healing for all human and nonhuman communities of life. Thus, the wilderness, rich in meaning, is central to the biblical narrative and the experience of God, is related to one's journey in faith, and is a sign of God's enduring promise of life-sustaining divine presence (cf. Jer 31:6).

The Wilderness as a Source of Inspiration and Healing for John Muir

Throughout the ages, the wilderness has continued to affect and influence people's lives and their work. One person whose love for the wilderness had a lasting effect on his life and his life's work as a naturalist is the world's preeminent conservationist, John Muir (1838–1914). Muir's enduring spiritual legacy retrieved from his writings indicates that, for him, the wilderness is a "Godful wilderness." In his journal entry of September 1, 1869, when he was near Tuohumne Meadows, Muir writes a simple yet profound reflection: "No other place has ever so overwhelmingly attracted me as this hospitable, Godful wilderness."[28] The wilderness becomes a refuge for Muir and a place of profound healing. He writes further: "But go to the mountains where and how you will, you will soon be free from the effects of this confusion, and God's sky will bend down about you as if made for you alone, and the pines will spread their healing arms above you and bless you and make you well again."[29]

In the wilderness of Alaska, Muir encounters God. Muir's July 13, 1890, journal entry features the following reflection:

> I am often asked if I am not lonesome on my solitary excursions. It seems so self-evident that one cannot be lonesome where everything is wild and beautiful and busy and steeped with God, that the question is hard to answer—seems silly.
>
> Every particle of rock or water or air has God by its side leading it the way it should go. How else would it know where to go or what to do?[30]

Pondering Muir's life and works, Max Oelschlaeger makes the point that "Muir ultimately found God and celebrated the divine presence in the wilderness. . . . He abandoned the anthropocentric theology of Calvinism, replacing it with a biocentric wilderness theology rooted in a consciousness of the sacrality of wild nature."[31] Thus, for Muir, the wilderness is sacred space and the dwelling place of God whose presence is felt everywhere and in everything. The wilderness poses a challenge to religious beliefs and has the potential of transforming them

[28] John Muir, *My First Summer in the Sierras* (New York: Random House, 2003), 326.

[29] John Muir, *The Life and Letters of John Muir*, vols. 1 and 2, ed. William Frederic Bade (Boston: Houghton Mifflin, 1924), 2:203.

[30] John Muir, *John of the Mountains: The Unpublished Journals*, ed. Linnie Marsh Wolfe (Madison: University of Wisconsin Press, 1938), 319.

[31] Max Oelschlaeger, *The Idea of Wilderness* (New Haven, CT: Yale University Press, 1991), 177.

as Muir himself had experienced. Finally, for Muir, the wilderness is a place of deep healing. He believed that if people would come to love the wilderness and experience its restorative and regenerative powers, then they would be more apt to protect it.[32] Muir's belief is so apropos for the reality of the wilderness today.

The Current State of the Wilderness and Its Gift of Hope to the World

Home to countless species, the wilderness is suffering from the devastating effects of human-caused climate change, which, in turn, has an adverse effect on Earth's entire web of life. Pope Francis writes:

> The loss of forests and woodlands entails the loss of species which may constitute extremely important resources in the future, not only for food but also for curing disease and other uses. Different species contain genes which could be key resources in years ahead for meeting human needs and regulating environmental problems.
>
> It is not enough, however, to think of different species merely as potential "resources" to be exploited, while overlooking the fact that they have value in themselves. Each year sees the disappearance of thousands of plant and animal species which we will never know, which our children will never see, because they have been lost forever. The great majority become extinct for reasons related to human activity. Because of us, thousands of species will no longer give glory to God by their very existence, nor convey their message to us. We have no such right.[33]

Francis highlights the relationship between the loss of forests and woodlands and the loss of species, and then he points out the effect that such loss will have on the human community. More important, however, he acknowledges from a nonutilitarian perspective the intrinsic goodness of the land and species whose deepest purpose in life is a spiritual one made manifest by their sheer existence now threatened predominately by climate change.

---

[32] See Tim Flinders, *John Muir: Spiritual Writings* (Maryknoll, NY: Orbis Books, 2013), 16.

[33] See Pope Francis, *Laudato Sì*, pars. 32 and 33.

In their article titled "The Wilderness Act and Climate Change Adaptation," Elisabeth Long and Eric Biber offer these observations:

> Climate change is already affecting wilderness areas, and will continue to do so. It will amplify and compound existing stressors to wilderness ecosystems, including invasive species, fire, pathogens, disease, insects, pollution, and extreme weather events. Other changes, including variations in the timing, amount, and type of precipitation (i.e., snow vs. rain), drought, and shifting species ranges will create a "kaleidoscope of new patterns and trends" and require new management strategies.[34]

They add further that:

> Climate change will also have dramatic effects on biodiversity. There is evidence that drought conditions are already negatively affecting pinyon-juniper woodlands in Arizona, shrub communities in the Colorado Plateau, amphibian species in Yellowstone National Park, and aquatic habitat in the Chugach National Forest. Certain public lands, including Bandelier National Monument and Mesa Verde National Park, are at risk of losing their forests altogether.
>
> Many species will likely respond to climate change by migrating northward and to higher altitudes; therefore, species that live at high elevation, where many wilderness areas are located, are especially vulnerable.[35]

These higher elevations, including alpine and sub-alpine wilderness areas, are already beginning to experience more severe and widespread storms, floods, drought, disease, insect infestation, fire, and species invasions.

Finally, the wilderness and its myriad species are the victims not only of climate change but also of the inordinate and unjust acts of certain human beings within the human community who seek to develop unprotected lands and to build roadways and highways through them. In the case of the rainforests, those of Sumatra and Tasmania are disappearing the fastest because of deforestation caused by logging and clear-cutting. In the case of the forests of Sumatra, British writer,

---

[34] Elisabeth Long and Eric Biber, "The Wilderness Act and Climate Change Adaptation," *Environmental Law* (Spring 2014): 5–6.
[35] Ibid., 7.

environmentalist, and political activist George Monbiot points out: "Those forests that remain have the highest diversity of plants on earth. Many of their large mammals—such as the tiger, orangutan, elephant and clouded leopard—are in danger of extinction. The clearance there affects everyone because it exposes one of the world's largest deposits of peat. When the peat is exposed and drained, it begins to oxidise, making carbon dioxide. Forest clearance is the reason why Indonesia now has the third-highest greenhouse gas emissions in the world, after the US and China."[36] Added to deforestation is the horrific crime of poaching that is specifically affecting the lives of elephants and rhinoceroses, moving them closer and closer to extinction. One has to think only of trophy hunting and remember, for example, the horrific death of Zimbabwe's beloved lion Cecil, who was lured out of his protected wilderness and killed for sport. Thus, climate change and other human acts that cry out for justice have led to the loss of wilderness space, the loss of habitat and species, and, ultimately, the loss of one's connection to the spiritual and the sacred, and the rupture of the entire web of life.

Ironically, alive within the wilderness that is endangered and being destroyed are the seeds of hope for the entire planet. The wilderness, just by its sheer existence, provides a critical means by which plants and animals can adapt to climate change. It protects and connects unfragmented natural areas and offers the least disturbed habitats and thus allows plants and animals to grow and migrate freely, all of which helps to reduce the adverse effects of climate change on ecosystems. Wilderness areas help to provide clean water, and watersheds that are healthy aid in maintaining healthy fish and wildlife populations. Wilderness areas also store water and release it slowly over time. This storage and slow release of water protects downstream communities from flooding. Functioning wetlands, streams, rivers, lakes, and other waterways within the wilderness assist in providing fresh water for domestic, agricultural, and industrial uses. Wilderness areas also help to suppress naturally the release of carbon dioxide gas, the "greenhouse" gas that is a leading cause of global warming. Last but not least, wilderness areas provide solitude,

---

[36] See George Monbiot's blog post on deforestation titled "Why Is a Former Greenpeace Activist Siding with Indonesia's Logging Industry?," *The Guardian* (December 2, 2010), http://www.theguardian.com/environment/georgemonbiot/2010/dec/02/sumatra-rainforest-destruction-patrick-moore.

aesthetic beauty, and recreation for all species of life. Hence, the great American writer Henry David Thoreau was so right when he declared that "in Wildness is the preservation of the World."[37]

A Concluding Thought . . .

An ancient biblical poet dubbed Isaiah once proclaimed:

> A voice cries out:
> "In the wilderness prepare the way of the Lord,
>   make straight in the desert a highway for our God." (Isa 40:3)

This ancient verse reflects the experience of our biblical ancestors who encountered their God in the wilderness, in the desert, and who have thus left us a legacy of poems and stories that remind us that creation is sacred and that the wilderness and all its magnificent species of life are imbued with God's presence. All is sacramental. I have argued in writing and speech that every time we lose a species unnaturally, we have lost something of the wonder, the beauty, and the mystery of God whose Spirit pulsates at the heart of all life.

Wallace Stegner once wrote:

> Something will have gone out of us as a people if we ever let the remaining wilderness be destroyed; if we permit the last virgin forests to be turned into comic books and plastic cigarette cases; if we drive the few remaining members of the wild species into zoos or to extinction; if we pollute the last clean air and dirty the last clean streams and push our paved roads through the last of the silence.[38]

The wilderness is a divine gift to the planet, and in its preservation and restoration lie the seeds of hope for our world and web of life living in the midst of peril and promise and so desperately in need of healing. If we agree with the ancient biblical wisdom writer that God's immortal Spirit is in all things, and if we acknowledge that the wilderness can and does play an important role in helping to reverse global climate change,

---

[37] Henry David Thoreau, "Walking," in *Excursions: The Writings of Henry David Thoreau*, ed. Joseph J. Moldenhauser (Princeton, NJ: Princeton University Press, 2007), 202.

[38] Wallace Stegner, "Coda: Wilderness Idea," in *The Sound of Mountain Water: The Changing American West* (Garden City, NY: Doubleday, 1969), 146.

then we need to realize that the Spirit of God is working through creation, through the wilderness to save us from devastation. Salvation, then, becomes a dynamic, ongoing experience that affects not only humankind but also the entire planet and all Earth's species of life. Would that one day the wilderness and dry land be glad, the desert rejoice and blossom, and all creation rejoice with joy and singing (see Isa 35:1-2). Isaiah's prophetic vision defines our ecological vocation, and as Elizabeth A. Johnson makes clear: "The long-term goal is a socially and environmentally sustainable society in which the needs of all people are met and diverse species can prosper, onward to an evolutionary future that will surprise."[39] The entire community of creation asks no less of us, and the wilderness waits to grace us.

---

[39] Johnson, *Ask the Beasts*, 285–86.

Part 2

Turning
To Ethical Action

Chapter 6

Thinking Beyond Theology

For Elizabeth Johnson

Ivone Gebara

"Turn to the Heavens and the Earth" is part of the title of Elizabeth Johnson's provocative lecture to the Catholic Theological Society of America in 1996. While at first glance the title seems clear, in reality, it has multilayered content and is immensely complex, as is our interpretation of this content. We stand on the Earth, and from it we turn our gaze and our awareness to something we call "the heavens." But what are these heavens we are talking about? Certainly not the heaven our catechisms used to tell us was the eternal home of our souls. Are we then referring to the Milky Way, or the endless expanse of the galaxies?

Elizabeth Johnson directs our attention to the cosmos—that is, the global reality, known and unknown, and the fullness of Creation—and the urgency of attending to it by the practice of justice and mercy. While it is true that cosmological and ecological awareness is more widespread than it was twenty years ago, it is also the case that the problems are much greater now because we continue to engage in the destruction of our greater body (an ecocide), which is the habitat of all living bodies. Among all living bodies, we who are human bodies have the use of reason and knowledge. In addition to making ourselves more aware of the destruction we cause, we are alerting one another to the urgent task of preserving life on the planet.

I wish to contribute to this raising of consciousness by highlighting the necessity of returning to an anthropology that is broader—that is to say, more inclusive and complex—than our traditional anthropologies. In other words, our cosmological and ecological discourse, as well as the new cosmologies and theologies we propose, are part of our anthropology. The reason to involve ourselves in anthropological reflection is because, whatever the understanding we arrive at, we are human beings who have to come to grips with all the different issues that challenge us. We cannot escape from our little dwelling place even though we may be talking about galaxies and the enormous creativity of the universe. As we broaden our knowledge, our feelings, and our perceptions, we reposition ourselves within the complex web of life. Through the diversity of their experiences and situations, human beings are able to embrace new ways of understanding themselves and the world.

We are coming to a new way of looking at the heavens and the earth because our first and main concern is with ourselves, with the search for knowledge, survival, and understanding. The challenging, fundamental problem for theology that Elizabeth Johnson set out nearly twenty years ago has helped me formulate some questions and misgivings that arise from the Latin American context and a feminist perspective. They are especially related to the articulation and the effectiveness of the contemporary theological response to issues surrounding the various forms of planetary destruction. The experience of these past twenty years has shown how difficult it is for countries, national and regional groups, and religious institutions to take up the issues of planetary destruction and respect for Creation as God's work. Often the "new histories of the universe," the Big Bang, and even ecological issues function as little more than trite illustrations appended to the superficial social conventions that have now become de rigueur. This new information, which is considered to be culturally important and politically correct, is often exploited by the churches, whose *modus agendi* is very similar to that of capitalistic enterprises that do not hesitate to use huge quantities of toxic agricultural chemicals while disseminating misleading statements about their care and concern for the environment. Exploitation, hypocrisy, and lack of moral fiber go hand in hand.

If we believed that the destruction of forests, rivers, seas, and many species of animals had no negative effects on human life, I am willing to bet that our selfishness and greed would be even more rampant. We would probably be perfectly willing to continue destroying the lives of many for the benefit of a few. All we have to do is point to the deforestation of large areas of the Amazon to build hundreds of private airports, or the indiscriminate logging of trees that are centuries old. The only reason many are now ready to "do something" is because drinking water is becoming increasingly scarce, or because carbon dioxide poisons our lungs, or because the unpredictability of the climate upsets our expansionist plans. The principal motivation of those who are now ready to "do something" is not love of neighbor, of the forest and its inhabitants, or of divine creation, but their concern to prolong their own lives and preserve their capital. The hope of continuing to make a profit is the motivation for more than a few of the initiatives that are being undertaken.

Theology and the Christian churches are not exempt from responsibility for the destruction of human lives and the world that is home to us all. As Elizabeth Johnson puts it, "ravaging of people and of land go hand and hand,"[1] and all of us to varying degrees are responsible for it. Today, xenophobia, Islamophobia, homophobia, capitalistic colonialism, abject poverty, and hunger express the unprecedented expansion of human wealth along with the natural resources of many peoples. However, I am suspicious about arguments from authority that appeal to an alleged "will of God" in relation to the Earth and to those living beings that are considered to be the image and likeness of God or divine sparks. It seems that this ancient tradition no longer has any ethical consequences. By that I mean that it does very little to bring about a change in behavior, especially with regard to modifying habits that are destructive of ecosystems. It seems to me that neither contemplation of the image of God nor its ethical application is any longer effective in bringing about a change of behavior. God has become little more than a useful "name" for many, especially on the lips of criminals and dictators of all kinds. They invoke an idol created in their own image and likeness, an idol that allows them to destroy lives for their own

---

[1] Elizabeth A. Johnson, "Turn To The Heavens and the Earth: Retrieval of Cosmos in Theology," *CTSA Proceedings* 51 (1996): 1–14, p. 11.

benefit. To be more precise, I believe that today very few of those who accept the doctrine of the divine image in us manage to control their passion for possessions, power, and outdoing others or the cruelty that results from that passion. Unbridled individualism and the excessive consumption of useless goods have blinded us to the dire situation of human beings and the planet and prevented us from opening our eyes to other ways of looking at the world. Deep down, we do not believe that we have the power both to save and to destroy ourselves, others, and the world. Moreover, we do not want to deprive ourselves of our privileged position and the comforts we have accumulated in order to be more considerate and respectful of many other lives. We do not want to admit that we too are responsible for them.

Today, *life* asks us to go beyond returning to the theology of Creation and integrating it into a new cosmology. Our declarations are not being heard, nor will they be. Our books will not be read by those who need to do more to avoid or prevent disasters. Perhaps we have come to a time when we need to be a little more reticent about the so-called truths of our faith and not rely so much on our theological traditions, even if we do reinterpret them. Maybe we need to give the name of "God" a rest and not call upon God every time there is a problem to be solved or some disastrous and corrupt policy to be supported. Confiding in our common responsibility, the creativity of our imagination, and the merciful kindness of our hearts, perhaps we can create a new humanist tradition for the twenty-first century. What is needed is a new consensus, a new social contract with cultural, social, and political dimensions. The starting point is no longer the motivation of our religious beliefs, nor is it given shape by traditional ecclesial ecumenism. Rather, beginning with an encounter with living and astonishingly diverse creatures, as well as an encounter with our own body, feelings, and emotions, we can go beyond being little more than the products of the current alienating consumerism. A new social contract that is personal and both local and international, a contract that calls for small daily activities aimed at a better quality of life and care for oneself and others is a pressing necessity. We are all aware of the limits and difficulties of such an undertaking, but the various means of communication that are available [on the internet] today offer us limitless possibilities to communicate with others and to form action groups in support of humanitarian causes. Let me repeat: humanitarian causes include rivers, seas, lakes, forests, animals, and even insects. They are not only about women who have been raped, children who have been abandoned, or refugees. Movements on behalf of the Earth are also humanitarian movements because they begin with us and include us as subjects and objects of the life for which we are struggling and of the complex, interdependent web of life of which we are only a part.

I would go so far as to say that this new venture, as necessary as it is, has no guarantee of victory, for we can no longer speak in terms of final victory. With regard to both cruelty and solidarity, human beings are unpredictable. For this reason, not a day goes by when we do not have to recommit ourselves to life. This commitment does not mean we assert ourselves as grandiose saviors of the planet earth, for this is an attitude that hides another form of impudent omnipotence. The commitment I am speaking of is a form of humility that simply commits us to be bold enough to learn to see the world as something very close to us. Life on the streets, in schools, in hospitals, the pleasant and repulsive odors we get used to or try to avoid, contain lessons we must be willing to learn. Similarly, the continued existence of air, clouds, forests, or beaches, with all the creatures that inhabit them, becomes meaningful to us because we draw our life from all these beings, learn with them, and are dazzled by their extraordinary beauty. The experiential, emotional closeness to the world we feel because our bodies are in touch with it may be one of many ways to awaken in us the desire to liberate or save the fragile life that inhabits us and in which we live. I will go so far as say that we open ourselves to a vision that is wider and more inclusive than can be contained in our different religious beliefs. What we need to do now is welcome the novelty of the moment, with all its questions and challenges, and graft our traditions onto them. Our world is different from that of our ancient religious traditions, myths, rites, and their way of speaking. Our new way of perceiving the connection of human beings with the bio-systems of the earth calls us to broaden our moral principles by introducing different solutions and clarifications and responding in a way that corresponds to what is required for the common good of all living beings. This new perception also calls us to marvel at the manifold beauty that is to be found on our tiny blue planet.

Even though we strive for national and local identities, we still belong to the community of the Earth. We are of many colors, but we still want to exclude those whose color is different from ours. We are of varying sexual orientations, but we still want to establish strict sexual dualities. We speak different languages, but we still want to insist on only one. Nevertheless, we are slowly waking up and shaking off our old securities and beliefs. Something new, painful, and salutary is taking shape. Horizons are already being widened by the many events, good and bad, that are mobilizing peoples from different parts of the globe. Many deaths, many survivals, and a sense of solidarity make it clear that the old ways of organizing the world no longer nourish us. Life, the life that we live today, demands more, much more, of us. The old wineskins have already burst, but we still do not realize that we are losing precious wine.

I have written these lines to express the hope that "the heavens and the earth" will unite as one flesh, as the love and hope of every living thing—hope expressed in human poetry and the "Hymn of the Universe" that are sung or contemplated every new day. In that same hope I celebrate and give thanks for the life of our beloved prophet and scholar Elizabeth Johnson and consider it a privilege to be able to add my voice to our common mission for the years to come.

Chapter 7

Choosing a Life of Exposure
Asking and Telling in the Face of the (Nonhuman Animal) Other

Michele Saracino

How many of us are anxious about admitting that we don't know something? How many of us think that our good isn't good enough or that we must be perfect to be loveable? How many of us are petrified to admit that we need others for help or companionship? Practically speaking, we should be comfortable asking questions and seeking out others, since we come by our neediness honestly. All creatures are limited, subject to the laws of physics, and bound by perspective—in other words all are needy and vulnerable. We cannot possibly know and do everything just by our being here or being there; we need to ask for and a lot of the time we could use the help of others. These realities are reflected in Christian anthropological claims that God as creator is infinite and perfect, while creation, including all animals and plants, is finite and imperfect. As foundational as these insights about vulnerability are to theology and life, we still seem to deny them.

In all fairness, it is not our malevolent intention to forget, downplay, or avoid appearing vulnerable; rather, it is more the case that we feel tremendous pressure by consumer culture to keep up the illusion that we have it all together and are not in need of anyone or anything. We are socialized to act as if we have all the answers and are doing great in all our relationships. Since vulnerability is conflated with our being weak, unattractive, and even unlovable, we find ourselves spending an exorbitant amount of resources to keep up the façade that we have it all together—that we are *not* vulnerable. This delusion, which upholds the idea that to be human is to surpass limits, have all the answers, and achieve perfection, is so powerful that we impute it onto others as well. It is my hunch that all of us are so fragile in our egos, abilities, age, looks, and so on that we look at the other and think he or she has it all together when in reality they too are probably on the verge of imploding. By denying our own frailties we prevent the other from expressing anxieties about theirs.

In her inspirational work *Bird by Bird: Some Instructions on Writing and Life*, Anne Lamott captures the toxic effects of our desires for perfection and anxieties about human frailty: "Perfectionism is the voice of the oppressor, the enemy of the people. It will keep you cramped and insane your whole life . . . [and] is based on the obsessive belief that if you run carefully enough, hitting each stepping-stone just right, you won't have to die."[1] Lamott's words emphasize the downside of the desire to control every aspect of our lives. It imprisons us and reduces our freedom, swaying us not to do the things we enjoy because we worry about failing or not being perceived as attractive. The fact is we are all imperfect and at times need to ask others to help us or be in relationships with us in order to have better lives. In our daily lives, the only thing for certain is that vulnerability is an undeniable aspect of the human condition.

Embracing vulnerability and our need for others are important themes in Elizabeth Johnson's work. Let's begin by considering the title of her recent work on theology and ecology, *Ask the Beasts: Darwin and the God of Love*.[2] In using that title, Johnson directs our attention to this passage in the book of Job: "Ask the animals, and they will teach you; the birds of the air, and they will tell you . . . and the fish of the sea will declare to you" (12:7-8; NRSV). Arguably what's most shocking

---

[1] Anne Lamott, *Bird by Bird: Some Instructions on Writing and Life* (New York: Anchor Books, 1995), 28.

[2] Elizabeth A. Johnson, *Ask the Beasts: Darwin and the God of Love* (London: Bloomsbury, 2014).

about this biblical passage is the mandate to engage nonhuman animals like one would humans, with enough respect for them to inquire of or about them. Some may wonder, nonetheless, why should humans care about nonhumans? What do *they* have to offer *us*? Do they, meaning nonhuman animals, have the same value as human animals? Are they subjects, so to speak, with rights, dignity, and the capacity for freedom? A second and perhaps even more stunning aspect of this scriptural text is the presumption that human beings don't have all the answers. Because we are limited, vulnerable, and uncertain, we humans need to ask the other—even the nonhuman other—for help, about their situation, and how their predicament affects our own.

No Questions Are Stupid, Really

All creatures are animals. What we are considering here is asking about nonhuman animals. This is a lofty and perhaps foolhardy goal. It is not as if communication with nonhuman animals is a simple matter. Even if we believe they, that is to say, nonhuman animals, have sophisticated forms of communication, human animals may not be able to converse with them in any concrete way. In an age of environmental crises and with rising extinction rates, this challenge is not an excuse *not* to ask and find out more about their plight and how our lifestyle impacts them. In fact, since we cannot communicate with them through ordinary means, we are obliged to learn more about them by asking about them.

"There is no such thing as a stupid question." Teachers love to say this in an effort to assure their students that it is better to ask a question than to remain in a state of ignorance. Still, the act of asking takes courage. In asking, we admit to being unsure, wrong even, and in need of the other. In asking, we expose our vulnerability. Moreover, when asking we have to prepare ourselves for new information that may change our outlook and may amplify our obligation to another. Related to the current crisis of environmental degradation, the facts are so stark and scary that many of us are apprehensive and overwhelmed by new information.

In his work on the practice of engaged Buddhism, *Being Peace*, Thich Nhat Hanh explains the momentous task of being open to intellectual change: "In Buddhism, knowledge is regarded as an obstacle to understanding, like a block of ice that obstructs water from flowing. It is said that if we take one thing to be the truth and cling to it, even if truth itself comes in person and knocks at our door, we won't open it. For things to reveal themselves to us, we need to be ready to abandon our views about them."[3] Keeping this in mind, it is not enough to ask; we need to be open to the potential emotional pushback from our asking. The other may not appreciate our asking. They may feel threatened by our asking. This is what makes asking so difficult. It opens us to the predicament of the other, a situation which is unpredictable and uncontrollable. What's more, even if our asking is welcomed by the other, we may not be prepared for the other's response to our questioning. The new information gathered in our asking could necessitate that we alter our views and even our values. When put this way, asking of any sort is trying. It demands a great amount of trust and hospitality from both parties. But what other choice do we have? While thinking, acting, and feeling as if we know something makes us feel safe and in control of our environment, it has the potential to be an obstacle to genuine understanding, limiting from developing life-giving relationships.

Throughout his career, Bernard Lonergan emphasized the complexity of human understanding and a similar sort of blockage, one which he called *scotoma*. A classical term used to talk about distorted or compromised vision, scotoma manifests in being unaware or not attentive to the problems, sin, injustices, and wrongs of our time. It is not the case that human beings inherently are malicious and/or stupid and their malevolence and/or ignorance prevent them from perceiving sinful situations and acting against these problems. On the contrary, Lonergan argues that there exist forces, including emotional and social pressures, that prevent one from seeing the totality of the situation and acting accordingly. We experience this blindness as bias, which becomes an obstacle to opening to new information and insights.[4] Bias is our metaphorical block of ice in that it prohibits our understanding of and love for the other. As ice impedes the flow of water, bias hinders our ability to connect with others in genuine ways. The Christian believer is accountable for overcoming or at least struggling against these blockages. In the face of environmental degradation, we are called to ask, so we can actuate our full humanity and open ourselves to the richest of lives

---

[3] Thich Nhat Hanh, *Being Peace* (Berkeley, CA: Parallax Press, 2005), 42.

[4] For a discussion of the four avenues by which bias occurs, see *Collected Works of Bernard Lonergan*, ed. Frederick E. Crowe and Robert Doran, vol. 3, *Insight: A Study of Human Understanding* (Toronto: University of Toronto Press, 1997), 214–20.

with the other. In the act of asking, we expose our limits, connecting with others in a deep way. We say implicitly, *I don't know everything; I need you.* This courageous questioning is a model for others, empowering them to do the same.

Asking takes many forms. It can plainly mean questioning others about themselves or something in their life. It can also refer to being with them to find out more about them and ourselves in the process. As such, witnessing to the other serves as a form of asking. Jean Vanier is a Canadian Catholic thinker and humanitarian who has devoted his life to asking about and witnessing to human vulnerability. In his earlier years, Vanier was struck by how people with intellectual and emotional challenges were treated as unlovable, deviant, and unworthy of friendship. In response to this social sin of marginalization and exclusion, he founded *L'Arche*, which is now a worldwide network of residential communities where abled and disabled individuals live in community, sharing in Christian fellowship.[5] For Vanier, exposing our vulnerability is a catalyst for enacting genuine freedom in our lives. Following Vanier's lead, how might human beings imagine living in community with the other, including the nonhuman other, with an openness to all the intricacies of asking?

At times it takes a life-changing event—conversion—to start asking the precarious questions. In *Ask the Beasts*, Johnson speaks of three simultaneous aspects of conversion, which she calls "turnings," that are necessary to change our world in light of environmental degradation. She first describes intellectual conversion as that which allows for one to transcend anthropocentricism, the belief that human animals are the center of the world and the most important creature in the cosmos. Then there is ethical conversion, which necessitates seeing morality beyond the landscape of human need. A third turning for Johnson is emotional conversion, which refers to the process of affectively connecting with all of creation.[6] Many of us have experienced some aspect of conversion. It's in our best interest to talk about this if we want human existence to take a new shape.

Seàn McDonagh, an Irish Columban priest, started asking about the cosmos and our place in it when he lived with the T'boli people in

---

[5] For more on *L'Arche*, see http://www.larcheusa.org/.
[6] Johnson, *Ask the Beasts*, 258–59.

the Philippines to protect the rain forests from human predation.[7] His conversion to working toward environmental justice was fueled by the staggering statistic that roughly twenty-seven thousand species are lost each year, rendering us in what Richard Leakey and Roger Lewin have called the "sixth mass-extinction event" of world history—a "spasm" caused by one single species: human beings.[8] In his book *The Death of Life: The Horror of Extinction*, McDonagh elaborates how human animals cause extinction by destroying and polluting habitats and introducing alien species into stable environments. In another of his works, *Climate Change*, McDonagh continues with his critique, lamenting the church's inconsistent engagement with global warming and its devastating effects—the likes of which we are already experiencing: violent weather, disappearing marine life as ocean temperatures change, and increased disease, not just because of melting polar ice caps, but because of desertification too.[9] Hopefully the tides are changing. In his recent and much-awaited environmental encyclical titled *Laudato Sì* (On Care for Our Common Home), Pope Francis inspires Catholic Christians everywhere to examine their engagement with the entire cosmos—for better or for worse. His call for conversion to reflect on the contemporary environmental crises, with attention to an unbridled anthropocentricism, is a much-needed wake-up call for all humans.

More Than Mind over Matter

While today Catholic Christian thinkers are definitely more attentive to questions of environmental degradation than in the past, there are lingering theological reasons for our misuse of the planet and its creatures. We cannot fully change our views and actions in regard to the ecological crises unless we grapple head on with the theological teachings that fuel the crises or at least rationalize our inaction in the face of them. One of the main reasons why Christians fail to embrace the gravity of environmental degradation, ask revealing questions, and give

[7] Seàn McDonagh, *The Death of Life: The Horror of Extinction* (Co Dublin, Ireland: Columba Press, 2005).

[8] Richard Leakey and Roger Lewin, *The Sixth Extinction: Patterns of Life and the Future of Humankind* (New York: Doubleday, 1995).

[9] Seàn McDonagh, *Climate Change: The Challenge to All of Us* (Co Dublin, Ireland: Columba Press, 2007).

themselves over to what Johnson notes as a "deep spiritual conversion to the Earth"[10] is due to dualistic thinking in traditional theology. Simply put, dualism is the separation of the mind, which is often conflated with the soul, from the body and the valorization of everything associated with the mind/soul over everything associated with the body. It is one of the biggest problems for being human in the midst of God and others because it could lead us to neglect and even hate our bodies or the bodies of others—both human and nonhuman others.

By way of example, McDonagh shows one of the places that dualism appears in theology is in the doctrine of Christology, specifically in emphasizing Jesus' divinity over his humanity, which in turn subordinates the material world to the spiritual world. Divinity-heavy christologies valorize mind over matter, obscuring the importance of Jesus' human, material nature and his connections with the Earth. Even more, divinity-heavy christologies have the potential to create a scenario in which Christians assume that because of the incarnation—because God became human—they (humans) are much closer to God than nonhuman animals. Such illogic concretizes the problematic binaries between human animals and nonhuman animals.

John Feehan, an Irish scholar and environmentalist, is likewise concerned with dualistic threads in Christian theology. In his poetic book *The Singing Heart of the World: Creation, Evolution and Faith*, Feehan claims that we need to think about the nonhuman animal as subject, for only then is it possible to dismantle the notion that a soul is the privilege of human beings alone and that we humans are the center of the world.[11] In the words of Feehan, this type of dualistic thinking exhibits a "failure of intelligence" that results in a failure to be human.[12] This failure of intelligence is not the fault of any one individual, rather a prevailing attitude that humans are more important than everyone and everything else in the cosmos, leading to a death-dealing anthropocentrism. When human communities, not just individuals, become so absorbed with their own prosperity that they become alienated from their connections with all of creation and the needs of all animals, not just human

---

[10] Johnson, *Ask the Beasts*, 258.

[11] John Feehan, *The Singing Heart of the World: Creation, Evolution and Faith* (Co Dublin, Ireland: Columba Press, 2010), 86.

[12] Ibid., 72.

animals, then we find social structures and institutions developing to protect these sinful attitudes and practices. Again, Pope Francis has been quite critical of the social sin that permeates our culture relative to issues of environmental degradation, echoing sentiments in which an anthropocentric mentality blinds us to seeing our connectedness to others—even nonhuman animal others.

Why is this social sin of anthropocentrism so prevalent? In *The Dream of the Earth*, Thomas Berry posits an explanation when he explains that anthropocentrism "is largely consequent on our failure to think of ourselves as species."[13] To embrace the notion that we are dependent on others—all species—we need to let go of the idea that we are self-sufficient and the center of creaturely existence. It feels comfortable to live as though humans are the most valuable creature. Even talking about the problems of this attitude can be unsettling. But if things are going to change, we need such honest talk. We need to dare not only to *ask* about the nonhuman animals in our midst but also to *tell* our stories about them.

Telling Our Stories

"We have to pay the closest attention to what we say. What patients say tells us what to think about what hurts them; and what we say tells us what is happening to us—what we are thinking, and what may be wrong with us. . . . Their story, yours, mine—it's what we all carry with us on this trip we take, and we owe it to each other to respect our stories and learn from them."[14] These words by physician and poet William Carlos Williams communicate the power of stories and storytelling. What might happen if we took stock of all our stories about nonhuman animals? Could the mere act of sharing them with others change our views about our connections with others—human and nonhuman?

It is worth asking, related to environmental degradation and even more specifically to the relations between human and nonhuman animals, whether we have been telling the wrong stories and have been too focused on our negative experiences surrounding them. Wallace

[13] Thomas Berry, *The Dream of the Earth* (San Francisco: Sierra Club Books, 1988), 21.

[14] Robert Coles, *The Call of Stories: Teaching and the Moral Imagination* (Boston: Houghton Mifflin Company, 1989), 30.

Nichols, a marine biologist, calls our attention to the power of telling our happy, joyful, and hopeful stories. Nichols is right to point out that individuals could feel overwhelmed by the doomsday scenarios about climate change, overfishing, and so on. In his book *The Blue Mind*, Nichols suggests an alternative, namely, that we tell our good stories about water to change our attitudes toward it: "We need to tell a story that helps people explore and understand the profound and ancient emotional and sensual connections that lead to a deeper relationship with water. The Blue Mind story seeks to reconnect people to nature in ways that make them feel good, and shows them how water can help them become better versions of themselves."[15] Telling stories in a way that pulls people into our passionate cause for justice for all creatures, rather than in a way that leaves individuals feeling guilty and powerless, is essential. Our stories must illustrate how each one of us is caught up with other creatures in intimate and mysterious ways, whether we realize it or not.

Kathy Rudy, in her work *Loving Animals*, argues for such personalized and positive storytelling. She begins her work by claiming that part of the challenge of animal justice issues is that we tend to be stuck in thinking about nonhuman animals as property or not property. As a way out of this impasse, she privileges human storytelling about nonhuman animals as a way to embrace an inclusive idea of creation, imaging them as our companions. Invoking the stories that changed our perspectives on nonhuman animals—such as Jane Goodall's and Dian Fossey's work with apes—Rudy claims that we become converted to the nonhuman animal other through story, through an "affective intervention that change[s] reality."[16] We might not be out in the jungle or rain forest, but many of us have these feeling stories if we were to give ourselves permission to tap into them and talk about them. Through my use of the phrase "feeling stories," I am pointing to those experiences with others that evoke something in us on the affective level and touch our hearts. This is the mystery of love; there are those moments when we

[15] Wallace J. Nichols, *The Blue Mind: The Surprising Science That Shows How Being Near, In, On, or Under Water Can Make You Happier, Healthier, More Connected, and Better at What You Do* (New York: Little, Brown and Company, 2014), 257–58.

[16] Kathy Rudy, *Loving Animals: Toward a New Animal Advocacy* (Minneapolis: University of Minnesota Press, 2011), 10.

are drawn to the other merely because they rouse our affections. What I am suggesting here is that sharing our affective or feeling stories about nonhuman animal others is a way to embrace even more confidently our connections with all of creation.

Stories—specifically, these mysterious love stories—about and with nonhuman animals are quite common. We hear of neighbors, friends, relatives, and colleagues who have pets as companions in the fullest sense of the word. They eat with them, sleep in the same space as them, play with them, cry with them, hold them, and care for each other. Perhaps, as Rudy puts it, this is another way of talking about queer love. She writes, "Queer theory teaches us to recognize various forms of intimacy that are often erased or invisible in our culture. It challenges us to resist the dominant forms of heteronormativity and celebrate differences of all sorts. Most important, it schools us to recognize that sexuality and intimacy have deep and varied connections." In pressing on with queer love as animal love, Rudy continues to share her "border-crossing" love for her dogs: "These canines teach me more about life and love than one human ever has or could. And so I ask again, isn't this queer?"[17] Rudy's reaction resonates with the reflections of Louis Herman, an expert in dolphin cognition. When asked if he would ever work with dolphins again after two of his subjects died from infection, Herman responded: "I loved our dolphins . . . as I'm sure you love your pets. But it was more than that, more than the love you have for a pet. The dolphins were our colleagues. That is the only word that fits. . . . When they died, it was like losing our children."[18] Both Rudy's and Herman's heartfelt comments strike a chord about the mystery of our connections with others—with all others, even the slippery, slimy, and furry kinds. The queer relationships between human and nonhuman animals are the stuff of great stories and moments of personal conversion.

Getting Personal

We all have stories related to nonhuman animals. Some are life-giving and others are traumatic, and sometimes they are both. When I gave a talk on the importance of sharing stories about our relationships with

[17] Ibid., 41.
[18] Virginia Morell, *Animal Wise: The Thoughts and Emotions of Our Fellow Creatures* (New York: Crown, 2013), 177.

nonhuman animals in an academic setting I was prepared for all sorts of intellectual pushback. I expected colleagues to question how personal narrative about their pets or their experiences in the wild has anything to do with changing our minds and actions in relation to the environment, that such storytelling is mere fluff. Was I wrong! My colleagues devoured the chance to share their stories with gusto and almost relief. It is like people are searching for moments to share their queer love stories. The stories all don't have to be about a favorite pet; they can be about confusing moments of cognitive and/or affective dissonance related to nonhuman animals.

Feeling safe with my colleagues, I then shared my queer love story. My son was a late talker. Even without spoken words, his love for marine animals was clear and present. Anything that lived in or near the big blue was his friend and still is. Etched in my memory is an ordinary day when he and his speech therapist were perusing a book on sharks—his queer love. On one of the pages was an image and description of shark finning. This is a torturous industry in which sharks are hunted for their fins. After their fins are sliced off, the marine animals are thrown back into the water finless. The sharks then suffocate to death because they need to swim to acquire oxygen, and without fins they cannot swim. My son had no verbal language to say anything with his mouth; yet the grief in his eyes was palpable and has stayed with me. *I* was converted in that moment. He called me by his silent grief to recognize the violence we have done and continue to do to the nonhuman animal other. His queer love has challenged me to think about my trespass and to ask for forgiveness. To be sure, my actions in relationship to water, the ocean, and marine animals are colored by his storytelling. To give one small example, after that experience I found myself wondering if I use anti-age creams that come from shark cartilage. Sometimes story, feelings, silence, or other unpredictable moments create opportunities for new ways of thinking and acting—for conversion. In those moments we experience empathy, imagining "how others are feeling even if we don't feel the same way ourselves."[19] Hopefully that empathy translates into changing our thoughts and ways.

On a different occasion, this time when attending a meeting to prepare parents for their child's first sacrament of reconciliation, I was

---

[19] Nichols, *Blue Mind*, 226.

thrown into a state of cognitive dissonance. While I was there for my child and the others for their children, I was struck by the tenor of the presentation. The talk was devoted primarily to conveying the idea of the human person being the crown of creation as portrayed in Genesis 1. While I appreciate the gender-inclusive language in the first book of Genesis, in which all humans—male and female—are described as created in the image of God, I lament having to sacrifice the inclusivity of all creation for gender balance. After all, only human animals seem to have the image of God in them. Still, the cognitive dissonance I experienced went deeper when I began to wonder what the others there thought of the presentation.

My friends and neighbors heard this with me, some of whom have deep connections with their pets. Perhaps they were not listening, on their phones, texting, checking their email, or just blocking it out. That probably was not a bad thing. If they heard this Christian story about human animals and nonhuman animals, as the former having dominion over the latter, they might have gotten seriously upset. I witness them with their nonhuman companions. They bury their pets in their well-manicured lawns. They sacrifice time and money to get them the best healthcare. They adore them. It is true queer love. At this preparation for the sacrament of reconciliation, I could not help feeling a strong disconnect between how they go about their daily lives and what we were hearing, explicitly that only humans are capable of full communion with God. I sat there in my struggle. We were there in the parish hall for a meeting about sin and reconciliation. Isn't it this—the devaluing of nonhuman animals, the sin of hubris, of narcissism, and of anthropomorphism—that needs to be told in the confessional? For reconciliation to occur in the fullest sense Christians might begin imagining themselves as species, creatures, and companions to all animal others in their midst.

Perhaps we have to think of our nonhuman animal friends as partners, as subjects. When we say one is a subject, we point to the value of the individual—their having rights and the potential for agency. Certainly some want to think about nonhuman animals as subjects. While understanding nonhuman animals as subjects most definitely has a role in the fight against environmental degradation and the specific problem of extinction issues, in what follows I suggest moving beyond the question of the subjectivity of nonhuman animals and grappling instead with their radical otherness from us.

Otherness of the Nonhuman Animal—A Helpful or Hurtful Frame?

Dwelling on nonhuman animal otherness may seem like a strange move. Why would one even consider framing the nonhuman animal as other, especially since the human/subject–animal/other border has been so vigorously patrolled, and everything labeled "other" seems to be automatically stigmatized? It is arguable that the animal-human border is another one of those constructed borders that work to keep one side empowered and dominant over the "other." So, one has to ask, since being an "other" has such a negative connotation, then why would anyone interested in ecological justice and extinction issues frame nonhuman animals as "others"?

There are a couple of responses here. For one, so much about subjectivity is wedded to damaging assumptions about what is normative; moving other species into that category does nothing to acknowledge that problem. One could keep the attitude *since they are like us, we don't need to find out more*. Put another way, imagining nonhuman animals as subjects does little to dismantle the dualism that drives exploitative anthropologies, while emphasizing their otherness has the potential to orient us to a new way of being that changes our reality. Moreover, framing nonhuman animals as others may actually be a positive move. When someone or something is different, it serves as a catalyst to find out more about them, to reflect on who they are and what they need. As others, they call us to ask questions such as these. They are not just like us, so who and what are they? How does human existence intersect with them? It may be the case that asking our questions and telling our stories about nonhuman animal others create openings for us to change our attitude and actions in relation to them. Put more boldly, regarding them as other may inspire us to have empathy for them.

Leslie Jamison, an American novelist and essayist, calls our attention to the complexity of empathy in a collection of essays titled *The Empathy Exams*. Her insights on empathy unfold in relation to her experience as a medical actor, a job she held when she was in graduate school. As part of Jamison's job, she acted out symptoms for medical students, so they could diagnose her and ultimately work on their empathy skills. Through her acting work, Jamison is changed and sees her thought on empathy as erroneous. Up until her experiences with medical acting and her own bout with illness, Jamison expected others to show empathy by feeling her pain. However, she has a series of conversions that challenge that assumption. Feeling another's pain or what she describes as "a bout of self-pity projected onto someone else" is not empathy as all, just "solipsism."[20] It is her boyfriend Dave, during her experience with having an abortion and then heart surgery, who really challenges her to rethink and redefine empathy. During Dave's two stays with her in the hospital, he reveals to her a higher purpose for empathy: just being there. "Dave doesn't believe in feeling bad just because someone else does. This isn't his notion of support. He believes in listening, and asking questions, and steering clear of assumptions. He thinks imagining someone else's pain with too much surety can be as damaging as failing to imagine it. He believes in humility. . . . I remember lying tangled with him, how much it meant—that he was willing to lie down in the mess of wires, to stay there with me."[21] In knowing that one does not know everything about the other and staying anyway to ask and tell, empathy is born. In the discourse of Emmanuel Levinas, the other becomes my concern without collapsing into me.[22] This is the power of otherness; it creates an opportunity for asking, for telling, and ultimately for a fresh sense of empathy to emerge in which one exposes oneself for the other.

Choosing a Life of Exposure—Asking and Telling in the Face of the Other

It may seem strange to use the word "exposure" here. Everything about the word "exposure" seems so tasteless. The term "exposure" conjures lewd images and scenarios. One thinks of individuals exhibiting inappropriate social behavior. Or perhaps exposure brings to mind a shameful moment of being caught cheating or stealing. It may be the case that the term "exposure" has too many negative connotations to be considered a good thing, never mind something life-giving. It is precisely because of the discomfort that it causes that exposure may present as a helpful term for reimagining human existence in terms of vulnerability being a virtue. Revealing one's humanity to the other—one's neediness, as awkward and unnerving as it is—through asking and telling, creates an opportunity for genuine and rich relationships.

[20] Leslie Jamison, *The Empathy Exams* (Minneapolis: Graywolf Press, 2014), 23.
[21] Ibid., 20–21.
[22] Emmanuel Levinas, *Otherwise Than Being or Beyond Essence*, trans. Alphonso Lingis (Pittsburgh: Duquesne University Press, 1998), 11–12.

Christians are called to choose a way of life—one rife with exposure, with asking and telling stories about the other. In relation to his research on water, Nichols underscores the grace in asking and telling when he writes: "Our eminence thus comes from realizing that the question mark is more powerful than the exclamation point."[23] Along these lines, we might seek out seeking as part of our life's journey, even our vocation. That is what Elizabeth Johnson has done for the entirety of her career and will undoubtedly continue to do in the future. She has been brave in asking the difficult questions about otherness in an ecclesial context that has not always been welcoming to such truth seeking and story-telling. How can each one of us live a life of exposure that is open to questioning, which entails being wrong, admitting uncertainty and limits, sharing queer love stories, and of course risking being scorned by others?

While we cannot channel Johnson, we can live with the courageous-ness of her spirit and dare to ask and tell. A first step in building a life of exposure, then, is to stop avoiding and concealing our human frailties. After all, if we cannot accept our own limits, how can we accept and aid others as they struggle with their human frailty? Hiding that we are needy serves no good purpose. It prevents us from getting the help and companionship we need as part of our embodied being; and it sets up a terrible example for others to hide their need too. It is not that we should not try to live independently or improve on this or that; rather, at a certain point we may hit our limit and be in need of assistance from others. That is okay, healthy even. What's more, accepting human frailty involves relinquishing the myth that we can somehow control every aspect of our embodied being. Our bodies are not machines. It is not the case that if we tinker around with them enough they will run just how we want.[24] That mentality just proves our need for control and perfection. There is very little in life we can control; even relationships have a life of their own. Sometimes, we can give our all to a relationship and it still dies.

A second step in saying yes to a life of exposure is overcoming an-thropocentricism. We are called to leave a privileged notion of the self

---

[23] Nichols, *Blue Mind*, 229.

[24] For more on the problem of controlling one's body, see Susan Wendell, *The Rejected Body: Feminist Philosophical Reflections on Disability* (New York: Routledge, 1996), 93–106.

behind. Sallie McFague in *Blessed Are the Consumers: Climate Change and the Practice of Self-Restraint*, describes this letting go in the Christian discourse of kenosis or self-emptying for the other. In an age of cosmic crisis, McFague urges Christians to embrace a broad sense of kenosis, which may unfold in "the recognition that restraint, openness, humility, respect for otherness, and even sacrifice (diminishment and death) are part of life *if* one assumes that individual well-being takes place within political and cosmic well-being."[25]

In addition to reflecting on the work of Christian thinkers, when talking about getting over our human selves, we might do well to learn from Buddhist thought and practice, particularly since in Christianity the notion of a core self or soul is so important. As mentioned earlier, believing that only human beings have a soul leads to a divinely ordained hierarchy with human beings at the top. This dualistic worldview justifies humans in their manipulation and exploitation of all other species below them without consequence. Alternatively, Buddhist teachings show how attachment to a privileged sense of self in the face of all others and a separation from others lead to suffering. To move beyond this cosmic suffering, we need to give up on the façade of not needing others and of being dependent on others. We are connected in this cosmos. In his work on water, Nichols describes this attitude as seeing ourselves as part of nature rather than separate from it in terms of biocentricism: "We move from 'humanity's needs first' to the recognition that we are participating in a dance of interdependence with our planet and its denizens, and that caring for our partners is, in fact, caring for ourselves. We understand that we have an interdependency that runs deeper than ecosystems, biodiversity, economics. Nature needs us, and we need nature. This enlightened self-interest is at the core of our very existence."[26] In daring to ask and tell we are compelled to take the steps toward a life of exposure. We have to admit our limits, give up on control, and decenter ourselves to make room for the other.

Ultimately choosing a life of exposure is at times emotionally messy and most always involves hard spiritual and psychological work. It demands an equal measure of intentionality and improvisation. Intention-

---

[25] Sallie McFague, *Blessed Are the Consumers: Climate Change and the Practice of Restraint* (Minneapolis: Fortress Press, 2013), 144.

[26] Nichols, *Blue Mind*, 250.

ality unfolds in our being aware of what we know and don't know, in asking questions, and by sharing stories. Christians ought to be deliberate in this work. Even with this work, however, we need to account for new information, insights, conversions, and the other's stories. We need to improvise. Mary Catherine Bateson provides an aesthetic model for thinking about how we live our lives with intentionality and improvisation when she speaks about how each one of us "composes" a life.[27] This metaphor of composition has an intentionality to it; one that is concerned with beauty and joy. So many of us feel overwhelmed by everything that is going on in our lives—at school, work, and home—that we feel powerless to make any changes, particularly ones connected to environmental degradation. We tend to try to juggle it all, leaving no room for change or growth. Juggling as a way of describing our life is negative and can leave us feeling overwhelmed, out of control, and trapped. There are other ways to conceptualize our experience to help us feel more empowered and confident. Instead of thinking that we have to frenetically juggle all of our responsibilities and obligations, we might think of our life as a work of art. Each stroke, lyric, and alliteration adds to the richness of it. Asking and telling—exposure—drives our life's work, fleshing it out, birthing it into beautiful being. This is the deep, gorgeous, mysterious, and awe-filled work Johnson has devoted her life to, creating a model for all Christians in the face of the other.

---

[27] Mary Catherine Bateson, *Composing a Life* (New York: Grove Press, 1989).

Chapter 8

Magnanimity
A Prophetic Virtue for the Anthropocene

Kevin Glauber Ahern

Few places on our planet highlight the failures of the anthropocene as much as the tropical islands dotting the Pacific Ocean.[1] After colonization by foreign powers, these vibrant ecosystems with their distinctive indigenous cultures became battlefields during the Second World War. As if such experiences of destruction and exploitation were not enough, many were subjected to nuclear weapons testing by the United States, the United Kingdom, and France. The "greatest" weapons ever created by the "greatest" empires on earth devastated local ecosystems and cultures. Today, these islands face a new threat with rising sea levels resulting from human-induced climate change.

The scars incurred by Pacific Island communities over the past two centuries illustrate in a stark way the misconceived notions of greatness and agency that underlie the anthropocene. What has been perceived as agency for "greatness"—empire, scientific progress, war, and fossil fuel

[1] Joseph Stromberg, "What Is the Anthropocene and Are We in It?," *Smithsonian Magazine* (January 2013), www.smithsonianmag.com.

consumption—has wreaked havoc on people and planet. Such patterns of exploitation and destruction, as Pope Francis writes in *Laudato Sì*, "have caused sister earth, along with all the abandoned of our world, to cry out, pleading that we take another course. Never have we so hurt and mistreated our common home as we have in the last two hundred years."[2]

Consider, for example, the atoll of Enewetak in the Marshall Islands. This group of islands formed partly by tiny coral organisms over thousands of years was the test site of nearly seventy weapons of mass destruction in the decade following the Second World War. After forcibly displacing the indigenous population, weapons testing poisoned the soil and beautiful lagoon with dangerous radioactive containments, such as plutonium-239, a carcinogenic isotope with a 24,000 year half-life. In 1979 the US Defense Department "cleaned up" the site for repopulation by gathering most of the contaminated soil into a bomb crater and covering it with the "Cactus Dome," a massive eighteen-inch-thick concrete casing—a temporary solution that is now threated by rising sea levels.[3]

From human-induced climate change and economic inequality to war and corruption, many of the multifaceted problems facing humanity today result from inordinate conceptions of greatness and agency. In order for the human family to address the present crisis, a profoundly new way of understanding great agency is needed to inspire bold, transformative, and concerted action at both the personal and collective levels. We need, as Pope Francis writes in *Laudato Sì*, "a bold cultural revolution" in which we "slow down and look at reality in a different way, to appropriate the positive and sustainable progress which has been made, but also to recover the values and the great goals swept away by our unrestrained delusions of grandeur."[4]

[2] Pope Francis, *Laudato Sì, On Care for Our Common Home* (Rome: Libreria Editrice Vaticana, 2015), par. 53.

[3] See Michael B. Gerrard, "A Pacific Isle, Radioactive and Forgotten," *The New York Times* (December 3, 2014), http://www.nytimes.com/2014/12/04/opinion/a-pacific-isle-radioactive-and-forgotten.html?_r=0; Christopher Jorebon Loeak, "A Clarion Call From the Climate Change Frontline," *The Huffington Post* (September 18, 2014), http://www.huffingtonpost.com/christopher-jorebon-loeak/a-clarion-call-from-the-c_b_5833180.html.

[4] Pope Francis, *Laudato Sì*, par. 114.

This essay explores how the Thomistic virtue of magnanimity, particularly when reclaimed through a prophetic-liberationist lens, might assist in bringing about such a bold cultural revolution. I will begin by highlighting two socially sinful models of agency for greatness, which underlie many of the destructive features of the anthropocene. I will then outline the distinctive elements of magnanimity as presented in the virtue ethics of Saint Thomas Aquinas. Rather than seeking greatness in a dominating agency, a Thomistic approach to magnanimity seeks greatness in empowered agency directed toward difficult goals, not for self-glorification, but for the common good. I will conclude by examining what this virtue looks like through a prophetic lens and how it can redefine what it means to be great in the anthropocene.

Social Sin in the Anthropocene

As with the threats facing the Marshall Islands today, our present global crises did not arise as so-called "natural disasters" or "acts of God." The ongoing destruction of human lives and ecosystems is a consequence of actions, structures, and cultural norms directed and initiated by human beings. Although this does not reflect well on us as a species, this is in some way good news. If oppressive and exploitive social arrangements result from the decisions of people, then another world is indeed possible.

From a theological perspective, destructive, exploitative, and unjust social relationships can be described with the language of social and structural sin, terminology first introduced by liberation theologies and later cautiously endorsed by official Catholic doctrine.[5] While every sin, even the most private, has a social dimension, the language of social and structural sin recognizes that there are cultural norms, institutions, and relational arrangements that are clearly not "in accordance with the plan of God, who intends that there be justice in the world and freedom and peace between individuals, groups and peoples."[6]

---

[5] John Paul II, *Reconciliatio et Paenitentia* (Rome: Libreria Editrice Vaticana, 1984), par. 16, John Paul II, *Sollicitudo Rei Socialis* (Rome: Libreria Editrice Vaticana, 1987), par. 36. See also Gustavo Gutiérrez, *A Theology of Liberation: History, Politics, and Salvation* (Maryknoll, NY: Orbis Books, 1988), 103.

[6] John Paul II, *Reconciliatio et Paenitentia*, par. 16.

Rather than abrogating personal responsibility and culpability by ascribing moral agency to some distant group, a framework of social sin offers a constructive lens to evaluate and change unjust social arrangements. A consciousness of the social and structural dimensions of sin takes on new urgency in the anthropocene, where ideologies, economic systems, and complex global structures threaten people and planet. But what enables this "deep sinfulness" to persist in the present context where most people know the dangers facing our global community?[7]

Domination and Consumption

Behind many of these destructive social relationships are two sinful approaches to greatness and agency. For many in the anthropocene, flourishing and greatness are measured by an ability to conquer, dominate, and possess. From the ancient petroleum deep underground to the trees that produce the air we breathe, the goods of creation are treated as mere commodities to be exploited, acquired, and discarded by those in positions of power. A dominating model of agency seeks greatness, not by "being more," but by "having more." This mind-set as, Pope John Paul II warns, easily leads to structural inequalities between the powerful few and the impoverished many.[8]

The obsessive desire to control and possess also extends to human beings. The same logic that makes it acceptable, as Elizabeth Johnson points out, to "prey without ceasing on natures' resources" supports the objectification, commodification, and exploitation of women, children and men.[9] At its worst, millions of human beings are bought and sold into situations of modern-day slavery. Those living in poverty are particularly vulnerable to objectification in the present economy since, as Gustavo Gutiérrez frequently laments, they are perceived as "insignificant." Stripped of their dignity and humanity, the poor in a hyper-consumerist culture become objects for the control of others. In *Evangelii Gaudium*, Pope Francis describes this mind-set in his critique of global capitalism: "Today everything comes under the laws of competition

---

[7] Elizabeth A. Johnson, "Turn to the Heavens and the Earth: Retrieval of the Cosmos in Theology," in *Proceedings of the Fifty-First Annual Convention of the Catholic Theological Society of America*, ed. Judith A. Dwyer (San Diego, CA, 1998), 9.

[8] See John Paul II, *Sollicitudo Rei Socialis*, par. 28.

[9] Johnson, "Turn to the Heavens and the Earth," 9.

and the survival of the fittest, where the powerful feed upon the power-less. As a consequence, masses of people find themselves excluded and marginalized: without work, without possibilities, without any means of escape. Human beings are themselves considered consumer goods to be used and then discarded. We have created a 'throw away' culture which is now spreading."[10]

The emergence of this "throw away culture" is not all that surprising in a hyper-individualistic context where free market capitalism goes largely unchecked and where everything, including those goods long recognized as basic rights (e.g., water, healthcare, education) are treated as commodities to be exploited. After all, as Timothy Radcliffe points out, the political, economic and cultural features of the so-called "west-ern world" were "founded on the harnessing of brute force, the force of steam and coal, the power of electricity, and ultimately the power of the atom. And this was linked with the triumph of imperial military powers competing to control the whole world."[11] In an almost Machia-vellian key, hard power, independence, and self-sufficiency, at both the personal and collective levels, define greatness and agency much more than service, dependence, and attention to the common good.

Passivity and Inaction

In the context of the anthropocene, there is another socially sinful model of agency that appears to oppose the first. Instead of promoting domination and control, this model encourages and imposes passivity in the face of injustice. Here, the sin is not in excessive and misguided efforts for greatness but rather in the failure to act. This is the flip side of domination. In order to thrive, most structures and systems of sin require both oppressive agency, acts of commission, and passive inaction, acts of omission. Prevailing structures of power, as Marxist analysis has rightly pointed out, be they political, economic, or religious, rarely en-courage critical reflection by the masses. This is particularly the case for unjust and exploitative social arrangements. Consider, for example, the

---

[10] Pope Francis, *Evangelii Gaudium* (Rome: Libreria Editrice Vaticana, 2013), par. 53.

[11] Timothy Radcliffe, *What Is the Point of Being a Christian?* (New York: Burns & Oates, 2005), 18.

many injustices where the majority of the population, most seemingly good people, failed to oppose the evils committed by others.

This passivity or non-agency has many causes. For many, it results from a *detachment* or disconnect between social realities and personal commitments. The most pervasive systems of sin engender a disconnect, if not a cognitive dissonance, between who people think they are and how they actually respond to injustice. The destruction of ecosystems and cultures on Enewetak, for instance, involved both assertive actions by the US government and the passive inaction by the majority of US citizens, most of whom did not know, and did not want to know, what was being done in their name. In a similar way, a sense of detachment is visible in our consumption patterns. Many, if not most, middle-class American Christians, for instance, profess a commitment to love of neighbor and care for God's creation. Nevertheless, this concern for others does not easily translate into sustainable consumption patterns. Even in places where it is very evident that one's present lifestyle is unsustainable and exploitative, such as water consumption patterns in California or the purchasing of clothing made in Bangladeshi sweat shops, it is difficult for people to voluntarily take action for the common good.

Pope Francis describes this detachment as the "globalization of indifference." While globalization brings us together, it also makes it easier to become indifferent to the sufferings of others. "Almost without being aware of it," the pope writes, "we end up being incapable of feeling compassion at the outcry of the poor, weeping for other people's pain, and feeling a need to help them, as though all this were someone else's responsibility and not our own."[12]

For others, passivity to injustice stems from a sense of *despair*. Unlike the indifferent and detached, those who despair *do* care about others. Nevertheless, they fail to take action because they feel as if they are unable to have an impact. The challenges of poverty, climate change, and inequality are so complicated, some say, "What can I do to change it?" They lack a sense of their own capacity and agency to change the status quo. They lack hope.

Inaction in the face of massive and complex problems can also result from what might be described as a type of selfish *cowardliness*. Here,

---

[12] Pope Francis, *Evangelii Gaudium*, par. 54.

people know what must be done and see the possibility to change the system but "sidestep the effort and sacrifice required" out of a concern for their own preservation and the maintenance of the status quo.[13]

Socially Enforced Passivity

This social sin of non-agency is linked to another destructive social pattern. Unlike those who choose to be passive in the face of injustice, there are others who are unable to respond because of cultural norms that engender or enforce a sense of passivity on certain groups. Patriarchy, for example, thrives in a context where some, namely, older (white) males, are dominant, while others are expected to remain passive. Far too often, a perverted understanding of the Christian virtue of humility has been used to reinforce not only systems of patriarchy but also racism, casteism, and ageism. Instead of instilling a proper sense of the self, this distorted notion of humility, forced on groups, has led to oppression and *humiliation*. This has been and continues to be intensely problematic for women as Valerie Saiving pointed out over fifty years ago in her seminal article, "The Human Situation: A Feminine View."

Responding to the work of Reinhold Niebuhr and other prevailing conceptions of sin as pride and Christian love as complete self-giving, Saiving highlights how the experience of sin for women is distinct from that of men. To perceive the human condition—and by extension our relationship to God—only through the experience of men is damaging to everyone. Rather than too much self-actualization—exercised in such a way as to be seen as a prideful overstepping of humanity's finitude—the experience of sin for many women can be summarized as "underdevelopment or negation of the self."[14] An all-too-common example of this is the mother who devotes all of her energy to her family and community so that she fails to take care of her own basic needs. In a context where many women suffer from a lack of self-actualization, an emphasis on sin as pride and love as sacrifice is inadequate and deeply dehumanizing.

---

[13] John Paul II, *Reconciliatio et Paenitentia*, par. 16.

[14] Valerie Saiving, "The Human Situation: A Feminine View," *The Journal of Religion* 40, no. 2 (1960): 37; see also Mark Douglas and Elizabeth Hinson-Hasty, "Revisiting Valerie Saiving's Challenge to Reinhold Niebuhr: Honoring Fifty Years of Reflection on 'The Human Situation: A Feminine View': Introduction and Overview," *Journal of Feminist Studies in Religion* 28, no. 1 (2012): 75–78.

In addition to calling theologians to pay greater attention to the actual experiences of women, Saiving also expresses concern for the social impact of this anthropology and moral vision on society as a whole, which may reduce persons to passive, "chameleon-like creatures" susceptible to the manipulation of others.[15]

In *Sex, Sin, and Grace*, Judith Plaskow develops Saiving's analysis of "women's sin" by examining more deeply the theology of Reinhold Niebuhr and Paul Tillich. For Plaskow, the theologies of both men are problematic in that they fail to contribute to self-actualization of women. Taking issue particularly with Niebuhr's strong emphasis on sin as pride and his near obsession with the dangers of turning toward the self, Plaskow laments how "for many women pride is a secondary phenomenon following on self-restriction." "Women's sin" is rather the opposite. It *"is precisely the failure to turn toward the self."*[16] It is not a question of forgetting God, but rather it involves the risk of forgetting to take care of the self.

In other words, excessive attention to sin as pride leads to a misconstrued notion of humility and agency, particularly for women in patriarchal cultures where certain men are seen as active agents and women as passive recipients whose dignity is found in responding to the needs of others. This dynamic has also been highly destructive for children, young adults, and people of color who are also treated as nonagents. It also extends to humanity's relationship to the earth. There is, in fact, a similar binary established where humanity is understood to be the active agent while the earth remains the passive object of humanity's actions. The connection here between women and "mother earth," as ecofeminists point out, is not a coincidence.[17] Like women in patriarchal cultures, the goods of the earth have been portrayed as passive objects, ripe and fertile fields for harvest, and passive wilderness zones that await the conquest of the white man for them to reach its supposed potential. Like the inherent dignity and value of women, the

---

[15] Saiving, "The Human Situation," 41.

[16] Judith Plaskow, *Sex, Sin, and Grace: Women's Experience and the Theologies of Reinhold Niebuhr and Paul Tillich* (Washington, DC: University Press of America, 1980), 151. Emphasis original.

[17] See, for instance, several of the essays in Mary Heather MacKinnon and Moni McIntyre, eds., *Readings in Ecology and Feminist Theology* (Kansas City, MO: Sheed & Ward, 1995), and Johnson, "Turn to the Heavens and the Earth," 11–12.

earth is far too often perceived as lacking any intrinsic value until the supposed "great" male agent enters the picture.

Several theological concepts have been used to support the suppression of women's potential to be great agents. Although space does not allow for a detailed analysis, two models are worth noting in this regard. Some interpretations of the christological model of *kenōsis*, for example, idealize Christ's sacrificial renunciation of divine power and identity (Phil 2:7) to the point of self-effacement and a destructive loss of the self.[18] Oppressed groups have been told to be patient, not call for change, and "take up your cross."

Even more destructive for Christian women, perhaps, has been a distorted portrayal of Mary, the mother of Jesus, as a passive suffering servant. Women have been urged to follow her example and to be obedient to male agents. The promotion of such a model has idealized non-agency for women around the world, as Elizabeth Johnson details in her work on Mary. "Presented with this ideal," she writes, "women learn that they find their true path to God by being obedient, submissive, self-sacrificing, silent, and deferential, rather than exercising independent, responsible thought and action, especially in the face of social and political ills. The construal of Mary the obedient handmaid legitimates the idea that women's virtue lies in being receptively obedient to the authority of males, be they divine or human, God, fathers, husbands or priests."[19]

Far from being a relic of the medieval past, the model of Mary as a passive non-agent continues to be articulated in ecclesiological and pastoral circles today. This can be seen in the work of Hans Urs von Balthasar, who distinguishes between the so-called Marian and Petrine

---

[18] See Sarah Coakley's analysis of *kenōsis* and agency in Sarah Coakley, "Kenosis and Subversion: On the Repression of 'Vulnerability' in Christian Feminist Writing," in *Swallowing a Fishbone? Feminist Theologians Debate Christianity*, ed. Margaret Daphne Hampson (London: SPCK, 1996), 82–111. See also Sarah Coakley, *Powers and Submissions: Spirituality, Philosophy, and Gender* (Malden, MA: Blackwell Publishers, 2002); and Carolyn A. Chau, "'What Could Possibly Be Given?': Towards an Exploration of Kenosis as Forgiveness—Continuing the Conversation Between Coakley, Hampson, and Papanikolaou," *Modern Theology* 28, no. 1 (January 1, 2012): 1–24.

[19] Elizabeth A. Johnson, *Truly Our Sister: A Theology of Mary in the Communion of Saints* (New York: Continuum, 2003), 26.

principles.[20] While highly praising Mary, this model reinforces non-agency on the part of women and the church as a whole in the face of social injustice. With its not so subtle sexual symbolism, this theological model uplifts the masculine God as the active agent and the feminine church as the passive recipient. In short, the church, the bride of Christ, should model Mary in its loving obedience and passive reception to the will of the masculine God. Such a rigid binary makes it nearly impossible to imagine Mary or any woman as an active agent in the struggle for a more just world.[21]

Like those models of agency that support domination and control, frameworks of agency that encourage or enforce passivity must also clearly be stated as sinful. We simply cannot hope to address the complex problems facing people and planet today with models that encourage non-agency. Inaction in the face of injustice only serves to reinforce the status quo. Clearly, the sins of those who have been forced into positions of submission and non-agency by dominant forces are distinct from sins of those who willfully fail to respond because of detachment, indifference, and cowardliness. Regardless of the cause, the failure to realize one's agency and strive for the common good reinforces the social and structural sins of the anthropocene.

Magnanimity: Between Domination and Passivity

In the face of these social sins, is there a model of agency for greatness that can serve as a middle ground between the prideful and inordinate domination of others and a humiliating or despairing failure to take responsibility for the demands of the common good? Here, a prophetic reading of the Thomistic virtue of magnanimity can be informative in rethinking ethical agency in the anthropocene.

---

[20] This was taken up in the gender complementary of John Paul II. See John Paul II, *Mulieris Dignitatem, On the Dignity and Vocation of Women* (Rome: Libreria Editrice Vaticana, 1988), par. 27.

[21] See Johnson, *Truly Our Sister*, 57, and Breandán Leahy, *The Marian Principle in the Church according to Hans Urs von Balthasar*, European University Studies, series XXIII, vol. 558 (Frankfurt am Main: Peter Lang, 1996).

Magnanimity for Aquinas

By its very name, magnanimity connotes a sense of "high minded-ness" or a "stretching forth of the mind to great things" and, in particular, great things that are difficult to achieve.[22] Following Aristotle, Thomas Aquinas takes up this "initiative taking virtue" in his *Commentary on Aristotle's Nicomachean Ethics*, in his treatise *On Kingship*, and in the second part of his *Summa Theologica*.[23] In the *Summa Theologica*, Aquinas situates this virtue, along with magnificence, patience, and perseverance as parts of fortitude, the cardinal virtue concerned with bringing about a firmness of mind in the face of difficulty by curbing the extremes of both fear and daring in irascible appetite.[24]

At first glace, this notion of striving for greatness and honor amid difficulty appears to support destructive and dominating models of agency. In Aristotle's framework, for example, magnanimity, which is often translated as the virtue of "pride," is generally reserved for the powerful, "self-absorbed" man.[25] For him, the ideal model of fortitude is the honorable soldier. Later, Machiavellian conceptions of greatness are even more problematic as they endorse duplicity in recognizing the necessity for the agent to engage in vicious deeds in order to support one's power, honor, and position in society.[26] There is no room in either approach for humility or a thick appreciation for our interdependent nature.[27] There is also little room for women and other marginalized

[22] Thomas Aquinas, *Summa Theologica*, trans. Fathers of the English Dominican Province, Complete English (Westminster, MD: Christian Classics, 1981), II-II, q.129, a. 1. (Hereafter ST).

[23] Craig Steven Titus, *Resilience and the Virtue of Fortitude: Aquinas in Dialogue with the Psychosocial Sciences* (Washington, DC: The Catholic University of America Press, 2006), 190.

[24] ST II-II, q. 129, a. 5, ad. 3.

[25] Titus, *Resilience and the Virtue of Fortitude*, 121; see Aristotle, *The Nicomachean Ethics*, trans. David Ross, Oxford World's Classics (New York: Oxford University, 1998), 4.3.

[26] Niccolò Machiavelli, *Machiavelli: The Prince*, ed. Quentin Skinner and Russell Price, Cambridge Texts in the History of Political Thought (New York: Cambridge University, 1988), 55. Departing from medieval Christian writings that urge rulers to be virtuous and follow the example of Christ, Niccolò Machiavelli constructs a model of a greatness that uplifts the Sicilian ruler Agathocles as a model. He argues, however, that the vicious rulers should attempt to hide their vices under an impression of virtue.

[27] See Aristotle, *The Nicomachean Ethics*, 4.3.

groups to be magnanimous. Understood in this way, magnanimity is more of a problem for the anthropocene than a solution.

Aquinas's approach to this virtue, however, is distinctive as he seeks a critical correction to the prideful notions of greatness and agency contained in Aristotle. It is a subtle, yet significant, move shaped by two christological elements, which are, understandably, absent from classical readings of greatness: the teleology of the reign of God and the virtue of humility.

God's Reign and the Common Good

Aquinas situates magnanimity within his larger teleological framework where the ends of an action specify its morality.[28] While the common good serves as an important proximate end for social life today, the ultimate end for humanity and all of creation is the complete happiness that comes about through a union with God or the participation in God's reign, which is the object of Christian hope.[29] The fallen human condition, however, prevents people from ever achieving this on their own without an infusion of God's grace and the theological virtues of charity, faith, and hope.[30]

While the reaching forth of the mind to this ultimate end involves the theological virtue of hope, the stretching forth of the self to more proximate goals that are great but difficult to achieve involves the acquired virtue of magnanimity.[31] But even here, the greatness of the agency must always be seen in relation to the other virtues and the demands of justice, prudence, and the common good.

In this way, Aquinas presents a model of agency that looks very different from Machiavelli's self-referential prince or the archetypal "self-made" American. For Aquinas, great rulers "should be ordained

---

[28] ST I-II, q.1, a. 3.

[29] ST I-II, q. 3, a. 2. See also II-II, q. 23, a. 7. In discussing hope in his *Compendium on Theology*, Aquinas relates the beatific goal to the biblical concept of the kingdom, or reign of God. See Thomas Aquinas, *Compendium of Theology*, trans. Cyril O. Vollert (St. Louis, MO: B. Herder Book Co., 1947), book 2, chap. 9.

[30] See ST I-II, q. 109.

[31] In this way, magnanimity functions to a large degree as the acquired counterpart to the theological virtue of hope. ST II-II, q. 17. See also Titus, *Resilience and the Virtue of Fortitude*, 190.

principally to eternal beatitude" and to the common good.[32] This teleology frames the model of greatness in at least three ways. First, it displaces individuals from the center of what they perceive as the ultimate goal. Second, it affirms the importance of being guided by virtues throughout life, since honor and glory come from true virtues, and not merely in the hypocritical appearance of virtue. For example, the ideal king, or great ruler, he argues, should embody virtue so as to instill "virtuous living in a multitude."[33] And, finally, the necessity for God's assistance dispels any notion of self-sufficiency. We need others to reach our goals.

As an acquired virtue, magnanimity guides an agency to excellence in great tasks for the common good.[34] When animated by the virtue of charity, an infused form of magnanimity can inspire excellent action to contribute to God's reign and bring the agent closer to union with God.[35] Though it relates directly to honor, since true honor is a reflection of great agency, the magnanimous agent does not strive toward honor for its own sake. Rather, situated with an eye on the final telos and the common good, magnanimity orients us in such a way so that any proximate good, such as honor or the so-called goods of fortune, must always be seen more broadly.[36] Importantly, for Aquinas, honor has a social and virtuous function. Recognizing great achievements can inspire others to be virtuous and work for the common good. Here, we might think of awards for exceptional service, such as Nobel Peace Prize. Nevertheless, one should not let the promise of such honors or the threat of unjust dishonor threaten or control one's self-confidence.[37] The goal of striving for peace, in other words, should not be winning an award but rather the common good and the telos of God's reign.

In fact, an excessive attention to honor or greatness for its own sake leads to several vices. For Thomas, *ambition*, the love of honor, becomes inordinate when one desires honor one does not deserve for one's own

---

[32] Thomas Aquinas, *On Kingship, to the King of Cyprus*, trans. Gerald B. Phelan (Toronto: Pontifical Institute of Mediaeval Studies, 1982), book 1, chap. 16.

[33] Ibid., book 1, chap. 16.

[34] The virtue addressing excellence or honors in ordinary tasks has no name. ST II-II, q. 129, a. 2.

[35] For more on the role of the infused moral virtues, see Thomas F. O'Meara, "Virtues in the Theology of Thomas Aquinas," *Theological Studies* 58, no. 2 (1997): 254–85.

[36] ST II-II, q. 129, a. 8.

[37] See ST II-II, 129, a. 2, ad. 3.

self-interest without "referring to God" or orientating it toward "the profit of others."[38] *Vainglory*, by contrast, is inordinate in that it desires rightfully deserved honors, but again without attention to the glory of God or the welfare of the neighbor.[39] This can lead to myriad other vices, including boastfulness, eccentricity, hypocrisy, obstinacy, discord, contention, and disobedience.[40]

With God's reign and the common good as broader ends, the magnanimous agent strives for more proximate goals that are difficult yet possible to achieve. In Thomistic framework, however, the more immediate goals, such as peace building or environmental conservation, must align with the ultimate ends.

In this way, magnanimity functions to a large degree as the acquired counterpart to the theological virtue of hope, the virtue that sustains the wayfarer in striving toward the ultimate good, which is difficult yet possible to achieve.[41] Like the other theological virtues of faith and charity, hope cannot be achieved without an infusion of God's grace. As an acquired virtue, magnanimity is attained by a diligent practice—although it could be argued that even here grace is never completely absent.[42]

Humility and Vulnerability

Aquinas also departs from Aristotle by approaching greatness and agency through faith in a kenotic God who humbled God's self in becoming human, vulnerable, and dependent (Phil 2:8). This reframes the traditional take on both humility and magnanimity. Humility, as Radcliffe writes, "was despised by pagan Rome and Greece. For Aristotle, humility was a vice. To be humble was to be low, despicable, beneath respect. Christianity turned this way of looking at the world upside down by proclaiming that humility is the typical Christian virtue and pride the greatest vice."[43]

---

[38] ST II-II, q. 131, a.1.

[39] ST II-II, q. 132, a.1.

[40] ST II-II, q. 132, a. 5. See also Aquinas, *On Kingship*, chap. 8.

[41] ST II-II, q. 17. See Titus, *Resilience and the Virtue of Fortitude*, 190.

[42] In addition to hope as a theological virtue, Thomas also describes the passion of hope. We are instinctively drawn toward good things. But a passion is not a virtue. The passion of hope cannot help someone endure the difficult task.

[43] Radcliffe, *What Is the Point of Being a Christian?*, 133.

In our present context, where humility is again perceived as a vice and where it has been (mis)used to suppress the agency of women and other groups, it is helpful to remember, as Josef Pieper writes, that humility for Thomas in no way suggests "an attitude, on principle, of constant self-accusation, of disparagement of one's being and doing, of cringing inferiority feelings, as belonging to humility or any other Christian virtue."[44] Rather, humility functions as proper self-understanding that takes into account one's weakness and strengths.

Since no two virtues should theoretically oppose one another, Aquinas has to address directly the apparent contradiction between humility and magnanimity in the Aristotelian tradition. In addressing both virtues, he directly responds to such objections by clearly stating how they are not opposed but rather complementary. In the question on magnanimity, he responds to an objection by differentiating between the two virtues. Magnanimity, he argues, inspires the agent to see himself "worthy of great things in consideration of the gifts he holds from God." Humility, by contrast, "makes the agent think little of himself in consideration of his own deficiency." So while they "tend in contrary directions," they are not contrary to one another.[45]

The magnanimous agent, in other words, is both honest and realistic about the limits and potential of her or his agency. Without such an appropriate appraisal, it is easy to give into two vices. If, on the one hand, one forgets one's limits, ignores one's state of dependence on others and God, and exceeds what is appropriate to one's ability, one is guilty of *presumption*.[46] On the other hand, if one "shrinks from great things" in failing to live up to one's potential, one is guilty of *pusillanimity* or cowardliness.[47]

Again departing from the philosopher, Aquinas understands the magnanimous agent as vulnerable and dependent. In the question on magnanimity, he responds directly to Aristotle's claim that the magnanimous person is wholly self-sufficient by pointing to our dependent nature as human beings. Everyone, he writes, relies on external assistance in at least two ways. First, we need assistance from God. Everything comes

---

[44] Josef Pieper, *The Four Cardinal Virtues: Prudence, Justice, Fortitude, Temperance* (Notre Dame, IN: University of Notre Dame, 1966), 189.

[45] ST II-II, q. 129, a. 3, ad. 4. See also ST II-II, q. 161, a.1, ad. 3.

[46] ST II-II, q. 130, a. 2.

[47] ST II-II, q. 133, a. 1.

from God, the "first mover." Within his overall theological framework, everything would fall apart without God's assistance. Human beings, in other words, are wholly dependent on God. Second, we depend on "human assistance," since human beings are "social animals."[48] Consequently, even the most magnanimous person is reliant on others. To forget this is to also give into *pride*, the vice that is most directly opposed to humility.[49] Though not developed by Thomas, we could add a third category that highlights our dependence on and profound interconnection with creation. Beyond the fact that we cannot survive without the food, water, and resources provided by the natural environment, humanity cannot be seen as independent from creation and the ongoing process of evolution, which connects us to nonhuman creation in the past, present, and future.[50]

Our dependent nature illuminates a reality that many seek to forget. We are vulnerable beings. While the magnanimous agent may achieve a certain sense of security in achieving great things, Aquinas insists that there can never be absolute security.[51] Indeed, as Josef Pieper points out, fortitude, the parent virtue of magnanimity, "presupposes vulnerability; without vulnerability there is no possibility of fortitude. . . . To be brave actually means to be able to suffer injury."[52]

Bold Humility

In the end, Thomas's reading of magnanimity offers a more constructive approach to great agency than many classical or contemporary approaches. For Aristotle, the exemplar is the soldier, a self-sufficient privileged male who strives for great deeds in the face of danger and difficultly. Like later self-serving approaches to greatness, the Aristotelian model can be seen as supporting dominating agency for a chosen few. Approaching the virtue in light of Christian faith, Thomas both develops and departs from Aristotelian conceptions of greatness and agency as he constructs a model that is both proactive and humble. While Aristotle's treatment of magnanimity has sometimes been translated

---

[48] ST II-II, q. 129, a. 6, ad. 1.
[49] ST II-II, q. 162.
[50] See Johnson, "Turn to the Heavens and the Earth," 6–7.
[51] ST II-II, q. 129, a. 7, ad. 2.
[52] Pieper, *The Four Cardinal Virtues*, 117.

as pride, Aquinas follows the Christian tradition in making pride a vice and humility a virtue. Instead of the solider as the model of fortitude, Aquinas uplifts the Christian martyr as the ideal fortuitous agent. This reading of the virtue is much more promising as humanity deals with the problems facing people and planet today. Rather than working for self-glorification, the end goal of magnanimity is the common good and the glorification of God.

In sum, Aquinas's virtue of striving for greatness looks beyond the self as it recognizes the demands of justice and the common good, the vulnerability intrinsic to human nature, and the ultimate goals of participating in God's reign and serving the common good. Such an approach stands in opposition to both the dominating models of agency, which have wreaked so much havoc in the anthropocene, and the passive modes of non-agency, which have inhibited people from taking action. Thus, his understanding of agency for greatness, of magnanimity, cannot be translated as pride in any way. Instead it might be better summarized by using Sarah Coakley's definition of *kenōsis* as "power-in-vulnerability" or David Bosch's description of the church's mission as a "bold humility."[53]

Magnanimity through a Prophetic Lens

Clearly, the Thomistic reading of magnanimity is an improvement over many classical and contemporary approaches to agency, but is it sufficient, by itself, to construct a model of greatness that can tackle the complex problems facing people and planet today? Though he greatly expands the understanding of the virtue, Aquinas is ultimately constrained by classical thinking that limits magnanimity only to those "men" with the resources to enable them to do great things.[54] A liberationist reading of this virtue, I would argue, has the potential to expand

---

[53] Coakley, "Kenosis and Subversion," 110; David Jacobus Bosch, *Transforming Mission: Paradigm Shifts in Theology of Mission*, American Society of Missiology Series 16 (Maryknoll, NY: Orbis Books, 1991), 489.

[54] In addressing magnificence, the virtue concerned with using great things, Aquinas shows an openness to expand his conception of greatness: "But goods of fortune are requisite as instruments to the external acts of virtue: and in this way a poor man cannot accomplish the outward act of magnificence in things that are great simply. Perhaps, however, he may be able to do so in things that are great by comparison to some particular work; which, though little in itself, can nevertheless be done magnificently in proportion to its genus" (ST, II-II, q. 134, a. 3, ad. 4).

his framework and adapt it to the present context by focusing on another exemplar of greatness: the prophet.

While liberation theologies certainly attend to the role of the martyr in the face of oppressive systems, they have also recovered the model of the prophet and the prophetic vocation of Christians in the world. In many ways, the biblical prophets embody in their own way, the type of action for greatness and bold humility inherent in Aquinas's reading of magnanimity. With their eye on God's reign and an openness to God's voice, the biblical prophets are not afraid to stand up to oppressive social forces and call for change. This magnanimous spirit is captured well in the prophet Micah's call to "do justice . . . to love goodness, and to walk humbly with your God" (Mic 6:8).

To be a prophet, one must be humble enough to listen to the call of God and the cries of the poor around oneself, yet bold enough to stand up for the great vision of God's justice. By being open to God of life and justice, the prophet "takes risks to denounce wrongdoing and to announce in hope a moral holistic vision of the community of life."[55] One must, in other words, be magnanimous, especially when forced to confront systems and structures of sin.

Mary of Nazareth

Among the biblical prophets who model a magnanimous spirit, Mary of Nazareth illuminates several dimensions of the virtue that are missing in the Thomistic reading. Mary's role as a biblical prophet and model for proactive agency has been recovered in recent decades by feminist and liberationist theologies, most notably in the work of Elizabeth Johnson.[56]

Mary's role as a prophet is most clearly presented in the Gospel of Luke and in particular in the *Magnificat*, her prophetic "canticle that joyfully proclaims God's gracious, effective compassion at the advent of the messianic age."[57] After hearing what to most would be unsettling

[55] Elizabeth A. Johnson, *Ask the Beasts: Darwin and the God of Love* (London: Bloomsbury Academic, 2014), 283–84.

[56] Johnson, *Truly Our Sister*, 258; See also Tissa Balasuriya, *Mary and Human Liberation: The Story and the Text* (Harrisburg, PA: Trinity Press International, 1997); Leonardo Boff, *The Maternal Face of God: The Feminine and Its Religious Expressions* (San Francisco: Harper & Row, 1987).

[57] Johnson, *Truly Our Sister*, 263.

news at the annunciation, Mary goes out to visit her friend Elizabeth. "Filled with the Holy Spirit" (Luke 1:41), Elizabeth praises the work of God in Mary who responds with a song that very clearly models the magnanimous combination of humility and bold proactive action.

This impoverished "lowly" woman living under foreign occupation praises the God of her ancestors and includes herself in a litany where God uplifts the poor and oppressed. It is a profound message that is anything but passive and pietistic. Echoing Luke's broader theme of the great reversal, the *Magnificat* makes clear that true greatness is not to be found where it is normally expected since, as Mary sings, the God of Abraham "has scattered the proud in the thoughts of their hearts. He has brought down the powerful from their thrones, and lifted up the lowly" (Luke 1:51-52). This is a powerful and dangerous prophecy, especially to come from the lips of a woman, as Johnson profoundly writes: "Here she takes on as her own the divine no to what crushes the lowly. She stands fearlessly and sings out that injustice will be over-turned. NO passivity here, but solidarity with divine outrage over the degradation of life, coupled with God's merciful promise to repair the world. In the process she bursts out of the boundaries of male-defined femininity while still every inch a woman."[58]

In contrast to Marian theologies that portray her as a passive, non-agent, the gospels describe Mary as an active figure who is alive in the Spirit. Beyond the *Magnificat*, Mary shows her empowered yet humble agency at the end of the gospels where she bravely remains close to her son even when his closest companions flee in fear. As Johnson shows, Mary can and should indeed be a role model for the church, but hers is a prophetic model of active and empowered agency and not, as some argue, a mere passive obedience.[59]

A Prophetic Magnanimity

Approaching magnanimity through a prophetic lens develops Aquinas's call for a bold and humble agency by emphasizing three aspects that are not as clearly stated in his formulation. First and foremost, a prophetic approach to magnanimity measures greatness with a concern

[58] Elizabeth A Johnson, *Abounding in Kindness: Writings for the People of God* (Maryknoll, NY: Orbis Books, 2015), 310.

[59] See ibid., 299.

for the experience of the poor and those on the margins. True greatness, to be clear, is not compatible with injustice and oppression. A prophetically magnanimous agent seeks to follow God in being attentive to "both the cry of the earth and the cry of the poor," which are too often ignored by prevailing power structures.[60] As receptive agents of God's Spirit, prophets, like Amos, Micah, and Mary, respond to the suffering of others by taking a vocal stance against oppressive social structures while also proposing new social patterns and arrangements that are more in line with God's will.

Second, a prophetic reading of magnanimity affirms the universality of a call to do great things. Great agency is not something reserved only to wealthy men. The model of Mary makes this clear. Even "the lowly" have the potential and responsibility to work for great things in a world broken by sin.

Finally, the prophetically magnanimous agent seeks greatness not in isolation but in relationships with others. Magnanimity, when seen through a Christian lens, is no cowboy virtue. In the present context, none of the great changes needed to address the problems of the anthropocene can happen without concerted and sustained efforts by groups and social movements. No individual can change the political structures or personal consumption patterns on one's own. Here, dialogue, as Pope Francis insists in his encyclical, is fundamental.[61] Dialogue is itself an act of bold humility and recognition of one's own vulnerability.

Difficult Questions

Reframing how we define great agency can go a long way in sustaining the efforts needed to bring about the "bold cultural revolution" that Pope Francis calls for in *Laudato Sì*. Rooted in contemplation, dialogue, and a willingness to adopt a more ascetic lifestyle, a prophetic approach to magnanimity demands that we strive for greatness at three levels. Globally, the human family must redefine flourishing. The recently articulated United Nations Sustainable Development Goals (SDGs) offer a good starting point, but they are not enough. We need to have the courage to ask some difficult questions. *What are end goals of our*

---

[60] Pope Francis, *Laudato Sì*, par. 49.
[61] Ibid., par. 14.

economic and political structures? What would the powerful nations and corporations have to give up to truly attend to the needs of the poor and the earth?

At the personal level, a prophetic magnanimity invites individuals and families to ask similar questions. *How do we define flourishing? What role models and lifestyles do we seek to emulate? How do we measure our own success? What are we willing to sacrifice in our consumption patterns?*

In the mediating space between the personal and the political, our institutions, churches, and social movements must also rethink what it means to be great. For example, *how do we rank the success of our universities? Where do our ecclesial and academic institutions invest their money? What are the ethical questions surrounding the honorary awards we give to individuals? How are ecclesial movements and structures involved in the broader movements for ecological and social justice? How can we form more creative communities and cooperatives to support sustainable and magnanimous lifestyles?*

Conclusion: Toward a Bold Cultural Revolution

In short, magnanimity, when seen through a prophetic lens, can be defined as empowered yet humble agency, exercised in a relationship with others that seeks to accomplish great things with a specific concern for those on the margins. Such a definition of striving for greatness helps to avoid both domination and passivity in the face of injustice.

In today's context, few things could be greater—and more challenging—than finding effective ways to address the complex questions that threaten both people and planet. The task ahead of us is daunting, and it is very tempting to look away. In order for the human family to reverse course we need a bold and transformative disposition, like magnanimity, to strengthen us as we seek to achieve what Elizabeth Johnson describes as a "socially just and environmentally sustainable society in which the needs of all people are met and diverse species can prosper, onward to an evolutionary future that will still surprise."[62] Short of the kingdom, can there be any greater goal to achieve than this?

---

[62] Johnson, *Ask the Beasts*, 285–86.

Chapter 9

Making the Cosmological Turn in Catholic Moral Theology

David Cloutier

Elizabeth Johnson's CTSA presidential address invites a cosmological turn in Catholic theology. As is characteristic of her work, the address develops a nuanced view of premodern Catholic theology. On the one hand, it is affirmed for being consistently cosmological. On the other hand, it lacks a sense of a dynamic, historical natural world that is the hallmark of modern science. Johnson narrates Catholic theology as at first shrinking from the challenges of modern science to the medieval cosmology, and then losing even that "ghost" of cosmology in the modern turns to the subject, to language, and to society. Vatican II "heightened our anthropocentric turn." Thus, there is a broad need in theology to "convert our intelligence to the heavens and the earth . . . by turning to the entire interconnected community of life and the network of life-systems in which the human race is embedded."[1]

---

[1] Elizabeth Johnson, "Turn to the Heavens and the Earth: Retrieval of the Cosmos in Theology," *CTSA Proceedings* 51 (1996): 1–14, here 1.

Johnson's essay raises the question of what kind of theology will be adequate to facing environmental crises. I want to sharpen that question by asking what kind of *moral* theology is needed. The importance of framing narratives for understanding moral reasoning has been pointed out by thinkers as diverse as philosopher Alasdair MacIntyre and psychologist Jonathan Haidt.[2] Johnson's essay is a matter of (re)framing the narrative for Catholic theology, and I want to pay particular attention to how Catholic moral theology has been framed since the council. I will start by noting the importance of a certain framing contrast in post–Vatican II moral thought: the move from a classicist to a historical-conscious worldview. A development of this framework is needed, because a moral theology attentive to issues of the environment cannot be one whose central preoccupation is how to interpret absolute norms. Debates over whether cars are "intrinsically evil" are dead on arrival. But there are also some challenges associated with the contrast itself when applied to environmental evaluation and action. This move is generally presented as a great advance, but it also represents a turn to the subject that Johnson cites as a central problem for environmental theology. Note that Pope Benedict insists that a sense of the creation as possessing an order or a grammar that is prior to us is central to his environmentalism; the emphasis on change, by contrast, in the advocacy for historical consciousness accords unfortunately well with the rhetoric of capitalist exploitation of the Earth.[3] But, as Johnson concisely explains, a simple return to medieval cosmology is not possible. Thus, the classicist/historical-consciousness dichotomy leaves moral theology with two inadequate frameworks for engaging questions posed by the environmental crisis. A truly cosmological approach to environmental problems requires a rethinking of the contrast. I will argue that a cosmo-

[2] Alasdair MacIntyre, *After Virtue* (Notre Dame, IN: University of Notre Dame Press, 1981), highlights both the importance of a historical narrative for understanding moral philosophy as a discipline, and also the role of narrative in moral agency. Haidt's work is summarized in "Morality," *Perspectives on Psychological Science* 3 (2008): 65–72. He is also interested in the broader historical narratives about what morality is, as well as in how these affect specific psychological constructions of morality in contemporary political discourse.

[3] See Benedict XVI, *Caritas in Veritate*, pars. 48–52, and David Cloutier, "Working with the Grammar of Creation: Benedict XVI, Wendell Berry, and the Unity of the Catholic Moral Vision," *Communio* 37 (2010): 606–33.

logical consciousness in moral theology involves attention to key aspects of both models, but expanded to encompass the ecological phenomena of durable natural patterns, which can then analogously be applied to a strengthened conceptual link between natural and cultural patterns. Such a framework can also make more precise Johnson's calls for moral theology to shift to a model of a dynamic cosmos, but one in which nature is accorded intrinsic value.

From Classicism to Historical Consciousness

There is no doubt that "change" becomes a dominant concept in Catholic moral theology in the conciliar era. Bernard Haring's book *Christian Renewal in a Changing World* (1964) exemplifies the spirit of the age. Featuring a foreword that highlights the discussion of the council on "The Presence of the Church in Today's World," the book begins with an italicized, *"We are living in a changing world."*[4] Haring notes the "stupendous transformation" of society and the "impressive signs" of automation, atomic energy, and space exploration, saying that "All these epoch-making achievements are unmistakable indications of 'a new era—a new world.'" In this new world, the Christian must "act in full accord with God's exhortation" to "fill the earth and subdue it."[5]

Haring's point, of course, is not to encourage ecological destruction. Rather, the historical context for his remarks is seeking to overcome "a stubborn adherence to empty forms and conventions"; in particular, he wants to surpass an understanding of God's Law in terms of "a multiplicity of regulations," in order to put in its place a spiritual vitality rooted in faith and charity, which calls for real conversion of life. That is to say, Haring's use of the framing narrative of rapid social and material change is supposed to connect to a development of moral theology beyond a deadening legalism toward a more responsive engagement with the world, and most especially with the actual life of persons.

The framing narrative of moral theology moving with a changing world rather than clinging to fixed rules continued to exert a powerful hold on moral theology in the wake of Vatican II, and perhaps especially after *Humanae Vitae*, which seemed to some to represent a reversion to fixed

---

[4] Bernard Haring, *Christian Renewal in a Changing World* (New York: Desclee, 1964), v, xvii.

[5] Ibid., xvii.

norms alienated from the life of faithful married Catholics. The contrast between a "classicist" worldview and a worldview characterized by "historical consciousness" becomes a dominant interpretative lens, one that "plays out in the Catholic Church throughout the second half of the twentieth century."[6] This move is called "the most important shift in theology which affects the entire enterprise of contemporary moral theology" by Richard Gula, in his influential 1989 textbook *Reason Informed by Faith*. Gula's text begins by noting three shifts in contemporary moral theology: this shift in worldview, a shift from a deductive to an inductive approach to moral reasoning, and a "shift in focus" away from laws and acts toward a scriptural and theological account of "the total human vocation of living in response to God's self-communication to us in creation."[7] This last shift, authorized by *Optatam Totius* (par. 16) and *Lumen Gentium* (pars. 38–42), was widely accepted in moral theology. But the question of continuity and change remained highly contested and is to some extent related to the contrast between deductive and inductive reasoning, as we will see.

Both contrasts have their roots in the work of Bernard Lonergan.[8] The contrast between classicism and historical consciousness was formulated in a concise essay in which Lonergan lays out the "enormous" differences between these two views.[9] He focuses on the contrast between anthropologies in the two approaches. Classicism understands the human person "abstractly through a definition that applies *omni et soli* and through properties verifiable in every man," and "because he is an abstraction, also is unchanging."[10] By contrast, a historical understanding sees "mankind as a concrete aggregate developing over time where the locus of development and, so to speak, the synthetic bond is the emergence, expansion, differentiation, dialectic of meaning and of meaningful performance." Such meaningfulness "is not fixed,

<hr/>

[6] James Keenan, *A History of Catholic Moral Theology in the Twentieth Century* (New York: Continuum, 2010), 115. See also Paulinus Odozor, *Moral Theology in an Age of Renewal* (Notre Dame, IN: University of Notre Dame Press, 2003), 181–82.

[7] Richard Gula, *Reason Informed by Faith: Foundations of Catholic Morality* (Mahwah, NJ: Paulist, 1989), 28–29.

[8] Keenan, *A History*, 111.

[9] Lonergan, "The Transition from a Classicist World View to Historical Mindedness," in *Law for Liberty*, ed. James E. Biechler (Baltimore: Helicon, 1969), 126–33, at 127.

[10] Ibid., 129.

static, immutable, but shifting, developing, going astray, capable of redemption."[11] While Lonergan makes it clear that he is not endorsing a worldview in which everything is endlessly in flux, he does indicate that the *aggiornamento* of the council is to be seen as a move toward a more historical approach to theology, a renewal that is not simply a reaction to the modern cultural context but a "mandate based on the very nature and mission of the Church."[12]

In the substantive vision of moral theology Gula offers, this worldview shift comes up chiefly in the treatment of natural law, especially in a rejection of "physicalism."[13] The question of physicalism has been closely associated with the debate over *Humanae Vitae*. Roughly speaking, the argument is that the church's prohibition on contraception rested on a physical definition of the finality of the sexual act, whereas the council's mature theology of marriage clearly marked a move to what Lonergan describes above as the "meaningful performance" of "a concrete aggregate developing over time." A thorough embrace of historical consciousness should have led the church to rethink the absolute norm against contraception.

Further evidence for this problem is typically the "majority report" of Pope Paul VI's birth control commission, which included much testimony from married Catholics and which recommended change. This would have been a sign of the related shift from a deductive to an inductive method, which Lonergan ties closely to the shift to historical consciousness. In another, longer essay, published around the same time, he makes clearer how what he is describing matters for how we do theology. Three developments are key. First, Lonergan outlines a move from a "deductive" to an "empirical science." Theology "was a deductive science in the sense that its theses were conclusions to be proven from the premises provided by Scripture and Tradition. It has become an empirical science in the sense that Scripture and Tradition now supply not premises, but data. The data has to be viewed in historical perspective."[14] Interpretation is required. Simple "demonstration"

---

[11] Ibid., 130.

[12] Ibid., 126.

[13] Gula, *Reason Informed by Faith*, 228–38.

[14] Lonergan, "Theology in Its New Context," in *Theology of Renewal*, vol. 1, *Renewal of Religious Thought*, ed. L. K. Shook (Montreal: Palm Publishers, 1968), 34–46, at 37.

is not possible. Instead, the goals are "new insights" and "the attainment of a more comprehensive view."[15] Interestingly, Lonergan dates the emergence of the deductive method to the seventeenth century, when "it replaced the inquiry of the quaestio by the pedagogy of the thesis."[16] Thus, the critique of classicist theology is not really aimed at the medieval scholastics themselves, still less at patristic authors. Johnson's address commendably helps us see how this is not so, and how premodern authors wrote out of a cosmological worldview that is neither (modern) classicist nor (modern) historicist. Less subtle presentations of this distinction imply that classicism has reigned over all theology prior to the twentieth century. We will return to this point later.

As an inductive, empirical science, theology is faced not with the task of producing "a new revelation or a new faith" but rather with two further turns.[17] One is the turn to "a new cultural context." Thus, all theology must be attentive to how its language is contextual, and thus how contexts change. This is equally true for ancient as for contemporary theology. Changing forms of expression, far from endangering the theological enterprise, in fact recalls it to its appropriate role as something serving "man's relations to God and to his fellow man," which are always concrete and historical. It does not do away with categories of "nature" or of "body and soul" but instead "adds" something that enriches and enlivens this analysis. This concern for a living Catholic theology is expressed by many of the important theologians of the Vatican II era, de Lubac and Ratzinger just as much as Lonergan and Rahner. The second turn is to "a new type of foundation."[18] Without any foundation, Lonergan notes, discernment is impossible, and the challenge of working in an inductive, contextually sensitive way heightens the imperative to "be able to distinguish tinsel and silver, gilt and gold."[19] For this, Lonergan refers to modern sciences, whose foundations are not any particular laws or conclusions of the science but "method." Summarizing some of his massive work, he notes that by "method" he means not a set of routine procedures but something more like "the grounds that governed" the giving of the procedures, which are themselves embodied in the scien-

---

[15] Ibid., 38.
[16] Ibid., 36.
[17] Ibid., 39.
[18] Ibid., 41.
[19] Ibid., 42.

tist.[20] Hence, the new foundation of theology is the theologian himself, in the sense of a formed practitioner who is "a particular, concrete, dynamic reality generating knowledge of particular, concrete, dynamic realities."[21] Lonergan explains the particular, ongoing experience of conversion as supplying theology "with a foundation that is concrete, dynamic, personal, communal, and historical."[22] His description of theology as an inductive science aware of historical context and concretely normed by the theologian him- or herself obviously manifests the historical consciousness identified in the other essay.

Even in these brief essays, Lonergan's work reflects a nuance and sophistication in making this contrast of worldviews; Keenan rightly notes that the distinction should be understood in terms of "degree," not of "kind," and that "no one is a pure classicist or historicist."[23] Yet the presentation of the contrast sometimes implied simple opposition. For example, Gula develops a table nearly two pages long that provides contrast after contrast of the two views, and little doubt is left in the reader's mind as to which view is to be adopted. While Gula suggests that "contemporary moral theology is not concerned with ignoring either classicism or historical consciousness,"[24] and instead is seeking a creative tension or synthesis, he also indicates that various areas of moral theology are more or less advanced in their adoption of the historical approach. Typically, modern Catholic social teaching is understood to have developed this sort of consciousness in ways that sexual teaching has not.[25] When the presentation is developed in such a contrastive way, it is difficult to understand exactly how to see the two approaches as anything but rivalrous.

The historical context for Gula's presentation is the shift in moral theology from the moral manuals to the approach of Vatican II, exemplified in *Gaudium et Spes*'s insistence on "reading the signs of the times."[26] Ideally, this context would be more clearly highlighted. As it is present in most histories of moral theology, it is generally agreed that

---

[20] Ibid., 43.
[21] Ibid., 44.
[22] Ibid., 45.
[23] Keenan, *A History*, 111.
[24] Gula, *Reason Informed by Faith*, 36.
[25] Ibid., 236–37.
[26] Ibid., 34.

the approach of the manuals does not adequately represent the work of scriptural, patristic, or medieval moral reflection. Thus, the danger in adopting this contrast of worldview as the primary hermeneutic for moral theology is the creation of a simple battle between progressives and conservatives, agents of change and agents of stability. Lonergan himself is wary even of adopting the term "historicist," cautions against using it simply to mean that everything is subject to change and process, and instead highlights the complexity of both progress and decline in action that involves "meaningful performance." He writes that "there is such a thing as historical process, but it is to be known only by the difficult art of acquiring historical perspective, of coming to understand how the patterns of living, the institutions, the common meanings of one place and time differ from those of another."[27]

The Contrast Reconsidered: Protecting the Environment and Historical Consciousness

I highlight this framing narrative in moral theology, and its limitations, in order to echo a concern expressed well in Johnson's essay. It is evident from these texts that the contrast comes into being at a time when the anthropological turn, or turn to the subject, was at its strongest in Catholic theology. Reaction against the dry textbook theology of neoscholasticism was widespread. In a striking 1942 address, Henri de Lubac diagnoses four internal problems in the church that contribute to a "loss of the sense of the sacred." The deepest problem is a "rationalist" tendency in theology, which he describes as follows: "Perhaps then we stroll about theology somewhat as if in a museum of which we are the curators, a museum where we have inventoried, arranged and labeled everything; we know how to define all the terms, we have an answer for all objections, we supply the desired distinctions at just the right moment."[28] Such a theology is cut off from the essential "feeling of Mystery" that connects the person to God.[29] Similarly, the moral manuals develop objective case studies and classifications in great detail, but their anthropology is a narrow vision of the bare individual

[27] Lonergan, "Transition," 129.

[28] De Lubac, *Theology in History*, trans. Anne Englund Nash (San Francisco: Ignatius Press, 1996), 233.

[29] Ibid., 234.

conscience with its acts before the letter of the law. In moral theology, the move from an "act-centered" to a "person-centered" approach is certainly to be applauded. Moreover, as mentioned, the context for the move was a debate over absolute norms and changing historical circumstances, especially as the Catholic theology of marriage made a clear move from a juridical to a personalist understanding of the sacrament. But as Johnson notes, the anthropological turn—especially in its attention to the subject's own experience—has the perverse and often unintended effect of driving out cosmology even further. As Gula notes in his contrasts, the "classicist" approach believes that "the world is marked by harmony of an objective order," whereas the "historicist" view sees the world "marked by progressive growth and change."[30] For all their problems, the manuals continued to express an understanding of the human person as placed within a given natural order, whose limits should be respected. The prioritization of "progressive growth and change," by contrast, makes it all too easy to believe that natural limits don't really exist, or are at least very flexible, and even if they do exist, technological solutions can be devised to deal with the limits, or at least with any bad effects of pushing the limits. If one is looking at a narrow, legalistic theology of the sexual act, the loosening of supposed natural limits may seem attractive; the same loss of a sense of order seems disastrous when caring for creation.

Therefore, I would suggest that Johnson's address should prompt Catholic moral theology to reexamine its turn to the subject, in order to develop a more sophisticated framing narrative for dealing with both stability and change as creatures within a larger cosmos. What is needed is not classicism or historical consciousness but a cosmological consciousness that incorporates and integrates aspects of each. Johnson herself suggests two key moves for the future of ethics. First, in her discussion of intellectual integrity, she suggests that, formerly, "natural law" theology meant "to transpose the order in the cosmos into human conduct." But how might this pattern of practical reason change, she wonders, if we recognize that the "laws of nature . . . are not eternal principles but only approximations read off from regularities, and that their working is shot through with chance and indeterminacy?"[31] Second, in facing

---

[30] Gula, *Reason Informed by Faith*, 32.
[31] Johnson, "Turn," 8.

the destructiveness of human behavior, she seeks "thought patterns that will transform our species-centeredness and enable us to grant not just instrumental worth but intrinsic value to the natural world."[32] Such a move allows for terms such as "compassion" and "solidarity" to be applied to our relations with the Earth.

I would like to jump off these two suggestions by noting that the contrasts Johnson suggests can be very helpful, if we do some work of historically contextualizing them. In so doing, we can be led to two key insights for the development of a moral theology for the environment, in which the classicist respect for order and limits can be combined well with the historicist sensitivity to circumstances and change.

Recall Lonergan's comment that the "deductive" and static approach to theology is not characteristic of the whole of Christian history but comes about in the seventeenth century. There is a similar case to be made for the "classicism" of the moral manuals. Servais Pinckaers traces these back to the reform of the seminaries subsequent to the Council of Trent, holding up the work of the Jesuit Juan Azor around 1600. In contrast to the patristic and scholastic organization of the moral life around happiness and virtue, Azor's work organizes the moral life around the response of conscience to the Ten Commandments and ecclesial law.[33] Such a change, Pinckaers claims, has its intellectual roots in late medieval nominalism, which sought to define freedom in terms of a radical autonomy of the will from any other power; in particular, this led moralists to separate freedom both from any final causes in the universe and from any inclinations natural to the human person.[34] This is the moral theology version of the loss of cosmology, as the human person no longer exists within a created cosmic order that is somehow "connatural" to his moral agency. The real problem here arises not in all pre-twentieth-century theology but in a specific period.

Johnson's two recommendations for ecological ethics should be contextualized similarly: her comments react against errors of early modernity. The idea that the "laws of nature" are "eternal principles" can be understood in two ways. It can mean that nature works according

[32] Ibid., 9.

[33] Servais Pinckaers, *The Sources of Christian Ethics*, trans. Mary Noble (Washington, DC: The Catholic University of America Press, 1995), 260–66.

[34] Ibid., 244–48.

to fixed machine-like mechanisms *or* it can mean that nature exhibits orderly, intelligent patterns that persist over long periods of time. R. G. Collingwood points out crucial differences in these two cosmologies. While both endorse the idea of an order in nature, the sort of order is different. The ancient view holds that "the world of nature is saturated or permeated by mind," which is "the source of that regularity or orderliness in the natural world whose presence made a science of nature possible."[35] Early modern thinkers deny, however, that the world is an "organism" and suggest that its order is "devoid both of intelligence and life." It does not move itself but is moved from without. "Instead of being an organism, the natural world is a machine" that is "set going . . . by an intelligent mind outside itself."[36]

While both views differ from the sense of evolutionary history bequeathed to us by Darwin, the earlier, ancient view is undoubtedly more congenial to a proper attention to and care for nature than is the early modern view. Johnson is making the contrast between mechanistic views of early modern science with the much more sophisticated evolutionary accounts of natural systems of the last 150 years. The chance and indeterminacy of natural systems should not obviate our ability to see the kinds of regularities and intricate patterns that are so characteristic of ecological studies. Indeed, when it does, appeals to evolutionary change threaten to become ideologies, as happened with "social Darwinism" in the late nineteenth century. Social reformers should get out of the way and not interfere with the contingencies of changes in society and work, they said. After all, natural systems show stability over time by rises and falls in different "populations" that have "differential responses to variable conditions."[37] Today, appeals to mere "approximations" and "chance" are common among climate change skeptics, in their attempts to deny the relationship between fossil fuels and global climate data. If we can't truly understand the natural order, then how can we know that this or that human action is destructive of it? Even amid change, the material base of the Earth is finite, and its cycles are subject to

[35] R. G. Collingwood, *The Idea of Nature* (New York: Oxford University Press, 1960), 3.

[36] Ibid., 5.

[37] Kevin McCann, "The Structure and Stability of Food Webs," in *The Princeton Guide to Ecology*, ed. Simon A. Levin (Princeton, NJ: Princeton University Press, 2009), 305–11, at 309.

the kinds of limits we find in human eating and sleeping—while there is some variation and elasticity in these patterns, they are subject to crashing if stretched too far.

Johnson is right that a renewed cosmology is absolutely essential for Catholic thought, and it must be one that appreciates BOTH the dynamisms built into nature AND the fragile but real complex order present there that calls for our humility and respect. The study of ecology is taken up with "determining how certain aspects of the natural world change or do not change."[38] Over long periods of time, and even in some cases in the face of destructive behavior, ecological patterns persist. Such systems demonstrate "resistance"—that is, the ability to "retain structure in the face of a perturbation"—but, even more important, "resilience," which enables a "dynamic response" to a "temporary perturbation."[39] It is important to recognize that the words "order" and "change" are inadequate to capture resilience. Ecologists also differentiate between "engineering resilience" and "ecological resilience." The former involves as rapid a response as possible to perturbation to return to a stable state, whereas the latter also seeks a stable state in face of perturbations, but it may not be a "return" to the previous state. Rather, it might be a different sort of stability. Ecological resilience is not a matter of simple passive reactivity but a matter of careful processes of "remembering" deployed in response to "revolt." Yet this remembering is not simply a pure return to the exact previous state. Engineering resilience is important because of its stress on "fail-safe" design; in other words, if something goes wrong, there is immediate response to avoid failure. Ecological resilience instead involves "safe-fail" design—where failure can be accommodated.[40] No doubt parents will recognize that both sorts of design are important for raising a child!

Why is this so important for Catholic environmental ethics? Preoccupied as it has been with absolute norms, moral theology has neglected the recognition and appreciation of what might be termed *durable natural patterns*. The overly stark dichotomy constructed between clas-

---

[38] Lawrence B. Slobodkin, *A Citizen's Guide to Ecology* (New York: Oxford University Press, 2003), 4.

[39] McCann, "Structure," 306.

[40] Lance Gunderson, et al., "Resilience of Large-Scale Resource Systems," in *Resilience and the Behavior of Large-Scale Systems*, ed. Lance Gunderson and Lowell Pritchard Jr. (Washington, DC: Island Press, 2002), 3–20.

sicism and historical change threatens to ignore or even obliterate these patterns. While Gula in his textbook explains that there is a "tension between the givenness of nature and human creative capacities," he then quotes Karl Rahner saying, "For contemporary man, nature is no longer the lofty viceroy of God, one which lies beyond man's control, but instead has become the material which he needs so as to experience himself in his *own role of free creator* and so as to build *his* own world for himself according to his own laws." While Rahner qualifies this slightly by noting that the material world has "laws proper to itself which will weigh heavily on man," he nevertheless concludes that humans are called to "a creativeness which forces nature into its own service."[41] The "push" of this language is clearly toward change and the authority of humans over nature. One could say the problem here is the perhaps unintended construction of an either/or, in which the laws of humans are totally their own. Obviously, this kind of use of historical consciousness in moral theology without attending to durable patterns (to which there may be exceptions and some range of variation) ends up veering toward a hubris that is extremely unhelpful for the environment.

Johnson's second claim also pushes against what might be termed an early modern problem: the view of nature in purely instrumental terms. Again, Johnson is right to suggest a moral theology that rejects such a view. Cardinal Turkson writes that Catholicism must view care for creation as "a virtue in its own right" and "a fundamental Christian duty," part of a "threefold relationship" to God, neighbor, and the environment in which "to violate one of these relationships is an offense, quite literally a sin."[42] The further development needed here is how to handle the claim "intrinsic value." The idea that nature has "intrinsic" value, without further definition and clarification, leads relatively easily to absolute conclusions about vegetarianism (that is, not killing animals). It also can suggest that we can simply somehow "leave nature alone," which is neither desirable or possible, since it almost makes it seem

---

[41] Gula, *Reason Informed by Faith*, 234, quoting Rahner, "The Man of Today and Religion," *Theological Investigations* 6, trans. Karl H. and Boniface Kruger (New York: Seabury, 1974), 8; italics in original.

[42] Cardinal Peter Turkson, 2015 Trocaire Lenten Lecture; http://www.catholic -bishops.ie/2015/03/05/cardinal-peter-turkson-delivers-trocaire-2015-lenten -lecture-saint-patricks-pontifical-university-maynooth/ (accessed June 1, 2015).

that "nature" is something "separate" from humans, that we either "use" or "respect."

Denis Edwards suggests a more complex, layered view, which he terms "theocentric." In this view, specific relationships to God contextualize other relationships. Humans have a unique dignity and commission, but to do so in the image of God means "to serve and protect the wider creation" as well as to develop the "cosmic humility" to recognize that we are not the creator, which enables us to then see ourselves properly as "part of the community of creation."[43]

In particular, Edwards's description is valuable because it does not avoid narrating dominion but subjects the concept to a larger cosmology. It is not first about the value of trees but about the responsibility of humans to God, within which we come to see trees (and ourselves) rightly. After all, the fundamental problem for Catholic environmental ethics is defining the right use of the environment. The centrality of "right use" is precisely the idea that is *not* captured by the instrumental value / intrinsic value contrast. Surely it is true that without a basic respect for all created things and the beauty of their design we are apt to think we can do whatever we want. I do not at all deny the need for starting with beauty and wonder.[44] The positing of intrinsic value for creation is correct, but it does not go very far in explaining right use. Right use will not be established by absolute norms, but neither will it be named by a pluralistic rejection of so-called speciesism. Instead, right use requires a recognition of ordered limits—an idea far more characteristic of a classicist worldview than one of historical consciousness. Yet these ordered limits of scale will not be definable in terms that completely ignore circumstance.

Thus, both of these contrasts move in the right direction for a cosmological moral theology and point us toward more development. A conception of the natural order requires attention to durable natural patterns understood in organic, rather than mechanistic or relativistic, ways. And an understanding of nature as having its own value requires

---

[43] Denis Edwards, "Humans and Other Creatures: Creation, Original Grace, and Original Sin," in *Just Sustainability*, ed. Christiana Z. Peppard and Andrea Vicini (Maryknoll, NY: Orbis Books, 2015), 159–70, 161.

[44] See the initial chapter on beauty in David Cloutier, *Walking God's Earth: The Environment and Catholic Faith* (Collegeville, MN: Liturgical Press, 2014), 3–11.

attention to how we rightly name our relationship with the rest of creation, in order to distinguish between proper and improper use.

Thus, the kinds of norms needed for an adequate and effective Catholic environmental ethics include aspects of the kinds of fixed limits advocated by one side of the debate, represented by classicism, and aspects of a recognition of the dynamism of natural systems, represented by the other side. A sense of fluid historical change and a sense of fixed laws on stone tablets are both needed but both by themselves are inadequate. Instead, we are in need of norms for restraint and creativity-within-limits; this kind of virtue understanding of norms would constitute the bulk of ethics after making the cosmological turn. An excellent representation of this kind of approach is found in Lisa Cahill's overview of the doctrine of creation. Referencing Johnson's call for a cosmological theology beyond a concern just with God and the self, Cahill insists on "an ethics of responsibility qualified by an ethics of restraint," one that crucially links the unrestrained consumption of the wealthy to the oppression of the poor and the destruction of the environment.[45] Responsibility *and* restraint name well the need for a real balance between the human agency in the developments of history and the human hubris throughout history that is supposed to be designated and constrained by "classicist" limits.

Environmental Ethics as Cultural Critique: Naming Natural Cultures as a Task for Moral Theology

But where are such limits to be enacted and enforced? Responsible right use and harmony with durable patterns cannot be codified precisely, but they are also not subjective. The kinds of norms that should govern right use of nature arise primarily from and are respected (or disrespected) by what we would now call "cultures." Therefore, perhaps the most important element for a genuinely cosmological ethics would be the development of "natural cultures"—a term whose awkwardness displays well the challenges to be faced.

For too long, nature and culture have been understood in a kind of opposition. In moral theology, the classicist/historical-consciousness

---

[45] Lisa Sowle Cahill, "Creation," in *The Oxford Handbook of Theological Ethics*, ed. Gilbert Meilander and William Werpehowski (Oxford: Oxford University Press, 2005), 7–24, at 15.

shift reinforces this opposition. This shift was encouraged by developments in both sexual and social teaching that came to view modern ideas like female equality, democracy, and religious freedom as attractive, despite some traditional reservation or even opposition to them. These developments generally took the form of a diminishment (of specificity) for claims about what was "natural"—in favor of a recognition that these previous claims were in fact claims not about nature but about specific cultural formations. This line of thinking, however, straightforwardly reinforces a dichotomy of nature and culture, which environmentalism calls into question. A cosmological approach calls us to renew the idea that there can be more and less "natural cultures." But this claim needs to be understood carefully.

Part of the problem is a very sloppy use of the term "culture." What we mean by "culture" is tricky. Kathryn Tanner's history of the term notes its gradual tacit expansion from a reference to a set of habits and practices marking the "cultured" (or "civilized") individual or society to a broader use indicating more generally "the customs of particular peoples viewed as distinct self-contained wholes."[46] This movement means that the term culture "has 'nature' . . . as its contrast term. What is not cultural is natural, in the sense of being merely 'physio-biological' or 'animal.' What is not cultural is, in short, subhuman."[47] Needless to say, this dichotomy will present problems for an environmental ethic. The most authoritative treatment of "culture" in the Catholic tradition is in a significant section of *Gaudium et Spes* (pars. 53–62). According to Tracey Rowland's exhaustive study of this issue, the document's use of the term is "extremely broad in coverage, but shallow in analysis" and seems to bear most affinity to Jacques Maritain's "general political project of rapprochement with the liberal-humanist tradition."[48] While not precise, the topic was treated more according to the latter view of diverse ways of life across the world and across time. *Gaudium et Spes* was an extremely important and innovative conciliar document in decisively overcoming the antimodern reactionary tendencies of Catholic thought and the ecclesial hierarchy. Nevertheless, theologians as diverse

---

[46] Kathryn Tanner, *Theories of Culture: A New Agenda for Theology* (Minneapolis: Fortress Press, 1997), 19.

[47] Ibid., 26.

[48] Tracey Rowland, *Culture and the Thomist Tradition: After Vatican II* (London: Routledge, 2003), 20–22.

as Karl Rahner and Joseph Ratzinger, supporters of the overall conciliar project, worried that the constitution combined a rather loose way of speaking with a questionable cultural optimism. Thus, while the general optimism is consistent with a move away from a fortress mentality toward an openness and pastoral mission toward the modern world, the document should not be read as a simple, passive acceptance of all culture, modern or otherwise.

The need for the church's moral theology to criticize cultures is exemplified in the use of the terms "culture of death" in John Paul II's writings and "culture of waste" in Francis's messages. Both of these manifest a clear rejection of certain modern cultural formations, and not simply individual acts. In *Evangelium Vitae*, Pope John Paul II analyzed a "new cultural climate" (4) that "can be described as a veritable structure of sin" (12). While sins against life are present in every age, the pope suggests that what is "even more sinister" in today's world is the justification and even legal sanction for the taking of life (4). In the encyclical, the pope links together poverty, militarization, and even "the spreading of death caused by reckless tampering with the world ecological balance" (10). All of this he traces basically to two sources in the culture: a mistaken view of human freedom that does not "grasp clearly the meaning of what man is" combined with "an idea of society excessively concerned with efficiency" (12). These two forces lead to a denial of solidarity and a profound isolation, which often drives people further into choices against life. Pope Francis's analysis of our "throwaway culture" in *Evangelii Gaudium* follows a very similar line: such a culture at its root is one of "exclusion" in which "everything comes under the laws of competition and the survival of the fittest" (53). Like our preoccupation with efficiency, the culture of waste is one in which "we calmly accept [money's] dominion over ourselves and our societies" (55). All of this, of course, traces back to the same misguided prioritization of individual freedom and deficit of social solidarity identified by John Paul II.

Both popes reject the idea that all cultures are equal, as well as the idea that cultural forms have an autonomy from theological concerns. Cultures are not neutral, morally or theologically. In both cases, the popes are pointing toward anti-*person* aspects of culture. But Francis's metaphor fills out John Paul's, by connecting our lack of attention to persons with our blithe attitude toward the rest of the natural world. Yet this is hardly novel, since John Paul himself coins the term "human ecology," and Benedict makes this term central in his explanation of the ecological crisis. In *Caritas in Veritate*, Benedict indicates that "the deterioration of nature is in fact closely connected to the culture that shapes human coexistence" and that "our duties towards the environment are linked to our duties towards the human person. . . . It would be wrong to uphold one set of duties while trampling on the other" (51).

These papal statements are not simply about norms; indeed, John Paul's use of the term indicates that structures of labor and urban planning are relevant to a genuinely human ecology, and these are evidently not going to generate many absolute norms. What is being offered here is something different, something much more sophisticated, which suggests a distorting cultural pattern that rests on wrong relationships among God, humans, and the natural world. The popes are of course not against freedom, or efficiency, or market transactions. But the moral theology they develop is highly critical of how cultures appropriate, understand, and practice such ideas.

A cosmological moral theology would be one that linked these anti-person aspects of cultural patterns with a similar analysis of a culture of "reckless exploitation" of nature.[49] A cosmological ethic links nature and culture together and expands the range of Catholic moral theology into what we would now call "social critique" or "cultural critique." Such a voice is, of course, easily seen in Scripture, in places like the Hebrew prophets and the exhortations of Paul's letters. While the prophets do not displace the law—indeed, their critique *depends* on it—they are also not simply engaging in scribal debate over the interpretation of law, which is also characteristic of moral theology debating between more classicist and more historically conscious positions on norms. Recovering this prophetic voice, but also not picturing it as a voice that rejects the voice of divine commandment, is crucial.

Naming these "unnatural" cultural patterns is a further task. Benedict echoes John Paul II in criticizing "hedonism and consumerism." Francis has tightly linked the "throwaway culture" to our willingness to "throw away" people, neglecting people who freeze to death on the street while pondering the loss of a few points on the stock market. Elsewhere, I suggest that one can name our cultural problem with nature in terms

---

[49] *Caritas in Veritate*, par. 48.

of three interrelated "diseases": scale, speed, and selfishness.[50] Each of these suggests a kind of sickening enlargement, which explain both our tendency toward consumptions and our ignoring of those who are trampled down in our wake. Smaller, slower, and with solidarity might be the cultural form of genuinely ecological life. In particular, our food, housing, and transportation systems are afflicted by these diseases and need to be transformed.

Yet one further insight will be needed: the development of a cosmological moral theology. Often enough, and in ways that are unquestionably well intentioned, environmentalist cultural critique becomes either rather hopeless or entangled in relatively trivial issues. A Catholic cosmological ethic will therefore pay most attention to *the most important relationships established between the cultural form of a society and the scale of natural resource use needed to support that form.* That scale was often threatened in premodern times by famine and scarcity; but today, some cultures, including our own, suffer from "superdevelopment," in which the primary problem is excessive use resulting in excessive waste. In both cases, the problem is sustainability, but sustainability is understood in different ways; we know, for example, that a human diet without sufficient food is unsustainable, but a human diet with too much food (and too much of particular foods) is also unsustainable. This attention to the scale of patterns within a culture will lead to further reflection on how such scale derives from an emphasis on speed and the selfishness inherent in modern individualism. Probably the two most important and consequential patterns in our own society are food and fossil fuel energy.[51]

Attending to these concrete cultural patterns is not a matter of invoking either the eternal fixed order of early modern classicism or simple appeals to historical context (especially when these implicitly include claims about inevitable historical progress). Instead, moral

---

[50] For more on scale, speed, and selfishness, see Cloutier, *Walking God's Earth*, 14–22.

[51] An example of this sort of analysis that demonstrates the complexity and precision needed for such judgments, in the area of energy ethics, see Erin Lothes Biviano, David Cloutier, Elaine Padilla, Jame Schafer, and Christiana Z. Peppard, "Catholic Moral Traditions and Energy Ethics for the Twenty-First Century," *Journal of Moral Theology* 5, no. 2 (2016): 1–36. On food, see especially Norman Wirzba, *Food and Faith: A Theology of Eating* (New York: Cambridge University Press, 2011).

theology requires a sense of the ordered durability of natural patterns that we have overshot in contemporary "superdeveloped" societies. Such a view requires us to step back from our individual lives and cultural contexts, in order to regain a sense that we live in a cosmos that we did not create. Moral theology can then develop a sensitivity to patterns of environmental use that undergird particular cultures, in order to evaluate them with sensitivity, care, and precision. And we can thank Beth Johnson, along with many others, for stirring us to awaken to this realization.

Chapter 10

Ask the Winds, Rains, and Waves around Us

Justice and Prudence in a Time of Planetary Emergency

William French

Elizabeth Johnson has inspired us and offered us much wisdom regarding the need for Christians to appreciate the great gift of all of creation and the rising threats to creation's integrity. Likewise, we have been instructed well by her strong feminist concerns and her exploration and display of the strong resources of the Christian tradition that support a critical feminist sensitivity. Johnson, in her wonderful book *Ask the Beasts*, draws on the words of the Hebrew Bible "ask the beasts and they will teach you" (Job 12:7) to suggest the importance of learning from the natural world about God, ourselves as a species, and the functioning of the community of creation all around us.[1]

In what follows I wish to offer my appreciation of her vision and leadership through the years by focusing my essay on the rapidly mounting concerns about global climate change. How should we act in such a planetary emergency? Years ago Al Gore, in his excellent book *Earth*

[1] Elizabeth A. Johnson, *Ask the Beasts: Darwin and the God of Love* (London: Bloomsbury Press, 2014).

in the Balance, called our attention to the similarities between our confronting the threat of rising climate change and that of Great Britain in 1936 confronting the growing threat of Hitler's rapid buildup of Germany's army and air force. Prime Minister Stanley Baldwin had promised the British people vigilance against the mounting German threat, but he delayed increasing Britain's military buildup for fear that increasing defense spending would hurt the economy and reduce his political popularity. On November 12, 1936, Winston Churchill rose in Parliament to give perhaps his finest speech.[2] Baldwin's unwillingness to act, Churchill argued, squandered years in which the opportunity for crucial preparation was wasted. These years are, he intoned, citing Joel 2:25, "the years the locust hath eaten." As he stated: "Owing to past neglect, in the face of the plainest warnings, we have now entered upon a period of danger. . . . The era of procrastination, of half-measures, of soothing and baffling expedients, of delays, is coming to its close. In its place we are entering a period of consequences."[3]

Churchill said he was "staggered" by the speed of the rise of the German threat. But even more, he was "staggered" by "the failure of the House of Commons to react effectively against those dangers. That, I am bound to say, I never expected."[4] Are we not similarly "staggered" at the rapid rise of the climate change threat and at the slowness of the international community to negotiate a treaty to begin to mitigate this threat? In particular are we not "staggered" especially by how so many political, corporate, and media leaders in America deny the existence of climate change or block efforts to push for solar and wind development in order to sustain current coal and oil company profits?

Sadly, the community of nations has failed across twenty years of UN-sponsored Climate Change Conferences to agree on any binding steps to reduce greenhouse gas emissions. During that time—from 1990 to 2013—global carbon emissions grew by 61 percent.[5] This fail-

---

[2] See Senator Al Gore, *Earth in the Balance: Ecology and the Human Spirit* (Boston: Houghton Mifflin Company, 1992), 196, 273.

[3] See David Cannadine, ed., *Blood, Toil, Tears and Sweat: The Speeches of Winston Churchill* (Boston: Houghton Mifflin Company, 1989), 127.

[4] Ibid., 128. For a magisterial treatment of Churchill's speech, see William Manchester, *The Last Lion: Winston Spencer Churchill; Alone 1932–1940* (Boston: Little, Brown and Company, 1988), 210–18.

[5] Naomi Klein, *This Changes Everything: Capitalism vs. The Climate* (New York: Simon & Schuster, 2014), 11.

ure occurred because the nations have disagreed over which frame of responsibility should take precedence. Should the emphasis center on a nation's historic contributions to the buildup of emissions or on current and projected levels of national emissions? Across these two decades repeated calls for "climate justice" have been voiced by island nations—like the Maldives and the Bahamas—who have played little role in causing climate change but who will be among the first to be massively damaged by it. They were joined by China, India, and others with large populations in the claim that they were not historically responsible for the massive buildup of emissions. In addition, these countries with many citizens mired in poverty have stressed that their need for economic growth means that they could not accept any caps on their ability to burn fossil fuels. Both groups, those poor island countries most negatively impacted by climate change and large-population countries who have not, historically, been responsible for large levels of emissions, have argued that the United States and other wealthy nations should bear the burden of caps on carbon emissions and a timetable for rapid emission reductions. But stalemate settled in when the United States and others noted how, over the years, China's and India's annual emissions have made them the number one and number three largest carbon emitters today. The US position rightly held that any treaty that exempted China and India from capping annual emissions would be worthless in actually protecting the global community from emissions buildup.

But there is hope that the stalemates and failures to compromise are coming to an end. Just last year China and the United States announced a major joint commitment to which India quickly joined. China committed to halt its emissions growth by 2030.[6] By the time this book is published we will know whether or not the Paris Climate Summit, held in late 2015, succeeded in establishing an international treaty holding all nations to some binding commitments for greenhouse gas emission reductions or whether more years will be needed to hammer out such a treaty.

My essay is situated in this context of urgency and opportunity with the goal of describing two moral frameworks for helping us to understand the scope of our climate responsibilities. The two frameworks have long shaped the debates and negotiation positions, and they will

---

[6] Mark Landler, "U.S. and China Reach Climate Accord after Months of Talks," *The New York Times* (November 11, 2014).

continue to do so. These frameworks I dub the climate justice framework and the climate prudence framework, respectively. They draw explicitly on classic discussions of the virtues and are being pressed into service today to illume key issues of ecological and climate responsibility. Together these two frameworks generate and justify important national and international policy recommendations.

The justice framework, when applied to the specifics of current pricing of fossil fuels, lumber, and other commodities, demands a "just pricing" that incorporates the "full-costs" of the production and consumption, including the cost of any damage or harm that flows onto society-at-large, ecosystems, and future generations. If those "external" costs are excluded from the market price, real harms go out of sight and out of mind, and consumers and producers get an incentive to continue "business as usual." Without full-cost pricing, the market price incentivizes continued consumption levels as rational and "good" when in fact they may often be ecologically disastrous and quite damaging to societies now and in the future.

The climate prudence framework, currently applied by ecologists, is often referred to as the "prudence principle." It holds that when the potential future harm is great, then robust action now to prevent such full-blown harm is demanded. As Churchill's speech makes clear, the very same core commitment to mitigate future threat lies at the heart of discussions about the prioritization of national security.

The Buildup to the Paris Climate Summit and Pope Francis's Watershed Encyclical

The year 2015 has been a time of drama in many spheres, both civil and ecclesiastical. As noted earlier, just before the Lima Conference of December 2014 began, the United States and China announced what may prove a game-changing agreement. China for the first time agreed that it would halt its carbon emissions growth in 2030, and the United States agreed to speed up its emission reductions. And India quickly joined in with its own commitment. Thus, for the first time the top three carbon emitting nations joined in binding caps and reduction levels. This agreement may well be the beginning of a thaw in the set of global negotiations that have been frozen in deadlock. Nations have been submitting their plans for carbon emission reductions to be ratified at the critically important UN Climate Summit to be held in Paris in December 2015. Many ecologists and leaders believe this summit is perhaps humanity's last hope for committing ourselves to a set of binding reductions that offer any hope of stabilizing global temperature rise to 2 degrees Centigrade (3.6 degrees Fahrenheit), the limit that the 2009 UN Climate Summit at Copenhagen endorsed as a relatively "safe threshold" we can reach with moderate impacts to which most societies can adapt.[7]

Pope Francis in his recent and historic encyclical *Laudato Sì* (On Care for Our Common Home) calls for a profound ecclesial and global mobilization of moral focus on climate change and development needs of the global poor.[8] With sustained passion he articulates the need for all humanity to care for our "common home," the Earth (pars. 1, 13). He stresses that we must give special attention and care for the global poor, for they suffer the stings of poverty and will suffer the heaviest burdens imposed by climate change. Accordingly, Pope Francis calls for an "integral ecology" that integrates concern for the sustainability of creation and concern to reduce the suffering of the world's poor (pars. 13–14).

The encyclical will be remembered as a pivotal moment when the church stepped forward to join the global effort to address climate change and to save the community of creation. As Pope Francis states: "Climate change is a global problem with grave implications: environmental, social, economic, political and for the distribution of goods. It represents one of the principal challenges facing humanity in our day" (par. 25). Whereas for years it has seemed to many that the Vatican has held abortion and birth control to be the distinctive special areas of Catholic moral concern, Francis has helpfully drawn attention to a broader circle of distinctively important concerns, among them justice for animal species, ecosystems, care for nature, ecologically responsible urban design, sustainable transit, and solar and wind energy production. He calls attention to the creation-centered sensitivities of Sts. Francis and Aquinas and the medieval church in general, and he reminds Catholics and all others of our responsibilities to care for the Earth. His call is a most helpful push for the nations to achieve success at the Paris Climate Summit.

---

[7] Klein, *This Changes Everything*, 12–13.

[8] See Pope Francis, *Laudato Sì* (Vatican City: Libreria Editrice Vaticana, 2015), for his stress that the Earth is our "common home" so that our security is only ensured through a common security commitment.

In what follows I sketch the main value concerns of the two moral frameworks and the two practical policy applications that draw direction and shape from those more general moral frameworks in light of the urgent international need to achieve a workable climate treaty. I will first sketch how climate justice is now understood and how justice grounds a powerful demand for national policies of "just pricing." Second, I will discuss climate prudence and show how powerful the appeal to prudence is when it is applied directly to the discussions of the prioritization of annual national spending to insure national security.

Climate Justice Framework and Just Pricing Policy

Much of our understanding of justice goes back to Aristotle's views in the *Nicomachean Ethics*. Justice is "regarded as the highest of all virtues" because it calls an individual to reach outside of mere self-regard to respect and promote the good of others.[9] Aristotle speaks of justice in the "distribution" of goods, benefits, and burdens, within a specific community. He stresses that justice is marked by "fairness."[10] When a relationship becomes unequal in terms of what Aristotle refers to as "loss" and "gain," justice seeks to balance the losses and gains between and among the parties involved.[11] "Rectification" promotes equality by seeking to compensate the party who experienced "loss" by transferring some of the "gain" from the other party.

Thomas Aquinas in his *Summa Theologiae* follows Aristotle's lead where Aquinas notes that the distinctive role of "justice . . . [is] to direct man to his relations with others" (ST 2.2, q. 57, a. 1).[12] He states that justice is "a habit whereby a man renders to each one his due" (ST 2.2, q. 58, a.1). Aquinas tellingly stresses the connection between justice and the moral priority of the "common good." Aquinas continues: "Wherefore when that which has been taken cannot be restored in

[9] Aristotle, *Nicomachean Ethics*, trans. Martin Ostwald (Indianapolis: Bobbs-Merrill, 1962), 114 (1129b.27–1130a.5).

[10] Ibid., 117–18 (1130b.30–1131a.25).

[11] Ibid., 120–22 (1131b.25–1132a.24).

[12] All citations to Aquinas's *Summa Theologiae* are from the following edition: St. Thomas Aquinas, *Summa Theologica*, trans. Fathers of the English Dominican Province, 5 vols. (Westminster, MD: Christian Classics, 1948).

equivalent, compensation should be made as far as possible" (ST 2.2, q. 62, a. 2).[13]

Applying the understanding of justice as rectification as expressed in the Aristotelian and Thomist traditions, though crucial, has proved extremely difficult. As noted earlier, deep disagreements about fundamental fairness and equity have been triggered across the last twenty years as the Climate Summit Conferences confronted the basic inequality between those nations most responsible for climate change and those most vulnerable to it. Nations—like the Maldives Islands, the Bahamas, and Bangladesh—are among the most vulnerable to climate change impact but are among those nations who have contributed almost nothing to the causes of climate change. Likewise many of the nations—like the United States, the United Kingdom, and Germany—that are (when measured on a per capita contribution) most massively responsible for the buildup of global atmospheric CO_2 and other greenhouse gases have great economic, geographic, and ecosystem advantages that will help them to adapt to climate change impacts.

This striking unfairness seems to justify a differential treatment of nations when we ask those most responsible for causing the problems to bear serious and binding caps on climate change emissions and to offer as a matter of restorative justice substantial financial contributions to funds to help poorer countries deal with climate change. "Climate justice" seems to demand these transfer funds now known as "climate finance."[14] This effort surely follows Aristotle's stress on "rectification" to bring balance back into the relationships between and among national communities.[15]

These developing nations emphasize data on the historical buildup of emissions by those developed nations who first launched the Industrial Revolution—namely, Great Britain, Germany, and the United States. When one asks about the top ten nations in overall historic contribution

[13] See how John Rawls follows out Aristotle's stress on "justice as fairness" in John Rawls, *A Theory of Justice* (Cambridge, MA: Harvard University Press, 1971), 11, 28–29.

[14] See Grantham Research Institute, "What Is Climate Finance and Where Will It Come From?," Environment, *The Guardian* (4 April 2013).

[15] See Pope Francis, *Laudato Sì*, par. 52, where he speaks of the "differentiated responsibilities." Rich nations have obligations to help relieve the burden on poorer nations of both poverty and climate change impacts.

of CO_2 emissions from 1850 to 2007, one finds the rank order is topped by the United States, responsible for 28.8% of the global total. China is number two with 9% (and that building up only in the last thirty years) and next comes Russia with 8%, Germany with 6.9%, and the United Kingdom with 5.8%. India has contributed a modest 2.4%.[16]

But on the other side of the negotiating table the United States and other rich and long-industrially developed nations have balked at accepting a regime of binding reductions imposed on themselves with no such binding caps or time lines for reductions imposed on China, India, Brazil, and other developing countries with large populations. They note that China's, India's, and Brazil's economic development has been surging for two decades. Indeed, in terms of current CO_2 emissions, China has, in the last few years, eclipsed the United States as the number one nation in total annual carbon dioxide emissions. China in 2011 was responsible for 28.6% of the world's total CO_2 emissions. The United States was number two with 16%, and India was number three with 5.8%.[17]

But the issue of climate justice is complex and the differing consumption levels are stark when one analyzes 2011 national emissions on a per capita basis. In terms of carbon emission intensity per person Saudi Arabia is first with 19 metric tons of CO_2 per person. Australia is second with 18 tons. The United States is third with 17, and Canada is fourth with 16. Interestingly, the European Economic Community come off with impressive and relatively low per capita emission levels. Germany stands at 9, the United Kingdom stands at 8, Italy stands at 6.5, France at 5.7, and Spain at 6.8. China stands at 6.5 while Brazil and India are much lower—2.4 and 1.4, respectively.[18]

This data highlights three important facts. First, the United States, Australia, and Canada have all developed energy-intensive societies marked by urban and suburban growth patterns that require high rates of automobile use for daily trips and high reliance on air travel for longer

---

[16] See Duncan Clark, "Which Nations Are the Most Responsible for Climate Change?," *The Guardian* (21 April 2011).

[17] Ibid.

[18] See "Each Country's Share of CO2 Emissions," Union of Concerned Scientists, http://www.ucsusa.org/global_warming/science_and_impacts/science/each-countrys-share-of-co2.html#.VhXaObmFNjo.

trips. Second, the core European nations, with more compact urban core areas, have sustained high gas taxes incentivizing greater reliance on walking, biking, and bus and rail use. Accordingly, the average European citizen contributes annually roughly half the carbon emission of the average citizen of the United States, Australia, or Canada. Third, per person carbon emission in China and India is much lower than even the relatively low figures for the European Economic Community. These differences surely must guide the allocation of levels of burden imposed by any new international climate treaties.

While the 2009 Copenhagen Conference failed to produce a treaty, it did achieve a commitment by wealthy nations to contribute to a climate finance scheme, to the tune of $100 billion annually beginning in 2020. There are a number of climate finance funds, but the international community is settling on the Green Climate Fund as the main fund for climate finance.[19] The wealthy nations have, however, been lagging in their contributions. Climate justice appeals are rhetorically potent, but it seems difficult for even wealthy nations to deliver on climate finance funding because it seems to their citizens to be a form of "foreign aid." But while such contributions to climate finance funds take money out of one's country, the purpose for the money used in other countries redounds back in an important strategic benefit to the United States and the other donor nations in that it helps to mitigate climate change impact everywhere.

"Just pricing" is a policy specification of the climate justice framework applied to how prices for goods and services are established. Price allows buying and selling, but price also shapes individual and societal decisions and behavior by incentivizing certain practices of consumption and disincentivizing others. Price sends critical information, but economists and ecologists note it can also send misinformation. In many cases the market interaction between buyer and seller ignores often heavy costs being displaced on unsuspecting third parties. These real costs are called "externalities" in that they lie to the side—or external to—the market price paid. Pollution cases are a classic case of "externalities" for the impact of the buyer/seller exchange redounds negatively on other living human beings and other species. Often the damage is spread

---

[19] Klein, *This Changes Everything*, 11–12. See also Grantham Research Institute, "What Is Climate Finance and Where Will It Come From?"

widely across geographic distances and also carried forward to impact communities and generations yet unborn. For this reason these "externalities" are often dubbed "hidden externalities" because their impact often goes unnoticed and undiscussed by general society.[20]

Across the last twenty years ecologists have noted that while the natural environment offers human communities many resources and "goods," it also offers a critically valuable array of "services" whose value must be acknowledged and protected. These services—forests providing flood control and emitting oxygen or wetlands serving as buffers against hurricane impact—have worked quietly and dependably for so long that their continued functioning is taken for granted. For example, the snow packs that build up vast glacier systems in the mountain ranges have long functioned as natural reservoirs whose melting in summers sustains river flows that allow irrigation for crops across the valleys and plains. This natural seasonal dynamic has operated undisturbed across the millennia so it is not surprising that societies have up until recently taken it for granted. Now as climate change melts back the glaciers our attention is concentrated on the profound agricultural, societal, and raw economic value of these glaciers' water delivery services.[21]

The current market prices of oil, coal, and gas benefit the producers/sellers with profits and give the consumer what we want—cheap fuel—but send other costs onto third parties who now bear and future generations who will bear the costs of the environmental damage, economic loss, and degraded health that rise with climate disruption. "Just pricing" demands "full-cost pricing" that includes production costs, a profit margin, and a compensatory assessment of the full social and ecological costs of the use of the good or service across the decades to come. Pricing that does not monetize the full pollution costs back into the purchase price sends a powerfully distorted message to society that

---

[20] On the critical importance of "hidden externalities," see Barry Commoner, *The Closing Circle: Nature, Man & Technology* (New York: Bantam Books, 1974), 249–91, and Gore, *Earth in the Balance*, 182–96. See also William French, "On Knowing Oneself in an Age of Ecological Concern," in *Confronting the Climate Crisis: Catholic Theological Perspectives*, ed. Jame Schaefer (Milwaukee: Marquette University, 2011), 145–75.

[21] See Gretchen C. Daily, ed., *Nature's Services: Societal Dependence on Natural Ecosystems* (Washington, DC: Island Press, 1997). See Lester R. Brown, *Plan B 4.0: Mobilizing to Save Civilization* (New York: W.W. Norton and Company, 2009), 6.

current practices of production and consumption are rational, sustainable, and "good."

Lester Brown and others argue rightly that coal, oil, and gas in the United States and many other countries are vastly underpriced, for the market price takes no account of the massive costs of rising climate change impacts caused by the production and consumption of those fuels. This underpricing incentivizes continued high rates of high fossil fuel consumption and undercuts public pressure to shift societies toward solar, wind, and geothermal power alternatives. Brown estimates that were we to monetize the full ecological costs of burning a gallon of gas, the United States government would need to place a $12 tax add-on, bringing the current market price at the pump to roughly $15 per gallon.[22] This would generate a large fund that could be used to help push domestic wind and solar production and a range of ecologically beneficial policies and programs. This fund could also help provide the US annual contribution to the Green Climate Fund. Likewise, the higher prices would incentivize individuals, families, and businesses to seek out ways to burn less fossil fuel. This would mobilize powerful societal and economic incentives pushing for more adequate mass transit, electric cars, and more national investment in solar and wind power production.

America has much to learn from Europe's patterns of transit, metropolitan design, and locally sourced agriculture. The average European consumes about half the fossil fuel as the average American, and one reason for this is surely explained by the societal ripple effect of the differential prices paid by drivers today for a gallon of gas. Overall, Europe's high gas taxes promote a widespread political pressure to sustain vibrant high population density urban centers where biking, walking, and public transit are encouraged. Recent figures of different nations' average gas prices illustrate the vast difference between European nations' history of imposing high gas taxes and the United States history of sustaining low gas taxes. In September 2015 the average US price of gasoline was $2.57 per gallon (US gallon). In Italy it was $6.44. In the United Kingdom it stood at $6.32. In Germany it was $5.65, and in France it was $5.54.[23] Prices incentivize certain choices and behaviors.

---

[22] Brown, *Plan B*, 16–17.

[23] See "Global Prices, US Gallons," http://www.globalpetrolprices.com/gasoline_prices/.

It is a matter of justice that the price Americans pay for gas, oil, and coal include the true costs of the ecological and societal damage that the consumption of fossil fuels brings. If America were to raise our gas taxes comparable to those of Western European countries, then we would gain a powerful incentive to follow European practices in adopting more energy-efficient transportation and metropolitan design practices. Convincing citizens of the need to raise gas taxes is a tough political sell, but it can be combined in a tax reform package that lowers income taxes as well. Such "tax shifting" schemes can make increasing gas taxes much more palatable to the general public.[24]

Climate Prudence and National Security Policy Ecologically Expanded

Where the call for "justice" is a rhetorically and morally powerful claim, the call for prudence is often heard as a more timid appeal to "be careful." Today the appeal for justice has clarity and drama, while the appeal to prudence sounds weak and ready to compromise. As Josef Pieper noted: "To the contemporary mind, prudence seems less a prerequisite to goodness than an evasion of it." "In colloquial use, prudence always carries the connotation of timorous, small-minded self-preservation, of a rather selfish concern about oneself."[25] But ironically, as in the 2014 agreement by the United States, China, and India, it seems that prudential calculations by many nations are pushing them to reassess their views of their raw self-interest, and they are coming to see that their national interests demand the compromises necessary to achieve an international regime of binding obligations to cut carbon emissions and to do it quickly.

For Aristotle *phronesis* or "practical wisdom" is the "capacity of deliberating well about what is good and advantageous."[26] "Practical wisdom," Aristotle holds, "is concerned with action and action has to do with particulars."[27] As Thomas Aquinas puts it: the prudent person "considers things afar off" (ST 2.2, q. 47, a.1). Prudence that is "directed

---

[24] Brown, *Plan B*, 244–47.

[25] Joseph Pieper, *The Four Cardinal Virtues* (Notre Dame, IN: University of Notre Dame Press, 1966), 4.

[26] Aristotle, *Nicomachean Ethics*, 152 (1140a.25–26).

[27] Ibid., 157 (1141b.15–16).

to the common good is called political prudence" (ST 2.2, q. 47, a. 10). He states: "prudence requires the memory of many things" (ST 2.2, q. 49, a. 1). Indeed, ecologists have long held prudence as a central obligation for thinking about our moral and policy responsibilities in an era of rising climate disruption. The "prudence principle" or "precautionary principle" lies at the core of environmental concerns.[28] It holds that where we face a potentially great future harm, we should err on the side of caution by taking steps now—even quite costly steps—to help us avoid greater costs in the future.[29] Prudence aims to anticipate rising threats and to take responsible steps now, both to reduce the scale of threat and to prepare the community to better deal with the uncertainties of the future.

It is ironic that while the appeal to prudence sounds timid, it must be recognized that its sustained focus on "threat reduction" means that prudence lies as the central value of national security policy. Lester Brown is right to stress our need in an era of climate change threat to commit to "mobilizing to save civilization" and his view that this "mobilization" must occur with "wartime speed."[30] I argue that when the nations acknowledge climate change as constituting a national security threat, then that demands a follow-through at the policy level of a robust national mobilization for climate security.

Realism and the Priority of Prudence in Mobilizing Action

Reinhold Niebuhr, perhaps America's most influential theologian, founded a movement called "Christian realism" that highlighted the ongoing relevance of Augustine's emphasis on the power of sin in human affairs. Niebuhr called on people not to be naïve about the sort of moral transformation that can occur in the political life of large groups. As Niebuhr puts it: Individuals "may be moral in the sense that they consider interests other than their own in determining problems of conduct, and are capable, on occasion, of preferring the advantages of others to their own. . . . But all of these achievements are more difficult, if

[28] See Pope Francis, *Laudato Sì*, par. 186.

[29] On prudence, see United States Conference of Catholic Bishops, *Global Climate Change: A Plea for Dialogue, Prudence and the Common Good* (Washington, DC: US Catholic Conference, 2001).

[30] Brown, *Plan B*, 23, 25.

not impossible, for human societies and social groups. In every human group there is less reason to guide and check impulse, less capacity for self-transcendence, less ability to comprehend the needs of others and therefore more unrestrained egoism than the individuals, who compose the group, reveal in their personal relationships."[31]

Niebuhr's point seems surprisingly relevant today for understanding the two-decade's long frustrations of the UN Climate Summits. Niebuhr's suggestion raises a stark question: are nations capable of altering core economic and daily life practices out of concerns for "justice," especially justice said to be owed to other peoples? While appeals to "climate justice" sound compelling to progressives and activists, in fact very few nations seem capable of being mobilized to act "for justice" in any way that undercuts their apparent national self-interest. That assessment seems to be borne out by the twenty years of failed climate negotiations.

While certainly discussions about justice remain important, it may well be that "prudence" is the real driver of nations today committing to step up and join in efforts at forging an international binding treaty to promote real Earth security. Prudence concerns are often more self-interested and thus more directly mobilizing of energies in response than appeals to other-regarding justice. But during the last three years or so it would appear that China, India, the United States and many other nations have been recalculating their negotiation positions based on the "prudence principle" and their careful assessment of their own "national interest." Increasingly, it seems that whether they like it or not many nations are now being forced, by rising winds, extreme rains, sustained droughts, and rising storm surges, to acknowledge that their national security is inextricably tied into the security of the whole community of nations. Prudence may be the core moral principle for ecologists, but it likewise remains the core moral principle for governments assessing national security threats and a responsible prioritization of spending on national defense.

For many decades ecologists have put forward the case that rising ecological threats constitute genuine national security threats and deserve to be attended to and responded to as we attend to the risks posed by

---

[31] Reinhold Niebuhr, *Moral Man and Immoral Society: A Study in Ethics and Politics* (New York: Charles Scribner's Sons, 1932), xi–xii.

hostile military threats.[32] But not many of our governmental, corporate, or media elites were listening. For example, not surprisingly, after 9/11 President Bush's administration concentrated intently on the threat of international terrorism and the need to get regime change in Afghanistan to eliminate any future threat posed by Al Qaeda's training camps. Sadly, during his eight years of leadership President Bush paid much less attention to rising climate change threats. Bush stressed that given the range of scientific uncertainty about climate change it would be imprudent to commit large funds now to address a future problem that might not even rise. We should ground "sound policy" on "sound science," and with broad uncertainty regarding the climate change possibilities he concluded that it would be imprudent to take any steps that might hurt America's economy. He claimed the Kyoto Protocol "would have required the United States to make deep and immediate cuts in our economy to meet an arbitrary target. It would have cost our economy $400 billion and we would have lost 4.9 million jobs." He stressed repeatedly that "economic growth and environmental protection go hand in hand."[33]

President Bush during his administration exhibited what I call the "asymmetry of threat recognition." When it came to national defense against hostile terrorist threats or military powers perceived as hostile—Afghanistan and then Iraq—no national expense was deemed too great to ensure American security.[34] But against rising ecological or climate change threats, the same invocation of prudence is made to justify the need to maintain American economic growth and to wait for "sound science" to establish greater certitude about climate change impact. When faced with uncertainties regarding the scale of the hostile military or terrorist threats, prudence is said to demand rapid response and vast increases in military spending for "homeland defense." But uncertainties regarding potential climate change impacts are held to warrant almost

[32] See Commoner, *The Closing Circle*, 214–43; Barry Commoner, *Making Peace with the Planet* (New York: Pantheon, 1975); and Norman Myers, *Ultimate Security: The Environmental Basis of Political Stability* (New York: W.W. Norton & Company, 1993).

[33] President George W. Bush, "George Bush's Global Warming Speech," *The Guardian* (February 14, 2002), http://www.theguardian.com/environment/2002/feb/14/usnews.globalwarming.

[34] For an analysis of a case of flawed decision making, see Thomas E. Ricks, *Fiasco: The American Adventure in Iraq* (New York: Penguin Press, 2006).

no national action other than adopting a "wait and see" attitude and a "business as usual" concern to protect American economic growth.

But under President Obama's administration it is clear that climate change concerns are being increasingly understood as grave national security threats, threats for which we do not have the luxury of delaying robust national response. The Pentagon released the *2014 Climate Change Adaptation Roadmap*, which holds that climate change poses an "immediate threat" to national security. In it, Secretary of Defense Chuck Hagel calls climate change a "threat multiplier" because it "has the potential to exacerbate many of the challenges we are dealing with today." It holds that "sound planning" for the nation's security requires that we attend to a "wide spectrum of possible threats."[35]

In his 2015 State of the Union Address President Obama rightly states: "And no challenge—no challenge—poses a greater threat to future generations than climate change."[36] Finally an American president named a critical climate reality. Once one acknowledges that climate change is a major national security threat, then addressing that threat must become a top national priority.[37]

Wide-Spectrum Threats Warrant Wide-Spectrum Security Spending

If we acknowledge climate change as a top national (and global) security threat, then we must either massively reallocate a large part of our current levels of military spending to try to mitigate climate change or increase overall levels of defense spending to include robust efforts to reduce climate change. The reallocation might seek to hold current national defense spending level and pivot, as soon as possible, a large percentage—say a half—of our current defense spending to help us switch from a coal- and oil-based economy to a solar- and wind-based economy.

[35] Carolyn Pumphrey, "Global Climate Change: National Security Implications" (May 2008), http://www.StrategicStudiesInstitute.army.mil/; and Department of Defense, *2014 Climate Change Adaptation Roadmap*, Office of the Deputy Under Secretary of Defense for Installations and Environment (Alexandria, VA: June 2014).

[36] President Barack Obama, State of the Union Address (January 20, 2015), http://www.whitehouse.gov/the-press-office/2015/01/20/remarks-president -state-union -address-january-20-2015.

[37] See Gore, *Earth in the Balance*, 269, where he holds that "we must make the rescue of the environment the central organizing principle for civilization."

In 2014 US defense spending totaled roughly $610 billion. So a reallocation approach would mean a shifting of, say, $305 billion toward ecological and climate security measures. This would be done on an annual basis. Surely such a reallocation would be met with incredulity and screams charging that this step would be leaving America militarily vulnerable, but it is all relative. China's military spending in 2014 was roughly $216 billion, and Russia's was roughly $84 billion. So the US military spending after the reallocation would still far outpace the next largest military budgets.[38]

If the nation found such a shifting of half of our current military spending to an ecological and climate security mission to be too risky, then we could simply hold our $610 billion level of military spending constant and add on a new budget line dubbed "ecological and climate security spending." We would simply add $305 billion for ecological and climate security on top of current military defense spending. That would raise overall national security spending to roughly $915 billion. That would take away the argument that America is being left militarily vulnerable but would trigger a new argument that America can't afford more federal spending. The predictable charge will invoke such terms as "Big Government," demanding higher taxes, and causing harm to America's economy.

But the American public would do well to note that our current levels of defense spending are relatively low in terms of a percentage of the gross domestic product (GDP) compared to the levels of most of our recent history. Many Americans admire the courage and sacrifices of the "Greatest Generation" who, during World War II, shouldered significant sacrifices to defeat Germany and Japan.[39] One of the ways wealthy Americans stepped up during the war was that they paid the highest tax rate ever imposed in American history. In 1944 the top marginal rate was "94 percent on taxable income over $200,000 ($2.5 million in today's dollars)."[40]

---

[38] See *SIPRI Fact Sheet*, Stockholm International Peace Research Institute, Sam Perlo-Freeman et al., "Trends in World Military Expenditure" (2014), books.sipri .org/files/FS/SIPRIFS1504.pdf.

[39] See Tom Brokaw, *The Greatest Generation* (New York: Dell Publishing, 1998).

[40] See "History of Federal Income Tax Rates: 1913–2014," Bradford Tax Institute, at bradfordtaxinstitute.com/Free_Resources/Federal-Income-Tax-Rates.aspx.

To win the war, the United States mobilized the entire economy and sent military spending through the roof. In 1944 US defense spending stood at roughly 43 percent of US GDP. Across much of the Cold War period Americans accepted the need to spend roughly 9 to 10 percent of GDP yearly on national defense. Since then, the economy has grown much larger, and after a buildup for the wars in Afghanistan and Iraq our military spending relative to GDP has declined. This year it is estimated to be roughly 4.5 percent of GDP.[41] So adding $305 billion for ecological and climate security on top of our current level of military spending would simply return us to a level of general security spending to which the nation has long been accustomed. Simply put, committing $305 billion per year in increased national spending is not an impossible task. We have sustained those levels of spending as a percentage of GDP for decades.

There is no question that steps to reduce the destructive impacts of climate change will force America and the rest of the world to bear huge costs. But did we not face huge costs during World War II or during the Cold War that the people judged were worth paying? Between 1940 and 1996 it is estimated that the United States alone spent $5.48 trillion just on nuclear arms.[42] That is a lot of money to spend for weapons created with the very intent that their presence on airfields and in missile silos would help ensure that they would never need to be used. In contrast, a similar, decades-long, massively expensive commitment to climate mitigation and adaptation seems smart and quite positive in comparison. Build a wind farm, and it will tap the free energy of the wind for the next forty years. That is positive and good for our economy. The development of solar, wind, and geothermal energy sources and all the retrofitting of urban regions with fuel-efficient mass transit and the development of electric cars and trucks all play positively into generating jobs and economic stimulation in ways that burying expensive weapons in dark silos does not.

[41] See Dinah Walker, "Trends in U.S. Military Spending," Council on Foreign Relations (July 15, 2014), http://www.cfr.org/defense-budget/trends-us-military -spending/p28855.

[42] See Matthew L. Wald, "Total Cost of U.S. Nuclear Arms Is Put at $5.48 Trillion," *New York Times* (July 1, 1998).

Conclusion

While climate justice is a critically important moral concern, it does not seem to be the primary mobilizing force pushing national decision making to join treaties that will cut against one's own perceived national self-interest. Climate prudence and national security concerns seem to be the primary powers that are mobilizing serious efforts toward an international agreement on binding caps on carbon emissions for all nations. In short, the self-interested character of prudence mobilizes the recognition that one's national security interest is now tightly tied to the national security of all other nations.

If climate prudence is the primary motive mobilizing action, then climate justice remains a critical guide for allowing different nations to make differential levels of contribution to the common climate security effort. It is climate justice concerns that will adjudicate the differential responsibilities for wealthy, climate perpetrator nations like the United States, Canada, and Australia to bear the highest burden of contributions in the Green Climate Fund. It is important to note that while some of the monies dispensed by the Climate Fund go to developing countries to help them build "resiliency" in levees, road nets, alternative crops, and such to help them adapt to climate change, much of the monies will go to help countries shift from coal and oil power to solar and wind power production. While these monies will be understood as "foreign aid," such projects directly serve the core well-being of the United States and the other donor nations. The United States has as much a direct security interest in helping others to shift to solar and wind as we do in helping ourselves to shift to solar and wind.

The analysis is informed by Aristotle's view that ethics and policy must be developed with an eye toward general principles but also deeply informed by the "ultimate particulars"—the concrete realities to which we must respond.[43] While I have made little explicit reference to the need to "care for creation" or our obligation to "love the neighbor," I believe that the mobilization to mitigate climate change is centrally related to both of these moral and religious obligations.

[43] Aristotle, *Nichomachean Ethics*, 158–61 (1141b.23–1142a.31). See also James M. Gustafson, *Varieties of Moral Discourse: Prophetic, Narrative, Ethical, and Policy* (Grand Rapids, MI: Calvin College and Seminary, 1988), where he argues that policy analysis is an important mode of moral analysis.

Part 3

Turning

To a New Creation

Chapter 11

Theology, Cosmos, and Hope

John F. Haught

During the late modern period Catholic theology handed over to science the task of understanding the natural world, reserving for itself the separate obligation of illuminating and healing human interiority, social evils, and economic injustice. In her 1996 CTSA address Elizabeth Johnson, however, spoke prophetically about the importance of bringing a sense of the cosmos back to the center of Catholic theological reflection. In a recent essay for *US Catholic* she shows how belief in the communion of saints, to give one example, can take on a cosmic significance in the age of science:

> The communion of saints has traditionally focused on humans and their companionship in the Spirit throughout space and time. As scientific discovery and ecological concern reposition the human race in relation to the natural world, however, the realization dawns that the greatest community of all is the world itself, which has spawned the human race and which sustains its life every moment. In a physical and biological sense, interrelationship is not an appendage to the natural order but its very lifeblood. Everything is connected to everything else, and it all flourishes or withers together. In a theological sense, the same divine creativity that fuels the vitality

of all creation also lights the fire of the saint. The communion of holy people is intrinsically connected to the community of holy creation, and they stand or fall together.[1]

Doing theology cosmologically—and cosmology theologically—has been an interest of mine as well. I am honored, therefore, to have the opportunity in this *Festschrift* to echo Johnson's hope that theologians will continue to bring the cosmos back into our explorations of the meaning of Christian faith.

This project would start with our developing an ever more organic sense of human connectedness to nature in view of recent biology, ecology, microphysics, and astrophysics. As Johnson's 1996 address made explicit, the new scientific sense of deep time, of spatial extension, and of the organic complexity brought about over the course of cosmic history should now encourage us to expand our sense of God, offering fresh opportunity for each soul to extend itself anew *ad magna*. Proportioning our sense of God to current and future cosmology is a project that not only links our new theological efforts tightly to the traditional sense of divine infinity, but it may also ensure that our sense of God will never again become smaller than the universe. Pictures of a one-planet deity may finally be permitted to disappear from our spiritual visions altogether.

Above all, however, Johnson's call for a renewed cosmological accent to theology is vital because Christian hope requires it. Hope would have little meaning, as Protestant theologian Jürgen Moltmann points out, unless the world continually allows for the actualizing of yet unrealized possibilities. If the universe itself had no prospect for future becoming, human hope would be reduced to the longing of solitary souls to escape "the prison of a petrified world."[2]

Geology, biology, and cosmology have now demonstrated that the universe is not petrified, nor has it ever been. It is still "unfinished," and this is good news for those who live in hope for a new future. Generally speaking, however, Christian theologians and religious educators, even if

---

[1] Elizabeth A. Johnson, "Circle of Friends: A Closer Look at the Communion of Saints," *U.S. Catholic* 64, no. 11 (November 1999): 12–18, http://www.uscatholic .org/2011/01/circle-friends-closer-look-communion-saints.

[2] Jürgen Moltmann, *Theology of Hope: On the Ground and the Implications of a Christian Eschatology*, trans. James W. Leitch (New York: Harper & Row, 1967), 92.

they are theoretically aware of new cosmological discoveries, continue unconsciously to fashion religious and ethical sensibilities in accordance with ancient images of a fixed universe and of a God who exists above or outside of the physical world. For the most part theologians have failed to draw out the spiritual implications of the spectacular shift the new sciences have wrought in the wider world of human understanding.

It is important for the full mobilization of hope, I am suggesting, that theologians explicitly embrace the new scientific sense that the whole universe is still on a long and far-from-finished journey. Over the last half century science has demonstrated that the universe is still building, still-aborning, a point that Pierre Teilhard de Chardin has emphasized more than any other recent religious thinker.[3] Christian eschatology, therefore, is irreconcilable with earlier modern assumptions that the cosmos is mainly a backdrop for the human drama. Moreover, our love for other persons, Earth, and life can thrive most meaningfully if we may plausibly assume that the universe itself still has room for realizing new possibilities. Contemporary scientific awareness that the universe is still coming into being provides an indispensable setting for the meaningful practice of justice and love.

Everything in theology, in fact, looks different once we become fully aware that the universe is still emerging. Early in the twenty-first century, however, Christian thought has yet to take full advantage of the hope-transforming implications of the new sense of nature entailed by biology, physics, cosmology, and other natural sciences. Johnson's impressive body of work is, in this respect, exceptional, especially among Catholic theologians. Prescientific, pre-Darwinian, and at times pre-Copernican cosmology still shapes the religious imaginations of countless Christians. Even though Galileo long ago insisted that mutability is more exciting than motionlessness, traces of the older suspicion of cosmic mobility are likely to persist wherever God is conceived of as an eternal present rather than an enlivening future. Ancient cosmology, in league with a persistently Parmenidean metaphysics, still provides an alluring setting for religious expectation, but it does so by steering human aspirations toward a spiritual heaven beyond the physical universe.

---

[3] Pierre Teilhard de Chardin, *The Human Phenomenon*, trans. Sarah Appleton-Weber (Portland, OR: Sussex Academic Press, 1999), 162–63.

A predominantly otherworldly kind of expectation is certainly understandable given the hopeless political and economic circumstances in which most human beings have lived. Yet the traditionally vertical brand of expectation has the disadvantage of tolerating despair about the final destiny of the cosmos that has given birth to us and all of life. The static universe taken for granted by traditional piety, since it undergoes no significant transformation itself, is destined eventually to be "left behind" as souls journey off to their final resting place elsewhere.

A scientifically informed sense of each person's connection to a still-emerging universe, on the other hand, forbids any decisive severance of human existence from nature. That the universe is still unfinished, Teilhard rightly insisted in trying to bring Catholic thought into the age of science, "is the basic truth which must be grasped at the outset and assimilated so thoroughly that it becomes part of the very habit and nature of our thought."[4] Regrettably, science's great new discovery of a still-emerging universe has yet to become habitual to Christian thought and spirituality. Were we to take science seriously, as Johnson has been doing for many years, everything in Christian life and thought would be enriched and ennobled. Above all, Abrahamic hope would find a more natural setting than has been available to it throughout most of Christian theological history.[5]

Meanwhile, the intellectual world at large remains mired in a pessimistic materialist understanding of physical reality, content with the prospect that nature is headed toward a final abyss of nothingness. The current invasion of secularist naturalism and cosmic pessimism into intellectual life is a threat to religious thought worldwide. Any theological apologetics comfortable with prescientific worldviews, however, has proven to be powerless in the face of this challenge. Within the Christian world, moreover, strong movements toward religious restoration—a nostalgia often endorsed at least implicitly by ecclesiastical leaders—still builds on prescientific pictures of the natural world.

Something radically new in cosmological sensitivity, consequently, is needed for Christianity's revitalization. Such a project, however, cannot

[4] Pierre Teilhard de Chardin, "The Meaning and Constructive Value of Suffering," in *Teilhard de Chardin, Pilgrim of the Future*, ed. Neville Braybrooke (London: Libra, 1964), 23.

[5] For an extended development of this point, see my book *Resting on the Future: Catholic Theology for an Unfinished Universe* (New York: Bloomsbury, 2015).

be intellectually or spiritually convincing as long as it avoids close contact with the natural sciences, especially recent cosmology, biology, geology, paleontology, and cognitive science. New ways of thinking about Christianity and its God in the age of science are vital, and Johnson's recent book, *Ask the Beasts*, is a splendid example of what I have in mind. It is an extensive and profound meditation on Darwin's *Origin of Species*, exposing theology adventurously to the strange and spiritually challenging story of life that evolutionary biology has recently revealed.[6] Most Christian theology, I fear, has barely begun to think about the God of love in a manner that takes new developments in scientific understanding so seriously. Unfortunately, those who have been involved in such attempts to rethink theology in the age of science are not always taken seriously either by the faithful at large or by secular thinkers. Seldom does their work appear in seminary curricula. I am convinced, however, that the survival of theology, and even of our faith traditions broadly speaking, requires the careful kind of encounter of religious hope with evolutionary biology and other sciences that Johnson has been working on so successfully.

If the universe is still coming into being, this can only mean that God's creation has at no time been paradisal. But it also means that something momentous may be taking shape up ahead, and that hope is necessary to greet the future of creation. Instead of hiding from the universe's persistent restlessness in the manner of acosmic Christian thought, we may come to realize, not without a throb of joy, that the doctrine of creation along with every other Christian teaching is now taking on fresh significance, as Johnson's work so persuasively exemplifies. Evolutionary biology and contemporary cosmology, if taken seriously, can have the effect of deepening human self-understanding, heightening our sense of freedom, expanding the horizons of hope, and giving new zest to our spiritual lives. A frank encounter with the world of Darwin, Einstein, and Hubble may let us hear with new ears that most challenging of all Christian instructions: *sursum corda*—lift up your hearts.

[6] Elizabeth A. Johnson, *Ask the Beasts: Darwin and the God of Love* (New York: Bloomsbury, 2014).

Chapter 12

Elizabeth A. Johnson and Cantors of the Universe

The Indwelling, Renewing, and Moving Creator Spirit and a Pneumatology from Below

Erin Lothes Biviano

Theology sings to set free, and now when creation is groaning, a song telling of the workings of the Creator Spirit, indwelling, renewing, and moving throughout the living world, sets free both our longing and our hopes for the liberation of Earth. Elizabeth A. Johnson stands among the "cantors of the universe" as one of theology's great singers and a pioneer in Catholic systematic theology's turn to the Earth. Her prophetic address to the Catholic Theological Society of America in 1996 challenged theology to reengage the cosmos as both a necessary framework and source of insights so that *fides quaerens intellectum* might honor its ancient faith in God as first of all faith in God the Creator; regain its authentic, "catholic" moral integrity; and heed the cry of the poor and the cry of the Earth.

This is a great and worthy challenge. As Johnson observed in 1996, much excellent foundational work had been done even at that time. Now, the field of religion and ecology has bloomed even more widely and deeply. When I was a doctoral student between 2000 and 2005,

174

with the good fortune to work with her, ecological theology was still a fairly marginalized topic. Now, blessedly, it is not. Yet what she calls for is not attention to cosmology or ecology as isolated motifs among the great fabric of theology (as she might say, don't "add Earth and stir"). The tapestry itself needs to be rewoven so that the essential strands relating Creator, creation, and humanity, once so evident in the medieval synthesis, are renewed and strengthened in the colors and fibers of our time. As she states, "We need to complete our recent anthropological turns by turning to the entire interconnected community of life and the network of life-systems in which the human race is embedded, all of which has its own intrinsic value before God. In a word, we need to convert our intelligence to the heavens and the Earth."[1]

In the process, theologians must direct their Earth-converted intelligence to reexamine basic categories and explore anew our traditional theological questions. For example, while listing categories of systematic theology to reexamine, Johnson raised pneumatology. She asks, "How to interpret the Spirit of the baptismal font as none other than the very Giver of Life to all the creatures of the rain forest?"[2] While all themes in the tapestry of systematic theology are relevant to the Earth—Christology, redemption, eschatology, anthropology—and that is exactly her point, there is a wonderful particularity to pneumatology. Hearing the cry of the Earth as a revelation of the compassionate concern of the Creator for the creation snaps our attention to the Spirit, the Giver of Life, like a sailboat's boom swinging in a gusting wind.

The classic theology of the Spirit is shaped by revelation as recorded in Scripture and Tradition. Its expression in the creed reflects classic trinitarian doctrine about the nature of God, doctrine that might be called a descending pneumatology or a pneumatology from above. But thinking about inspiration may also lead to a theology of the person who is inspired. That is, the nature of the work of the Holy Spirit may also be described on the basis of the experience of inspiration. The human experience of inspiration is a source for what theologians would name a pneumatology from below—a theology that searches human experience for encounters with, and language about, God.

---

[1] Elizabeth A. Johnson, "Turn to the Heavens and the Earth: Retrieval of the Cosmos in Theology," *CTSA Proceedings* 51 (1996): 1.

[2] Ibid., 8.

A brief detour to trace Karl Rahner's expression of a Christology from above will illustrate this. Rahner notes that a "descending or incarnational Christology presupposes the classical theology of the *Trinity*. . . . This trinitarian theology says: there are three 'persons' in God who are distinct from one another: one of them, the second person, is the 'Logos' from all eternity and independently of the Incarnation of the 'Son.'"[3] Rahner elsewhere calls this a "metaphysical Christology." The assumptions of this descending, incarnational, metaphysical, theology "are properly speaking based not upon the experience in saving history of the crucified and risen Jesus, but are made known through verbal teaching by this same Jesus. . . . This is not a justifiable interpretation of a more original experience of saving history, but the supreme and primary axiom of this Christology."[4] In that sense this descending Christology comes "down from on high." As Johnson explains, "Thus the genuine descent of the eternal Word into human existence is a redemptive event par excellence; Jesus Christ's metaphysical identity is the ground of his function as Redeemer of the human race."[5]

By contrast, ascending Christology—a Christology from below—takes its starting point from "the simple experience of the man Jesus, and of the Resurrection in which his fate was brought to its conclusion."[6] An ascending Christology begins with the events of salvation history and considers the teaching, healing, activities, death, and resurrection of Jesus. Johnson writes: "Thus the genuine ascent of the ministering-crucified-risen Jesus into the life of God is a redemptive event par excellence."[7] Scripture offers paradigms for both Christologies. Descending Christology takes its paradigm from the Gospel of John; ascending Christology from the Synoptic Gospels.[8]

Johnson has pioneered Christologies from below, anthropologies from below, Mariologies from below. Here I wish to honor her feminist insight that emphasizes the revelatory nature of experience: experience

---

[3] Karl Rahner, *Foundations of Christian Faith: An Introduction to the Idea of Christianity*, trans. William V. Dych (New York: Crossroad, 1994), 286.

[4] Karl Rahner, "The Two Basic Types of Christology," *Theological Investigations* 13 (New York: Seabury Press 1975), 218.

[5] Elizabeth A. Johnson, *Consider Jesus: Waves of Renewal in Christology* (New York: Crossroad, 1990), 70.

[6] Rahner, "The Two Basic Types of Christology," 215.

[7] Johnson, *Consider Jesus*, 74.

[8] Ibid., 70, 74.

is a source for theology. The experience of faith-based environmentalists, I propose, contributes to the ongoing tradition from biblical times forward, of living in the Spirit. More specifically, the transcendental openness of human experience to the "holy mystery," to the indwelling Spirit, forms the condition of possibility for inspiration. Thus I propose to explore a pneumatology from below through my ethnographic study of persons deeply committed to caring for the Earth precisely as faith-based environmentalists.[9] In other words, this paper seeks to reflect on the Earth-loving Spirit through observing the human experience of being inspired to care for the Earth. These persons had certainly turned "to the heavens and the Earth." Their witness in congregational environmental advocacy bears the marks of "genuine conversion of mind and heart."[10] In their work we can see the Lord, the Giver of Life, at work in them, giving testimony to how the Spirit loves the Earth. What we know of the Spirit through revelation thus links with what we are learning about the Spirit from humanity's work to love and heal the Earth. This "pneumatology from below" converges with the pneumatology from above, the powerful accounts of the workings of the Spirit told in revelation and lyrically recounted by Johnson, to offer a thicker description of the workings of the Earth-renewing Spirit.

The convergence I will trace here takes up Johnson's invitation to "a fully inclusive turn to the heavens and the Earth, a return to cosmology," and marries that with the observed spirituality of faith-based environmentalists. Rather than reinscribe the risky and narrow focus on the human subject of some early modern theology, indeed, on the human soul, whose morally meaningful life occurred in history but precisely *not* in nature, I hope this amounts to a turn to the ecologically conscious subject, the Earth-converted, faithful subject.

Johnson offers a formal treatment of pneumatology in her Madaleva lecture *Women, Earth, and Creator Spirit*, where she lyrically traces the three dynamics of the Spirit as the Creator Spirit who indwells, renews,

---

[9] The study involved over twenty-five focus groups with people from congregations representing multiple Christian and other religious traditions throughout the United States that were working toward ecological justice. See Erin Lothes, "Worldviews on Fire: Understanding the Inspiration for Congregational Religious Environmentalism," *CrossCurrents* 62, no. 4 (December 2012): 495–511; also Lothes, *Inspired Sustainability* (New York: Orbis Press, 2016).

[10] Johnson, "Turn to the Heavens and the Earth," 8.

and moves in creation. In the first part of this essay I will outline that triad dynamic of the workings of the Spirit. In the second part I will suggest a parallel triad dynamic within the human experience of being inspired to care for the Earth: the indwelling of noticing and favoring the Earth; the renewing of love to prioritize the Earth; and the movement in charity and justice to act for the Earth. Finally I will lift up the circles of relationality that bind this love together, calling us to act in solidarity for our common home, at an appropriately Earth-scaled level of response to the ecological crisis.

Elizabeth A. Johnson and the Creator Spirit

As Johnson writes, "The Spirit is God who actually arrives in every moment, God drawing near and passing by in vivifying power in the midst of historical struggle."[11] The Spirit is the presence of God active and alight in the world of history, active in time and space. Indeed, when people speak of the experience of God, "more often than not they are referring to the Spirit," were they to view God's activity according to a trinitarian lens.

The Spirit is most significantly identified with her creative power. Expressed in the Nicene Creed, Johnson reminds us, the Spirit is *vivificans*, life-giver, the creative origin of all life. This is an ongoing, continuous, "unceasing, dynamic flow of divine power that sustains the universe, bringing forth life." And from this creedal core, three dynamics of the Spirit's sustaining dance spin forward.

First, the Spirit is the "Giver of life," the third person of the Trinity who participates in the mystery of Creation with God the Father, the Creator of Heaven and Earth, and the eternally begotten Word of God, through whom all things were made. Second, the Spirit indwells the community, moving with them as they go forward in history. Third, the Spirit is a renewing power.[12] This threefold scriptural account of the power of the Spirit is the foundation for the revelation-rich pneumatology from above captured in the creed as the giver of life, worthy of worship, and the one who has spoken through the prophets.

---

[11] Elizabeth A. Johnson, *Women, Earth, and Creator Spirit* (New York: Paulist Press, 1993), 42.

[12] Ibid.

Indwelling

The Spirit is immanent in the historical and natural world: "where can I go from your Spirit?" (Ps 139:7). The Spirit transcends the universe, embracing the cosmos, bringing all life "within the sphere of the divine." This panentheistic embrace offers one theological explanation for what Gerard Manly Hopkins might call the instress, or inner imprint, of the Spirit, whose inspiration imparts freedom, community, and solidarity. For, as Johnson describes it, the concept of panentheism teaches that "the universe, both matter and spirit, is encompassed by the Matrix of the living God in an encircling that generates freedom, self-transcendence, and the future, all in the context of the interconnected whole. . . . The Spirit's encircling indwelling weaves a genuine solidarity among all creatures and between God and world."[13]

The Spirit is the life-giving and creative breath of God for the human community and the cosmos. Denis Edwards notes that the biblical image of the Spirit breathing life into all creatures belongs to one set of Hebrew Bible texts, alongside others that associate the Spirit with prophecy, kingship, or the renewal of Israel.[14] In both the Hebrew Scriptures and New Testament, the Spirit of God means the divine power active in the world, especially in bringing forth and sustaining life, and empowering the community. The Spirit acts in history, calls out to chosen individuals, and gives salvation to all (Pss 51:12; 143:10). In the Christian Scriptures, the Spirit drives the ministry of Christ and is promised to his followers. The gift of the Spirit at Pentecost constitutes the church community.[15]

The movement of the Spirit summons forth our most imaginative and powerful symbols. Christian feminist theology treasures the founding texts, traditions, and riches of women's experience as it constructs a rich imagining of the reign of God "that Jesus preached and that the Spirit brings forth: a new world and a new way of being in the world that holds a blessing for all life—women, men, and their children, all

---

[13] Ibid., 43.

[14] Denis Edwards, *Breath of Life: A Theology of the Creator Spirit* (Maryknoll, NY: Orbis Books, 2004), 35. An explicit Christian theology of the Spirit was not developed until the Council of Nicaea in 325 established the divinity of the Word, and theologians could turn to consider the Spirit; see page 37.

[15] Michael Schmaus, "Holy Spirit," in *Sacramentum Mundi*, vol. 3, ed. Karl Rahner (New York: Herder and Herder, 1968), 53–59.

races, the poor, and the Earth included."[16] These powerful symbols for the Spirit include a great wind, the lifting breath, the transfiguring fire, Woman Wisdom, the generous hostess, life-giving water, the midwife, the mother hen.

The Spirit moves the faithful to praise and thanksgiving, encourages them to live by imitating Christ, and empowers new life in every form of daily activity. The individual Christian and the church community are temples for the indwelling Spirit.[17] In all these ways the Spirit is the source and flow of living freedom from and through God and the universe.

Renewing

As a continuous creative force, the Spirit is a renewing power pouring forth new vitality on the brokenness of creation. "This divine creative power assumes the shape of a rejuvenating energy that renews the face of the Earth (Ps. 104:30)."[18] Johnson observes that the psalms, the Pentecost hymn *Veni Creator Spiritus*, and the very testimony of Jesus the healer point to the power of the renewing and healing Spirit. "The Spirit of the Lord is upon me, because he has anointed me to bring good news to the poor," reads Jesus from Isaiah (Luke 4:18; Isa 61:1). The hopes of creation and all creatures for renewal is linked to the desire of human creatures for liberation, for the poor seeking the Good News, for the captives waiting to be set free. The nexus of poverty and ecological degradation underscore this link all the more today. The inseparability of the poor, of all humanity, and of the ecosystems of creation is newly affirmed by *Laudato Sì*. "All is connected," teaches Pope Francis:

> The New Testament does not only tell us of the earthly Jesus and his tangible and loving relationship with the world. It also shows him risen and glorious, present throughout creation by his universal Lordship. . . . Thus, the creatures of this world no longer appear to us under merely natural guise because the risen One is mysteriously holding them to himself and directing them towards fullness

---

[16] Johnson, *Women, Earth, and Creator Spirit*, 24.

[17] Schmaus, "Holy Spirit," 55.

[18] Johnson, *Women, Earth, and Creator Spirit*, 43.

as their end. The very flowers of the field and the birds which his human eyes contemplated and admired are now imbued with his radiant presence.[19]

Johnson similarly expresses this beautiful spirituality of resurrection as a revelation of the Spirit, writing that the "resurrection of Jesus from the dead into a new life of glory is but the most surprising revelation of this characteristic of the Creator Spirit," the Giver and Renewer of life.[20]

The Earth and her creatures cry out for renewal as never before in our time of climate change and ecological crises. Neglecting the mystery and power of the Spirit's renewing activity risks despair, for "what is being neglected is nothing less than the mystery of God's personal engagement with the world in its history of love and disaster; nothing less than God's empowering presence active within the cosmos from the beginning, throughout history and to the end, calling forth life and freedom."[21]

Johnson reminds us that our hope for renewal is well founded, for "precisely as the giver of life the creative Spirit cherishes what has been made and renews it in myriad ways."[22] One of these myriad ways God's compassion breaks forth is through the emergence of Earth-conscious care: mending the world, the *tikkun olam* of Jewish environmental theology.[23] This renewing Spirit, the living presence and action of God, inspiring the energy to care for creation, will be discussed later as observed from below.

Moving

The Spirit is never still; Johnson cites Genesis 1:2 and Revelation 21:5 to recall that the Spirit moves in a continuous fruitful dance from the ancient waters of chaos to the end times when all will be made new.

---

[19] Francis, *Laudato Sì* (On Care for Our Common Home), http://w2.vatican .va/content/francesco/en/encyclicals/documents/papa-francesco_20150524 _enciclica-laudato-si.html.

[20] Johnson, *Women, Earth, and Creator Spirit*, 43.

[21] Ibid., 20.

[22] Ibid., 43.

[23] Hava Tirosh-Samuelson, "Nature in the Sources of Judaism," *Daedalus Special Issue: Religion and Ecology: Can the Climate Change?* 130, no. 4 (2001): 99–124.

Through the novel improvisation of evolution, the Spirit enlivens the blooming and buzzing diversity of life.[24] The Earth's tremendous dynamism prompts new insights about the nature of the Spirit. As Johnson writes, "Realization of its energy, diversity, relationality, fecundity, spontaneity, and ever surprising mixture of law and chance makes the times ripe for a rediscovery of the neglected tradition of the Creator Spirit."[25] By enlarging the notion of the *imago Dei* to include all creation, Johnson invites an even larger idea of God. "What must the Creator be like, in whose image this astounding universe is created?" The "astounding universe" is analogically created in the image of the relational, spontaneous, and surprising God. In the ongoing relationality of creativity, the Earth's dynamism is reflected in the energy of green spirituality in human persons, themselves an image of God.

Through the intelligent lure of Wisdom calling to holy souls, the Spirit creates community and justice in her circling spheres of relationship. "Throughout the process, the Spirit characteristically set us bonds of kinship among all creatures, human and non-human alike, all of whom are energized by this one Source."[26] As Roger Haight observes, there are two dimensions of God as Spirit that encourage the religious imagination and empower hope: the Spirit as divine power and as infinite caring love. "The creating Spirit of God readily encourages the religious imagination to conceive God as the inner power of an emergent universe . . . [and the] Spirit that symbolized God's awesome power also signals God's faithful and loving care for each creature."[27] The emergence of Earth-conscious awareness and advocacy is part of that emerging and healing power of the universe. We may reimagine the world—we may be moved to bring into being what we dream, inspired by the Earth-loving Spirit.

A Response to Elizabeth Johnson: Pneumatology from Below

Now I turn to the discussion of the actual experience of the Earth-loving Spirit as described to me by my research participants—the

---

[24] Elizabeth A. Johnson, "Does God Play Dice? Divine Providence and Chance," *Theological Studies* 57, no. 1 (1996): 2–18.

[25] Johnson, *Women, Earth, and Creator Spirit*, 40.

[26] Ibid., 44.

[27] Roger Haight, "Holy Spirit and the Religions," in *The Lord and Giver of Life*, ed. David H. Jensen (Louisville: Westminster John Knox Press, 2008), 61, 67.

pneumatology from below. Language about the transcendent is limited by culture, self-deception, and bias, and interpreted through a filter of symbols and psychological needs.[28] Nonetheless, however difficult it is to make precise claims about experiencing the divine, it is clear that religious experiences of inspiration exist. In my research with religious environmental advocates, I observed a triadic working of the Spirit that is harmonious with the triad dynamic of Spirit described above. At the outset, I note that not all of the participants were Christian, or mono-theistic, nor did they share scriptural language of "Spirit." Much more needs to be said than space will allow about how to discuss "inspiration" when religious language and beliefs about the numinous realities that "inspire" differ. Yet a similar pattern is perceptible in the advocacy of diverse faith-based environmentalists. By observing a parallel triadic dynamic within the human experience of being inspired to care for the Earth, I will suggest a Christian theology of inspiration that heeds the call from the indwelling Spirit. This triadic dynamic reflects the threefold dance of the Spirit with (1) the indwelling of noticing and favoring the Earth; (2) the renewing of love that prioritizes the Earth and brings hope; and (3) the movement in charity and justice to act for the Earth. The triadic dynamic I observed characterizes the work of persons who have already turned to the Earth with attention, love, and committed action, so their naming of the work of the Spirit can and should contribute to Christian weaving of new theological tapestries.

With some trepidation, I conduct this pneumatological investigation in an anthropological key, turning both to the Earth and to the subject. I will devoutly try to look outward, however, "turning to the entire interconnected community of life and the network of life-systems in which the human race is embedded," as Johnson calls us to do, but firmly planted in the conditions of possibility for sensing the movement of the Earth-loving Spirit—as a theologian and a pragmatic empirical researcher.

Three observations about the dynamics of the experience of Earth-oriented inspiration as I have observed them in my research par-ticipants follow. First, the human experience of inspiration to care for the Earth begins with noticing and favoring the Earth. Second, the human experience of the renewing Spirit is the healing of despair and

---

[28] Edwards, *Breath of Life*, 52.

the reordering of our concerns, giving the Earth greater priority. Third, the human experience of the moving Spirit is feeling oneself moved to action and advocacy, with the freedom to choose a new way of living.

Noticing: The Indwelling Inspiration which Embraces God's Favor for the Earth

Noticing is the condition of possibility for effective inspiration, and holy noticing is itself the gift of the Spirit. The Spirit is calling us to notice creation and our communion with all life. Inspired attention to the planet gives the Earth new beauty, new significance in our eyes. Noticing something is especially spiritual when the beauty of a thing summons awareness of the presence of God. "An everyday reality can seem to become transparent to the light of the Spirit shining through it. A person can . . . gaze at the stars on a moonless night, and can find in the experience a sense of wonder, mystery, and gracious presence."[29]

The gift of noticing forms a blessed unity between creation and the human observer, herself part of creation. Kathy, a leader in a Catholic parish, had a gift for noticing beauty as a child, which both led her to God and inspired one of the longest careers in faith-based environmental advocacy of anyone I met.[30] She had been at it since at least 1991.

The power of Kathy's love for nature, born from noticing things within a small city park, never fails to move me profoundly.

> *Kathy (Catholic): I grew up in an apartment house in the city, but there was a park across the street, a couple blocks long. I spent a lot of time there. I also wasn't really raised a Catholic. I wasn't really raised in any religion. So I had a lot of communing with God through nature long before any of this advocacy happened.*

---

[29] Ibid., 54.

[30] I emphasize that my research engaged persons from thirteen Christian communities and nine other-than-Christian groups, ranging from Jewish to Jain to Navajo to Islamic. In this essay I focus on Christian theology of the Spirit and grace drawn from the common Abrahamic texts. Yet the universality of the experience of being inspired, however conceived, accompanies the universal call to "notice," reminding one of contemplative practice in all traditions: Buddhist mindfulness, Ignatian "situating in time and place," and Bernard Lonergan's first epistemological imperative, "to be attentive."

Regarding such ecological awareness, Jay McDaniel retrieves the teaching of the seventeenth-century mystic Brother Lawrence, who calls us to "practice the presence of God."[31] Becoming open to this kind of spirituality occurs through "the help of the universe": friends and strangers, plants and animals, spirits and ancestors, rivers and stars. The practice of noticing all these fellow creatures to whom we are kin increases our awareness of the "presence of God," who is the Creator of all.

This kind of noticing becomes a special means of communion with the divine when the Spirit moves the soul to see nature with God's love for creation. God's love for creation is among the very first messages of Genesis: creation is very good. Humanity's affirmation of nature's worth is expressed in our loving attention to it, thus reflects God's gracious affirmation of humanity and creation. Instead of a passing glance at the world that turns right back to the paper or the iPad or the project, simply "looking" becomes a holy noticing that takes on God's favor for the Earth. Thus I suggest that the "nature" of holy noticing is that form of inspiration, of God's indwelling love, that was expressed by the Hebrews as *hen*. *Hen* is a scriptural term for God's benevolent glance on humanity and creation that means "finding favor in God's eyes."[32] For example, "Noah found favor in the sight of the Lord" (Gen 6:8). *Hen* and *hesed*, which denotes loving-kindness and mercy, are both translated as *charis* (grace) in the Greek Septuagint. I would like to consider *hen* here first and return to *hesed* below.

The link between the terms *hen* and *charis* (grace) spills over into an association with the Spirit. This is a complex relationship, but it follows from the scriptural links that James Dunn notes between Spirit and the Christian theological concept of grace. Dunn writes, "Like 'Spirit,' with which [grace] overlaps in meaning (cf., e.g., [Rom] 6:14 and Gal 5:18), it [grace] denotes effective divine power in the experience of men."[33]

Thus, in a view of inspiration from below, human attention to creation parallels divine attention, and we can speak of the Earth finding favor anew in our eyes. In other words, inspired noticing is the human experience of *hen*—and it is a response to the gift of grace. Here I

[31] Jay B. McDaniel, *Living from the Center: Spirituality in an Age of Consumerism* (St. Louis, MO: Chalice Press, 2000), 12.

[32] William L. Reed, "Some Implications of Ḥēn for Old Testament Religion," *Journal of Biblical Literature* 73, no. 1 (March 1954): 36.

[33] James D. G. Dunn, *Romans 1–8* (Dallas: Word Books, 1988), 17.

invoke a classic interpretation of grace as the inner working of the Spirit that is the prior gift, the first mover of the heart, from the God we love because God first loved us. As Karl Rahner emphasizes, God is immediately present to the subject through the prior offer of God's free self-communication.[34]

Furthermore, we notice what should not be, and yet what tragically is: the desecration of our common home, the negative contrast of ecological devastation. Inspiration leads people to notice the transcendent beauty of the Earth and to see ever more clearly its tragic devastation.[35] Paul, an Evangelical Christian in my study, connected this perceptive insight directly to the Spirit (and to Jesus the Word of God):

> Paul: I think we can depend on God and be led by his Spirit and his Word. I think that people can look at a beautiful sunset and know that's good, and they can look at a polluted lake and know that's bad. It doesn't take a rocket scientist to figure that out. I think if we're led by God's Spirit and by his Word we'll go in the right direction.

A pneumatology from below that attends to the indwelling of the Earth-loving Spirit thus implies a theology of attention that fruitfully reclaims the ancient meaning of *hen*. Favorable attention is not passive looking and admiring, however. Twentieth-century theology restores a sense of the eventful, personalist nature of grace, the self-communication of God active and effective in human experience. The grace of the person inspired to show favor to the Earth, then, is energized by the Spirit to turn his attention to favor the Earth actively—to love and value our common home, to mourn its devastating losses.

A theology of attention shifts the responsibility for the gracious observation of nature onto humankind. It is not just God but we who must look intently at the Earth. We too must see that it is very good and re-view how intently we are acting to sustain its goodness. We must look at what is bad and work to restore it. The Eastern Orthodox liturgy confirms this sign, insisting over and over, "Let us attend!" To

---

[34] God's self-communication is first of all the "gratuitous miracle of God's free love. . . . The spiritual creature is constituted to begin with as the possible addressee of such a divine self communication" (Rahner, *Foundations*, 122–23).

[35] I have more fully described the characteristics of "green spirituality," including freedom, a strong sense of interdependence, and social justice, in "Worldviews on Fire," 495–511.

see attention as part of the doctrine of grace highlights our vocation to look graciously on the Earth.

Being Renewed for Love of the Earth

Many of my research participants experienced a shift in priorities that favored the Earth, as well as energy that was sustained by virtue, if not always by hope. They (along with many others in society) feel overwhelmed and depressed by the magnitude of climate change. Having communed with God in nature, they experienced the diminishment of creation's beauty as a spiritual loss and shared their grief for the near impossibility of extricating themselves from moral enmeshment in society's destructive systems. Charlie, a highly effective Presbyterian leader, stated, *"I'm suffering from mass depression sometimes, thinking that what I do is going to touch somebody negatively, and that upsets me."*

Religious values motivated Charlie and others to keep working despite a sense that "the system" and the tides of time were against them. Jim is a Unitarian leader who said, *"It doesn't matter to me whether I am optimistic or pessimistic—my values are robust enough so that it's important to keep working even though actually I'm very pessimistic about the overall situation."*

Not all have Jim's grim fortitude. Environmental decision theorists emphasize that exceeding one's "finite pool of worry" threatens most people's ability to continue with environmental advocacy.[36] Being overwhelmed is a serious damper to environmentalist energy, and consumerism can stifle any faint signs of environmentalist concern in the first place. Johnson has critically analyzed consumerism as a worldwide religion that promotes overconsumption and a constant orientation toward producing, purchasing, achieving, improving one's social appearances and seeking greater affluence.[37] Economically, consumerism is a threat to the Earth that absorbs outsized amounts of time, attention, and money.

---

[36] Elke Weber, "Doing the Right Thing Willingly: Behavioral Decision Theory and Environmental Policy," in *The Behavioral Foundations of Policy*, ed. E. Shafir (Princeton, NJ: Princeton University Press, 2007).

[37] Elizabeth A. Johnson, "'And God Saw That It Was Good': Why Religion's Resources for Ecological Ethics Are Not More Effective," in *Moral Heat: Ethical Dimensions of Environmental Regulation and Economics in the 21st Century* (New York: Fordham University Press, 2010).

Spiritually, consumerism constricts our openness to the presence of God by compelling our attention to things that are not of God.

Yet the Spirit as a renewing power may rekindle the energy and the focus to care for the Earth against the competing priorities and distractions of consumerism. How exactly does the Spirit renew love of Earth against what some described as the "onslaught" of consumerism? Precise dynamics are hard to pin down in this limited space, but naming the onslaught of consumerism as a threat fuels the power to resist it. Anger fuels a refining fire that intensifies one's care for the Earth and lets trivial pursuits fall away. This prioritization is part of an unfolding relationship between the person and the world she notices, empowering a sacrifice of lesser priorities to advocate for the Earth.[38] As Johnson writes, "Every act of resistance to the history of radical suffering is fueled by the inexhaustible source of new being."[39]

Healthy energy spills forth from the anger of frustration and despair as well as from joy and peace. As Nancy Victorin-Vangerud notes, the Spirit may bring forth fruits from that anger to fuel resistance—the gifts of "self-determination, risk, resistance, willfulness, defiance, courage, confrontation, conflict, and voice."[40] But courage only endures so long; hope must be renewed to console the stalwart and energize the more fainthearted. The Spirit lifts up persons who struggle with too many concerns in the "finite pool of worry," overwhelmed by the magnitude of the crisis, and over the gaps, healing the blues. Hope is renewed by recalling the ongoing and future-directed providence of God against the weight of pessimism. As Pope Francis has said, hope is not the same as optimism, which is a psychological attitude. But hope is of God. Invoking an ancient Christian image of the anchor connecting the believer to the distant shore of anticipated salvation, Francis preaches that hope "carries us onwards," like an anchor pulling toward the future.[41]

---

[38] I discuss this further in my forthcoming book, *Inspired Sustainability*.

[39] Johnson, "Turn to the Heavens and the Earth," 13.

[40] Nancy M. Victorin-Vangerud, *The Raging Hearth: Spirit in the Household of God* (St. Louis, MO: Chalice Press, 2000), 202.

[41] Address of the Holy Father during a pastoral visit to Cagliari, Meeting with the Workers, September 22, 2013; http://w2.vatican.va/content/francesco/en/speeches /2013/september/documents/papa-francesco_20130922_lavoratori-cagliari.pdf; Francis Rocca, "Pope Says Hope Is Not Mere Optimism But a Link to Eternal Life," *The Catholic Spirit* (October 29, 2013), http://thecatholicspirit.com/news

Shonto, a Navajo artist and activist, likewise looked to future generations to call forth the hope that would sustain his care for the Earth.

> *Shonto: I have to be hopeful. It would be hard to be gloomy and seeing everything just hopeless. Then you affect your own environmental spirituality, and introduce hopelessness into that. That's not good. So always be hopeful. The Native people, when we talk about saving the Earth or saving the land or saving a grove of trees, it's always not for us, it's always seven generations from now. That's how we keep the hope.*

Being Moved to the Freedom of New Actions for Justice

The inspiration for Earth care that I have observed is liberating in at least two senses: it empowers the freedom of a new life, and it seeks justice that liberates the Earth's living communities from oppression. These are two of the characteristics emphasized by liberation theologian José Comblin, who also characterizes the experience of the Holy Spirit as an experience of action, of freedom, of the word, of community, and of life.[42] Conceiving inspiration as "being moved" is an essential third dynamic because it is all too clear that even the ecologically conscious subject may still not be moved to action, still not yet vigorously inspired to do . . . something. But those who are inspired by the Spirit of Creation to adopt actively her loving concern for the Earth, those effectively "converted to the heavens and the Earth," seize the moment to act, quickening the pulse of a global movement.[43]

Being moved by the Spirit to environmental action is an experience of freedom. Spurred on by what they see (noticing and finding favor) and caring (renewed priorities), faith-based environmentalists find the freedom to change old habits. Theologian Wendy Farley puts it this way:

/nation-and-world/from-the-pope/pope-says-hope-mere-optimism-link-eternal
-life/.

[42] José Comblin, "The Holy Spirit," in *Mysterium Liberationis: Fundamental Concepts of Liberation Theology*, ed. Ignacio Ellacuría and Jon Sobrino (Maryknoll, NY: Orbis Books, 1993).

[43] For a discussion of the worldwide environmental movement as the Earth's own "immune response," see Paul Hawken, *Blessed Unrest: How the Largest Movement in the World Came into Being and Why No One Saw It Coming* (New York: Viking Press, 2007).

her relationship with the "blessed Trinity compels [her] to seek that beauty and power in all of the cosmos and in every religious tradition."[44] As she ponders "the interior dynamics of bondage and liberation," the human experience of obstacles to realizing our visions, these common human realities "will help remind us that there is only one freedom and one command and they are the same: to know ourselves beloved of God and to allow that love to flow within and through us toward all the world." Thus the human experience of the moving Spirit is feeling oneself being moved. It is the freedom of choosing a new way of living.

Choosing new lifestyles is not easy, and from within our consumerist culture the price of conversion can seem quite high. Earth advocates must accept the potential of conflict and recognize the sociopolitical dimensions of the crisis.[45] Conversion to the Earth not only invites revisions to prayer and theology but also challenges daily priorities and actions, investment decisions, and institutional economic and power structures.

Grappling with these challenges, the research participants wanted to understand what worked most effectively to move others to create new habits and build sustainable communities. As one Catholic leader, Marie, lamented, *"The one thing we lack is an ability to be able to make an analysis of what's happening in people's lives or thinking."* Understanding the Spirit's work as empowering freedom is key—it is a power that makes possible radically new action on behalf of the Earth. The Spirit empowers people to freely respond to what Karl Rahner calls the self-communication of God as Spirit.[46] Similarly, Edward Schillebeeckx speaks of a distinctive category for an experience of grace that is "being redeemed for community . . . freedom for self-surrender in love for fellow men [*sic*]; that is abiding in God. Ethics, and above all love of one's neighbor, is the public manifestation of the state of being redeemed."[47] Freedom empowers "love in deed," that justice-seeking aspect of inspiration as "being moved": love for the neighbor throughout the world, the neighbor impacted by climate change and all the living neighbors, flora and fauna, of each threatened ecosystem.

---

[44] Wendy Farley, *The Wounding and Healing of Desire: Weaving Heaven and Earth* (Louisville: Westminster John Knox Press, 2005), xix.

[45] Edwards, *Breath of Life*, 160.

[46] Haight, "Holy Spirit and the Religions," 63, 64.

[47] Edward Schillebeeckx, *Christ: The Experience of Jesus as Lord*, trans. John Bowden (New York: Crossroad, 1981), 495.

A compassionate commitment to social justice born of love of neighbor is the fundamental motivation for Earth advocacy.[48] The Spirit pours out this love in human hearts, enabling people to hear the cry of the Earth and be moved to action that seeks justice. This invites attention to the biblical understanding of *hesed*. The indwelling movements of compassion links *hen* with *hesed*, noticing and favorable affirmation with compassionate action. All of these flow into the experience named by the Christian Scriptures as grace, which is fulfilled in love of neighbor. As James Dunn observes, *charis* combines the sense of both *hesed* and *hen*, and denotes the active, experienced, and effective experience of God's love: "In Paul . . . χαρις [*charis*] is never merely an attitude or disposition of God (God's character as gracious); consistently it denotes something much more dynamic—the wholly generous *act* of God."[49] For Klaus Berger, *charis* refers to the whole gift of salvation offered by God in Christ: the freely offered relationship between humanity and God. "Hence, in contrast to our notion of grace, *hesed* may be attributed to both partners in the relationship between man and Yahweh."[50] Thus the relational experience of compassion, or *hesed*, is a vocation for the believer as well as the generous act of God, a lived response to inspiration: a sign of pneumatology from below. *Charis* is "relationship to another in loving compassion . . . set up by God's mercy in the salvation which came in Jesus Christ."[51] Today that loving compassion requires justice and healing for the Earth.

In sum, the ancient experiences of divine *hesed* and *hen* express the active quest for justice inspired by the indwelling, renewing Spirit of creation who moves in human hearts. Through loving awareness that looks favorably on the Earth, persons are moved by the Spirit to offer creation God's own gracious benevolence and establish their own covenant of justice with the Earth community.

Conclusion: Cosmic Community—Relationality and Justice

Johnson writes, "Regarding humanity's connection to the Earth, women's wisdom suggests that the relation is not one of 'over against'

---

[48] Lothes, "Worldviews on Fire."

[49] Dunn, *Romans 1–8*, 17.

[50] Klaus Berger, "Grace: Biblical," in *Sacramentum Mundi*, vol. 2, ed. Karl Rahner (New York: Herder and Herder, 1968), 409–10.

[51] Ibid., 411.

and 'superior to' but 'together with,' moving in an interactive circle of mutual kinship."[52] Having traced three dynamics within the human experience of being inspired to care for the Earth—the indwelling of noticing and favoring the Earth, the renewing of love to prioritize the Earth, and the movement to act for justice for the Earth—let us trace the circles of relationality that bind this love together.

First, the Spirit empowers mutual kinship by guiding the community. *"You know in the United States, we've become such individualists we forget about the community. And the church's blessing of the Holy Spirit was sent upon on the community, not the individual,"* said Jack, an Episcopal priest from North Carolina. Jack reminded his groups that inspiration itself has a communal aim and purpose. Jack added, *"For me, the environment has had a growing sense of urgency. And that if I look at it from a theological standpoint, the main thing Christians today of all denominations really need to refocus on is our need to be stewards of creation."* While theological reflection at times correlates spirituality with individual experiences, in Pauline theology the gifts of the Spirit do originate in the community, to build up the community (1 Cor 12:7, 26). Inspiration is thus given and fulfilled in action that renews the community.

That new urgent focus on the Earth of which Jack speaks is borne by today's greater awareness of the needs of the global community. Here is a second relational dimension of inspiration: the Spirit empowers awareness of global community and kinship. This global community is widely recognized by faith-based environmentalists. Dr. Hunter, a leading Evangelical environmentalist, and pastor of a Florida megachurch, shared his own interpretation of the movement of the Spirit as a rapid revolution in global awareness. With his gift for metaphor, he compared the inspiration of religious environmentalists to a computer "reboot." And as a scientifically informed evangelist, he compared sustained inspiration to evolutionary periods of punctuated equilibrium.

> *Dr. Hunter: I think that God has different times in the world where he remakes the world. He reboots us, so to speak, and you could see that in Scripture. The flood was a reboot, you know, the destruction of Jerusalem was a rebooting. Even in evolutionary biology, they have the phrase called punctuated equilibrium, where you don't just [see*

---

[52] Johnson, *Women, Earth, and Creator Spirit*, 28.

steady development; the Earth's changes] just kind of go boom, boom, boom. I think what's happening right now is that we have reached a turning point in many ways in our world, the communications revolution has put us together so that we're now more in touch with what is happening in the rest of the world.

Dr. Hunter points to the communications revolution which spurs global awareness of the Earth's crises, enabling worldwide "noticing" that inspires a turn to the heavens and the Earth. Granting attention to the Earth is an aspect of self-transcendence, an emerging awareness of the Earth's true situation. Self-transcendence includes the intellectual and moral capacity to transcend an initially limited perspective, through the freedom to attend to challenging realities about the environment. This freedom may be seen as a phenomenon of emergence, which Karl Rahner interprets as the evolution of greater complexity from the capacity for self-transcendence that is given to creation.[53]

Carol from the Towson Presbyterian Church agreed that ours is a globally conscious generation. *"The world around us is changing and becoming more aware."* In this changing world, greater awareness of the reality of the Earth's history and current crisis sparks a spiritual Copernican revolution. If early modern astronomy displaced the Earth from its pious place at the center of the universe, the Earth is again becoming central to the vocation of persons from many religious traditions. This new cosmology both decenters humanity within an ancient, vast, evolving universe and highlights humanity's unique role as cantors of the universe able to celebrate and renew the Earth in this unprecedented time of crisis.[54]

Third, scriptural promises ground the hope that mutual kinship will be fulfilled in cosmic salvation. Johnson frequently emphasizes the consoling and profound teaching that the "glory of God is the human person, fully alive." The hope for cosmic salvation is deeply rooted in scriptural visions of the redemption of the whole creation. Edward Schillebeeckx confirms that "the believer's concern for God's honor is also a struggle for more justice in the world, a commitment to a new

---

[53] Edwards, *Breath of Life*, 46.

[54] Mary Evelyn Tucker, "Worldly Wonder: Religions Enter Their Ecological Phase," *Religion East & West: Journal of the Institute for World Religions* 2 (2002): 1–31.

Earth and an environment in which human beings can live fuller lives. Christian salvation is not simply the salvation of souls but the healing, making whole, wholeness, of the whole person, the individual and society, in a natural world which is not abused."[55]

A young evangelical leader, Sarah, spoke of that hoped-for renewal as already underway:

> *Sarah (Evangelical): I think the end of the story is a new heaven and a new Earth. The Shalom that is talked about in the Old Testament and that Christ calls us to, being at peace with our brothers and sisters. And I think it's happening now. It's not just in the future but we are really called to be a part of that process.*

Thousands of faith-based environmental leaders worldwide have been living out the conversion to the Earth that Elizabeth Johnson calls theology to take, and they have consciously engaged the power of spirituality to empower creative and lasting commitments to the Earth.[56] What I hope to suggest for a pneumatology from below, from observing their experience of being inspired to care for the Earth in an intensifying, accelerating movement of concern and action, is that the Spirit is revealing her intensifying presence and accelerating renewal of the creation she indwells, in our time when creation is indeed groaning for profound renewal.

What have I learned from Beth's warm and deep wisdom? That in God is a Spirit that is intelligent, holy, unique, manifold, subtle, mobile, clear, unpolluted, distinct, invulnerable, loving the good, keen, irresistible (Wis 7:22), far above our ways, but intimately present, and lovingly indwelling. Though the divine holy mystery transcends all our names, yet She Who Is bends over the world with great compassion, yearning

---

[55] Edward Schillebeeckx, "I Believe in God, Creator of Heaven and Earth," in *God among Us: The Gospel Proclaimed* (New York: Crossroad, 1983), 100.

[56] See the websites of OurVoices (http://ourvoices.net/), Interfaith Power and Light (http://www.interfaithpowerandlight.org/), Religions for the Earth (http://unionforum.org/religions-for-the-Earth/), Alliance of Religion and Conservation (http://www.arcworld.org/), GreenFaith (http://www.greenfaith.org/), Yale Forum on Religion and Ecology (http://fore.yale.edu/), Catholic Youth Network for Sustainability in Africa (http://cynesafrica.webs.com/), and the Global Catholic Movement (http://catholicclimatemovement.global/), to name only a few.

for her beloved children, all creatures, the pebble and the peach and the poodle and the person. That God's compassion embraces each beloved in and through their experience, even and especially their suffering, for that belongs to the horizon of their being and the condition of the possibility for experiencing the inspiration of the Spirit of God. And the expanding horizon of our collective being, our ecological, cosmological being, is a circle of relationships, an outward expanding ring of music, whose cantors sing of the relationality of all things, called to be in harmony with God.

Chapter 13

Evolution, Evil, and Christian Ethics

Lisa Sowle Cahill

Elizabeth Johnson's gifts as a theologian are abundant and distinctive. She breaks new and fertile ground in Christology, trinitarian theology, feminist theology, interreligious theology, and now a theology of God's beautiful and bruised creation, the planet Earth. A reader can count on the fact that, behind soaring prose and inspirational visions, there is a theological infrastructure that has been very carefully conceived and constructed. Key for me as a Christian social ethicist, Johnson unfailingly links Christian identity to the suffering and flourishing of all beings, affirming justice analysis and advocacy for change in both church and world.

Among Johnson's writings, the book that has most influenced my thought and sense of the divine is *She Who Is: The Mystery of God in Feminist Theological Discourse*. Like *Ask the Beasts*, this work begins with a concrete injustice: the violence suffered by women across all eras and cultures and the complicity if not direct engagement in this violence by the Christian churches and their theologies. As the earlier book repeatedly declares, "the symbol of God functions."[1] The way we

[1] Elizabeth A. Johnson, *She Who Is: The Mystery of God in Feminist Theological Discourse* (New York: Crossroad, 1994), 5, 36.

talk about God shapes the way we envision God and humanity's relation to God and one another. Exclusively masculine God-language partakes in a worldview in which men are more God-like than women, while women are lesser creatures, whose human dignity can be questioned. In *She Who Is*, Johnson proposes the symbol of God as *Sophia* to reenvision the Trinity and to speak about the mystery of God in a way that is both faithful to the authentic traditions of Christian faith and "will serve the emancipatory praxis of women and men, to the benefit of all creation, both human beings and the earth."[2] *Ask the Beasts* serves that same "emancipatory praxis," turning the focus from the plight of women to that of the earth itself and its myriad species, whose extinction human behavior has accelerated at an unprecedented rate. It is the accompanying theological infrastructure of *Ask the Beasts*, particularly the relevance of its account of natural evil to Christian ethics, that will be my focus here.

The primary challenge of the science of Darwinian evolution to contemporary Christian theology is not that it opposes a literal, historical interpretation of Genesis. Mainstream Christian churches and theologians accept critical biblical studies and do not regard it as the purpose of Scripture to present a historical record of every event its narratives contain, including creation.[3] The problem is not evolution as such but that evolution takes place on the basis of contingency and randomness, and that evolution entails suffering and death, most troublesome for sentient beings, as species and their individual members are replaced. Johnson avoids calling pain, suffering, and death "evil," presumably because to do so would seem to prejudge the question whether they are justified. While agreeing that the justification of natural evils as compatible with the Christian view of God is precisely the problem to be addressed, I will term the pain, suffering, and death of sentient creatures natural evils, relying on the definition Marilyn McCord Adams provides in analyzing "the problem of evil." "In this context, 'evil' is given the widest possible scope to signify all of life's minuses. Within this range, philosophers and theologians distinguish 'moral evils' such as

---

[2] Ibid., 8.

[3] In 1950, Pius XII affirmed that science and the theory of evolution are not opposed to faith and the theology of creation. See *Humanae Generis*, no. 36 (http://w2.vatican.va/content/pius-xii/en/encyclicals/documents/hf_p-xii_enc_12081950_humani-generis.html).

war, betrayal and cruelty from 'natural evils' such as earthquakes, floods and disease. Usually the inescapability of death is numbered among the greatest natural evils."[4]

Adams explains further that the "problem" of evil arises from the conjunction of five claims in Christian theism: God is omnipotent, omniscient, and perfectly good; evil exists; a good being would eliminate evil as far as it could; an omniscient being would know all about evils; and there are no limits to what an omnipotent being can do. Only four of these claims can be maintained simultaneously; to hold four entails the denial of the fifth.[5] This explanation of the problem of evil translates easily into the terms of Christianity's engagement with evolutionary science.

How could a completely good and all-powerful Creator make a world that operates on the principle of "the survival of the fittest," requiring competition, predation, death, and dominance? The modern science of evolution confronts us anew with some age-old questions. If there is only one just and omnipotent God, who has created the entire universe, where does evil come from? Why does God allow it to exist? Since it does exist, does that either undermine monotheism, or undermine faith in the goodness and power of God?

Johnson disavows that her project is a "theodicy,"[6] which she does not define, but which may be understood as "an attempt to give a morally sufficient reason for God's allowing evil to exist."[7] Johnson grapples with natural evil by bringing Darwin into conversation with a theology of "continuing creation." God is a dynamic, active presence within creation that "undergirds, enfolds, and bears up all evolutionary process."[8] Nevertheless, the natural world has "its own operational autonomy," since the Spirit of God sustains creatures "in, with, and under their own naturalness."[9] "In its free working evolution brought forth the

---

[4] Marilyn McCord Adams, "Evil, Problem of," *Routledge Encyclopedia of Philosophy* (1998), https://www.rep.routledge.com/articles/evil-problem-of/v-1/.

[5] Ibid.

[6] Elizabeth A. Johnson, *Ask the Beasts: Darwin and the God of Life* (London: Bloomsbury, 2014), 187.

[7] Eleonore Stump and Mike Rea, "Religion, Philosophy of," *Routledge Encyclopedia of Philosophy* (2015), https://www.rep.routledge.com/articles/religion-philosophy-of/v-2/philosophy-and-belief-in-god.

[8] Johnson, *Ask the Beasts*, 123.

[9] Ibid., 124.

kind of life that always entails death and, in its later development, pain and suffering." This renders life on earth "tragic in some dimension," yet suffering is a result of creation's contingent development, not "the eternal will of a good and gracious God."[10]

Suffering and death are too great an enigma to bring under the control of theological logic; yet humans must relieve "unwarranted" suffering where possible. This ethical mandate, however, does not remove the biological fact that pain, suffering, and death are "irreplaceable" in "the emergence of complex and beautiful life forms."[11] Death is essential to "the creative process on this planet," a process of which "the creating Giver of Life has to be part."[12] Yet, although the emergence of new forms requires "the suffering and death of billions of creatures," God also draws the world toward a "redeemed end-time," when all creation will be transformed "in an unimaginable way in new communion with divine life."[13]

To craft a theological response to the reality of natural suffering as required by the de facto conditions of life on this planet, Johnson invokes a theology of continuing creation and a theology of continuing redemption, which includes "deep incarnation"[14] and "deep resurrection."[15] The compassion of God is present within "the shocking enormity of pain and death. The indwelling, empowering Creator Spirit abides amid the agony and loss,"[16] in a transformative way. Johnson is receptive to the hypothesis of Christopher Southgate that God's personal presence even alleviates creaturely agony in the moment of death (an idea perhaps belied by Jesus' cry of forsakenness on the cross).[17]

In summary, I understand Johnson to be making four claims about God, suffering, and ethics: (1) The presence of pain, death, and suffering in this world is ultimately an enigma and a tragedy.[18] (2) God

---

[10] Ibid., 191.

[11] Ibid., 188.

[12] Ibid., 189.

[13] Ibid., 123–24.

[14] Ibid., 196. The phrase is borrowed from Niels Gregerson and signifies that the embodiment of the Word or Wisdom as "flesh" encompasses all material reality.

[15] Ibid., 208. The phrase captures the insight of John Wesley, Denis Edwards, and others, that all creation is redeemed in Christ and resurrected in the Spirit.

[16] Ibid., 191.

[17] Ibid., 206.

[18] Ibid., 187, 191.

empowers and sustains nature and its evolutionary processes as free and autonomous, and evolution requires suffering.[19] (3) God is in solidarity with all suffering creatures, sustaining, incarnate in, and resurrecting each and all, as Creator, Redeemer, and Spirit.[20] (4) For humans, there is a "moral imperative" to "promote life's flourishing" as "an expression of love of neighbor deeply intertwined with love of God."[21]

Johnson's rendition of God's creative, compassionate, healing, and resurrecting presence to and in creation is eloquent and compelling. Yet I am left with doubts and questions about the relation of God to natural evil that her vision of creation entails, and particularly about the mandate for human action that it might imply. My concerns focus on the second claim. If natural "agony" is truly an enigma (first claim), then it cannot be explained theologically by saying that it is necessary to God's continuing creation of the world. If God is in healing solidarity with suffering (third claim), then it seems contradictory to hold that God is at the same time sustaining the suffering that occurs in nature (natural evil), even indirectly, or through "secondary causality." Finally, if the Christian moral life revolves around the revelation of God's love in Jesus Christ (fourth claim), then to say that God's creative action is behind "natural" suffering either undermines the ultimate coherence of nature and grace, or suggests that life in imitation of God can include violence equally with love.

In an essay on evil and political theology, William Desmond offers four models of theodicy that usefully further reflection on these problems.[22] One is "free-will theodicy," in which God's granting of freedom to creatures must involve the power to revolt against good. In my view, a general liability of such theories is that they fail to explain why creatures in unity with God by the grace of "original righteousness"[23] would choose to turn in another direction, since they already see, recognize,

---

[19] Ibid., 188.

[20] Ibid., 191–92.

[21] Ibid., 187–88.

[22] William Desmond, "On Evil and Political Theology," *Political Theology* 16, no. 2 (2015): 93–100.

[23] The grace by which humans are said to have enjoyed, before the Fall, "original righteousness" or "original justice" establishes the unity of creatures, especially humans, with God as their natural good or end. It may be distinguished from supernatural grace, the grace of redemption, or the beatific vision. See the *Catechism of*

and enjoy the one supreme good. To propose that they do seems to assume that there is another source of attraction that is opposed to the divine goodness. This, then, is incompatible with the idea that there is one Creator responsible for all that exists. Alternatively, if there is one Creator, then that Creator must have established factors in creation that could distract humans and other creatures from their original unity or harmony with God. Yet this premise is incompatible with the idea that God is all-good.

Johnson's explication of natural evil reflects "free will" theodicy insofar as she attributes the suffering caused by evolution to the freedom, autonomy, and contingency of the process itself, enabled by the creative power of God. It thus encounters the difficulties outlined. Moreover, when the rubric of "freedom" is applied to the natural world, the anthropomorphism involved makes the coherence of this model even more tenuous. Evolution as a whole is not a willful agent; the emergence, adaption, and demise of species is dependent on contingent and random features of environments and their inhabitants. In sum, God's beneficent and graceful presence within creation—immanent, continuously creating, and even continuously redeeming—sits uneasily with the idea that, notwithstanding God's intimate and all-pervasive presence, nature is at its heart an "evolutionary" display of competition, violence, and death.

A second model is what Desmond calls "virtue theodicy." Applied to human suffering, it explains evil as a school of virtue or "soul-making." Evil is a means to something greater. This model too has much in common with Johnson's view that the suffering entailed by evolution leads to the emergence of more rich and beautiful life-forms. The problems with this model are that it portrays God as causing natural evil, instrumentalizes innocent suffering, and avoids the fact (not avoided in *She Who Is*[24]) that some suffering is simply destructive, annihilating the victim without leading to any greater good.

A third model is termed "aesthetic theodicy," referring to the idea that the suffering of some is part of the beauty of a greater whole. This too closely resembles Johnson's explanation of natural evil as nec-

---

the Catholic Church, pars. 374–84, http://www.vatican.va/archive/ccc_css/archive/catechism/p1s2c1p6.htm.

[24] Johnson, *She Who Is*, 261.

essary to the entire evolutionary process producing ever-richer forms. Within this model may be differentiated two versions, one in which lesser creatures are sacrificed in a hierarchy of life, with humans at the top.[25] In Calvin's rather more scary version, God has a "double will."[26] God mysteriously wills realities that are repugnant to a human sense of justice, such as the predestination of some to damnation from the moment of their creation. How this fits into the beauty of the whole is not for us to know. Scripture reveals only what is "conducive to our interest and welfare," namely, the mercy of God shown to the elect through Christ the Mediator. "Secrets" such as predestination remain concealed in God's "eternal wisdom."[27] Johnson's vision resembles this model, insofar as the Creator "enigmatically" empowers suffering, while the Redeemer opposes and heals it. (Johnson's position is different in that she does not see God as causing suffering to some creatures while redeeming others; she sees God as both enabling the evolutionary suffering of all living things and redeeming all.)

If God empowers, enables, and sustains the evolution of violence and destruction, and at the same time is in healing solidarity with the suffering caused by this very destruction, doesn't that put God as Creator and God as Redeemer in an oppositional relationship?[28] Or does it lead to the logical conclusion framed by the Reformed theologian James Gustafson—God is not in fact in "solidarity with" every individual sufferer? For Gustafson, God is "the ultimate power that has brought worlds into being, sustains them, *bears down upon them*, and determines their ultimate destiny."[29] He adds, "To assure people that the reason that bad things happen to good people is because there is chance in the

[25] Thomas Aquinas, *Summa Theologiae*, II-II, 64, "Of Murder," a.1, "Whether It Is Lawful to Kill Any Living Thing?"

[26] John Calvin, *Institutes of the Christian Religion* 3.21.5, 3.22.10-11, vol. 2, trans. Henry Beveridge (Grand Rapids, MI: Eerdmans, 1962), 206, 223–24. For further discussion in relation to theodicy, see John E. Thiel, *God, Evil, and Innocent Suffering: A Theological Reflection* (New York: Crossroad, 2002), 92–93.

[27] Ibid., 3.21.1, 204.

[28] God "creates and empowers the evolutionary world" but also is in solidarity with those who suffer the dire consequences of God's own action, entering "into the nothingness of death, to transform it from within" (Johnson, *Ask the Beasts*, 192).

[29] James M. Gustafson, *Ethics from a Theocentric Perspective*, vol. 2: *Ethics and Theology* (Chicago: University of Chicago Press, 1984), 320. Italics added.

world, and in the next breath to assure them once again that God is ultimately concerned for their own individual well-being, or is 'just,' strikes me as an incongruity."[30]

A fourth model is evil as privation of the good, a theodicy going back to Augustine. This model overlaps with the free will model, as its second step. When free creatures turn away from God, they defect from the good, but there is no reality of evil that is the specific cause of the resulting privation. Desmond comments perceptively that the idea that evil is simply a "falling away" from the good underestimates the power and attraction of evil itself: we "do not see the reversed energy of nihilation involved in privation."[31] This observation takes us back to the question whether there is some power of evil that exists outside divine goodness, creativity, and uniting love.

Desmond's "nihilation" twist on the privation model does not resemble Johnson's theology of natural evil, but it might be worth further consideration. I would not endorse an explanation of evil that involves an evil person or power that coexists with God and is equally powerful, or that denies monotheism, or the divine attributes as traditionally understood in Christian theology. Rather, I suggest that this philosophically indebted Western framework be provisionally set aside, in favor of an imaginative engagement with some "unorthodox" biblical allusions. In ways that are both puzzling and provocative, biblical narratives portray evil in terms of agents and structures whose existence is not clearly due either to divine intention or human freedom, entities that confront and challenge God but are ultimately defeated. This possibility will be addressed further under the rubric of "the biblical imagination."

As far as theodicies framed in the terms of "classic" theology are concerned, I am forced to concur in the judgment of Terrence Tilley, John Thiel, and others that theodicy is an unsuccessful and even wrongheaded theoretical and theological project. Johnson asserts rightly that natural pain, suffering, and death are enigmas, and the discussion should be left at that, not extended into an inquiry into the necessity of evil in a process of "continuing creation" sustained and empowered by God. Such an inquiry amounts, in effect, to a theodicy. Natural evil should in

---

[30] Ibid., 292n11.
[31] Desmond, "Evil and Political Theology," 93.

no way be associated with the Creator's will, directly or indirectly.[32] As Tilley asserts, "theodicy is legerdemain."[33] Thiel insists, "the suffering and death human beings do not do, since they lie beyond their power, are not done by God either." As far as the origin of such evils is concerned, the "answer can only be an admission of ignorance."[34] Theodicies not only verge on blasphemy but also are morally offensive, as will be addressed under the heading of "theological ethics."

The Biblical Imagination

The Bible does not attempt to explain why natural evil is necessary, or to justify God's actions. Instead it proclaims God's sovereignty. "I form the light and create darkness, I bring prosperity and create disaster; I, the LORD, do all these things" (Isa 45:7; NIV). Yet there is a wide range of biblical materials that deal with evil and suffering—its causes, its consequences, and the human and divine response.[35] Of these, "the Book of Job is the longest sustained exploration of the mystery of suffering."[36] The meaning of this complex narrative has been highly debated, for it demonstrates how difficult (if not impossible) it is to give a satisfactory response to the fact of innocent suffering. Johnson takes her title from a passage in the book of Job, in which Job names his sufferings, contrasts the good fortune enjoyed by the wicked, and rejects the idea that his misfortunes are his own fault. The lesson of the animals is that the good and the bad in human life come from the hand of God.

> But ask the animals, and they will teach you;
>   the birds of the air; and they will tell you; . . .
> Who among all these does not know
>   that the hand of the LORD has done this?

[32] According to Thiel, "God neither permits, nor wills, nor causes any kind of suffering at all" (*God, Evil*, 64). A necessary qualification is that God as Redeemer does will suffering, not in itself or directly, but as a cost of the love that heals evil.

[33] Terrence W. Tilley, "Prologue," in *The Bible on Suffering: Social and Political Implications*, ed. Anthony J. Tambasco (New York: Paulist Press, 2001), 1.

[34] Thiel, *God, Evil*, 98.

[35] See Daniel J. Harrington, *Why Do We Suffer? A Scriptural Approach to the Human Condition* (Franklin, WI: Sheed and Ward, 2000); and Richard W. Miller, ed., *Suffering and the Christian Life* (Maryknoll, NY: Orbis Books, 2013).

[36] Harrington, *Why Do We Suffer?*, 31.

> In his hand is the life of every living thing
> and the breath of every human being. (Job 12:7, 9-10)[37]

Job asks God for the chance to plead his case but acknowledges that mortals "lie down and do not rise again" (14:12). Just as the mountains fall and the water wears away stones, "so you destroy the hope of mortals" (14:19).

When "the Lord" finally answers Job "out of the whirlwind," it is to challenge Job's boldness, contrasting the smallness and powerlessness of a human being to the awesomeness of the Creator and Destroyer of all that exists. The mountain goats give birth, the wild ass runs free, the horse is mighty, and the hawk soars, because the Almighty has decreed it. The ostrich deserts its eggs in the earth and "deals cruelly with its young," because "God has made it forget wisdom" (39:13-17). God elaborates rhetorically, "Have you comprehended the expanse of the earth? Declare, if you know all this" (38:18).

Johnson proposes that interrogation of the beasts and plants "will lead your mind and heart to the living God, generous source and sustaining power of their life" for "they witness to the overflowing goodness of their Creator."[38] Job, on the contrary, is led to a confession of God's power, to repentance, and to self-despising (42:1-6). Nevertheless, Job has seen God personally, has been answered by God, and experiences God's presence in suffering, even if its rationale is never explained. Divine power is more central to the story of Job than divine beneficence.

The book of Job supports Johnson's view (claim 2 above) that divine creativity is behind and within the evolutionary process, somehow empowering death and destruction along with flourishing and new life (also the view of James Gustafson). It fails to confirm the thesis that suffering is both an enigma and a tragedy (claim 1), or that God is in solidarity with suffering and heals it (claim 3). The idea that humans should alleviate suffering (claim 4) may be inferred from the efforts of Job's friends, as well as from Job's righteousness as including aid to the poor (29:12). Yet from the book's final perspective, the natural evils of pain, death, loss, and adversity are neither a mishap nor a defect and might be explained very simply, by God's power and will. Hope for Job lies in continuing relationship with God, and from seeing God's nature

---

[37] Unless otherwise noted, biblical quotations are taken from the NRSV.
[38] Johnson, *Ask the Beasts*, 2.

more clearly. Job now realizes that "divine justice cannot be measured by the narrow criteria of human justice."[39]

Johnson invokes Gustavo Gutiérrez's christological interpretation of Job to surpass the terms of the original narrative. Job "deeply grasps that God's love . . . like all true love operates freely in a world of grace that completely enfolds and permeates him, even in pain," so that he can move "toward healing and peace."[40] I am hesitant to inject a Christian interpretation into this Israelite expression of struggling faith. On its own, the book of Job allows us to confront the fact that the mystery of God and of human existence before God is not penetrable by human theologies, and that we have no analytical control over the specification of divine "goodness."

As a Christian theologian, however, Johnson anchors her over-arching vision in the Christian Scriptures. These allow her to maintain that human death and loss are evils, that God is in healing solidarity with and resurrects sufferers, and that the mediation of divine love in Jesus Christ and the Spirit must shape the Christian life (claims 1, 3, and 4). These are convictions compellingly expressed. As in *She Who Is*, Johnson's ecological theology receives a trinitarian formulation, focused through the divine Word, Wisdom, or Sophia—active in creation, incarnate in Jesus Christ, and transformative in history as the liberating Spirit of divine love. *Ask the Beasts* follows earlier works by adopting a Christology in which God in Christ suffers (albeit analogically) but emphasizes that the Word is incarnate in all flesh, not merely human beings. Likewise, the resurrection of Christ and his sending of the Spirit include all. "For human beings and other organisms as well, the promise of final redemption in both a general and particular sense seems fitting in view of the goodness of God whose love treasures every creature."[41]

Ask the Beasts concludes on an ethical-political note by emphasizing human responsibility to strive for "the flourishing of all" in the interdependent "community of creation."[42] By characterizing this responsibility as an "ecological vocation," Johnson conveys not only that it requires

[39] Harrington, *Why Do We Suffer?*, 47.

[40] Johnson, *Ask the Beasts*, 271. Johnson cites Gustavo Gutiérrez, *On Job: God-Talk and the Suffering of the Innocent* (New York: Orbis Books, 1987).

[41] Johnson, *Ask the Beasts*, 231; see 231–35. Johnson here draws centrally on the works of systematic theologian Denis Edwards.

[42] Ibid., 280.

a multitude of overlapping practices but that it demands conversion of worldviews, attitudes, personal habits, local practices, and global policies. Ecological responsibility has its prophets, heroes, and martyrs. Yet there are signals that an ecological consciousness has begun to emerge.

Insights from Theological Ethics

The role of the ethicist includes at least three closely related tasks: to provide an accurate *descriptive* account of the conditions and situations of the moral life; to make *normative* judgments about what goals, goods, and virtues should guide morality; and to foster *practical* actions and relationships that are possible within the human condition properly understood and coherent with the normative framework proposed. As Johnson says, theology "seeks to understand faith more deeply in order to live more vibrantly."[43] Theological *ethics* seeks to specify *what it means* to "live more vibrantly" in light of the human and natural sciences, Scripture and tradition, philosophical reflection on values and virtues, contemporary theology and experience, and social-political opportunities in the appropriate contexts of action. Any theology that has a practical point of origin and a practical vision of human life (and I would say this includes all theology) must describe the human situation accurately, make coherent normative claims, and empower moral-political action that accords with its norms.

The human, species-wide, and planetary situation includes the rapid extinction of species and ecosystems at human hands, a disproportionate effect on the human poor, and the suffering of other species with intrinsic value. The gospels prioritize love of God and neighbor manifest as special care for the poor, which contemporary theology expands to all creatures and the earth itself. Theology and Christian experience proclaim that God as Creator, Redeemer, and Spirit is already empowering the transformation of concrete historical conditions, though the hold of evil survives.

Traditional theodicies have been criticized precisely on the ground that they do *not* provide a theological rationale for the practical, political, and historical transformation of violence and oppression. Terrence Tilley complains that, although theodicies may seem like purely intellectual

[43] Ibid., 2.

exercises, "not addressed to people who sin and suffer," they in fact devalue the practical, marginalize suffering, and divert attention from actual structures of evil. Ultimately, they defend evil's continuing existence.[44] Johnson cites Celia Deane-Drummond and John Haught, who express similar concerns. If evil is part of the natural and good existence of things, why should it not be tolerated; what rationale is there for opposition?[45] Mark Stephen Murray Scott insists that the problem of evil be reframed from an intellectual to "an existential and ethical enterprise." The moral standard is set by Matthew 25, for God is the defender of the poor and abandoned. Theodicy should consist in a concrete process of solving specific problems of evil and should be informed by the insights of feminist, black, and liberation theology about God and God's ways with the world.[46]

One way in which theodicies minimize the actual and concrete horrors of evil is to separate natural from moral evil and to see God as responsible for only the former or to see God as "permitting" human evil, which distorts all creation. Natural evil remains extrinsic to the spiritual and moral identities of persons. When its effects on agency itself are considered, natural evil is taken to another level of profundity.

Johnson does not take natural evil lightly. She offers disturbing though familiar examples of the suffering of animals whose deaths benefit other species or the survival of their own. The most poignant case is "the backup pelican chick," whose parents hatch two eggs. Unless one chick meets an untimely death, the weaker of the two is eventually nudged from the nest and left to starve.[47] Yet, in the case of humans, evil is of a greater range, reflexivity, and therefore intimacy and personal and interpersonal intensity. The same may be true of other species with high intelligence, wide emotional range, and complex social relations. When humans are forced to abandon or otherwise dispose of children due to adverse conditions of family survival, they are capable of a depth of suffering equal to or greater than that of the child.[48]

---

[44] Terrence Tilley, *Evils of Theodicy* (Eugene, OR: Wipf and Stock, 2000), 229, 238, 250.

[45] Johnson, *Ask the Beasts*, 188–91.

[46] Mark Stephen Murray Scott, "Theodicy at the Margins: New Trajectories for the Problem of Evil," *Theology Today* 68, no. 2 (2011): 149–52.

[47] Johnson, *Ask the Beasts*, 185–86.

[48] Chris Buckley and Thomas Fuller, "A Migrant Mother's Anguished Choice: Lost in the Diplomatic Wrangling over the Fate of the Rohingya Fleeing Myan-

At the same time, humans are also capable of harming children (or other innocent persons) with no feelings of guilt or regret whatsoever, inventing rationalizations to justify their actions. While it is customary and sometimes right to chalk such behavior up to evil character, vice, blameworthy lack of empathy, and pure selfishness, recent studies in fields such as evolutionary psychology, neuropsychology, behavioral genetics, and social psychology show that the natural and moral causes of evil are interdependent and entwined. There is no bright line between natural and moral evil.

As a species with a long evolutionary history, humans display a complex variety of traits and behaviors that are not all morally beneficent. Many of these traits evolved because they were supportive of the goals of reproduction and survival, enabling humans to adapt to the environments of their hunter-gatherer ancestors.[49] It was an evolutionary advantage for humans to form groups to protect insiders, aggressively fend off outsiders, and capture as many resources for the group as possible, including fertile females. Considered from the standpoint of individual members of the species, "survival of the fittest" also means exercising dominance over competitive adults in the group and maximizing one's own opportunities for reproductive and social success.

Survival and adaptation also favor the evolution of group cohesion, cooperation, loyalty, altruism within the group, emotional and social intelligence, reproductive pair-bonding, and protective care toward offspring. Yet these traits can conflict with traits such as aggressiveness and maximization of reproductive opportunity; both types of traits vary in intensity from individual to individual, and to some extent among the sexes. Furthermore, in-group reciprocity can directly enhance the innate human drive to dominate and control outsiders, by validating and collectivizing it under the aegis of group identity and ideology. In

---

mar Are the Harrowing Personal Consequences," *New York Times* (July 5, 2015), http://www.nytimes.com/2015/07/06/world/asia/myanmar-rohingya-refugee-crisis-malaysia.html.

[49] James Waller, *Becoming Evil: How Ordinary People Commit Genocide and Mass Killing* (Oxford: Oxford University Press, 2002), 145–49. For general background, see David M. Buss, *Evolutionary Psychology: The New Science of the Mind*, 5th ed. (East Sussex, UK: Psychology Press, 2014). For an extensive treatment of evolutionary psychology in relation to religion and ethics, see Stephen J. Pope, *Human Evolution and Christian Ethics* (Cambridge and New York: Cambridge University Press, 2007).

his treatment of the social factors that help marshal human behavior around evil and genocide, James Waller identifies three evolved tendencies of human nature that create a human "capacity for extraordinary evil—ethnocentrism, xenophobia and the desire for social dominance."[50]

Evolution has not only furnished humans with ethically troubling species-typical survival traits but also resulted in the presence of unusually commanding destructive impulses in some "atypical" individuals. When linked to innate traits of individual genetics or brain function, antisocial predispositions put a special strain on the agent's capacity for moral self-determination. An easily recognized case is severe mental illness, in which the individual does not grasp the full interpersonal and social reality of his or her actions. Even in extreme cases, however, the social, legal, and judicial response is very often to moralize the problem, avoiding recognition of the extent of human moral vulnerability.

Recent research has shown that even individuals not affected by any recognized mental illness can be prompted to antisocial and immoral behavior by biological as well as social conditions. For example, underlying causes of domestic abuse can include genetic and biochemical factors, as well as changes in brain development owing to physical or social trauma.[51] War veterans who have experienced "perpetrating, failing to prevent, or bearing witness to acts that transgress deeply held moral beliefs and expectations" suffer emotional, psychological, spiritual, social, and behavioral "moral injury," significantly impairing future moral agency. They may suffer involuntary symptoms of a partly biological nature, such as flashbacks, extreme and disabling emotions of shame, or neurotic defense mechanisms.[52] Acts of unjustified violence in war are themselves partly due to group bonding around the ethnocentrism, xenophobia, and desire for social dominance identified by James Waller.

In his studies on the minds of violent criminals, Adrian Raine uses brain imaging on imprisoned convicts to show that there is a "biological basis" to "recidivist violent offending."[53] For example, a significant

---

[50] Waller, *Becoming Evil*, 153.

[51] David A. Wolfe and Peter G. Jaffe, "Emerging Strategies in the Prevention of Domestic Violence," *Domestic Violence and Children* 9, no. 3 (1999): 134.

[52] Brett T. Litz et al., "Moral Injury and Moral Repair in War Veterans: A Preliminary Model and Intervention Strategy," *Clinical Psychology Review* 29 (2009): 695–706.

[53] Adrian Raine is the author of *The Anatomy of Violence: The Biological Roots of Crime* (London: Penguin Random House, 2013). See his interview

number of violent psychopaths who seem to be "without conscience" also have shrunken amygdalae, a probable cause of lower emotional capacity, and a lack of normal feelings of connection to others. These offenders are abnormally impulsive and may seek emotional stimulation by extreme means (and with little consideration of its effect on victims) because it is a dimension of human experience they lack. This of course raises the prospect that more socially conformist individuals may also be "naturally" handicapped in moral response by lack of the underlying emotions that enable other-concern.

The "natural" human traits supported by the "evolutionary process" are multiple, often disharmonious, sometimes conflicting, and frequently conducive to behavior that harms the self or others. Evolution has produced "natural" affective, emotional, and cognitive characteristics in humans that undermine "moral" identity, agency, discernment, and action. This evidence implicating "natural" causes in "moral" behavior does not mean that moral agency and responsibility disappear (except in extreme cases). Emotions can result from complex networks of environmental, experiential, psychological, and neurological causes, and agents have responsibility to repress, rechannel, sublimate, or cultivate their own emotions.[54] But not all moral agents are dealt the same hand or "working material," and the cultivation of moral virtue can be immensely more difficult for some than for others.

Evolutionary science can sometimes be reductionist, downplaying the possibility of any moral judgment on human phenomena such as dominance, violence, or sexual promiscuity—or for that matter, as empathy, generosity, and altruism. Ethicists, however, assume the reality and necessity of moral agency and make normative judgments about the ideals and goals that *should* control human behavior. They use terminology like respect, equality, justice, human rights, empathy, solidarity, and justice. From the ethical point of view, it is not possible to regard evolved traits that are especially conducive to others' suffering as simply part of the free evolutionary process enabled and sustained by God as "continuing Creator." Reinhold Niebuhr identified exclusive tendencies

---

on National Public Radio: *Fresh Air*, "Criminologist Believes Violent Behavior Is Biological" (April 30, 2013), http://www.npr.org/2013/05/01/180096559/criminologist-believes-violent-behavior-is-biological.

[54] Diana Fritz Cates, *Choosing to Feel: Virtue, Friendship, and Compassion for Friends* (Notre Dame, IN: Notre Dame Press, 1996).

of group behavior as "collective egotism" and as unqualifiedly sinful.[55]
Natural traits can inhibit the *moral* traits that ethicists and theologians
prize as normative and virtuous. The personal moral integrity of affected
individuals is undermined by "natural" evil. How is this development in
any way supported by "the ineffable God of mercy and love recounted
in the Nicene Creed"?[56] *The symbol of God functions.* Should and will
human beings imitate a God whose wisdom envisions and upholds the
agony of God's beloved children? Or does such a vision of divine providence undermine the heart of Christian ethics as an option for the poor?

A related basis of Christian ethics, traditionally termed "natural law,"
is a hermeneutics of human experience (both individual and social) in
which certain components or aspects are identified as "goods" commanding moral choice because they contribute to human "flourishing,"
while their opposites are rejected and avoided. Theologically, natural
law is understood as humanity's participation in divine being. Although
concepts of goods, evils, and flourishing can be informed by religious
insights, their basic content is common to all humans, even though speci-
fications may vary with context and culture. An easy example is the good
of life as commanding protection, while killing is to be avoided, if not
always condemned in rare instances, such as protection of innocent life.

Yet Johnson proposes that natural pain, suffering, and death are
valuable, particularly in the emergence and demise of species. Such
evils are "morally neutral" because they are "the natural working out
of life's creative processes."[57] Then why see humanity's destruction
of species and ecosystems (even its own) as "unwarranted killing"? If
"survival of the fittest" is the principle of evolutionary change, then
why should humans not dominate other species? If species go out of
existence, so what? In fact, humans probably can't destroy the planet,
just ourselves and other life forms. But others will grow up and replace
us. That's "evolution."

My rejoinder is that evolution is a fact, but the evil it involves is
not "created"—nor can it be explained. Thomas Aquinas says, "there
was no pain before sin," encapsulating the discredited view that even

---

[55] Niebuhr, *Moral Man and Immoral Society*; and *The Nature and Destiny of
Man*, vol. 1: *Human Nature* (New York: Charles Scribner's Sons, 1941), 218–19.
[56] Johnson, *Ask the Beasts*, xv.
[57] Ibid., 185.

natural evil is due to human fault but surmising rightly that it is not part of creation.[58] We know simply that natural evil is "redeemed" by God's immanence, Jesus' solidarity, and the Spirit's power. John Thiel proposes that God's omnipotence be envisioned not as divine power to do anything but to act everywhere: "God's unlimited power is the divine love that, as grace, is utterly disposed toward healing all the guilty and innocent suffering that precedent sin and precedent evil bring to human life." The evidence for this claim is neither the human historical record, nor modern science, but "actual experiences of need, hope, and reconciliation that are formed in an existential encounter with the living God."[59] Humans are called to imitate God by confronting, naming, and resisting evil, particularly in the form of concrete instances of violence and oppression, where basic human flourishing is denied and the cry of the poor unheeded. We are called to mediate love, hope, and reconciliation.

An Alternative Biblical Imagination

In conclusion, let us consider a completely different set of biblical images for grappling with the reality of evil, its relation to God, and Christian ethics as participation in strategies of change. Contrary to classical theology and theodicy, the Bible does not rule out forces of evil that are separate from God and not causally linked to God; yet they are secondary to God's power and goodness, and eschatologically overcome by God. Paul refers to these forces as principalities and powers, among other terms (in Rom, 1 and 2 Cor, and Gal, as well as the possibly pseudonymous 2 Thess and Col).

In an intriguing study,[60] Robert Ewusie Moses argues that Western theology is too quick to "demythologize" such references. Contemporaries in Paul's Greco-Roman and Jewish milieux, as well as virtually all peoples on the African continent, take for granted that the natural world and human life are affected by unseen spiritual forces of a sometimes "demonic" nature. In Africa, virtually without exception, people believe that although one Supreme Being created the universe, there are myriad

---

[58] Aquinas, *Summa*, I.Q. 92, "Of the Production of Woman," a. 3, r. ad. 3.

[59] Thiel, *God, Evil*, 138.

[60] Robert Ewusie Moses, *Practices of Power: Revisiting the Principalities and Powers in the Pauline Letters* (Minneapolis: Fortress Press, 2014).

invisible spirits who affect the physical world and can be invoked for good or ill. These beliefs should not be dismissed as superstition, for they are "based on experiences and deep reflection."[61] The important question is not where the powers come from, or what they mean for "classical" divine attributes, but how specific human practices cooperate with or resist their dominion.

Reviewing the work of important scholars, Moses proposes that the powers have both a spiritual, personal reality and a material and structural reality. They are not merely or only the "interior" or personal aspect of social structures of sin, and they can exist in a spiritual realm independent of the physical.[62] The powers defy the limitations of human language, shattering normal categories, even that of "spiritual being." They operate at all levels of existence simultaneously. "From the bondage of creation (Rom. 8:18-39; 1 Cor. 10:19-20; Gal. 4:3; Col. 2:8, 20) to social and individual degeneration (1 Cor. 6:7-25) and death in the human race (Rom. 5:12-6:23, 1 Cor. 15:26), Paul discerns the work of the powers."[63]

The powers can be associated with Satan, demons, and angels, who line up opposite to God and Christ and exercise dominion in the "present evil age." Their dominion, authority, and strength can even corrupt the church. Neither Paul nor his churches, nor other early Christian writers, dispute the existence of the powers. Instead, their message is that Christ defeats them. Through the death and resurrection of Jesus Christ, the efficacy of the powers has been broken, and a new age is beginning.[64] The powers are not conquered by earthly force or violence. Rather, Christians counteract them by cultivating a *habitus* of discipleship through baptism, Eucharist, prayer, proclamation, and the relational practices of the body of Christ and new family of brothers and sisters in Christ (1 Cor 11, 13).

Moses insists that *practices* are key to understanding how evil works in the world, as well as how it is overcome in Christ. Johnson does justice to the social, structural, and global reach of Christian practices when she situates the Christian *habitus* within a "community of creation."

[61] Ibid., 218–19.
[62] Ibid., 37.
[63] Ibid., 211.
[64] Ibid., 208.

Johnson's practical and political refrain is the goal of "a socially just and environmentally sustainable society," in which basic human needs are met and "diverse species prosper."[65] The evils creatures suffer are mysterious in origin, but their mechanisms may be discerned, and their effects allayed. Hope, not the necessity of suffering, is the luminous touchstone of Johnson's theology. Hope flows from "the life-giving presence of the Spirit who empowers all creation [and] is also the power of resurrected life for all creatures."[66] This presence can seem evanescent in the face of nature's tooth and claw. Yet Darwin's God can be enlarged by the witness of those who sense a power of life at the center of things. The poet Mary Oliver does not shy away from predators, prey, and the assured vanishing of every life. But the natural world still hints at something larger, and ineffable.

> This morning
> the beautiful white heron
> was floating along above the water
>
> and then into the sky of this
> the one world
> we all belong to
>
> where everything
> sooner or later
> is a part of everything else
>
> which thought made me feel
> for a little while
> quite beautiful myself.[67]

---

[65] Johnson, *Ask the Beasts*, 285–86.

[66] Ibid., 231.

[67] Mary Oliver, "Poem of the One World," in *A Thousand Mornings* (New York: Penguin, 2012).

Chapter 14

Truly Our Sister

In Celebration of Dr. Elizabeth Johnson

Jeanette Rodriguez

Blessed is she who has believed that the Lord would fulfill his promises to her!"

—Luke 1:39-45[1]

In gratitude and humility, I offer these reflections in celebration of Dr. Elizabeth Johnson for her contribution to the theological enterprise, her engaging presence of the last four decades, and her commitment to humanity and all of creation. In this essay I will address three areas in particular where I find my work both dovetailing with and enhanced because of Dr. Johnson's work: the revisiting and retrieving of the communion of saints, her contribution and understanding of Mary, and the return to a healthier, more interdependent relationship with the Earth.

---

[1] All biblical citations are taken from the New International Version of the Bible.

On a Personal Note

When I reflect on the person and the work of Dr. Elizabeth Johnson, a couple of things come to mind. I am reminded of my early upbringing where my parents emigrated from Ecuador and raised my brothers, sisters, and me in the projects of New York City. Dr. Johnson's community, that is, the Sisters of St. Joseph of Brentwood, were a viable and healing presence, not just to my family, but to our neighbors. It was the sisters, in conjunction with our parents, who understood how important it was to invest in our education. At different times these sisters of St. Joseph brokered with our parents to allow us to move out of traditional gender roles to become educated professionals. During the racial riots of the 1960s and 1970s, many of those in the helping and ministerial professions abandoned our communities. I don't blame them. It was pretty scary. But the memory of our communities is and will always be that the sisters never left us.

Second, I was fortunate enough to be born and raised in the spirit of Vatican II. This *renovación de la Iglesia*, "renewal of the church," opened the door for more inclusive participation in ministry and diverse, global theological reflection of our tradition. Those of us laypeople and particularly women, like a flower seeking the sun, sought individuals we could learn from and emulate in order to incarnate our faith. Elizabeth Johnson was one such person to emulate with her dedication and knowledge of the tradition, her courage to speak out, her integrity, and her ability to articulate the hopes and aspirations, joys and sorrows of a generation of women.

And finally, I remember my father telling me that in this broken world there might come a time when it feels like the other is taking everything away from me. In fact, they may be. But the one thing they will never be able to take he would say is *tu palabra de honor* or "word of honor," your integrity. This understanding was reinforced by the sisters as we have seen most recently in how the Vatican has treated our sisters and, in particular, Elizabeth Johnson. Yet what we have witnessed is that her real victory was in her integrity, a victory that she does not claim individually. Johnson articulated in her keynote address to the Leadership Conference of Women Religious (LCWR) on August 15, 2014, that she is where she is because of the many women who have mentored and nurtured, directed and supported her in the same way she has done for others. Elizabeth Johnson, reclaims, revitalizes, and retrieves the manner in which the people of God experience the living church today.

Revisiting and Retrieving the Communion of Saints

One of the many important works that have impacted my own work was her revisiting and rearticulating the importance of the communion of saints, as articulated in her book, *Friends of God and Prophets* (1998). In this book she defines the communion of saints as a Christian symbol that speaks of profound relationships. This spoke to me, a US Latina Catholic, especially when she pointed to the ongoing and unbreakable connection between the living and the dead, and all of creation.[2] In her CTSA presidential address, "Turn to the Heavens and the Earth: Retrieval of the Cosmos in Theology" (1996), Johnson reminds us of the wisdom of the early Christian and medieval theologians who recognize that "God has put two books at our disposal, the book of sacred scripture and the book of nature."[3] In his recent encyclical, *Laudato Sì*, Pope Francis reaffirms this interconnection of all creation; all life as a part of this network. Pope Francis affirms a strong sacramental view of creation, wherein "soil, water, mountains: everything is, as it were, a caress of God."[4]

By lifting up this unbreakable connection among the living, the dead, and all creation, and by providing a sustained and deep reflection about this image of the communion of saints, Johnson invites us to participate in the holiness of God. In so doing, she restores a liberating dignity to humanity and creation—where all are equal, have inherent dignity, and are called to participate in the building of the reign of God.

When *Friends of God and Prophets* came out I was in El Salvador to remember and celebrate the martyred Jesuits, their housekeeper Elba, and her daughter, Celina. Thousands of Salvadorans and visitors from all over the world gathered to remember those who had died— who had either been killed or disappeared. The death of the Salvadorans and their beloved Archbishop Oscar Romero, along with the church of the

---

[2] Elizabeth A. Johnson, *Friends of God and Prophets: A Feminist Theological Reading of the Communion of Saints* (New York: Continuum Publishing, 1998), 19.

[3] Elizabeth A. Johnson, "Turn to the Heavens and the Earth: Retrieval of the Cosmos in Theology," *CTSA Proceedings* 51 (1996): 2.

[4] Francis, *Laudato Sì* (Vatican City: Libreria Editrice Vaticana, 2015).

poor and the church of the martyrs, renewed and strengthened the faith of not only the people of El Salvador but the universal church as well. The church of the poor evangelized the larger church in spirit through its witness of faith steeped in the blood of martyrs.

Johnson reminds us that memories are important and that in particular memories of hope must be practiced in "faithful deeds of discipleship."[5] Every few years, I return to San Salvador to celebrate with the people. I meet with former guerrillas, contemporary human rights activists, church workers, and a women's collective; all speak about solidarity in terms of profound relationships that have had an impact on the meaning and value of their lives. Their faith-filled lives are passed on in song, stories, and rituals in everyday discourse.

The concept of the communion of saints has almost been lost in the contemporary Anglo US church. Perhaps even more disturbing for me is when Johnson states that the dead are no longer "accessible to the living."[6] What I have learned from the Latin@ culture and in particular the Salvadoran experience is from the people's ability to step into or open the portals of space and time and call forth in memory those who have gone before us in order to draw on their faith, commitment, and strength. This is a manifestation of the communion of saints that I have grown to know in my own cultural experience and that Johnson revitalizes and translates for the North American church.

Those of us who work with the faith-filled and marginalized communities, particularly of Latin America, owe a debt of gratitude to Johnson because she brings to the table of accepted theological practices those values and constructs that have been too long marginalized but that give our life and work meaning. Instrumental to this is a paradigm of God who is imminent, accessible, and incarnated in the intimate, loving relationships of those who have gone before us and of those with whom we are in solidarity today.

Johnson's reflection on the significance of storytelling as a form of keeping memory alive speaks intimately to my experience. She contends:

> These memories carry a vital élan that inspires and energizes action for the good. Thus, by their inner dynamism, "the communities of memories that tie us to the past also turn us to the future as com-

---

[5] Johnson, *Friends of God and Prophets*, 9.
[6] Ibid., 19.

munities of hope. They carry a context of meaning that can allow us to connect our aspirations for ourselves and those closest to us with the aspirations of the larger whole. . . . People growing up in communities of memory not only hear the stories that tell how the community came to be, but what its hopes and fears are, and how its ideals are exemplified in outstanding men and women."[7]

In my work on cultural memory, I have found that the narratives of and about Archbishop Oscar Romero serve to keep the memories of martyrdom and the church of the poor alive for future generations.[8]

Mary, Our Sister

Johnson's reflection on Mary argues against gender dualism which has produced idealized and damaging images for women. When I was writing my dissertation, subsequently published as *Our Lady of Guadalupe: Faith and Empowerment Among Mexican American Women*,[9] I turned to the writings of Johnson for a solid reading of the tradition. In my desire to move toward more gender-inclusive theology of God, the Marian tradition offers me its powerful maternal and other female images of the divine.

The Marian phenomenon has been powerful throughout history precisely because it is a female representation of the divine, bearing attributes that have been excluded from mainstream Christian perceptions of God as Father, Son, and Spirit. The feminine face of God has been suppressed and excluded, and female images of God have migrated to the figure Mary through a long process of patriarchalization. As a result of this process, the divine image became more remote and judgmental, while Mary became the beloved "other face" of God. Intellectually a distinction was maintained between adoration of God and veneration of Mary, but on the affective, imaginative level people experienced the love of God and the saving mystery of divine reality in the figure of Mary.[10]

---

[7] Ibid., 22–23; citing Robert Bellah, et al., *Habits of the Heart: Individualism and Commitment in American Life* (San Francisco: Harper and Row, 1985), 153 and 154.

[8] See Jeanette Rodriguez and Ted Fortier, *Cultural Memory: Resistance, Faith, and Identity* (Austin: University of Texas Press, 2007).

[9] Jeanette Rodriguez, *Our Lady of Guadalupe: Faith and Empowerment Among Mexican American Women* (Austin: University of Texas Press, 1994).

[10] Ibid., 70–73.

Some Catholics, along with Johnson, call for the theological necessity of expressing the mystery of the Christian God more comprehensively. That is, God must be envisioned in ways inclusive of the reality of women and other marginalized groups. Those elements in the Marian symbol that probably properly belong to divine reality must be retrieved.[11] Through this process of integration, the figure of Mary no longer has the burden of keeping alive female imagery of the divine. The Marian image is not meant to replace but to enhance the person of God.

According to Catharina Halkes, the fact that Mary's "hearing and keeping the word of God went together with motherhood and were even the preconditions for it" is not emphasized enough.[12] This combination of hearing and keeping God's word as a faithful believer and, thus, listening and responding to God's word, is modeled in Mary as an example for us to follow, and, as a result, Mary is seen as a symbol of the community of redeemed humanity. Gifted with the healing grace of God, she responds wholeheartedly and is called to the mission of spreading the Gospel in the world and to healing those who have suffered. Devotees look to Mary's unique ability to accompany them in their suffering while at the same time trusting and believing in the promises of God. Although the mother of Jesus appears in all four gospels and is featured in 152 verses of the New Testament, of which ninety verses come from the gospel attributed to Luke, there are "relatively few, but meaningful, words about her."[13] Simply stated, according to Christian sources, Mary was a first-century Jewish woman who lived under Roman occupation, gave birth to Jesus in a manger, and became the mother of the Christ. During her lifetime, she endured poverty, experienced refugee status, and watched in horror as her son was unjustly judged and brutally crucified. Following the death of her son and as a widow, she continued to trust in God and lived as an elder dependent on others. This background is important as we recognize that "in all of these

---

[11] Elizabeth A. Johnson, "Mary and the Female Face of God," *Theological Studies* 50, no. 3 (1989): 500–501, cited in Rodriguez, *Our Lady of Guadalupe*, 153–54.

[12] Catharina Halkes, "Mary and Women," in *Concilium: Religion in the Eighties: Mary in the Churches*, ed. Hans Küng and Jürgen Moltmann (New York: Seabury Press Inc., 1989), 70.

[13] Diego Irarrázaval, "Mary in Latin American Christianity," in *The Many Faces of Mary*, ed. Diego Irarrázaval, Susan Ross, and Marie-Theres Wacker (London: Concilium Press, 2008), 98.

moments, she is sister to the unchronicled lives of marginalized women throughout the ages, and to all who stand in solidarity with them."[14]

Among these marginalized women, of course, are Latinas, whose devotion to Mary takes a wide variety of forms. What accounts for Hispanics' massive and persistent devotion to Mary? Latin American and US Hispanic theologians view Marian images from a liberationist theology point of view: Mary's cult appeals strongly to the oppressed because she gives dignity to downtrodden people and thus renews their energy to resist assimilation into the dominant culture. Further, as Virgilio Elizondo points out, the cult not only liberates downtrodden peoples from social and political oppression but also liberates us from a restrictive idea of God.[15] Within the Roman Catholic tradition Our Lady of Guadalupe is a Marian image, and within the Hispanic culture she is a *mestiza*, a person with a mixture of both Spanish and Indian blood. The event and figure of Our Lady of Guadalupe combined the Nahuatl female expression of God with the Spanish male expression of God that had been incomprehensible to the Indians' duality—their belief that everything perfect has a male and female component.

Our Lady of Guadalupe manifests God as mother. Our Lady of Guadalupe identifies herself as Our Loving Mother and people see her as a mother, a maternal presence, consoling, nurturing, offering unconditional love, comforting—qualities that tell us that mother is an appropriate metaphor for God. As I have argued elsewhere: "Transferring this maternal language back to God enables us to see that God has a maternal countenance. All that is creative and generative of life, all that nourishes and nurtures, all that is benign, cherishes, and sustains, all that is solicitous and sympathetic originates in God/Her."[16]

Popular religion as a *locus theologicus* of US Hispanic/Latin@ theology is highlighted and continues to be highlighted because of the very clear demonstration that people's identity is so interconnected with their religious symbols, their faith, and their struggle for liberation. Marian devotion is no exception to this. We are indebted to Orlando O.

---

[14] Elizabeth A. Johnson, "Truly Our Sister: A Feminist Hermeneutical Disciplinary Approach," in *The Many Faces of Mary* 4, ed. Diego Irarrázaval, Susan Ross, Marie-Theres Wacker (London: Concilium Press, 2008), 14.

[15] See Virgilio Elizondo, *Guadalupe: Mother of the New Creation* (New York: Orbis Books, 1997), 199.

[16] Rodriguez, *Our Lady of Guadalupe*, 155–56.

Espín for his sensitive and scholarly retrieval of Latin@ popular Catholicism as a *locus theologicus*. As Roberto S. Goizueta explains, "what he [Espín] calls for is not simply an 'openness' to other cultures and religious experiences, nor simply an 'understanding' or 'appreciation' of Latino popular Catholicism. . . . Rather, what he calls for is a different starting point for the theological enterprise, the *privileging* of a different 'way of being Catholic,' as a place wherein the God of Jesus Christ, about whom we Catholic theologians claim to speak, has chosen to be revealed . . . the God who has chosen to be revealed preferentially in the lived faith of the poor is a God whose love extends to all."[17]

One of the most common forms this popular Catholicism takes for Latin@s is rituals that involve acting or dramatizing religious stories such as the narrative of Our Lady of Guadalupe, Las Posadas (Mary and Joseph's search for a room before the birth of Jesus), and the Passion of Jesus. Religious symbols, stories, and rituals draw individuals and community into a deeper understanding of God by accessing the mind and heart (devotion to the Sacred Heart, rosary, baptism, blessings). In Latin@ culture, everything is interrelated, interconnected, and interdependent, and people identify themselves through their relationships to others (hence the importance of *compadrazgo*).[18] These relationships among people also apply to the relationships between people and the Divine. The saints are Jesus' friends and, therefore, friends of mine: Jesus is my brother, God is my father, Guadalupe is my mother. Through popular religion, the presence and message of Our Lady of Guadalupe has empowered people as they interact with society in the United States. The emphasis on family values, the ability to hope against all hope, a spontaneous feeling of connection and relationality, the unquestioned sense of God's providence as it is delivered through Our Lady Guadalupe, the warm conversational sense of the presence of God, respect and love for all creation—all of these are found in the narrative, rituals, and the image of our lady of Guadalupe.[19]

---

[17] Roberto S. Goizueta, foreword to *The Faith of the People: Theological Reflections on Popular Catholicism*, by Orlando O. Espín (Maryknoll, NY: Orbis Books, 1997), xiii; emphasis original.

[18] *Compadrazgo* is a traditional ritual kinship involving a set of responsibilities and duties not limited to co-parenting, which provides a network of relationships.

[19] Rodriguez, *Our Lady of Guadalupe*, 146.

Every Creature A Word of God

Would reclaiming the knowledge that the Earth is in fact our first and oldest home have an impact on the experience of displacement and aloneness that humans feel with the onset of civilization that ruptures the human-nature relationship? I believe this ancestral memory of Earth as our home is deep within us. If we are to recall the wisdom of that memory, we must be able to stand firmly on the Earth and in reverential silence recall the interdependence and intricate relationship we have, not just with the world, the Earth, and the land, but with the universe. As Pierre Teilhard de Chardin reminds us, "We are the universe reflecting on itself."[20] I find that consciousness and awareness about our common birth home is a starting point for this reflection.

As Johnson has articulated in her CTSA address, the intellectual integrity of theology must be in dialogue with cosmology. We now know through contemporary science that this world is organic, self-organizing, indeterminate, boundless, and, ultimately, a mystery.[21] As a result of these insights, that is, of the unimaginable age of the planet, of its dynamic and organic connection to everything else, we can now be open to other discoveries of contemporary science that call us into the new interpretations.

In light of the inequity, poverty, and suffering of both humanity and the Earth, the turn to the heavens and the Earth "bears the marks of genuine conversion of mind and heart."[22] This conversion must include a posture of humility and a reexamination of both our values and our relationships. Moreover, awareness of our common birth home initiates our understanding that this sacred place on which we stand and on which we make our habitat holds for us the secret of our relationships. In other words, our relationship with the Earth is the context of all contexts.

New Testament accounts reveal that Jesus himself walked, prayed, preached, and ministered within the "Cathedral of Creation," making references to the desert, garden, lake, field, and mountain. His parables include birds and sheep as well as seed, wheat, and harvest. Similarly, the accounts of the first communities recorded that "All the believers were one in heart and mind. No one claimed that any of their possessions was

---

[20] Lorna Green, *Earth Age: A New Vision of God, This Human and the Earth* (Mahwah, NJ: Paulist Press, 1994), 125–26.

[21] Johnson, "Turn to the Heavens and the Earth," 5.

[22] Ibid., 9.

their own, but they shared everything they had" (Acts 4:32-34; NIV). Not surprisingly, then, the teaching body of the church has articulated and reflected on such themes as property, the role of earthly goods, and demands of social justice. While the church has always recognized the right of all people to property, it has also held that a right to property "constitutes for no one an unconditional and absolute right. There is no reason to reserve for one's exclusive use that goes beyond our need while others are lacking essentials."[23]

In 1980 Guatemalan bishops used this process of reflection in their pastoral letter concerning land. "It is a cry from 'The People of Corn' who, on the one hand, identify with furrows, sowing, and harvest. And who, on the other hand, find themselves expelled from the land by an unjust and punitive system."[24] In this pastoral letter, the bishops highlight agrarian problems in Guatemala and critique the political system of land ownership that has existed since colonial times to the present, the unequal distribution of land, and the discriminatory practices and marginalization of the *Campesinos*. The bishops' theological insights focus on the Earth as a gift of God. They refer to the first oral traditions of Genesis that, first of all, acknowledge and recognize the dignity of the human person. In the context of systemic and institutional violence, bishops remind believers of the inherent dignity of the human person as expressed both in the Scriptures and in the subsequent theological constructs. They move on to expressions of joy in the psalms (Pss 67:7; 85:13), which pronounce humanity's joy at the fruit of their labors on the earth, the joy with which the people gather their fruits, culminating with the fiesta in God's honor (Deut 16:1-15). They note that the earth is a sign of a covenant between God and humanity and that the earth does not belong to humanity but to the *Dios de la Vida*, or God of Life. Finally, the letter denounces avarice and excessive wealth, urging believers to imitate Jesus' encounter and commitment to the poor.[25]

It is because we are the creation of a loving and relational God that *la tierra* becomes a gift to all creatures. When we forget our identity, place,

---

[23] "Cry for the Land: Joint Pastoral Letter by Guatemalan Bishops' Conference," in *"And God Saw That It Was Good": Catholic Theology and the Environment*, ed. Drew Christiansen and Walter E. Grazer (Washington, DC: United States Catholic Conference, 1996), 286; citing Paul VI, *Populorum Progressio* 23.

[24] Ibid., 275.

[25] Ibid., 275–76.

and inherited relationships, God in God's goodness sends the prophets, artists, "ordinary" saints and mystics to remind us of our communal relationship with all creation. Mystics and saints like Benedict of Nursia, Hildegard of Bingen, and Francis of Assisi have given us a language in which to nurture and sustain our relationship with Brother Sun, Sister Moon.[26] Latin American theologian Leonardo Boff comments: "None of these masters believed that knowledge was a form of appropriation or of domination of things, but rather a form of love and of communion with things."[27] Theologian Thomas Berry beautifully invites us to move from being a collection of objects to a communion of subjects. It is through our embodied selves in the context of being a part of creation and living upon this earth that we experience God. The whole universe is God's dwelling. Earth, a very small blessed corner of the universe, gifted with unique natural blessings, is humanity's home, and humans are never so much at home as when God dwells with them.[28] This is the basis of La Tierra theology.

One of the most controversial issues that arises within the environmental movement is the understanding that the impoverishment of people, and, in particular, the most vulnerable of people, is closely related to how natural resources, technology, and commerce are exploited, processed, and distributed. It is evident that the level of energy consumption, especially in First World countries, is a key issue. Today, in the United States communities of color and of low income are in distress reflecting "disproportionate placement of landfills, incinerators, coal-fired power plants, and other environmental hazards."[29]

In the encyclical *Laudato Sì*, Pope Francis lays the blame for environmental degradation on the ideologies of power and profit and critiques the style of leadership that is more interested in domination than in service.[30] The statistics of environmental injustice that bear witness to the truth of Pope Francis's claims are staggering. Some of the statistics

[26] See Regis Armstrong, "Canticle of the Creatures," in *Francis of Assisi: Early Documents*, vol. 1 (New York: New City Press, 1999), 113–14.

[27] Leonardo Boff, *Ecology and Liberation: A New Paradigm* (Maryknoll, NY: Orbis Books, 1995), 38.

[28] "Renewing the Earth: An Invitation to Reflection and Action on the Environment in Light of Catholic Social Teaching" (A Pastoral Statement of the United States Catholic Conference, Washington, DC, November 14, 1991), 6.

[29] Jacqui Patterson, "Right to a Healthy Environment," *A Matter of Spirit* 86 (2010): 1.

[30] Francis, *Laudato Sì*.

that can be cited are the following: "71% of African-Americans live in counties that violate federal air pollution standards, compared to 58% of the white population. . . . African Americans are hospitalized for asthma at more than three times the rate of the white population," and "much of the mining for uranium used in nuclear power takes place on indigenous lands."[31]

Increasingly experts are convinced that the way our generation is using energy will not leave enough for future generations. By future generations, we mean the total web of life of which humans are just one part.[32] The web of life is one. Human mistreatment of the created world not only diminishes our dignity but also destroys the resources made available to us. Perhaps more frightening is that this mistreatment destroys the resources for our future generations.

The most difficult challenge will be to move away from the sole interest in individual lifestyles and Western ethnocentrism to a more adequate structural and systemic concern, or—as our Christian Tradition has called for—a commitment to the common good, a common good that includes reading the "book of nature" God has provided so that we might hear God's Word more comprehensively.

We had lost the ability to hear God's Word in nature. We are, however, slowly attempting to retrieve it. Perhaps at this time it would make sense to open the discourse in dialogue with our native brothers and sisters. Indigenous people around the world have seen firsthand the impact of destructive actions against the Earth and her fruits. In a statement at the United Nations in September 2014, indigenous people from around the country acknowledge that while the elders and medicine people of their nations are not scientists, they are connected to a source of truth in life. Their counsel is this: "to survive climate change and see the future, we must restore the sacred in ourselves and include the sacredness of all life in our discussions, decisions and actions."[33] In their statement, they go on to say,

[31] Patterson, "Right to a Healthy Environment," 1.

[32] See US Catholic Conference of Bishops, "Global Climate Change: A Plea for Dialogue, Prudence, and the Common Good" (2001).

[33] Indigenous Elders and Medicine Peoples Council, "Beyond Climate Change to Survival on Sacred Mother Earth" (message to the United Nations Climate Summit, September 21, 2014), 2; http://spiret.org/wp-content/uploads/2014/09/COUNCIL_FORMAL_STATEMENT_UN_CLIMATE_SUMMIT.pdf.

> We are the people of the earth united under the creator's law, with
> a sacred covenant to follow and uphold and a sacred responsibility
> to extend Life for all future generations. We are expressing deep
> concern for our shared future and urge everyone to awaken spir-
> itually and take action. It is critical that we come together with
> good minds and prayer as a global community of all faiths, to honor
> the Creator and the Creator's Gift by restoring the Sacredness in
> ourselves. We must work in unity to help mother earth heal so
> that she can bring back balance and harmony for all her children.[34]

It is imperative to understand that the key issue is survival itself, especially as it affects the survival of the more marginalized. K. C. Abraham,
director of the South Asian Theological Research Institute, argues that
political and social justice are linked to ecological health. He cites connections between economic exploitation and environmental degradation.
Global atmospheric changes result from the destruction of forests, and
poor and indigenous peoples are driven away for the sake of "development." The uneven distribution, control, and use of natural resources
are just a few of the serious justice issues. For example, the natural
resources needed to maintain the lifestyle of one person in the United
States are equal to what is required for two hundred or three hundred
people in Asia.[35] The rapid depletion of nonrenewable natural resources
further raises the question of our responsibility for future generations.

The indigenous traditions teach us that when we separate our existence from the processes of the landscape our hearts become fragmented and all that is "other" is objectified. *La Tierra* theology reminds
us that the land is the source of our nourishment, survival, identity,
and indeed life. Therefore, the contemporary ecological crisis must
impress upon our consciousness a new awareness of our dependence on
the Earth and each other. We must help our communities understand
that we share a common destiny. This common destiny is linked with
the Earth because we belong to the Earth. It calls for the reembracing
of values laden with the heartfelt meaning of our interconnectedness
with creation.

[34] Ibid., 3.
[35] K. C. Abraham, "A Theological Response to the Ecological Crisis," in *Ecotheology: Voices from South and North*, ed. David Hallman (Maryknoll, NY: Orbis
Books, 1994), 69–70.

On December 10, 1992, designated as Human Rights Day, the official opening ceremonies for the International Year of the World's Indigenous Peoples was held at the United Nations in New York City. At that gathering, twenty leaders from indigenous nations from all over the world came to address the General Assembly. This was significant because it was the first time in history that indigenous peoples were able to bring their issues directly to an international body.

Oren Lyons, faith keeper of the Onondaga Nation of the Haudenosaunee, in his address to the assembly, provides an insight into his nation by referencing the Great Law of Peace: "We were instructed to create societies based upon the principles of peace, equity, justice, and the power of the 'good mind.' Our societies are based upon great democratic principles of authority in the people and of equal responsibilities for the men and women. . . . Our leaders were instructed to be men with vision and to make every decision on behalf of the seventh generation to come."[36] After providing the assembly with a sense of his people, Lyons continues:

> We were told that there would come a time when the world would be covered with smoke, and that it would take our elders and our children. . . . We were told there would come a time when we could not find clean water to wash ourselves, to cook our food, to make our medicines, or to drink, and there would be disease and great suffering. . . . We were told that there would come a time when tending our gardens we would pull up our plants and the vines would be empty. Our precious seed would begin to disappear. There are some specific issues that I must bring forward on behalf of our nations and peoples.[37]

With this eloquent opening, faith keeper Oren Lyons spells out the various issues that affect his people, which include but are not limited to the violation of treaties, the refusal to recognize and support religious freedom, the appropriation of intellectual property, violence against women, and, of course, the basic rights of water and land. Ingrid Washinawatok-El Issa, a member of the Menominee Indian Tribe of

---

[36] Alexander Ewen, ed., *Voice of Indigenous Peoples: Native People Address the United Nations*, with an introduction by The Native American Council of New York City (Santa Fe, NM: Clear Light Publishers, 1994), 33.

[37] Ibid., 33–34.

Wisconsin writes: "Virtually every Indian community has a struggle of some kind or another, yet some of the most pressing issues involve defending the earth."[38] She cites the struggle of the Navajo against the removal from their lands, a struggle in Nevada between the Western Shoshone and the Bureau of Land Management, the Lummi of the Northwest coast trying to stop the clear-cutting of forests, and "in the East the Mohawks of Akwesasne are fighting the smelters and other heavy industries that have virtually destroyed the St. Lawrence Seaway and surrounding regions with toxic wastes and heavy metals, poisoning the reservation's water supply and lands."[39]

Despite placing these very difficult issues before the General Assembly, Lyons presents the global community with alternatives and options, prompting us to remember that we need "to have the courage to change our values for the regeneration of our families and the life that surrounds us."[40] He concludes by making reference to the Two Row Treaty, stating: "Even though you and I are in different boats—you in your boat and we in our canoe—we share the same river of life. What befalls me, befalls you. And downstream, downstream in this river of life, our children will pay for our selfishness, for our greed, and for our lack of vision."[41]

Today, humanity still struggles with greed and a lack of vision. At a meeting held at the United Nations on September 21, 2014, indigenous people gathered once again to address climate change and the survival of Mother Earth. Native peoples issued their plea to protect the Earth, warning that "there is no more time for discussion on preventing 'Climate Change.' That opportunity has passed."[42] They argue that we have passed the point of discussion because the air, water, plants, animals, and all others on the Earth are not the same anymore. They issue their passionate plea underscoring that "all that is Sacred in Life is vanishing because of our actions. The truth is [that] we have moved beyond climate change to survival on Sacred Mother Earth."[43] In order to rectify

---

[38] Ibid., 134.
[39] Ibid.
[40] Ibid., 36.
[41] Ibid., 35.
[42] Indigenous Elders and Medicine Peoples Council, "Beyond Climate Change," 1.
[43] Ibid.

the situation, the Council of Elders believes that we must restore the sacredness in ourselves and honor our obligation to care for all life in our discussions, decisions, and actions, and by instilling respect into our very culture.

Hispanic Catholics in the United States are more tuned into these needs than other US Catholics. In November 2014, the Public Religion Research Institute (PRRI) found that 73 percent of Hispanic Catholics in the United States are "very" or "somewhat" concerned about climate change, higher than any other religious/ethnic group in the study's breakdown.[44] Perceived vulnerability to the impact of climate change could explain this level of concern expressed by Latin@s. In addition, according to Adrianna Quintero, executive director of the Latino environmental advocacy group Voces Verdes, Latin@s have a "deep personal sense of our global interconnectedness . . . not only to our family members . . . but for our extended network of cousins, aunts and grandparents whether they live here in the U.S. or abroad."[45] Katie Rose Quandt, a freelance social justice journalist, comments, "That could be why 86 percent of Latinos in the NRDC [National Resources Defense Council] study cited a 'moral duty' to preserve the planet for children and to respect ancestors' legacy of care for the earth."[46]

Johnson brings to these specific cultural experiences of Indigenous and Latin@ peoples a theoretical framework that helps us to understand how traditions of hierarchical dualism have led to the degradation of marginalized communities and of the planet. She argues against the radical dualism between matter and spirit. Central to her work is the starting point of spirit. Beginning with the experience of Spirit means starting with the experience of the origin of the cosmos: it is an ecological, or cosmological, beginning. It is faithful to Christian traditions, because Spirit was present before Christ's incarnation, and it is also respectful of religious plurality.[47] Her challenge to dualistic thinking

---

[44] Katie Rose Quandt, "Hispanics Lead U.S. Catholics on Climate Change," *Commonweal Magazine* (March 11, 2015), https://www.commonwealmagazine .org/hispanics-lead-us-catholics-climate-change.

[45] Ibid.

[46] Ibid.

[47] Jessica Fraser, "Where the Divine Meets the Created: The Feminist and Ecofeminist Trinitarian Theologies of Elizabeth A. Johnson and Ivone Gebara," *Religious Studies and Theology* 23, no. 2 (2004): 56.

reminds me of my community's passionate narratives about embodied involvement in the natural world. They draw on the many resources of Latin@s' memory, including oral traditions, poems, stories, music, literature, and emergent virtual discourses. Deep metaphors speak to experiences of rootedness, interconnectedness, and interdependence of humans. These images are heightened by peoples' shared experience of their environment impacted by (im)migration and sense of homelessness and return.

In *Voices of Time: A Life in Stories*, Eduardo Galeano[48] tells the story of a Catholic priest hearing confessions of the indigenous people in their Tojolobal language in 1992. As the priest listened to the confessions, the translator Carlos Lenkersdorf began to think that "no one could make sense of such mysteries." These "mysteries" referred to the sins Carlos translated for the people:

- He says he abandoned his corn . . .
- He says the cornfield is very sad. Many days since he last went.
- He says he abused the fire.
- He says he defiled the land.[49]

Moreover, "The priest had no idea what to do with these things that don't appear anywhere on Moses's list."[50] Perhaps the translator felt that no one could "make sense of such mysteries," because of the different cultural context. Latin@s' relationships appear to go beyond the individual/interpersonal level to a broader field of relating, which includes family, land/place, and ancestors. This broader field of relating may include animate and inanimate things—or anything that reminds us or connects us to where we come from or to whom we belong. These relationships reflect the deep connection between *adamah* and God's breath.[51]

---

[48] Eduardo Galeano, *Voices of Time: A Life in Stories*, trans. Mark Fried (New York: Metropolitan Books, 2006).

[49] Ibid., 84.

[50] Ibid.

[51] Jeanette Rodriguez, "La Tierra: Home, Identity, and Destiny," in *From the Heart of Our People: Latino/a Explorations in Systematic Theology*, ed. Orlando O. Espín and Miguel Díaz (Maryknoll, NY: Orbis Books, 1999), 189–208.

All great religious traditions recognize and acknowledge that life is a sacred gift. Ecologists, scientists, and theologians are asking how we can live with our Mother Earth in a way that promotes sustainability. And as we come to learn from La Tierra theologies, the concept of *pacha mama* is integral to the identity and culture of the people. For the Quechua and Aymara people of the Peruvian highlands, the land that they inhabit is more than just a commercial commodity; it is not a commodity to be bought and sold. Similarly, Kenyan environmentalist, political activist, and 2004 Nobel Peace Prize laureate Wangari Maathai once said, "We are called to assist the earth to heal her wounds and in the process heal our own—indeed, to embrace the whole creation in all its diversity, beauty, and wonder."[52] Clearly, members of communities of faith are not the only ones challenging the tradition and other religious communities to respond to this crisis. La Tierra theologies join the voices of ecologists to reclaim and reinterpret symbols and imagine new and hopeful ways to affirm life. The theologies honor the subject, respect the language and affectivity of the heart, realize the importance of teaching our future generations how to humanize their will, and increase one's ability to understand and draw from an intuitive nature of thinking that is dynamic, fluid, creative, searching, and excludes no one. These theologies call for a radical openness to all, placing as paramount the work of relationships as a consequence of being. We, as theologians, must play an active role in this conversation and bring to the table both the life-affirming aspects of our religious and cultural traditions and our skills and commitment to transformation.

Conclusion

I began this essay on a personal note, identifying my social location as the daughter of Ecuadorian immigrants and identifying with a larger group of marginalized and transplanted communities. As I grew, especially in my faith, I found a message of liberation in the dominant/traditional church. It was the priests and sisters who committed themselves to serve our impoverished communities who provided me hope for the future. They ensured my success by nurturing and investing in

---

[52] Wangari Maathai, "Nobel Lecture" (December 10, 2004), http://www.nobelprize.org/nobel_prizes/peace/laureates/2004/maathai-lecture-text.html.

me and providing me with a worldview that affirmed my dignity and called me to mission. These formative years enriched my life, ministry, and academic endeavors.

The key question of our generation was, essentially, how do we, the marginalized, find our voice in order to be heard? How do we attain the keys to a sense of power so we might endeavor for much needed systemic change? And how do we accept the authority to call on those who already have assumed their own voice, power, and authority to heed our call for justice? It is by binding ourselves to allies, such as Elizabeth Johnson, that the Gospel values of true liberation from enslavement to the false idols of hierarchical status and alienation from our mother Earth is possible. I found as I progressed in my scholarship that the prophetic voice of Elizabeth Johnson brought together the unity of our common struggle in the voices of the saints, both living and dead, the reclaiming of the nurturing face of our Mother-Creator, and the return to the roots of our true home—the Earth. The support and intellectual and spiritual integrity of Elizabeth Johnson is a beacon to my own work, and continues to provide direction and guidance for generations of theologians who thirst for justice and peace promised to us by our Creator.

And finally, thank you Dr. Johnson for reimagining and revealing to us through the layers of experience of both the people of God and living church that the God we believe in is beyond our imagination.

Chapter 15

Thinking the Unthinkable
The Theologian and the Planetary Emergency

Richard W. Miller

1. The Problematic Situation[1]

In 2012, twenty past winners of Blue Planet Prize (often referred to as the Nobel for environmental sciences) published a synthesis paper for the United Nations Environment Program (UNEP) in which they maintained the following: "In the face of an absolutely unprecedented emergency [i.e., climate change] society has no choice but to take dramatic action to avert a collapse of civilization. Either we will change our ways and build an entirely new kind of global society, or they will be changed for us."[2]

---

[1] This chapter has to do with spirituality not in terms of the discipline-specific practice of spiritual theology but in a more general sense. A sense captured by the definition of spirituality of Daniel Groody: "Christian spirituality is about following Jesus through the power of the divine breath, living out the values of the kingdom of God and generating a community transformed by the love of God and others. It makes present a kingdom of truth and life, of holiness and grace, of justice, love and peace" (Dan Groody, "Globalizing Justice: The Contribution of Christian Spirituality," *International Review of Mission* 98, no. 2 [2009]: 261).

[2] Gro Harlem Brundtland and others, "Environment and Development Challenges: The Imperative to Act" (The Asahi Glass Foundation, 2012), 7.

Why is climate change not just another serious public problem like income equality but rather a planetary emergency? Because we are committing the human community and the natural world to catastrophic impacts that will last for millennia, and to avoid impacts that could threaten civilization requires immediate and unprecedented global reductions in greenhouse gases. Let me provide a glimpse of the timing and magnitude of some of the forecasted impacts as revealed in important published climate science studies. In May 2014, two studies were published that maintained that six glaciers on the West Antarctica ice sheet are now in a phase of unstoppable melt that will lead to a sea level rise of 1.2 meters (4 feet). This means that if these studies hold up, then we have already condemned Charleston, New Orleans, Fort Lauderdale, Tampa, Saint Petersburg, and Miami to destruction. These estimates do not factor in storm surge damage, which is likely to ravage our coasts much earlier. One study suggests that a five-foot sea level rise, which is likely when we factor in contributions from Greenland, would cause Hurricane Sandy–type storm surges every other year along the East Coast, putting our cities under siege.[3] We have condemned much of the rice-growing regions of Asia to destruction, including 50 percent of the rice fields in Bangladesh (home to 160 million people, with projections of 250 million by 2050) and more than half of those in Vietnam (the world's second largest rice exporter).

Unless we reduce greenhouse gas emissions within the next few years to decade at an unprecedented rate, it is likely that this sea level rise is only the beginning. Our current atmospheric carbon dioxide (CO_2) levels of 400 ppm are way outside the range in which civilization developed (the past ten thousand years of relative global climate stability) when CO_2 levels were around 280 ppm. In fact, CO_2 levels have not been this high for 3 million years,[4] when sea levels were between 50 and 80 feet higher than today,[5] and then 15 million years ago,[6]

[3] Mark Fischetti, "Sea Level Rise 5 Feet in New York City by 2100," *Scientific American* (May 14, 2013).

[4] M. E. Raymo and others, "Mid-Pliocene Warmth: Stronger Greenhouse and Stronger Conveyor," *Marine Micropaleontology* 27 (1996): 313–26.

[5] James Hansen and others, "Assessing 'Dangerous Climate Change': Required Reduction of Carbon Emissions to Protect Young People, Future Generations and Nature," *PLoS ONE* 8, no. 12 (2013): 1-26, at 6.

[6] Aradhna K. Tripati, "Coupling of CO_2 and Ice Sheet Stability Over Major Climate the Last 20 Million Years," *Science* 326, no. 5958 (2009): 1394.

when sea levels were between 80 and 130 feet higher than today.[7] In addition, multi-meter sea level is a possibility that is much closer than we had previously thought. Though it is too early to see if this trend will continue, Dr. James Hansen has argued for years that ice sheet loss is a nonlinear process, and his calculations show that a continued five-year doubling time (a worst-case scenario on our current path) in ice mass loss would generate a 1 meter (3.3 feet) sea level rise by 2045 and 5 meters (16.5 feet) by 2057.[8] With half the world's population living within forty miles of the sea, and three-quarters of the world's largest cities located directly on the coast,[9] a multi-meter sea level rise would likely generate conflicts from "forced migrations and economic collapse,"[10] which "might make the planet ungovernable, threatening the fabric of civilization."[11]

While rapid sea level rise could be much closer than we realize, the transition to a more arid climate in the US Southwest and northern Mexico might already be underway.[12] And as we continue on our present path we increase the risk of locking in, within decades, permanent dustbowl conditions in the US Southwest, southern Europe, northern Africa, southern Africa, and Western Australia.[13] Historically, mega-droughts have led to the collapse of civilizations.

When looking at the earth's history coupled with present observations and the conclusions of climate models, it is becoming increasingly clear that current CO_2 levels are too high and must be brought down to safe levels by the end of the century to avoid multi-meter sea level

---

[7] Ibid.

[8] James Hansen and others, "Ice Melt, Sea Level Rise and Superstorms: Evidence from Paleoclimate Data, Climate Modeling, and Modern Observations that 2° C Global Warming Is Highly Dangerous," *Atmospheric Chemistry and Physics Discussions* 15 (2015): 20059–20179. See figure 8a at 20157. See also an earlier statement with more precision: James Hansen and Makiko Sato, "Update of Greenland Ice Sheet Mass Loss: Exponential?" (2012), 2. Can be accessed at http://www.columbia.edu/~jeh1/mailings/2012/20121226_GreenlandIceSheetUpdate.pdf.

[9] United Nations Environment Programme, "Cities and Coastal Areas," http://www.unep.org/urban_environment/issues/coastal_zones.asp.

[10] Hansen, "Ice Melt, Sea Level Rise and Superstorms," 20119.

[11] Ibid.

[12] Richard Seager and others, "Model Projections of an Imminent Transition to a More Arid Climate in Southwestern North America," *Science* 316 (2007): 1181–84.

[13] Susan Solomon and others, "Irreversible Climate Change Due to Carbon Dioxide Emissions," *PNAS* 106, no. 6 (2009): 1704–9.

rise. Because of the long life of CO_2, 25 percent of which lasts in the atmosphere for at least a thousand years, it is not enough to reduce the level of carbon dioxide emissions; rather, there is only a certain amount of carbon dioxide we can put into the atmosphere. To achieve atmospheric CO_2 levels of 350 ppm we need to remove 367 billion metric tons of CO_2 from the atmosphere by the end of the century through improved forestry and agricultural practices. In addition, we need to reduce CO_2 emission globally by at least 6 percent per year, waiting until 2020 pushes required global reduction rates to 15 percent per year.[14] To have an idea of the staggering scale of this carbon reduction challenge, it is important to recall that the only time that emission reductions over a ten-year period have been more than 1 percent per year was during the economic collapse (i.e., a halving of the economy) of the former Soviet Union after the fall of the Berlin Wall when emissions declined 5.2 percent per year.[15]

In this emergency situation where the human community is now making choices between different levels of catastrophe and "climate change is a clear and present danger to civilization,"[16] how must we envision the theological task? We are faced with the terrible situation that as we write and reflect on God and all things as they are ordered toward God (theology) and more specifically the relationship between human beings and nonhuman nature to construct a theology of creation adequate to the intellectual horizon of our age (ecotheology), we are involved in a system that is committing humanity to ever higher sea level rise that will displace tens of millions of people.

In a 2014 interest group session on discipleship and sustainability at the CTSA, I quickly ran through some of the science of climate change and asked attendees (around thirty people) whether the conclusions from the climate science community permeated their universities. Only one person said that they did. Do these startling conclusions permeate the theological community? In her 1996, CTSA presidential address, Elizabeth Johnson argued that there had been in theology a neglect

[14] See Hansen, "Assessing 'Dangerous Climate Change,'" 10.

[15] Nicholas Stern, *The Economics of Climate Change: The Stern Review* (Cambridge: Cambridge University Press, 2007), Box 8.3, 231.

[16] Lonnie G. Thompson, "Climate Change: The Evidence and Our Options," *The Behavior Analyst* 33, no. 2 (2010): 155. Thompson is perhaps the most distinguished glaciologist of mountain glaciers in the history of climate science.

of "the whole world as God's good creation."[17] Surveying Catholic theology over the past five to ten years indicates that there has been a much greater attention to ecological theology, but does the emergency character of our situation permeate the theological community? Though there has been considerable uptick in interest in the past few years, culminating with Pope Francis's encyclical *Laudato Sì*, I would say the gravity of the situation and a real cognizance of what we are unleashing does not permeate the theological community. Why not? The advance of knowledge means greater and greater specialization; no one person can be an expert in all areas of theology, much less be an expert in multiple fields of inquiry. Thus, theologians, by and large, receive their information regarding the earth sciences from the prestige press. In the late 1970s and 1980s as family-owned newspapers were purchased by large corporations, which were traded on Wall Street, science journalism began to be slashed to cut costs and increase profits to meet the insatiable earning expectations of Wall Street. The quality of science journalism began to decline and continues to decline.[18] In addition, while the prestige press in the United States, in the late 1980s, reported on the emerging scientific consensus regarding the reality of climate change and the need for immediate mandatory action,[19] by the 1990s, the press, following the journalistic norm of balance, gave equal space to scientific consensus reports by specialists and the contrarian views of a small group of scientists, many of whom were not climate scientists and were affiliated with conservative think tanks.[20] This has sown confusion, for decades, about the reality, timing, and magnitude of the climate problem both in the wider public and, by extension, in the theological community.

[17] Elizabeth Johnson, "Turn to the Heavens and the Earth: Retrieval of the Cosmos in Theology," *CTSA Proceedings* 51 (1996): 1.

[18] Robert McChesney and John Nichols, *The Death and Life of American Journalism: The Media Revolution That Will Begin the World Again* (New York: Nation Books, 2010), 25.

[19] Maxwell T. Boykoff and Jules M. Boykoff, "Balance as Bias: Global Warming and the US Prestige Press," *Global Environmental Change* 14 (2004): 129–33.

[20] Among the vast literature on this topic, see Peter J. Jacques, "The Organisation of Denial: Conservative Think Tanks and Environmental Skepticism," *Environmental Politics* 17, no. 3 (2008): 349–85.

There is a further problem. A recent influential work in social psychology has persuasively argued that even when people know about the seriousness of climate change social "norms of conversation, emotion, and attention assist people in keeping troubling emotions at bay and simultaneously produce a 'double reality.'"[21] There is a mutually reinforcing dynamic between the desire not to talk about truths (conversation) that make one feel guilty, fearful, and helpless (emotions) and the socially accepted norms not to talk about truths (conversation) that make others feel guilty, fearful, and helpless (emotions). In this state of individual and social avoidance, one will either avoid those truths or not pay attention to them when they cross one's awareness (attention). As such, one will live in denial. This I would suggest is the most common form of denial, which has led to climate change becoming background noise in the United States.[22] This also is likely contributing to the fact that the climate emergency does not permeate the theological community and the universities in which they work.

There is a related danger among those who write in ecological theology; namely, we will lose hold of our subject matter. This is the risk that our reflections will not be sufficiently grounded in the multiple lines of evidence revealed in a host of scientific disciplines but also, more importantly, for this paper, because the planetary emergency requires us to think the unthinkable. That is to say, even if one glimpses the gravity of the problem, which I have briefly tried to provide in this opening section, and breaks through the sociological norms of conversation, emotion, and attention, one is susceptible to the feeling of powerlessness and angst. And, "it is this quality of angst, a condition that social psychologists tell us we are profoundly motivated to avoid, that essentially makes climate change 'unthinkable.'"[23] Let me illustrate this dynamic from my own experience. After presenting a paper on scientific research on planetary boundaries, which included a section on possible ways out of our predicament (grounds for hope), and its relationship to theology, a colleague admitted to me that he thought my paper "shut down conversation." His comment struck me because he was probably right. I

---

[21] Kari Marie Norgaard, *Living in Denial: Climate Change, Emotions, and Everyday Life* (Cambridge, MA: MIT Press, 2011), 201.

[22] See ibid., 177–205.

[23] Ibid., 197.

adhered closely to the scientific literature and thus my reflections were grounded in our best approximation of the truth of the climate change problem; nevertheless, the "truth" (as our best approximation) shut down conversation in an academic setting. What was going on here? When confronted with the science, we feel the terrible guilt about what we have wrought, especially in the United States, which is responsible for a quarter of all historical emissions[24] and has done more than any other country to inhibit a binding global climate change treaty. We also feel our powerlessness, a loss of personal agency. We want, with the full power of our being, to make it otherwise. This desire, however, is frustrated. Theological reflection in a conference setting seems of little importance compared to the overwhelming truth that has been thrust in front of us. We are, however, theologians, and the theological task is essential for our humanity and for the human community, as I will show momentarily, so theology must go on. Yet, it must go on firmly in contact with the awful truth of climate change.

If the truth of catastrophic climate change can pull agency, including conversation, out from under us, then one path to recover power and agency, and thus conversation, is to theologically treat ecological issues, most especially climate change, as if they are problems that can be addressed on our terms over the next several decades rather than emergencies that must be responded to immediately according to nature's timetable. In the implicit desire to recover agency and conversation, we are susceptible to distancing ourselves from the truth of things as revealed in the scientific literature. As such, we can lose hold of our subject matter. In her 1996 CTSA address, Elizabeth Johnson maintained that theologians neglecting creation as a central theme in their theologies ran the risk of offering "interpretations of reality far removed from the way things actually work [and actually are]."[25] Now, twenty years later, I would like to take up her original concern (i.e., theologians providing interpretations that are not in line with reality) in the present context of the climate change emergency that requires theologians to confront the overwhelming truth of the unfolding climate change tragedy. The questions then become, in light of the terrible truth of the unfolding climate change tragedy, how can theology, especially ecotheology and

---

[24] Hansen, "Assessing 'Dangerous Climate Change,'" 17, fig. 11.

[25] Johnson, "Turn to the Heavens and the Earth," 5.

all the various political theologies and theologies of liberation, hold on
to its subject matter? How must we understand the theological task
such that theology can think the unthinkable?

To respond to these questions, I will rethink the classic Anselmian
definition of theology as faith seeking understanding through a theological anthropology informed by transcendental and existential Thomism
and illuminated by several central Christian doctrines. Let me be more
specific and provide an overview of the argument. First, I argue that the
discipline of theology is grounded in the activity of the human subject
and thus in anthropology (section 2). Second, anthropology reveals that
the intellect and will mutually interpenetrate and inform each other
(section 3). The implications of this mutual interpenetration of the
intellect and will are not adequately captured by the classic Anselmian
definition of theology as faith seeking understanding. Thus the turn to
an anthropology illuminated by the central doctrines of Christianity will
lead to an expansion of the definition of theology (section 6). Third,
Christian anthropology finds its ultimate roots in an ontology informed
by the doctrine of the Trinity. Here we see that the dynamism of the
intellect is a moment within the dynamism of the will toward self-
fulfillment (*eros*) and self-communication (*agape*) of the goods (in this
case theological knowledge, section 6) we possess (section 4). This argument provides the grounds for expanding the definition of theology to
include not only faith seeking understanding but also word spirating love
(section 6). Fourth, the height of agapic love of the finite (the height of
willing in relation to the finite) is revealed in the incarnation, understood
in a unity with creation (i.e., God creates in order to give God's self),
where love is creative (it creates the conditions for its own acceptance)
and incarnational (it is realized in the concrete reality) (section 5.1).
Fifth, the dynamism of the subject toward Infinite Truth and Goodness
that was developed in the preceding anthropology and ontology is not
concerned with nature isolated from grace (i.e., pure nature) but is a
reflection of God's grace (section 5.2). In addition, grace is not simply
received by the human being passively, but grace moves the human
being toward participating in Christ's mission of inaugurating the reign
and kingdom of God (section 5.3). If theology is going to be true to the
activity of the graced human subject, then theology must be understood
not only as faith seeking understanding and word spirating love but also
love participating in incarnating the kingdom (section 6). Sixth, the
pluralism of methods and disciplines and the institutional structures by

which we do theology are expressions of the intellect and will as they mutually interpenetrate each other in their dynamism toward Infinite Truth and Goodness (sections 2, 3, 4, 6). Current institutional structures in the theological community are not adequate to the dynamism of the intellect and will informed by grace and by extension the threefold character of theology. Thus I propose establishing several institutional structures that would set the stage for the flourishing of theology in its threefold character. Finally, these proposed structures could create the conditions of the possibility for theologians to hold on to their subject matter and to think the unthinkable unfolding climate change tragedy.

2. The Theologian, the Dynamism of the Intellect, and the Word "God"

Early Christian writers, beginning with Origen, "used the term *theologia* to mean 'teaching about God' and *theologein* [i.e., to theologize] to mean 'to speak about God,' in either an everyday way or a scientific way."[26] Theologians were not necessarily a specialized group but included all those who spoke about God—poets, "inspired writers and even to the angels who sing hymns to God."[27] To speak of the word "God," to theologize, is not reserved for professional theologians operating in a university setting; rather, the word "God" "confronts us [all of us] with ourselves and with reality as a whole, at least as a question."[28] We are by nature, in our intellectual capacity, an unrestricted desire to know all being, and our apprehension in every act of questioning that being is intelligible is a pre-apprehension (*Vorgriff* in Rahnerian terms) of being as such, as the ground, goal, and condition of the possibility of all our intellectual activity. As the being who affirms herself as questionable, the human being is confronted with the question of the totality and ultimate meaning of her existence. This infinite reality is what we call "God." This word is not our creation; rather, we are born into languages that use this word "God." If the word "God" in the future disappeared

---

[26] Angelo Di Berardino and Basil Studer, eds., *History of Theology*, vol. 1, *The Patristic Period*, trans. Matthew J. O'Connell (Collegeville, MN: Liturgical Press, 1996), 3.

[27] Ibid.

[28] Karl Rahner, *Foundations of Christian Faith: An Introduction to the Idea of Christianity*, trans. William V. Dych (New York: Crossroad, 1984), 51.

without a trace, "neither would these two things exist any more for man, the single whole of reality as such and the single whole of human existence in the mutual interpenetration of both aspects."[29] Without the word "God," the human being would lose hold of her humanity and diminish to a clever animal.[30]

The human being really exists as a human being when she uses the word "God." Thus theologizing, as speaking about God, is not the purview of a specialized academic discipline; rather, all human beings in their humanity are called to theologize. As such, trained theologians sacramentalize what all human beings are called to in their graced humanity. As the mind moves ceaselessly toward knowing all there is to be known about all of reality (and reflects on knowing itself) various ways or methods of knowing are discovered and differentiated. The specialization and the pluralism of methods within theology are an expression of the human being's unrestricted desire to know as concretized and institutionalized in various disciplines and methods.

3. The Theologian and the Dynamism of the Will

The human being is not simply a desire for truth but also a desire for goodness. The will is that capacity within us (i.e., an active potency) that desires and seeks that which we perceive as good. The dynamism of the intellect and the will are distinct in their formal object, that is, the aspect under which they are oriented toward being. The intellect is oriented toward being as true. The will is oriented toward being as good. There is a further distinction between intellect and will that should be noted. While the dynamism of the intellect moves "toward making its object present in some intentional mode of idea or image,"[31] the will is an existential dynamism. It moves toward "concrete possession of, or existential union with, the being itself in its concrete reality as good."[32] While distinct, the intellect and will mutually interpenetrate each other such that the dynamism of the intellect toward the true is in a *peri-*

---

[29] Ibid., 47–48.

[30] Ibid., 48.

[31] W. Norris Clarke, "Freedom as Value," in *Freedom and Value*, ed. Robert O. Johann (New York: Fordham University Press, 1976), 12.

[32] Ibid., 13.

choresis[33] with the dynamism of the will toward the good. The desire to know is a moment within the desire for the good. The only reason I desire the truth is because I recognize it as good; indeed, I recognize it as my good. Conversely, I can only desire the good if I know it in some way. Furthermore, the horizon of being as the good like the horizon of being as the truth is infinite and unlimited.

4. The Trinity and the *Perichoresis* of Truth and Goodness

God is *ipsum esse subsistens*, the subsisting act of existence. The inner trinitarian life, as the exemplar of the act of existence, reveals that being itself is self-communicative and self-expressive. It is of the very nature of God "to pour over into two supreme eternal acts of self-communication of the perfection of its nature, first from the Father to the Son, then from the Father and Son together to the Holy Spirit: the procession of the Son or Logos according to self-knowledge, and the procession of the Holy Spirit according to self-love."[34] God in God's self is supremely self-communicative, and this is God's goodness. All created beings participate in the plenitude of existence in a limited way. If God is "to be itself," while creatures are "to be in a limited way," then the characteristic perfections of the act of existence (i.e., *esse* or "to be") are found less intensely in the creature. As such, all beings are self-communicative and self-expressive. While God is self-communicative as an aspect of God's perfection (i.e., God's goodness), finite beings are self-communicative for two reasons. First, because they are rich.

---

[33] The Greek term *perichoresis* can be translated as "interpenetration." The idea finds its roots in the New Testament, especially in John's gospel where the Son states "Believe me that I am in the Father and the Father is in me" (John 14:11; NRSV). In the history of the development of the doctrine of the Trinity this idea of the mutual interpenetration of the Father and the Son was extended to the Holy Spirit. Though the notion of mutual interpenetration was found in Hilary of Poitiers and Gregory of Nazianzus, the term *perichoresis* is first used by Maximus the Confessor to speak of the mutual interpenetration of the two natures of Christ. It was extended to the doctrine of the Trinity in the work of St. John Damascene. See Gilles Emery, *The Trinitarian Theology of St. Thomas Aquinas*, trans. Francesca Aran Murphy (Oxford: Oxford University Press, 2007), 298–300.

[34] W. Norris Clarke, "Action as the Self-Revelation of Being: A Central Theme in the Thought of St. Thomas," in *Explorations in Metaphysics: Being—God—Person* (Notre Dame, IN: University of Notre Dame Press, 1994), 49.

The creature is receiving the perfection of existence from God at every moment according to its limited form and actively communicates itself as the natural outflowing of the act of existence (*agere sequitur esse*). Second, because they are poor. They lack the fullness of existence and in striving to obtain the richness of being corresponding to their nature, must "enrich themselves from the richness of those around them."[35] For nonintellectual beings their self-communication is unconscious and unaware. For intellectual finite beings their self-communication flows from the subject itself as aware of itself through knowledge and as possessing itself through free choice. There is then the possibility of a free self-communication, a free gift of self to the other. Conversely, there is the negative capacity to withhold oneself from the other. Because the dynamism toward self-communication is a feature of the human being *qua* existent, it is "connatural for a human person to be a lover, to go out towards others we love, sharing what we have and wishing them the good they need for their own flourishing."[36] This willing of the good of the other is to love agapically.

The central metaphor for God in the New Testament is that God is *agape*. *Agape* is a type of self-giving love whose focus is not on the lover's good but on the good of the beloved. Thus, the least wrong way to speak of the God of Jesus Christ, as revealed in the New Testament, is that God is self-giving love (*agape*; 1 John 4:8, 16). When the human being freely gives of herself (to love agapically) the human being freely affirms her own being as self-communicative and shares in God's life of self-giving love through which she foretastes her end of abiding in union with God. As 1 John teaches, "God is love [*agape*], and those who abide in love abide in God, and God abides in them" (4:16; NRSV).

Agapic love is a conscious and free acceptance of what we are in our very being. Agapic love is the meaning of being when being exists at an ontological intensity where being is conscious of itself and takes possession of itself, that is, when being is at the level of personal being. While God communicates God's self out of pure self-presence and perfection, the human being in her imperfection is in a process of development. The whole dynamism of the human being is toward

---

[35] W. Norris Clarke, *Person and Being* (Milwaukee, WI: Marquette University Press, 1993), 10.
[36] Ibid., 76.

possessing or being in union with Infinite Truth and Goodness (God) as her fulfillment, completion, and end. This dynamism toward self-fulfillment is *eros*. In loving agapically we abide in God's life and we foretaste ultimate union with God who is Infinite Truth and Goodness. For the human being there is a dynamic spiral of self-development in the interplay between the drive toward self-fulfillment in reaching out toward Infinite Truth and Goodness, as we know and love finite truths and goods, and the self-communication of the riches one attains in the drive toward self-fulfillment. Without the self-communication of the good we possess, there is no self-fulfillment; without the dynamism toward self-fulfillment, there is not the dynamic movement to expand and enrich ourselves further as we asymptotically move toward Infinite and Truth and Goodness.

5. Incarnation, Grace, and the Kingdom of God

5.1. Incarnation

The perfect, supreme, and necessary divine self-communication is the self-communication in the inner life of God. God, in contemplating and loving God's own goodness, perceives it not only as God's proper perfection but as able to be given to others and thus recognizes the sufficient reason (no necessity here) for freely sharing God's self.[37] God creates the universe (a gift that has its being by receiving it from God) in order to give God's self (incarnation, grace, and ultimately union with the triune God). The final cause of God's creative act is union with God, and the proleptic final cause is the self-communication of God in the missions of the Son and the Spirit. The unity (one person: the person of the Logos) and plurality (two natures: divine and human) of Christ is grounded in God's free absolute decision to create in order to give God's self. A plurality cannot ground a unity; thus in order for there to be a unity in plurality, "the plurality must be seen as plural moments arising from a single being, for a subsequent conjunction of elements existing separately on their own cannot form an essential unity."[38] Creation, as

---

[37] See John H. Wright, "Divine Knowledge and Human Freedom: The God Who Dialogues," *Theological Studies* 38, no. 3 (1977): 455.

[38] Joseph H. P. Wong, *Logos-Symbol in the Christology of Karl Rahner* (Roma: Las, 1984), 77.

a gift, exists for God to communicate God's self. God creates beings and the whole interconnection of beings turned toward each other (*universum*, turned toward unity) in order to communicate God's self as Father, Son, and Holy Spirit. In God's agapic love outside the inner life of God as revealed to us in the sending of the Son who enters into our concrete history and the Spirit who is present in the spiritual depths of our existence,[39] God's love created human beings as capable of receiving God's self. God's agapic love of the finite is creative and incarnational.

While the human being does not create ex nihilo, the conscious self-communication of the human being (agapic love) is in its deepest roots not simply about modifying the present structures but is truly creative. The incarnation, understood in a unity with creation, reveals what self-communicative love of the finite is at its height; namely, it creates in order to communicate itself.[40]

5.2. Grace

Since the purpose (final cause) of God's creating was in order to give God's self, the purpose or final cause necessarily effects an ontological change in all human beings, ordering them in knowledge and love toward union with God through the self-communication of God in the mode of offer (what Rahner calls the supernatural existential). As such, "transcendence towards being in general, the natural openness for being as a whole, cannot be clearly distinguished in subsequent re-flexion from the supernatural transcendence, the openness of the soul informed by grace."[41] Thus while nature and grace are distinct, nature can never be found separated from the concrete determination of the supernatural existential.

Rahner's analysis focuses on the inability to distinguish graced nature and the underlying nature and speaks specifically of a "metaphysics of

---

[39] Rahner, *Foundations of Christian Faith*, 137.

[40] This does not mean that God is more agapic for becoming incarnate. That is to say, God's agapic love in God creating in order to give God's self as revealed in the sending of the Son and the Spirit does not add anything to God's self-giving love in the inner life of the Trinity. Rather, it reveals to us what God is in God's self and what the height of love is outside the inner life of God.

[41] Karl Rahner, "Nature and Grace," in *Theological Investigations 4: More Recent Writings*, trans. Kevin Smyth (London: Darton, Longman and Todd, 1966), 178.

knowledge" focusing on the dynamism of the intellect. Nevertheless, "transcendence towards being in general, the natural openness for being as a whole,"[42] includes not only the dynamism of the intellect toward the whole of being as true but also the dynamism of will toward the whole of being as good. We not only receive God's grace, but that grace has a dynamic influence on us. The real active influence of grace on us moves us to act according to the spirit of Christ. What does it mean for us to act according to the spirit of Christ? Here we will turn to the central teaching of Jesus, namely, that in him the reign and kingdom of God are at hand.

5.3. *The Reign and Kingdom of God*

There is a "wide consensus in biblical scholarship that the Kingdom of God was the overarching theme of the historical Jesus and the Bible in general."[43] The coming of God's reign and kingdom was the centerpiece of Jesus' ministry, with the expression "reign of God" occurring 150 times in the New Testament.[44] Establishing the reign and kingdom of God "means the transformation not only of the human heart but of the

---

[42] Ibid.

[43] Mark Saucy, *The Kingdom of God in the Teaching of Jesus in 20th Century Theology* (Dallas: Word Publishing, 1997), 254. Hebrew term *melek* and the Greek *basileus* mean "king," but because this metaphor is understood in dynamic terms in the Scriptures these terms are often translated as "reign" rather than the more static term "kingdom." The expression "reign of God" more accurately captures the dynamic character of God's rule over creation, and history and the expression is more gender inclusive than "kingdom of God," which can lead to a male imaging of God. There is, however, an embodied and concrete character to God's transformative action and rule in history that is better captured by the phrase "the kingdom of God." The concrete character of the kingdom can be glimpsed in the images of assurance that the oppression of the poor will be overcome. Jesus guarantees to the poor in spirt that they will "possess the land" (Matt 5:5). There is the notion of "entry into the kingdom" (Matt 5:20; 7:21; 18:3; 19:23, 24; Mark 9:47; 10:23-25; Luke 18:25; John 3:5). In the judgment scene in Matt 25:31-46 the kingdom has been prepared for the blessed from the foundation of the world. During the Last Supper meal Jesus promises his disciples that they "may eat and drink at my table in my kingdom and you will sit on thrones judging the twelve tribes of Israel" (Luke 22:30; NRSV). In light of the dynamic and concrete character of God's transformative rule of history, I will use the phrase "God's reign and kingdom" to capture both meanings.

[44] Donald Senior, "Reign of God," in *The New Dictionary of Theology*, ed. Joseph A. Komonchak, Mary Collins, and Dermot A. Lane (Collegeville, MN: Liturgical Press, 1990), 856.

oppressive social structures that dehumanize and exclude the poor and defenseless from participation in the family of Israel."[45] For, the reign and kingdom of God is "characterized by forgiveness and reconciliation, by universal justice and peace."[46] While the reign and kingdom of God pervade all aspects of existence, including social systems and structures,[47] it can never be identified with any particular social organization or political structure. In Jesus the kingdom of God has come near so the kingdom of God is at hand (Luke 17:20; see also Luke 10:9, 11); nevertheless, the New Testament clearly indicates that there is a future character to the kingdom.[48] While the kingdom is present, it is not yet realized. As not realized and the domain of God as Lord of history, the kingdom cannot be identified with a particular political structure.

The dynamic influence of grace moves us toward participating in the inauguration of the kingdom of God such that "the future kingdom of God provides the horizon and goal for Christian action in the present."[49] Yet, "it remains God's prerogative to bring it in its fullness. We do not bring it or build it up."[50]

6. The Theologian, the *Perichoresis* of Truth and Goodness, and the Planetary Emergency

The central questions that arose in the first section's analysis of the problematic situation were these: In light of the terrible truth of the

[45] Ibid., 858.

[46] Ibid.

[47] The miracles, which are signs of the kingdom, indicate that the kingdom is not simply about the interior life of the person but about "the physical condition of the human body and nature itself" (Saucy, *The Kingdom of God in the Teaching of Jesus*, 323). Furthermore, Jesus' miracles not only heal the physical conditions of the human body but also draw the person, who was often an outcast of society, back into society and heal their alienation while simultaneously transforming the character of the community.

[48] Among other textual evidence, the parables of Jesus, as Joachim Jeremias argued, do indicate that in Jesus the kingdom is present, but the kingdom is not realized, for the parables of the mustard seed, the leaven, the sower, and the patient husbandman all "looked forward to the future culmination of something begun in the present." (Saucy, *The Kingdom of God in the Teaching of Jesus*, 20).

[49] Daniel Harrington, "Kingdom of God," in *The New Dictionary of Catholic Social Thought*, ed. Judith A. Dwyer (Collegeville, MN: Liturgical Press, 1994), 512.

[50] Ibid.

unfolding climate change tragedy, how can theology, especially ecotheology and all the various political theologies and theologies of liberation, hold on to its subject matter? How must we understand the theological task such that theology can think the unthinkable? In this final section, I will bring together the various threads of the argument in theological anthropology, draw out their implications, and offer a proposal for the doing of theology in the planetary emergency.

The pluralism of methods and disciplines and the institutional structures by which we do theology are concrete expressions of the dynamism of the human spirit toward Infinite Truth and Goodness. There is a mutual interpenetration of truth and goodness as transcendentals that express a mode of being not expressed by the term "being." Since the human spirit is conformed to reality there is a corresponding *perichoresis* between the dynamism of the intellect toward being as true and the dynamism of the will toward being as good. The desire to know is a moment within the desire for one's good (i.e., one's fulfillment). The dynamism of the will in a finite subject is both a dynamism toward possession of the good (*eros*) and the communication of the good (*agape*). This twofold dynamism of the graced human being finds its deepest root in God's communication of God's self within the inner life of God. It is an ordered self-communication first from the Father to the Son through the procession of the Son or Logos according to knowledge, then through the procession of the Holy Spirit according to love.[51] What it means to communicate to the finite the good one possesses is revealed in God's creative and incarnational love that creates conditions for its own communication and acceptance.

The institutional structures that have been established by the theological community for the doing of theology are concrete expressions of the dynamic spiral of personal development between self-fulfillment and self-communication of a finite graced subject who is oriented toward Infinite Truth and Goodness.[52] They also reflect the creative and

---

[51] See Clarke, "Action as the Self-Revelation of Being," 49. The use of the terms "first" and "second" in reference to the procession of the Son and Spirit should not be understood in temporal terms because God is eternal; rather, they need to be understood in terms of a natural order of priority.

[52] The structures in any historical period are conditioned by historical circumstances; nevertheless, the underlying ground for these structures is the invariant character of the subject as a dynamism toward Infinite Truth and Goodness.

incarnational love that creates conditions for its own communication and acceptance. The dynamism of the intellect in its search for truth is reflected in the creation of a pluralism of methods and subdisciplines within theology. The dynamism of the will toward self-fulfillment and self-communication are reflected in the institutional structures that have been created to advance conversation (academic societies, academic journals, published books, and universities as places of conversation and teaching). These institutions were created to foster conversation among scholars across space and time in order to expand their knowledge in the drive toward self-fulfillment and to allow scholars to communicate the good they possess (i.e., knowledge) to other scholars and students. In light of the core doctrines of the faith illuminating an anthropology influenced by transcendental and existential Thomism, we see that the communicative character of theology, as an expression of the twofold dynamism of the human being, indicates that theology is not simply faith seeking understanding (*fides quaerens intellectum*) but also the word spirating love (*verbum spirans amorem*).

The dynamism of the will not only is in service to knowing the truth (as the subject moves toward her self-fulfillment) and communicating the truth that is known (as the subject is freely faithful to her natural dynamism toward self-communication) but also informs the intellect in another crucial way. What the subject gives itself to in inquiry is informed by what the subject perceives is of interest and value, that is, what it perceives is good and worthy to know. While the will is open to the Infinite Good it is always within the world choosing finite goods. As such, the range of the subject's concerns is conditioned by her cultural and social location. All cultures and societies fall far short of the reign and kingdom of God as they are vulnerable to power operating in opposition to truth and love. In this situation, one can shrink in upon oneself and miss that one's good is caught up with the good of all,[53] that one's fulfillment is realized in giving oneself away. Thus, one is susceptible

---

[53] The dynamism of the person toward the good is a dynamism for her fulfillment, for her completion, for her happiness. One of the central desires of the human being is for peace, which can be understood (at a minimum) as the cessation of conflict—internal conflict and conflict with others. When faced with the truth of the suffering of others, a human being, who has not diminished her humanity, will at the very least be unsettled by this truth. One's peace is caught up with the peace of all others. Thus, one's desire for fulfillment is linked to the fulfillment of all others.

to veiled self-interest and blindness of the other. In the *perichoresis* of knowledge and goodness, this blindness will affect the range of one's questioning and inquiry. As liberation theologians rightly point out, knowledge is never neutral but reflects the cultural environment and values of the social circumstances of the time.

The necessary general corrective for such blindness is the recognition that the promise of the reign and kingdom of God is for universal peace, justice, and flourishing. The particular concrete corrective is a hermeneutic from the margins or a preferential option for the poor. The preferential option for the poor does not mean that one loses one's focus on the common good and limits oneself to a particular experience of a particular group (though that group is the majority globally); rather, it recognizes that in light of the susceptibility of the will to distortion and the concomitant constriction of the range of inquiry of the intellect, the preferential option for the poor and marginalized becomes the necessary hermeneutical principle through which one examines society in relationship to the hoped-for kingdom of God. It is a necessary hermeneutic so that the dynamism of the graced human being to truth and goodness remains open to being as true and good in light of the dynamism toward the reign and kingdom of God in its promise of universal peace, justice, and flourishing.

This theology from the margins is already operative in many of the post–Vatican II turns in theology that Elizabeth Johnson pointed to in her CTSA address: "the turn to the subject under threat or defeated, in political theology; the linguistic turn, reintegrating the subject to community; the turn to the nonperson through the praxis of justice in liberation theologies as well as in feminist, womanist, *mujerista*, and Third World women's theologies."[54] In light of the work of Elizabeth Johnson and others, there has been a turn to creation, to Earth; now there must be a deepening of that turn such that theology is done in the truth of the planetary emergency. Deepening this turn to creation will deepen the other aforementioned turns while adding young people (especially poor young people) to the list of those who are treated as nonpersons, who must be liberated through a praxis of injustice, in the global Ponzi scheme that is bringing climate chaos into their lives and the lives of future generations. While the various turns operate within

[54] Johnson, "Turn to the Heavens and the Earth," 4.

the *perichoresis* of the intellect and will, they are incomplete in terms of the dynamism of the will, which as an existential dynamism moves toward a praxis centered on the concrete realization of the good. Here the notion of the kingdom of God becomes crucial for informing the dynamism of the graced will as it moves (as an existential dynamism) toward realization of the good in the concrete. In light of the dynamism toward the kingdom, theology is not only faith seeking understanding and word spirating love but also love participating in incarnating the kingdom. The theological community, however, has not sufficiently institutionalized the dynamism toward the realization of the reign and kingdom of God in the concrete.

An adequate reflection on possible institutional structures faithful to the dynamism of the will in its *perichoresis* with the intellect would require another paper, but let me briefly provide some examples in terms of broadening the reach of the scholarly and educational work of the theological community. First, the theological community could establish a separate theological society or establish a society adjoined to the Catholic Theological Society of America or College Theology Society for theologians to produce consensus documents, which would be circulated to audiences outside the academic community. These consensus documents would critique, through a theological lens in dialogue with other disciplines, the many facets of the social, economic, and political systems that have led to the planetary emergency while offering alternative visions for our global community. Second, this society or another group of theologians could establish a peer-reviewed journal dealing with the emergency. Relationships could be established with online publications that have a wide online reach (*National Catholic Reporter, America, Commonweal*, etc.) such that a link to the new journal was provided at those sites. Articles would have two versions—a nontechnical summary version for the lay reader and a technical version for the professional theologian. This would try to combine the peer-reviewed requirements for serious scholarship with the need to reach a wider audience. Third, the theological community could engage presidents of the Catholic colleges and universities in the United States, seeking to educate them about the gravity of the problem and how universities could respond to the emergency. Fourth, theology departments could make a commitment to hire theologians to do political theology in the mode of social outreach, publishing in academic journals but also seeking venues to reach a wider audience.[55] Each one of these four proposals would have to be worked out with much greater detail, but they offer introductory suggestions that would not hurt the academic rigor of our discipline; instead, they would likely enhance it. It bears repeating: this social outreach is not social activism at the periphery of what it means to do theology; rather, in light of this rethinking of theology through theological anthropology, this social outreach is now understood as integral to the discipline of theology.

According to Kari Marie Norgaard's influential work in social psychology, which I referenced earlier, it is the feeling of powerlessness in the face of the overwhelming truth of climate change that generates angst, which "we are profoundly motivated to avoid."[56] It is this recoiling from angst that influences our retreat into lived climate denial and "essentially makes climate change unthinkable."[57] Since the feeling of powerlessness generates lived denial, the way out of lived denial is empowerment. In the process of creating the aforementioned structures in fidelity to the *perichoresis* of the dynamism of the intellect and will and to leverage our power in the service of the kingdom, we empower ourselves and thereby create conditions for moving out of the double life and lived denial. The structures will also provide a social context in which colleagues within the theological community, our universities, our students, fellow Catholics, and citizens can become empowered and capable of living in the truth. When we live in the truth our interpretations of reality will not risk "being far removed from the way things actually are."[58] As such, we could begin to think the unthinkable and authentically do theology in our emergency situation. Tragically, there is a great deal that will be unthinkable in the days ahead.[59]

---

[55] This understanding of social outreach is influenced by the notion of *proyección social* that was developed by Ignacio Ellacuría, SJ, and set in motion by Ignacio Martín Baró, SJ, Segundo Montes, SJ (all of whom were murdered in the 1989 Jesuit Massacre at the UCA), and others, including Jon Sobrino, SJ, and Dean Brackley, SJ. The full implications of this notion for Catholic universities and theologians is the subject matter of another paper.

[56] Norgaard, *Living in Denial*, 197.

[57] Ibid.

[58] Johnson, "Turn to the Heavens and the Earth," 5.

[59] I ended with thinking, but in the *perichoresis* of intellect and will, in their dynamism toward the reign and kingdom of God, the movement does not stop at thinking but will move further in social outreach, and social outreach will increase our capacity to confront further overwhelming truths.

Epilogue

Reverence for the Earth—
Friendship with the Wild Beasts
Two Footnotes to Ecological Theology

Jürgen Moltmann

1. "Reverence for Life," proclaimed Albert Schweitzer and remembered animals and human beings. Animals and human beings, however, are living from the earth. The earth is "bringing forth living creatures, cattle and everything that creepeth upon the earth" (Gen 1: 24). All "living things" are called "alive" because they reproduce themselves, but the earth is "alive" because she does produce all living things but does not reproduce herself. Also we human beings are taken from the earth, and shall again return to the earth. We are children of the earth and the earth is rightly called "our mother," because she is the mother of all living beings. We humans are members of the great community of life on earth. Should not the "reverence for life" begin with the reverence for the earth? But what do we mean by "the earth"?

We are speaking of the earth when we mean the land on which we stand: earth, sea, and air. We are speaking of the earth when we mean the creation of heaven and earth. We are speaking of the earth when we admire satellite photos of our "blue planet." Then we have the whole of

256

the earth before our eyes, the land, the sea, the clouds, and the winds, and we discover that we the human race do not live on the earth but in the earth. All life, human life included, takes place in the earth. The planet earth embraces us from all sides like a living organism, taking care of fortunate living conditions.

Before we are taking care for our life the earth cares for us. Before we are claiming the earth is given in our hands, we are given in the hands of the earth, and we must confess that her care is generally speaking a good care. The planet earth can survive without us humans and did so for millions of years, but we can't live without the earth. As the creation story and the theory of evolution are telling us, we humans are late-comers. This doesn't mean we are the "crown of creation," but rather we are the most dependent creatures. We are dependent on the life of animals, the life of plants and trees, the existence of the land, the water and the air, the light of the day, and the darkness at night. We must learn cosmic humility instead of the modern arrogance of world domination. We must integrate ourselves into the life-community of the earth.

2. Israel's prophet promised not only a new earth and a new heaven but also a messianic kingdom of peace for humankind and animals, where there is no killing anymore. Children will play with snakes, and lions will eat straw (Isa 11:6-8). This indicates that meat-eating humans and the beasts of prey are peaceless creatures. The future doesn't belong to them. The messianic kingdom is without violence. The present situation in the human and the animal world is not in the order of their creator, though some say fight of competition with the result of the survival of the fittest is the given law of nature. At the end of his temptations by satan, it is told that

> Jesus was with the wild beasts,
> and the angels ministered unto him. (Mark 1:13)

Jesus doesn't "dominate" over the animals, as humans should do according to the creation story (Gen 1:26). He was "with the wild beasts" as with his friends. But he "dominates" over the inhabitants of heavens; they are his servants, a strange reversal of what we may have expected. The "wild beasts" may have smelt the creation-peace going out from Christ. Of some saints it is told they were seeking and finding peace with the "wild beasts." There was Saint Francis of Assisi who preached to the birds and they listened to him. I suppose he also listened to the sermons of the birds as I do every morning. And there was Saint Sergius of Radonesh, who lived with the bears in the Russian woods and healed their wounds.

Select Bibliography of the Works of Elizabeth A. Johnson

Books

Consider Jesus: Waves of Renewal in Christology. New York: Crossroad, 1990.

She Who Is: The Mystery of God in Feminist Theological Discourse. New York: Crossroad, 1992. Paperback edition: New York: Crossroad, 1993. Tenth anniversary edition with new preface, 2002. Twenty-fifth anniversary edition with "history of reception," forthcoming, 2017.

Women, Earth, and Creator Spirit. Madeleva Lecture in Spirituality. New York: Paulist Press, 1993.

Friends of God and Prophets: A Feminist Theological Reading of the Communion of Saints. New York: Continuum; Ottawa: Novalis Press, 1998. Paperback edition: London: SCM Press, 1998.

The Church Women Want: Catholic Theology in Dialogue. (Editor and Contributor.) New York: Crossroad, 2002.

Dangerous Memories: A Mosaic of Mary in Scripture. New York: Continuum Publishers International, 2004.

Truly Our Sister: A Theology of Mary in the Communion of Saints. New York and London: Continuum Publishers International, 2003. Paperback edition: New York: Continuum, 2006.

Quest for the Living God: Mapping Frontiers in the Theology of God. New York: Continuum Publishers International, 2007. Paperback edition: New York: Continuum, 2011.

Ask the Beasts: Darwin and the God of Love. London & New York: Bloomsbury, 2014.

Abounding in Kindness: Writings for the People of God. Maryknoll, NY: Orbis Books, 2015.

The Strength of Her Witness: Jesus Christ in Women's Global Voices. (Editor.) Maryknoll, NY: Orbis Books, 2016. (Forthcoming)

Documentation and Discussion of Elizabeth Johnson's Interaction with US Bishops' Committee on Doctrine in 2011

Richard Gaillardetz, ed., *When the Magisterium Intervenes: The Magisterium and Theologians in Today's Church.* Collegeville, MN: Liturgical Press, 2012. Part 3 of this book includes a dossier of Elizabeth Johnson's interactions with the USCCB Committee on Doctrine in 2011.

Horizons: Journal of the College Theology Society 38, no. 2 (Fall 2011): 284–337: Theological Roundtable: "The Johnson Case and the Practice of Theology: An Interim Report," with analysis by Cristina Traina, Francis Schüssler Fiorenza, Robert Masson, Richard Gaillardetz.

Articles in Professional Journals

"The Right Way to Speak about God? Pannenberg on Analogy." *Theological Studies* 43 (1982): 673–92.

"The Ongoing Christology of Wolfhart Pannenberg." *Horizons: Journal of the College Theology Society* 9 (1982): 237–50.

"Resurrection and Reality in the Thought of Wolfhart Pannenberg." *Heythrop Journal* 24 (1983): 1–18.

"The Theological Relevance of the Historical Jesus: A Debate and a Thesis." *The Thomist* 48 (1984): 1–43.

"The Incomprehensibility of God and the Image of God Male and Female." *Theological Studies* 45 (1984): 441–65.

"Mary and Contemporary Christology: Rahner and Schillebeeckx." *Eglise et Théologie* 15 (1984): 155–82.

"Christology's Impact on the Doctrine of God." *Heythrop Journal* 26 (1985): 143–63.

"Jesus, The Wisdom of God: A Biblical Basis for Non-Androcentric Christology." *Ephemerides Theologicae Lovanienses* 61 (1985): 261–94.

"The Marian Tradition and the Reality of Women." *Horizons: Journal of the College Theology Society* 12 (1985): 116–35.

"The Symbolic Character of Theological Statements about Mary." *Journal of Ecumenical Studies* 22 (1985): 312–35.

"The Legitimacy of the God Question: Pannenberg's New Anthropology." *Irish Theological Quarterly* 52 (1986): 289–303.

"Images of the Historical Jesus in Catholic Christology." *The Living Light* 23 (1986): 47–66.

"Christology and Social Justice: John Paul II and the American Bishops." *Chicago Studies* 26 (1987): 155–65.

"May We Invoke the Saints?" *Theology Today* 44 (April 1987): 32–52.

"Feminist Hermeneutics." *Chicago Studies* 27 (1988): 123–35.

"Mary and the Female Face of God." *Theological Studies* 50 (1989): 500–526.

"The Maleness of Christ." In *Concilium: The Special Nature of Women?*, ed. Anne Carr and Elisabeth Schüssler Fiorenza, 107–16. London: SCM Press, 1991/6.

"Author's Response," in "Review Symposium of *She Who Is*." *Horizons: Journal of the College Theology Society* 20 (Fall 1993): 339–44.

"Jesus and Salvation." *Proceedings of the Catholic Theological Society of America* 49 (1994): 1–18.

"Feminist Theology: A Review of the Literature: Introduction." With Susan Ross. *Theological Studies* 56 (1995): 327–30.

"Turn to the Heavens and the Earth: Retrieval of the Cosmos in Theology." *Proceedings of the Catholic Theological Society of America* 51 (1996): 1–14.

"Does God Play Dice? Divine Providence and Chance." *Theological Studies* 57 (1996): 3–18.

"Trinity: To Let the Symbol Sing Again." *Theology Today* 54 (October 1997): 299–311.

"Community on Earth as in Heaven: Jewish and Christian Roots of the Communion of Saints." *Union Seminary Quarterly Review* 52 (1998): 49–66.

"Author's Response," in "Review Symposium: *Friends of God and Prophets*." *Horizons: Journal of the College Theology Society* 26 (Spring 1999): 127–35.

"A Community of Holy People in a Sacred World: Rethinking the Communion of Saints." *New Theology Review* 12 (May 1999): 5–16.

"Tectonic Shifts: Catholic Theology as American, Lay, and Pluralistic." *Horizons: Journal of the College Theology Society* 26 (1999) [Twenty-Fifth Anniversary Issue]: 295–98.

"Naming God 'She': Theological Implications." *Princeton Seminary Bulletin* 22 (2001): 134–49.

"A Critical Reading of the Marian Tradition." *Theology Digest* 47 (2001): 317–25.

"Author's Response," in "Review Symposium of *Truly Our Sister*." *Horizons: Journal of the College Theology Society* 31 (Spring 2004): 174–86.

"Frontiers of the Quest for the Living God." *Sewanee Theological Review* 48, no. 3 (Pentecost 2005): 273–86.

"The Living God in Women's Voices." *Sewanee Theological Review* 48, no. 3 (Pentecost 2005): 287–300.

"The Living God in Cosmic Perspective." *Sewanee Theological Review* 48, no. 3 (Pentecost 2005): 301–15.

"One Fire Kindles Another: Crisis and the Leadership of Holy Men and Women." In *Concilium: Christianity in Crisis?*, ed. Jon Sobrino and Felix Wilfred, 108–14. London: SCM Press, 2005/3.

"*Truly Our Sister*: A Feminist Hermeneutical Disciplinary Approach." In *Concilium: The Many Faces of Mary*, ed. Diego Irarrázaval, Susan Ross, and Marie-Theres Wacker, 11–18. London: SCM Press, 2008/4.

"Galilee: A Critical Matrix for Marian Studies." *Theological Studies* 70 (June 2009): 327–46.

"Female Symbols for God: The Apophatic Tradition and Social Justice." *International Journal of Orthodox Theology* 1, no. 2 (2010): 40–57.

"Creator Spirit and Ecological Ethics: An Ancient Frontier." *Concilium: Lord and Life-Giver: the Spirit Today*, ed. Paul Murray, Diego Irarrázaval, Maria Clara Bingemer, 23–31. London: SCM Press, 2011/4.

"Is God's Charity Broad Enough for Bears?" *Irish Theological Quarterly* 80 (November 2015): 283–93.

Chapters in Edited Books

"Marian Devotion in the Western Church." In *Christian Spirituality: High Middle Ages and Reformation*, ed. Jill Raitt, 392–414. Vol. 17, *World Spirituality: An Encyclopedic History of the Religious Quest*, ed. Ewert Cousins. New York: Crossroad, 1987.

"Mary and the Image of God." In *Mary, Woman of Nazareth*, ed. Doris Donnelly, 25–68. New York: Paulist Press, 1989.

"Reconstructing a Theology of Mary." In *Mary, Woman of Nazareth*, ed. Doris Donnelly, 69–91. New York: Paulist Press, 1989.

"Jesus Christ." In *The Universal Catechism Reader*, ed. Thomas Reese, 70–83. San Francisco: Harper & Row, 1990.

"Theology and Science: A Response." In *John Paul II on Science and Religion: Reflections on the New View from Rome*, ed. Robert Russell, William Stoeger, George Coyne, 37–39. Rome: Vatican Observatory Pub., 1990.

"Mary in Praxis-Oriented Theology: Memory, Narrative, Solidarity." In *Kecharitomene: International Festschrift for René Laurentin*, ed. Paul Cardinal Poupard, 467–82. Paris: Desclée, 1990.

"The Greater Glory of God: Women Fully Alive." In *A Spirituality for Contemporary Life* (The Ignatius Anniversary Lectures), ed. David Fleming, 64–81. St. Louis, MO: Review for Religious, 1991.

"The Saints and Mary." In *Systematic Theology: Roman Catholic Perspectives*, vol. 2, ed. Francis Schüssler Fiorenza and John Galvin, 143–77. Minneapolis: Augsburg Fortress Press, 1991.

"Mary as Mediatrix: History and Interpretation." In *The One Mediator, the Saints, and Mary: Lutherans and Catholics in Dialogue*, vol. 9, ed. George Anderson, et al., 311–26. Minneapolis: Augsburg Fortress Press, 1992.

"Redeeming the Name of Christ." In *Freeing Theology: The Essentials of Theology in Feminist Perspective*, ed. Catherine LaCugna, 115–37. San Francisco: HarperSanFrancisco, 1993.

"Wisdom Was Made Flesh and Pitched Her Tent Among Us." In *Reconstructing the Christ Symbol: Essays in Feminist Christology*, ed. Maryanne Stevens, 95–117. New York: Paulist Press, 1993.

"Between the Times: Religious Life and the Postmodern Experience of God." In *The Future of Religious Orders in the United States: Transformation and Commitment*, ed. David Nygren and Miriam Ukeritis, 103–26. New York: Praeger Pub., 1993.

"Powerful Icons and Missing Pieces." In *Preserving the Creation: Environmental Theology and Ethics*, ed. Kevin Irwin and Edmund Pellegrino, 60–66. Washington, DC: Georgetown University Press, 1994.

"Toward a Theology of Mary: Past, Present, and Future." In *All Generations Shall Call Me Blessed* (Keynote Address: Proceedings of the Twenty-Sixth Theology Institute of Villanova University), ed. Francis Eigo, 1–38. Villanova, PA: Villanova University Press, 1994.

"Heaven and Earth Are Filled with Your Glory." In *Finding God in All Things* (Essays in Honor of Michael J. Buckley, SJ), ed. Michael Himes and Stephen Pope, 84–101. New York: Crossroad, 1996.

"On Not Going Fishing: Papal Primacy and the Words of Women." In *The Exercise of the Primacy: Continuing the Dialogue, Archbishop John R. Quinn and the Oxford Lecture*, ed. Phyllis Zagano and Terrence Tilley, 47–55. New York: Crossroad, 1998.

"Forging Theology: A Conversation with Colleagues," in *Things New and Old: Essays on the Theology of Elizabeth Johnson*, ed. Terrence Tilley and Phyllis Zagano, 91–123. New York: Crossroad, 1999.

"A Theological Case for God-She." In *Commonweal Confronts the Century: Liberal Convictions, Catholic Tradition*, ed. Patrick Jordan and Paul Baumann, 299–307. New York: Simon and Schuster, 1999.

"Ecological Theology." In *Vision and Values: Ethical Viewpoints in the Catholic Tradition*, ed. Judith Dwyer, 53–69. Washington, DC: Georgetown University Press, 1999.

"Losing and Finding Creation in Christian Tradition." In *Christianity and Ecology*, ed. Dieter Hessel and Rosemary Radford Ruether, 3–21. Cambridge, MA: Harvard University Press, 2000: 3-21.

"The Word Was Made Flesh and Dwelt Among Us: The Impact of Jesus Research on Christian Faith." In *Jesus: A Colloquium in the Holy Land*, ed. Doris Donnelly, 146–66. New York: Continuum, 2001.

"Passion for God, Passion for the Earth." In *Spiritual Questions for the Twenty-First Century*, ed. Mary Hembrow Snyder. 118–25. Maryknoll, NY: Orbis, 2002.

"Worth A Life." In *Vatican II: Forty Personal Stories*, ed. William Madges and Michael Daley, 200–204. Mystic, CT: Twenty-Third Pub., 2003. Revised edition: Maryknoll, NY: Orbis, 2012: 236–40.

"Horizons of Theology: New Voices in a Living Tradition." In *New Horizons in Theology*, Proceedings of the College Theology Society, vol. 50, ed. Terrence Tilley, 3–15. Maryknoll, NY: Orbis Books, 2004.

"They Have No Wine: The Compassion of Mary in the Light of Feminist The-ology." In *La Categoria Teologica della Compassione: Presenza e Incidenza nella Riflessione su Maria di Nazaret*, ed. Ermanno Toniolo, 161–75. Rome: Edizioni Marianum, 2007.

"El Dios de la Vida en la Teología Feminista de Liberación." In *Libertad y Es-peranza: a Gustave Gutiérrez por sus 80 años*, ed. Consuelo de Prado and Pedro Heghes, 313–29. Peru: Centro de Estudios y Publicaciones - Instituto Bartolomé de las Casas, 2008.

"Articulating the Vision Anew: The Banquet of the Creed." In *Prophetic Witness: Catholic Women's Strategies for Reform*, ed. Colleen Griffith, 6–15. New York: Crossroad, 2009.

"Jesus of the People." In *Holiness and the Feminine Spirit: The Art of Janet McKenzie*, ed. Susan Perry, 69–73. Maryknoll, NY: Orbis Books, 2009.

"The Banquet of the Creed." In *Theology: Faith, Beliefs, Traditions*, ed. Gloria Schaab, 325–38. Dubuque, IA: Kendall Hunt Pub., 2010.

"Deep Christology: Ecological Soundings." In *From Logos to Christos: Essays in Honor of Joanne McWilliam*, ed. Ellen Leonard and Kate Merriman, 163–80. Waterloo, Ontario: Wilfrid Laurier University Press, 2010.

"Communion of Saints and Mary." In *Systematic Theology: Roman Catholic Perspectives*, ed. Francis Schüssler Fiorenza and John Galvin, 431–60. Rev. ed. Minneapolis: Fortress Press, 2011.

"Ecological Theology in Women's Voices." In *Faith + Feminism: Ecumenical Essays*, ed. B. Diane Lipsett and Phyllis Trible, 189–202. Louisville, KY: Westminster John Knox Press, 2014.

"Pneumatology and Beyond: Wherever." In *The Theology of Cardinal Walter Kasper: Speaking Truth in Love*, ed. Kristin Colberg and Robert Krieg, 98–109. Collegeville, MN: Liturgical Press, 2014.

"Jesus and the Cosmos: Soundings in Deep Christology." In *Incarnation: On the Scope and Depth of Christology*, ed. Niels Gregersen, 133–56. Minneapolis: Fortress Press, 2015.

Lectures Printed by University Presses

"Feminism and Sharing the Faith: A Catholic Dilemma." The Warren Lecture. Tulsa, OK: University of Tulsa, 1994.

"The Search for the Living God." John M. Kelly Lecture. Toronto: University of St. Michael's College, 1994.

"Community on Earth as in Heaven: A Holy People and a Sacred Earth To-gether." Santa Clara Lecture. Santa Clara University, October 1998.

"Jesus-Sophia: Ramifications for Contemporary Theology." The Mary Ward Lecture. Cambridge, UK: Margaret Beaufort Institute of Theology, 1999.

"Feminine Faces of the Divine." Women of Spirit Lecture. Rockville Centre, NY: Siena Women's Center, Molloy College, 1999.

"The Ethical Implications of Naming God 'She.'" The Boardman Lecture. Philadelphia: University of Pennsylvania, 2001.

"Mary of Nazareth: Friend of God and Prophet." Mackey Marianist Lecture. Honolulu, HI: Chaminade University, 2001.

"Seeking the Living God: Nourishing Faith with the Living Tradition." Myser Lecture on Catholic Identity. St. Paul, MN: College of St. Catherine, 2008.

"Creative Giver of Life: An Ecological Theology of the Holy Spirit." The Spiritan Lecture. Pittsburgh, PA: Duquesne University, 2008.

"Deep Incarnation: Prepare for Astonishment." The Albertus Magnus Lecture. River Forest, IL: Dominican University, 2009.

"Quest for the Living God." The Carondelet Lecture. St. Louis, MO: Fontbonne University, 2009.

"Creation: Losing and Finding an Ecological Belief." The Mary Milligan Lecture. Los Angeles: Loyola Marymount University, 2014.

"The Mighty from Their Thrones." The Theotokos Lecture in Theology. Milwaukee, WI: Marquette University, 2015.

"Evolution and the Cross." Myser Lecture on Catholic Identity. St. Paul, MN: St. Catherine University, 2015.

Theological Writings for a Wider Public

"Discipleship: Root Model of the Life Called Religious." *Review for Religious* 42 (1983): 864–72.

"Women Religious in the United States: A Report."*Religious Life Review* 24 (1985): 135–41.

"Dissent In and For the Church." *Newsletter*, Leadership Conference of Women Religious, USA (June 1986): 5–7.

"Recovering Women's Faith Experience from Scripture." *Miriam's Song II* (1987): 7–10.

"Why the Decline in New Adult Catholics?" *Catholic Evangelization* 1 (1988): 5–10.

"Mary in the Life of the Church." *Khulisa: South African Journal of Christian Formation* 9 (1988): 27–31.

"Communion of Saints: Partners on the Way." *Church* 5 (Summer 1989): 17–21.

"The Image of God Male and Female." *Khulisa: South African Journal of Christian Formation* 10 (1989): 22–24.

"God in the Image of Women." *The Catechist's Connection* 4, no. 54 (December 1989): 1–2.

"Jesus Christ in the Catechism." *America* 162, no. 8 (March 3, 1990): 206–8, 221–22.

"Lutherans and Catholics: Breakthrough on Christ, the Saints, and Mary." *Ecumenical Trends* 19 (July/August 1990): 97–101.

"Christ—Savior of the Whole World." *Praying* 37 (July–August 1990): 10–11.

"Theological Foundations of Catholic Social Teaching." *The Living Light* 28 (1991): 3–6.

Professional Approaches for Christian Educators. Huntington, IN: Our Sunday Visitor, 1991:

  "The Humanity of God With Us" (January): 153–56.

  "The Story of God With Us" (February): 193–96.

  "In the Voices of the Oppressed" (March): 233–36.

  "The Cosmic Compassion of God" (April): 275–77.

"How Complete Is Your Picture of Jesus?" The Editors' Interview. *U.S. Catholic* 57 (April 1992): 6–13.

"No Contradiction Between Catholicism, Feminism." *Long Island Catholic* (June 24, 1992): 9.

"Images of the Historical Jesus in Catholic Christology." *The Catholic World* 236 (January/February 1993): 24–29.

"A Theological Case for Naming God 'She.'" *Commonweal* 120 (February 29, 1993): 9–14.

"The Author Replies." *Commonweal* 120 (March 26, 1993): 30–31.

"A Modern Mary: Sister, Companion, Friend"; and "What About Apparitions?" *Praying* 54 (May–June 1993): 4–8.

"Don't Make Mary the Feminine Face of God." *U.S. Catholic* 59, no. 4 (April 1994): 30–32.

"God Poured Out: Recovering the Holy Spirit." *Praying* 60 (May–June 1994): 4–8, 41. (Catholic Press Association Journalism Award: Best Article, Prayer and Spirituality.)

"The Search for the Living God." *Grail: An Ecumenical Journal* 10, no. 3 (September 1994): 11–29.

"May the Circle Be Unbroken: Why Catholics Treasure Their Saints." *U.S. Catholic* 59, no. 11 (November 1994): 12–16.

"Remembering the Holy Spirit." *Catholic Update* (June 1995): 1–4.

"And Their Eyes Were Opened: The Resurrection as Resource for Transforming Leadership." CMSM/LCWR Joint Assembly, Anaheim, CA, August 1995.

"Nevertheless, It Moves." *New Women, New Church* 18, no. 2 (Fall 1995): 14.

"Resurrection: Promise of the Future." *Sisters Today* 67 (November 1995): 404–11.

"The Church in the Year 2000" (with Avery Dulles). *Fordham* 29, no. 2 (Winter 1995–1996): 16–19.

"Disputed Questions: Authority, Priesthood, Women." *Commonweal* 123, no. 2 (January 26, 1996): 11–12.

"The Cosmos: An Astonishing Image of God." *Origins* 26, no. 13 (September 12, 1996): 206–12.

"Sacred Ground at the Bedside: The Hospice Caregiver as Partner of God's Compassion." *Connecticut Medicine* 61 (December 1997): 787–88.

"*Communio Sanctorum* in a Cosmic Vision." *The Living Light* 35 (Winter 1998): 53–58.

"Trinity and Christian Life" (with Julia Brumbaugh). *Scripture from Scratch*. (May 1999): 1–4.

"Feminist Christology." *Women and the Australian Church News* 6, no. 1 (June 1999): 1–8.

"Jesus, Wisdom and Our World." *Priests and People* 13, no. 7 (July 1999): 260–65. (Published by *The Tablet* of London, UK).

"My Greatest Hope." *U.S. Catholic* 64, no. 8 (1999): 14–15.

"Circle of Friends: A Closer Look at the Communion of Saints." *U.S. Catholic* 64, no. 11 (November 1999): 12–18.

"The City Gate." *Scripture Forum* 4, no. 2 (Autumn 1999): 10–11. (Principia College, IL).

"Galileo's Daughters: What Error Looks Like Today." *Commonweal* 126, no. 20 (November 19, 1999): 18–20. [Seventy-Fifth Anniversary Issue: Symposium on the Church and Error].

"Madeleva Manifesto: A Message of Hope and Courage." Saint Mary's College, Notre Dame, IN (April 29, 2000).

"Feminine Faces of the Divine: Dangers, Theological Meaning, and Prophetic Power." *Women of Spirit* 3 (Rockville Centre, NY: Molloy College Siena Center, 2000): 19–30.

"Holy Wisdom and Women's Spirituality." *Newsletter: Margaret Beaufort Institute of Theology* 6 (Spring 2000): 2–3.

"Mary of Nazareth: Friend of God and Prophet." John Courtney Murray Lecture. *America* 182, no. 21 (June 17–24, 2000): 7–13.

"Holy Wisdom: Image of God's Saving Presence." *The Living Pulpit* 9, no. 3 (Summer 2000): 6–7.

"Like the Earth, Women Image the Creator Spirit." Call to Action Spirituality / Justice Reprint (July 2000).

"Five Elements of Compassion." *FSM Magazine* 12, no. 1 (Winter–Spring 2001): 2–3.

"In Search of the Real Mary." *St. Anthony Messenger* 108, no. 12 (May 2001): 22–26.

"God's Beloved Creation." *America* 184 (April 16, 2001): 8–12.

"Mary of Nazareth: Friend of God and Prophet." *The Living Pulpit* 10, no. 4 (Fall 2001): 12–17.

"Passion for God, Passion for the Earth." *Scripture from Scratch* (October 2003): 1–4.

"The Prophetic Message of the Magnificat." *U.S. Catholic* (December 2003): 12–17.

"S. Elizabeth Johnson: A Theologian for the 21st Century: The Work of the Theologian." *Liguorian* 92 (April 2004): 20–23.

"The Hidden Strength of the Magnificat." *Catholic Digest* (May 2004): 62–64.

"Women's Place: Two Conflicting Views." *Boston College Magazine* 64, no. 3 (Summer 2004): 20–22, 26–28.

"Remember the Ladies." The Jerome Award Remarks at NCEA Prayer Breakfast, Boston, April 16, 2004; in *Catholic Library World* 74, no. 4 (June 2004): 42–45.

"Cracking the *DaVinci Code*: Theologian Elizabeth Johnson on Mary Magdalene." *St. Anthony Messenger* 112, no. 2 (July 2004): 12–17.

"Mary's Role in the Church Today: She Should Be Honored as a Woman of History." *The Brooklyn Tablet* (August 14, 2004): 24. Originally published on the Web, *Catholic News Service*, "Viewpoints," August 2004.

"Mary, Mother of God." *The Mirror* (Diocese of Springfield–Cape Girardeau) 40, no. 30 (December 24, 2004): 8–9, 14.

"A Historian's Faith and Hope: Eamon Duffy and the Uses of Tradition." *Commonweal* 132, no. 5 (March 11, 2005): 16–18.

"Dear Pope Benedict . . ." *U.S. Catholic* 70, no. 6 (June 2005): 37.

"Pierre Teilhard de Chardin, *Pensées* from the *Hymn of the Universe*" (selected by Elizabeth Johnson), *Grace and Truth: A Journal of Catholic Reflection for Southern Africa* 22, no. 2 (April 2005).

"*Truly Our Sister: A Conversation with Elizabeth Johnson on Mary*" (with Clint Schnekloth). *Word and World* 25, no. 1 (Winter 2006): 68–75.

"You Did It to Me: Lenten Mediation on Torture." *America* 196 (February 26, 2007): 14–16.

"Making a Way: The New Challenge of Catholic Higher Education." *Centennial Year Remembrances* (College of New Rochelle, 2007): 53–57.

"The God of Surprises: Discerning God's Call." *Novena of Grace in Honor of St. Francis Xavier* (Fordham University, 2007): 21–23.

"Jesus e as imagens sobre Deus: para além do masculino e do feminine." *Revista Instituto Humanitas Unisinos* 7 (December 2007): 23–25.

"Honor your Father and Mother." *U.S. Catholic* 73, no. 1 (January 2008): 24–29.

"An Earthy Christology: For God So Loved the Cosmos." *America* 200, no. 12 (April 13, 2009): 27–30.

"Christ and the Earth: Prepare to be Astonished." *Benedictines* 65, no. 2 (Fall/Winter 2012): 6–16.

"Darwin's Tree of Life." *Commonweal* 141, no. 2 (January 24, 2014): 10–13.

"At Our Mercy: The Tree of Life Now Depends on One Twig." *Commonweal* 141, no. 3 (February 7, 2014): 13–16.

"Jesus and Women: You Are Set Free." *Catholic Women Speak: Bringing Our Gifts to the Table*, ed. Tina Beattie, 19–22. New York: Paulist Press, 2015.

Further Reading

Select Scholars Serving Our Cosmological Conversion

Abrahm, David. *The Spell of the Sensuous: Perception and Language in a More-than-Human World*. New York: Pantheon Books, 1996.

Agyarko, Robert Owusu. "God of Life: Rethinking the Akan Christian Concept of God in the Light of Ecological Crisis." *The Ecumenical Review* 65, no. 1 (March 2013): 51–66.

Ahn, Ilsup. "From Colonizing Contract to Decolonizing Covenant: The Case for Ecological Justice in Maquiladoras and a New Covenantal Approach to Christian Environmental Ethics." *Cross Currents* 65, no. 1 (March 2015): 30–56.

Alexander, Kathryn B. *Saving Beauty: A Theological Aesthetics of Nature*. Minneapolis: Fortress Press, 2014.

Baker-Fletcher, Karen. *Sisters of Dust, Sisters of Spirit: Womanist Wordings on God and Creation*. Minneapolis: Fortress Press, 1994.

Bartholomew, Ecumenical Patriarch. *On Earth as in Heaven: Ecological Vision and Initiatives of Ecumenical Patriarch Bartholomew*. Orthodox Christianity and Contemporary Thought. Edited by John Chryssavgis. New York: Fordham University Press, 2011.

Bergmann, Sigurd. "The Legacy of Trinitarian Cosmology in the Anthropocene: Transcontextualising Late Antiquity Theology for Late Modernity." *Studia Theologica* 69, no. 1 (2015): 32–44.

Berry, Thomas. *The Dream of the Earth*. San Francisco: Sierra Club Books, 1988.

Berry, Wendell. *Sex, Economy, Freedom, and Community: Eight Essays*. New York: Pantheon, 1993.

Birch, William, William Eakin, and Jay B. McDaniel. *Liberating Life: Contemporary Approaches to Ecological Theology*. Maryknoll, NY: Orbis Books, 1990.

Boff, Leonardo. *Towards an Eco-Spirituality*. Church at the Crossroad, a Series of Global Marking Posts. Translated by Robert H. Hopke. New York: Crossroad Publishing Co., 2015.

Botas, Athanasios. "The Orthodox Ecological View as a Tool in Environmental Education and the Care of the Ecumenical Patriarch for 'Green Development.'" *The Greek Orthodox Theological Review* 57, nos. 1–4 (2012): 81–104.

Bouma-Prediger, Steven. *For the Beauty of the Earth: A Christian Vision for Creation Care*. 2nd ed. Grand Rapids, MI: Baker Academic, 2010.

Brown, Lester. *Plan B: 4.0: Mobilizing to Save Civilization*. New York and London: W.W. Norton and Company, 2010.

Cahill, Lisa Sowle. *Global Justice, Christology and Christian Ethics*. New Studies in Christian Ethics. New York: Cambridge University Press, 2013.

Carpenter, Colleen Mary, ed. *An Unexpected Wilderness: Christianity and the Natural World*. College Theology Society Annual Volume 61. Maryknoll, NY: Orbis Books, 2016.

Carson, Rachel. *Silent Spring*. With an Introduction by Linda Lear. Fortieth Anniversary Edition. New York: Houghton Mifflin Company, 2002.

Chimhanda, Francisca Hildegardis. "African Theology of Land: A Shona Perspective." *Journal of Theology for Southern Africa* 148 (March 2014): 33–47.

Choi, Kwang Sun. "Ecological Themes in *Evangelii Gaudium*, Together towards Life, and The Cape Town Commitment for Fraternity with God's Creation." *International Review of Mission* 104, no. 2 (November 2015): 278–91.

Christie, Douglas. *The Blue Sapphire of the Mind: Notes for a Contemplative Ecology*. New York: Oxford Press, 2013.

Chryssavgis, John, and Bruce V. Foltz, eds. *Towards an Ecology of Transfiguration: Orthodox Christian Perspectives on Environment, Nature, and Creation*. With a prefatory letter from Ecumenical Patriarch Bartholomew and a foreword by Bill McKibben. New York: Fordham University Press, 2013.

Clough, David. *On Animals: Volume I, Systematic Theology*. New York: T & T Clark, 2012.

Cloutier, David. *Walking on God's Earth: The Environment and Catholic Faith*. Collegeville, MN: Liturgical Press, 2014.

———. *The Vice of Luxury: Economic Excess in a Consumer Age*. Moral Traditions Series. Washington, DC: Georgetown University Press, 2015.

Coakley, Sarah. "Kenosis and Subversion: On the Repression of 'Vulnerability' in Christian Feminist Writing." In *Swallowing a Fishbone? Feminist Theologians Debate Christianity*, edited by Margaret Daphne Hampson, 82–111. London: SPCK, 1996.

Cobb Jr., John B., and Herman E. Daly. *For the Common Good: Redirecting the Economy Towards Community, the Environment, and a Sustainable Future*. Boston: Beacon Press, 1989.

Conradie, Ernst M. "Towards an Agenda for Ecological Theology: An Intercontinental Dialogue." *Ecotheology: Journal of Religion, Nature & the Environment* 10, no. 3 (December 2005): 281–343.

Daedalus, Journal of the American Academy of Arts and Sciences (Fall 2001): Religion and Ecology: Can the Climate Change?

Daly, Herman E., and Joshua Farley. *Ecological Economics: Principles and Applications*. 2nd ed. Washington: Island Press, 2010.

Delio, Ilia, Keith Douglass Warner, and Pamela Wood. *Care for Creation: A Franciscan Spirituality of the Earth*. Cincinnati, OH: St. Anthony Messenger Press, 2008.

Deane-Drummond, Celia. *The Wisdom of the Liminal: Evolution and Other Animals in Human Becoming*. Grand Rapids, MI: Eerdmans, 2014.

Deane-Drummond, Celia, Rebecca Artinian-Kaiser, and David Clough, eds. *Animals as Religious Subjects: Transdisciplinary Perspectives*. New York: Bloomsbury, 2013.

Deane-Drummond, Celia, and David Clough, eds. *Creaturely Theology: On God, Humans and Other Animals*. London: SCM Press, 2009.

Dempsey, Carol J., and Russell A. Butkus, eds. *All Creation Is Groaning: An Interdisciplinary Vision for Life in a Sacred Universe*. Collegeville, MN: Liturgical Press, 1999.

Dempsey, Carol J., and Mary Margaret Pazdan, eds. *Earth, Wind, and Fire: Biblical and Theological Perspectives on Creation*. Collegeville, MN: Liturgical Press, 2004.

de Waal, Frans, *The Bonobo and the Atheist: In Search of Humanism Among the Primates*. New York: Norton, 2013.

Christiansen, Drew, and Walter Grazer, eds. *"And God Saw that It Was Good": Catholic Theology and the Environment*. Washington, D.C.: United States Catholic Conference, 1996.

Edwards, Denis. *Ecology at the Heart of Faith*. Maryknoll, NY: Orbis Press, 2007.

———. *Partaking of God: Trinity, Evolution and Ecology*. Collegeville, MN: Liturgical Press, 2014.

Edwards, Denis, ed., *Earth Revealing—Earth Healing: Ecology and Christian Theology* Collegeville, MN: Liturgical Press, 2001.

Ewan, Alexander, and The Native American Council of New York City, eds. *Voice of Indigenous Peoples: Native People Address the United Nations*. With a preface by Rigoberta Menchú, a foreword by Boutros Boutros-Ghali, and an epilogue by Oren Lyons. Santa Fe, NM: Clear Light Publishers, 1994.

Foley, Edward, ed. *The Wisdom of Creation*. Collegeville, MN: Liturgical Press, 2004.

French, William. "Common Ground, Common Skies: Natural Law and Ecological Responsibility." *Journal of Ecumenical Studies* 42, no. 3 (Summer 2007): 373–88.

———. "Natural Law and Ecological Responsibility: Drawing on the Thomistic Tradition." *University of St. Thomas Law Journal* 5, no. 1 (Winter 2008): 12–36.

Gebara, Ivone. *Longing for Running Water: Ecofeminism and Liberation*. Minneapolis: Fortress Press, 1999.

———. *Out of the Depths: Women's Experience of Evil and Salvation*. Minneapolis: Fortress Press, 2000.

Haught, John. *The Promise of Nature: Ecology and Cosmic Purpose*. New York: Paulist Press, 1993.

———. *Is Nature Enough? Meaning and Truth in the Age of Science*. Cambridge: Cambridge University Press, 2006.

Hawken, Paul. *Blessed Unrest: How the Largest Social Movement in History Is Restoring Grace, Justice, and Beauty to the World*. New York: Viking Press, 2007.

Hessel-Robinson, Timothy, and Ray Maria McNamara. *Spirit and Nature: The Study of Christian Spirituality in a Time of Ecological Urgency*. Princeton Theological Monograph Series. Eugene, OR: Pickwick Publications, 2011.

Hogan, Linda, and Agbonkhianmeghe E. Orobator, eds. *Feminist Catholic Theological Ethics: Conversations in the World Church*. Catholic Theological Ethics in the World Church, 2. Maryknoll, NY: Orbis Books, 2014.

Jenkins, Willis. *Ecologies of Grace: Environmental Ethics and Christian Theology*. New York: Oxford University Press, 2008.

Jensen, David, ed. *The Lord and Giver of Life: Perspectives on Constructive Pneumatology*. Louisville: Westminster John Knox Press, 2008.

Kearns, Laurel, and Catherine Keller, eds. *Ecospirit: Religions and Philosophies for the Earth*. Transdisciplinary Theological Colloquia Series. New York: Fordham University Press: 2007.

Keller, Catherine. *The Face of the Deep: A Theology of Becoming*. New York: Routledge Press, 2003.

———. *Cloud of the Impossible: Negative Theology and Planetary Entanglement*. Insurrections: Critical Studies in Religion, Politics and Culture Series. New York: Columbia University Press, 2014.

Klein, Naomi. *This Changes Everything: Capitalism vs. The Climate*. New York and London: Simon & Schuster, 2014.

Koosed, Jennifer, ed. *The Bible and Posthumanism*. Atlanta: Society of Biblical Literature, 2014.

Lai, Pan-chiu. "God of Life and Ecological Theology: A Chinese Christian Perspective." *The Ecumenical Review* 65, no. 1 (March 2013): 67–82.

Lane, Belden. *Landscapes of the Sacred: Geography and Narrative in American Spirituality*. Exp. ed. Baltimore: Johns Hopkins University Press, 2001.

Leal, Robert Barry. *Wilderness in the Bible: Toward a Theology of Wilderness*. Studies in Biblical Literature 3. Edited by Hemchand Gossai. New York: Peter Lang, 2004, 2008.

Lothes Biviano, Erin. *Inspired Sustainability: Planting Seeds for Action*. Maryknoll, NY: Orbis Books, 2016.

Lothes Biviano, Erin, David Cloutier, Elaine Padilla, Christiana Peppard, and Jame Schaefer. "Catholic Moral Traditions and Energy Ethics in the 21st Century." *Journal of Moral Theology* 5, no. 2 (June 2016): 1–36.

Macy, Joanna, and Thich Nhat Hanh, eds. *Spiritual Ecology: The Cry of the Earth*. Point Reyes Station, CA: The Golden Sufi Center, 2013.

McDonagh, Seàn. *The Death of Life: The Horror of Extinction*. Co Dublin, Ireland: Columba Press, 2005.

McFague, Sallie. *Super, Natural Christians: How We Should Love Nature*. Minneapolis: Fortress Press, 1997.

———. *A New Climate for Theology: God, the World, and Global Warming*. Minneapolis: Fortress Press, 2008.

McKibben, Bill. *The End of Nature*. New York: Random House, 1989. Reprint with new introduction, 2006.

Miller, Richard W., ed. *God, Creation, and Climate Change: A Catholic Response to the Environmental Crisis*. Maryknoll, NY: Orbis Books, 2010.

Moe-Lobeda, Cynthia. *Resisting Structural Evil: Love as Ecological-Economical Vocation*. Minneapolis: Fortress Press, 2013.

Moltmann, Jürgen. *God in Creation: A New Theology of Creation and the Spirit of God*. Translated by Margaret Kohl. Minneapolis: Fortress Press, 1993.

Moore, Stephen, ed. *Divinanimality: Animal Theory, Creaturely Theology*. New York: Fordham University Press, 2014.

Nadkarni, Nalini M. *Between Earth and Sky: Our Intimate Connections to Trees*. Berkeley: University of California Press, 2008.

Nichols, Wallace J., *Blue Mind: The Surprising Science That Shows How Being Near, In, On, or Under Water Can Make You Happier, Healthier, More Connected, and Better at What You Do*. New York: Little, Brown and Company, 2014.

Northcott, Michael S. *The Environment and Christian Ethics*. New York: Cambridge University Press, 1996.

———. *A Political Theology of Climate Change*. Grand Rapids, MI: Eerdmans, 2013.

Peacock, Arthur. *Paths from Science toward God*. Oxford: Oneworld, 2002.

Peppard, Christiana. "Fresh Water and Catholic Social Teaching: A Vital Nexus." *Journal of Catholic Social Thought* 9, no. 2 (Summer 2012): 325–52.

———. *Just Water: Theology, Ethics and the Global Water Crisis*. Maryknoll, NY: Orbis Books, 2014.

Peppard, Christiana, and Andrea Vicini, eds. *Just Sustainability*. Maryknoll, NY: Orbis Books, 2015.

Persoon, Joachim. "Towards an Ethiopian Eco-theology with Inspiration from Monastic Spirituality." *Svensk Missionstidskrift* 98, no. 2 (2010): 211–37.

Pinckaers, Servais. *The Sources of Christian Ethics*. Translated by Mary Noble. Washington, DC: CUA Press, 1995.

Plaskow, Judith. *Sex, Sin, and Grace: Women's Experience and the Theologies of Reinhold Niebuhr and Paul Tillich*. Washington, DC: University Press of America, 1980.

Pope Francis, *Laudato Sì (Encyclical Letter on Care of our Common Home)*. Vatican City: Libreria Editrice Vaticana, 2015.

Pope, Stephen J. *The Ethics of Aquinas*. Washington, DC: Georgetown University Press, 2002.

Pui-Lan, Kwok. "Ecology and Christology." *Feminist Theology: The Journal of Britain and Ireland School of Feminist Theology* 15 (May 1995): 113–25.

———. *Postcolonial Imagination and Feminist Theology*. Louisville, KY: Westminster John Knoxx Press, 2005.

Rasmussen, Larry L. *Earth-Honoring Faith: Religious Ethics in a New Key*. New York: Oxford University Press, 2015.

Rhoads, David, ed. *Earth and Word: Classic Sermons on Saving the Planet*. New York: Continuum, 2007.

Rodriguez, Jeanette. "La Tierra Theologies' Contribution to Creation Theologies." In *In Our Own Voices: Latino/a Renditions of Theology*, edited by Benjamin Valentin, 21–40. Maryknoll, NY: Orbis Books, 2010.

Rudy, Kathy. *Loving Animals: Toward a New Animal Advocacy*. Minneapolis: University of Minnesota Press, 2011.

Ruether, Rosemary Radford. *Gaia and God: An Ecofeminist Theology of Earth Healing*. San Francisco: HarperSanFrancisco, 1992.

Ruether, Rosemary Radford, ed. *Women Healing Earth: Third World Women on Ecology, Feminism, and Religion*. Maryknoll, NY: Orbis Books, 1996.

Schabb, Gloria. *The Creative Suffering of the Triune God: An Evolutionary Theology*. New York: Oxford University Press, 2007.

Schaefer, Jame. *Theological Foundations of Environmental Ethics: Reconstructing Patristic and Medieval Concepts*. Washington, DC: Georgetown University Press, 2009.

Schaefer, Jame, ed., *Confronting the Climate Crisis: Catholic Theological Perspectives*. Milwaukee: Marquette University Press, 2011.

Schaefer, Jame, and Tobias Winright, eds. *Environmental Justice and Climate Change: Assessing Pope Benedict XVI's Ecological Vision for the Catholic Church in the United States*. Lanham, MD: Lexington Books, 2013.

Stoknes, Per Espen. *What We Think about When We Try Not to Think about Global Warming: Toward a New Psychology of Climate Action*. With a foreword by Jorgen Randers. White River Junction, VT: Chelsea Green Publishing, 2015.

Taylor, Sarah McFarland. *Green Sisters: A Spiritual Ecology*. Boston: Harvard University Press, 2009.

Theokritoff, Elizabeth. *Living in God's Creation: Orthodox Perspectives on Ecology*. Crestwood, NY: St. Vladimir's Seminary Press, 2009.

Titus, Craig Steven. *Resilience and the Virtue of Fortitude: Aquinas in Dialogue with the Psychosocial Sciences*. Washington, DC: Catholic University of America Press, 2006.

Tomasello, Michael. *A Natural History of Human Thinking*. Cambridge, MA: Harvard University Press, 2014.

Tucker, Mary Evelyn. *Worldly Wonder: Religions Enter Their Ecological Phase*. Master Hsuan Hua Memorial Lecture. With a commentary by Judith Berling. Chicago: Open Court, 2003.

Vaillant, John. *The Golden Spruce: A True Story of Myth, Madness, and Greed*. New York: W. W. Norton, 2005.

Winright, Tobias, ed. *Green Discipleship: Catholic Theological Ethics and the Environment*. Winona, MN: Anselm Academic, 2011.

Select Scholarly Work on the Theological Contributions of Elizabeth Johnson

Ashley, Benedict. "Elizabeth Johnson's '*She Who Is*.'" Appendix 2 in *Justice in the Church: Gender and Participation*, 189–205. Washington, DC: Catholic University of America Press, 1996.

Bracken, Joseph. "Quaestio Disputata: Response to Elizabeth Johnson's 'Does God Play Dice?'" *Theological Studies* 57 (1996): 720–30.

Dallavalle, Nancy. "Neither Idolatry nor Iconoclasm: A Critical Essentialism for Catholic Feminist Theology." *Horizons: Journal of the College Theology Society* 25 (1998): 23–42.

Dorrien, Gary. "Feminist Interruptions: Anne Carr and Elizabeth Johnson." Chapter 7 in *The Making of American Liberal Theology: Crisis, Irony, & Postmodernity 1950–2005*. Louisville, KY: Westminster John Knox Press, 2006.

Doyle, Dennis. "Communion Ecclesiology on the Borders: Elizabeth Johnson and Roberto Goizueta." In *Theology: Expanding the Borders*, ed. Maria Pilar Aquino and Roberto Goizueta, 200–218. Annual Publication of the College Theology Society. Vol. 43. Mystic, CT: Twenty-Third Pub., 1998.

———. "Communion on the Borders: Elizabeth Johnson and Roberto Goizueta." Chapter 9 in *Communion Ecclesiology*. Maryknoll, N.Y.: Orbis Books, 2000.

Fox, Patricia. "The Trinity as Transforming Symbol: Exploring the Trinitarian Theology of Two Roman Catholic Feminist Theologians." *Pacifica* 7 (1994): 273–94.

———. *God as Communion: John Zizioulas, Elizabeth Johnson, and the Retrieval of the Symbol of the Triune God*. Collegeville, MN: Liturgical Press, 2001.

Greene-McCreight, Kathryn. *Feminist Reconstructions of Christian Doctrine.* New York: Oxford University Press, 2000. See esp. chapters 4–6.

Grenz, Stanley. "The Trinity as Sophia: Elizabeth Johnson." Chapter 5 in *Rediscovering the Triune God.* Minneapolis: Fortress Press, 2004.

Hunt, Anne. "Christian Feminist Liberation Theology." Chapter 2 in *What Are They Saying about the Trinity?* New York: Paulist Press, 1998.

Jones, Serene. "Between A Rock and A Hard Place: Feminist, Womanist, & *Mujerista* Theologies in North America." In *Horizons in Feminist Theology: Identity, Tradition, and Norms,* ed. Rebecca Chopp & Sheila G. Davaney, 33–53. Minneapolis: Fortress Press, 1997.

Masson, Robert. "Analogy and Metaphoric Process." *Theological Studies* 62 (2001): 571–96.

McDonnell, Kilian. "Feminist Mariologies: Heteronomy / Subordination and the Scandal of Christology." *Theological Studies* 66 (2005): 527–67.

Molnar, Paul. *Divine Freedom and the Doctrine of the Immanent Trinity.* London, New York: T & T Clark, 2002. See esp. "Feminist Concerns / Elizabeth Johnson," 9–25.

Ormerod, Neil. "Elizabeth Johnson." Chapter 17 in *Introducing Contemporary Theologies: The What and Who of Theology Today.* Maryknoll, NY: Orbis Books, 1997.

Rakoczy, Susan. "The Theological Vision of Elizabeth A. Johnson." *Scriptura* 98 (2008): 137–55. [University of Stellenbosch, South Africa].

———. "Women Consider Jesus." In *Religion and the Reconstruction of Civil Society,* edited by J.W. de Gruchy and S. Martin, 244–60. Pretoria: University of South Africa, 1995.

Schaab, Gloria. "Of Models and Metaphors: The Trinitarian Proposals of Sallie McFague and Elizabeth A. Johnson." *Theoforum* 33, no. 2 (2002): 213–34.

Schindler, David. "Creation and Nuptiality: A Reflection on Feminism in Light of Schmemann's Liturgical Theology." *Communio* 28 (Summer 2001): 265–95, at 285–94.

Schlumpf, Heidi. *Elizabeth Johnson: Questing for God.* People of God Series. Collegeville, MN: Liturgical Press, 2016.

Schrein, Shannon. *Quilting and Braiding: The Feminist Christologies of Sallie McFague and Elizabeth Johnson in Conversation.* Collegeville, MN: Liturgical Press, 1998.

Teevan, Donna. "Challenges to the Role of Theological Anthropology in Feminist Theologies." *Theological Studies* 64 (2003): 582–97.

Tilley, Terrence, and Phyllis Zagano, eds. *Things New and Old: Essays on the Theology of Elizabeth Johnson.* New York: Crossroad, 1999.

Wells, Harold. "Trinitarian Feminism: Elizabeth Johnson's Wisdom Christology." *Theology Today* 52, no. 3 (1995): 330–43.

Contributors

Editors

Julia Brumbaugh is an associate professor of religious studies at Regis University in Denver, Colorado. She holds a PhD from Fordham University in contemporary systematic theology. She is active in the Catholic Theological Society of America where she is co-convener of the Women's Consultation in Constructive Theology. Her teaching and writing focus on spirituality and ecclesiology.

Natalia Imperatori-Lee is associate professor of religious studies at Manhattan College in Riverdale, New York. She teaches in the areas of contemporary Catholicism, US Latino/a theology, and gender studies. She earned a PhD in systematic theology from the University of Notre Dame and is currently working on a monograph for Orbis Books on the importance of narrative in Catholic ecclesiology. She lives in the Bronx with her spouse and her two young sons.

Contributors

Kevin Glauber Ahern, PhD, is assistant professor of religious studies at Manhattan College where he directs the Labor Studies and Peace Studies programs. From 2003 to 2007 he served as the president of the International Movement of Catholic Students (Pax Romana). He is the editor of *The Radical Bible* and *Visions of Hope: Emerging Theologians and the Future of the Church* (Orbis Books, 2013). His most recent book, *Structures of Grace: Catholic Organizations Serving the Global Common*

Good (Orbis Books, 2015), examines the role of church organizations in the struggle for social justice. @kevin_ahern.

Lisa Sowle Cahill is the J. Donald Monan, SJ, Professor at Boston College. She received her PhD at the University of Chicago Divinity School. She is past president of the Catholic Theological Society of America and the Society of Christian Ethics, and she is a fellow of the American Academy of Arts and Sciences. Her works include *Global Justice, Christology and Christian Ethics* (Cambridge, 2013), *Theological Bioethics: Justice, Participation, and Change* (Georgetown, 2005), *Sex, Gender, and Christian Ethics* (Cambridge, 1996). She serves on the editorial boards of the *Journal of Religious Ethics* and the international journal *Concilium*.

Colleen Mary Carpenter is associate professor of theology and the Sister Mona Riley Endowed Professor of the Humanities at St. Catherine University in St. Paul, Minnesota, where she has taught since 2006. She is the author of *Redeeming the Story: Women, Suffering, and Christ* (Continuum, 2004) and numerous articles in ecotheology and ecospirituality. Before coming to St. Catherine, she worked with the School Sisters of Notre Dame at EarthRise Farm, an organic farm and retreat center in western Minnesota. In addition to ecological issues, her research focuses on feminism, theological aesthetics, and the imagination.

David Cloutier holds the Knott Professorship in Catholic Theology at Mount St. Mary's University (Maryland), teaching in moral theology and Catholic social ethics and directing a year-long university-wide seminar for tenure-track faculty on the Catholic Intellectual Tradition. His books include *The Vice of Luxury: Economic Excess in a Consumer Age* (Georgetown University Press) and *Walking God's Earth: The Environment and Catholic Faith* (Liturgical Press). He is a coeditor of the Moral Traditions series at Georgetown University Press and blogs at catholicmoraltheology.com and dotCommonweal. He also serves on the Board of Directors at the Common Market, his consumer food cooperative.

Kathy Coffey is the the author of *Hidden Women of the Gospels* (Orbis Books, 2012), *When the Saints Came Marching In* (Liturgical Press, 2015), and fourteen other award-winning books. She gives retreats and workshops nationally and internationally. For more information, see her website: kathyjcoffey.com.

Carol J. Dempsey, OP, is professor of theology (biblical studies) at the University of Portland, Oregon. She holds a BA from Caldwell University, New Jersey, an MA from St. Louis University, Missouri, and a PhD in biblical studies from The Catholic University of America in Washington, DC, where she studied both Old and New Testament and biblical languages. Her area of expertise is the Prophets, with additional interest in gender studies, ethics, and environmental studies. She has published widely and serves on several editorial boards. Her most recent works include *The Bible and Literature* (Orbis Books, 2015) and *Amos, Hosea, Micah, Nahum, Zephaniah, Habakkuk* (Liturgical Press, 2013). She is a member of the Dominican Order of Caldwell, New Jersey.

Denis Edwards is a professorial fellow in theology at Australian Catholic University, Adelaide campus, and is a priest of the Catholic Archdiocese of Adelaide. He is a member of the ACU Institute for Religion and Critical Inquiry, has been involved with international dialogues on science and religion, and is a member of the International Society for Science and Religion. He is part of the national Lutheran–Roman Catholic Dialogue and the national Australian Anglican–Roman Catholic Commission. Recent books include *Ecology at the Heart of Faith* (2007), *How God Acts: Creation, Redemption and Special Divine Action* (2010), and *Partaking of God: Trinity, Evolution and Ecology* (2014).

William French is an associate professor of theology at Loyola University Chicago. He received his MDiv from Harvard University and completed his PhD at the University of Chicago. His main research interests are religious ethics, ecological ethics and policies, and war and peace issues. He has written articles and book chapters on such topics as global climate change, land use issues, ecological security, just war theory, the moral status of animals, the Catholic natural law tradition, biblical views of creation, gun violence, and comparative religious ethics. He serves on the advisory board of the National Catholic Center for Holocaust Education.

Ivone Gebara is a Brazilian feminist philosopher and theologian. She taught several years in the Institute of Theology of Recife and gave alternative theological formation to the leaders of Christian Communities and Social Movements. Presently, she is living in São Paulo and is invited by different universities and religious centers in Brazil and internationally to lecture. She is the author of several books and articles from a feminist and ecological perspective and adviser for different publications in Brazil.

John F. Haught (PhD, The Catholic University, 1970) is Distinguished Research Professor, Georgetown University, Washington, DC. He was formerly professor in the Department of Theology at Georgetown University (1970–2005) and chair (1990–95). His area of specialization is systematic theology, with a particular interest in issues pertaining to science, cosmology, evolution, ecology, and religion. He is the author of twenty books and numerous articles and reviews, and he lectures internationally on many issues related to science and religion. In 2002 he was the winner of the Owen Garrigan Award in Science and Religion, in 2004 the Sophia Award for Theological Excellence, and in 2008 a "Friend of Darwin Award" from the National Center for Science Education. He testified for the plaintiffs in the Harrisburg, Pennsylvania, "Intelligent Design trial" (Kitzmiller et al. vs. Dover Board of Education). In April 2009 he received an honorary doctorate from Louvain University in Belgium. He is the author most recently of *Resting on the Future: Catholic Theology for an Unfinished Universe* (York: Bloomsbury Press, 2015).

Mary Catherine Hilkert, OP, is professor of theology at the University of Notre Dame where she specializes in theological anthropology, fundamental theology, and feminist theology and spirituality. A former president of the Catholic Theological Society of America, she is the author of *Naming Grace: Preaching and the Sacramental Imagination* (Continuum/Bloomsbury, 1997), *Speaking with Authority: Catherine of Siena and the Voices of Women Today* (Paulist, 2008), *The Praxis of the Reign of God: An Introduction to the Theology of Edward Schillebeeckx* (co-editor with Robert Schreiter, Fordham University Press, 2002), and numerous articles on theology, preaching, and spirituality. She is currently working on a volume titled *Words of Spirit and Life: Pneumatology, Preaching and Spirituality*.

Erin Lothes Biviano is assistant professor of theology at the College of Saint Elizabeth, Morristown, New Jersey. She received a PhD in contemporary systematic theology from Fordham University, an MA in theology from Boston College, and an AB in English from Princeton University. As a 2007–2010 Earth Institute Fellow at Columbia University, she conducted theological, ethnographic, and social science research to write *Inspired Sustainability: Planting Seeds for Action* (Orbis Books, 2016). She is also author of *The Paradox of Christian Sacrifice: The Loss of Self, the Gift of Self* (Herder and Herder, 2007) and articles on environmentalism, including the coauthored "Catholic Moral Traditions and Energy Ethics for the Twenty-First Century," *Journal of Moral Theology*.

Sallie McFague is currently the Distinguished Theologian in Residence at the Vancouver School of Theology in Vancouver, British Columbia. She teaches a course on reimagining how we speak of God and the world in a time of climate change. She taught at Vanderbilt University Divinity School for many years and is the author of books tackling the same issues Elizabeth Johnson has addressed in her writings, such as the power and authority of religious language, the "nature" of nature, and the contribution of the religions, especially Christianity, for both the problem of climate change and its possible solutions. See especially *Blessed Are the Consumers: Climate Change and the Practice of Restraint* and *A New Climate for Theology: God, the World, and Global Warming* (both published by Fortress Press). She presently lives in Vancouver, holding dual citizenship in Canada and the United States.

Eric Daryl Meyer currently serves as postdoctoral faculty fellow at Loyola Marymount University, having earned his PhD in theology from Fordham University in 2014 under Elizabeth Johnson's supervision. He specializes in theological anthropology, examining theological views of animals as they influence accounts of human nature and purpose. This focus on animals and humans grows from an interest in developing effective responses to ecological degradation. His work connects the study of late Ancient Christianity, contemporary constructive theology, critical animal studies, and poststructural philosophy. Outside of academic contexts, he has worked in wilderness education and environmental advocacy for over a decade.

Richard W. Miller is associate professor and director of the MA in theology program in the theology department of Creighton University in Omaha, Nebraska. He has a PhD in systematic theology from Boston College, is the editor of seven books, and is the author of many articles on themes in Catholicism and American public life, spirituality, and ecology. Notably, the collection *God, Creation, and Climate Change: A Catholic Response to the Environmental Crisis* (Orbis Press, 2010) received the 2011 Catholic Press Association of the United States and Canada book award in the faith and science category.

Jürgen Moltmann is professor emeritus of systematic theology at the University of Tübingen, in Germany. His widely influential works in the field of systematics are too numerous to list but include *The Crucified God* (1972), *God in Creation* (1985), *Science and Wisdom* (2002), and most recently *The Ethics of Hope* (2012). His *The Coming of God* (1996) was awarded the Louisville Grawmeyer Award in Religion in 2000.

Jeanette Rodriguez is a professor at Seattle University and teaches in the departments of theology and religious studies, women studies, and the graduate School of Theology and Ministry. Rodriguez is the author of several books and articles concentrated in the areas of US Hispanic theology, theologies of liberation, peacebuilding, and genocide studies. Her works include *Our Lady of Guadalupe: Faith and Empowerment Among Mexican American Women*; *Stories We Live*; coauthor with Dr. Ted Fortier of *Cultural Memory: Resistance, Faith and Identity*; and coeditor with Dr. Maria Pilar Aquino and Dr. Daisy Machado of *A Reader in Latina Feminist Theology*. She has served as board member for the Academy of Hispanic Theologians in the United States and as vice chair for Pax Christi USA. Presently she is on the board of the *National Catholic Reporter*. Rodriguez holds a PhD in religion and personality sciences from the Graduate Theological Union, Berkeley, California.

Michele Saracino is professor of religious studies at Manhattan College in Riverdale, New York. Her research focuses on the intersections among theological anthropology, contemporary continental theory, psychologies of the self, and expressions of religiosity in everyday life. She is the author of four books and various essays. Her most recent, *Christian Anthropology: An Introduction to the Human Person* (Paulist Press, 2015), is a textbook for undergraduate and seminary students and deals with the sacred relationship between human and nonhuman animals. Currently she is working on the spirituality of water and water-related practices, including baptism, bathing, and swimming.

Index